Because
They Were Jews

Recent Titles in
Contributions to the Study of World History

The Myth of the Revolution: Hero Cults and the Institutionalization
of the Mexican State, 1920–1940
Ilene V. O'Malley

Accommodation and Resistance: The French Left, Indochina
and the Cold War, 1944–1954
Edward Rice-Maximin

Genocide and the Modern Age: Etiology and Case Studies of Mass Death
Isidor Wallimann and Michael N. Dobkowski, editors

Because They Were Jews

A History of Antisemitism

MEYER WEINBERG

CONTRIBUTIONS TO THE STUDY OF
WORLD HISTORY, NUMBER 4

GREENWOOD PRESS
NEW YORK • WESTPORT, CONNECTICUT • LONDON

Library of Congress Cataloging-in-Publication Data

Weinberg, Meyer, 1920–
  Because they were Jews.

  (Contributions to the study of world history,
ISSN 0885-9159; no. 4)
  Bibliography: p.
  Includes index.
  1. Antisemitism—History. I. Title. II. Series.
DS145.W45 1986   305.8'924   86–15013
ISBN 0–313–25606–3 (lib. bdg. : alk. paper)

Library of Congress Catalog Card Number: 86-15013
ISBN: 0–313–25606–3
ISSN: 0885–9159

First published in 1986

Greenwood Press, Inc.
88 Post Road West, Westport, Connecticut 06881

Printed in the United States of America

The paper used in this book complies with the
Permanent Paper Standard issued by the National
Information Standards Organization (Z39.48–1984).

10 9 8 7 6 5 4 3 2 1

Copyright Acknowledgments

The following publishers graciously gave permission to use extended quotations from copyrighted works: From *The Politics of Genocide. The Holocaust in Hungary*, 1 (1981), by Randolph L. Braham. Reprinted by permission of Columbia University Press. Reprinted from *The Bulgarian Jews and the Final Solution, 1940–1944* by Frederick B. Chary by permission of the University of Pittsburgh Press. From *History of the Jews*, 2 (1968), by Simon M. Dubov, translated by Moshe Spiegel. Reprinted by permission of the publisher, Thomas Yoseloff. From *Anti-Semitism in the Soviet Union*, edited by Theodore Freedman. Copyright 1984 Anti-Defamation League of B'nai B'rith. Used by permission. From *Hitler, Germans, and the "Jewish Question"* by Sarah Gordon. Copyright © 1984 by Princeton University Press. Reprinted by permission of the publisher. From "Roumania" by Daniel Labin in *Universal Jewish Encyclopedia* (1943). Reprinted by permission of KTAV Publishing House, Inc. From *Mussolini and the Jews. German-Italian Relations and the Jewish Question in Italy, 1922–1945* (1978) by Meir Michaelis. Reprinted by permission of Oxford University Press. From *The Jews of Argentina from the Inquisition to Perón* (1979) by Robert Weisbrot. Reprinted by permission of the Jewish Publication Society.

Anyone who closes his eyes to the past is
blind to the present.
—Richard von Weizsäcker, 1985

CONTENTS

Acknowledgments   ix

Introduction   xi

1. A Noah's Ark of Bigotry: Argentina   3

2. A Tradition of Tolerance: Bulgaria   27

3. A Cycle of Centuries: Egypt   33

4. Isolated Fidelity: Ethiopia   53

5. From Jew to Citizen: France   65

6. The Classic Catastrophe: Germany   83

7. On Being Used and Being Useful: Hungary   133

8. Two Destinies in One Land: Italy   143

9. The Continuity of Oppression: Poland   153

10. The Struggle for Civic Status: Rumania   169

11. Long Winters of Dark Nights: Russia/USSR   181

12. The Toleration of Tolerance: United States   207

13. Similarities and Differences   237

14. The World of Antisemitism   245

Bibliographic Essay   265

Index   271

ACKNOWLEDGMENTS

I wish to thank the members of the library staff at the University of Massachusetts, Amherst, for their unstinting cooperation in supplying valuable materials for this study. A sabbatical leave in 1984 provided an indispensable opportunity for me to write. My research assistant, Ali Munif Seden, was helpful in many ways, including assembling data for table 1 and aiding in the making of the index. Angela Hoover Morrison edited the copy with great care and sensibility, and Todd Adkins, production editor, made certain there was a book at the end of the road. Betty Craker typed the manuscript with her usual high ability and practical sense.

INTRODUCTION

Antisemitism is not a Jewish disease. It is an illness of the non-Jewish world.

—Yehuda Bauer, 1982

This book examines the development of antisemitism in twelve countries from earliest times to the present. While the emphasis is necessarily on Europe, also included are countries in Africa, the Near East, and North and South America. During the half-century before 1980 these twelve countries accounted for more than four-fifths to somewhat less than two-thirds of the world's Jews (see table 1). This falling percentage after 1945 is accounted for mainly by the birth of Israel in 1948. In 1980, for example, most of the world's Jews not living in any of the twelve countries resided in Israel.

Quite possibly some seventy-five countries have a significant element of antisemitism in their history. To select twelve required criteria that would yield a representative group. This was assured in part by including the eight European countries most populous with Jews. Also, the countries included, taken as a whole, portray a wide range of conditions. In some, Jews made up less than 1 percent of the population, in one other they amounted to as much as 10 percent. These are, in addition, countries with or without state churches; either possessing or lacking a "Jewish question"—countries like Germany, with a centuries-old record of antisemitism, or Bulgaria, without one; and Muslim countries, like Egypt, where both Jews and Christians were religious minorities, and Ethiopia, where both Jews and Muslims were ruled by a Christian majority.

Ideally, antisemitism in any country ought to be treated as part of the country's general history, and every major aspect of the history of Jews in that country should be detailed. Except for specialists, with far

Table 1
Approximate Number of Jews in Twelve Countries, 1930–80

	1930	1945	1955	1965	1980
Argentina	215,000	350,000	360,000	460,000	242,000
Bulgaria	48,398	46,500	6,000	7,000	3,500
Egypt	63,550	75,000	40,000	2,500	250
Ethiopia	51,000	51,000	12,000	12,000	32,000
France	225,000	180,000	300,000	520,000	535,000
Germany	499,682	85,000	25,000	31,000	33,500
Hungary	475,949	200,000	135,000	80,000	65,000
Italy	47,485	52,000	31,000	35,000	32,000
Poland	2,978,000	120,000	50,000	25,000	5,000
Rumania	900,000	300,000	225,000	120,000	33,000
Russia/USSR	2,638,275	2,000,000	2,000,000	2,486,000	1,700,000
United States	4,228,029	5,000,000	5,200,000	5,720,000	5,690,000
Twelve countries	12,370,368	8,459,500	8,384,000	9,488,500	8,371,250
World total	15,200,000	11,000,000	11,908,000	13,400,000	13,028,000
Twelve Countries as % of World Total	81.4	76.9	70.4	70.8	64.4

All data were derived from various volumes of the *American Jewish Year Book*. Many of the figures are estimates.

more than a single volume at hand, this is impractical. For the general reader, the author has focused on the most important of the essentials, sketching very broadly, whenever appropriate, the general background. Many sources are cited so that interested readers may read further.

In this work, antisemitism is understood as systematic opposition to Jews because they are Jewish. To antisemites, simply *being* Jewish is offensive. Yet, it is well to remember Gertrude Stein's sage comment: "Remarks are not literature." That is, literature is a great deal more than isolated clever and striking assertions. Similarly, neither are mere remarks antisemitic. It is not the isolated, rare negative remark that constitutes antisemitism but a characteristically anti-Jewish pattern of thought in which Jews are held to be at fault almost regardless of the problem. The same holds true of a national society or local community. In the following chapters we are seeking the characteristic responses of each society rather than a compendium of all the negative (or positive) instances we can find.

Nor is it sufficient to equate the oppression and suffering of Jews with antisemitism. In the history of Muslim countries it has not been unusual for Jews to be oppressed or regulated closely; it is almost unheard of, however, for Jews to be oppressed in such countries without Christians suffering as well. In nineteenth-century Russia, part of the Jews' extreme poverty reflected official discrimination; another portion of it arose from the fact that Russia was a poor country. On the other hand, part of the reason for the relative prosperity of many American Jews is the lack of religious oppression; another is the fact that the United States is a wealthy country. The real question is: when distinctions affecting Jews are drawn whether this is because they are Jews. Sometimes a great deal of research is required to establish the truth of the matter.

We do not know whether antisemitism will prove eternal. Certainly, it has not always existed. In the ancient Near East and classical Greece and Rome little systematic antisemitism can be found. As we shall see, local conditions sometimes provided exceptions, as in Alexandria, Egypt, both in the first century as well as during the ninth through thirteenth centuries. At the same time, it was unknown in nearby places such as Cairo. During the days of the early Christians, in the first two centuries after Christ, Jew-hate was virtually unknown. As the Roman Catholic church matured and its institutional interests took shape, antisemitism was formulated and propagated by church officials on many levels. If religion is to be turned against a people, one must work hard at it. Poland illustrates this process all too well.

The absence of antisemitism during these early times implies something encouraging. Antisemitism always involves a denial of the humanity of the Jew. In this regard, antisemitism is strongly akin to racism and sexism. There, too, the "other"—a black, a woman—is not considered fully human. The other lacks human dignity and therefore does not deserve to be treated equally. Those who deny a causal connection between antisemitism and the Final Solution type of thought should contemplate the loss of humanity of the hated object that is integral to both.

A truthful history of antisemitism cannot help but contain a catalog of horrors. As the story moves from one country to another, the indignities appear and reappear. Their force, it should be remembered, rests upon a simple calculation. Jews, as a small minority in most places, were greatly outnumbered and thus unable to resist effectively in an open confrontation. The threat of force was a principal horror. Extra-legal group attacks known under their Russian name "pogroms" were launched against Jews. Individual attacks by private citizens or police officers were common. The burning of houses and shops appears repeatedly in historical accounts.

Legal compulsion has been sweepingly employed against Jews. For a listing of the principal laws and regulations against Jews passed in a single country—Rumania—during one century, see chapter 10. Elsewhere, some measures related to the person of the Jew—the types and colors of clothing or hairstyle were prescribed, and where the use of horses was forbidden to Jews, they were required to walk, not ride, in the presence of certain others. Control of residential space was legislated extensively. In tsarist Russia, Jews were restricted to one region of the country—the Pale of Settlement—and excluded from the rest. In Germany, walls and locked gates surrounded Jewish ghettos. In Poland, Jews were restricted to certain sides of streets in Warsaw. Economic regulations were the most plentiful. Jews were excluded from most ordinary trades, at times from agriculture, and were compelled to pay special taxes. Access to education, especially higher education, was severely controlled.

Civic exclusion was widely practiced. Jews could not be equal citizens, nor could they run for office or even vote. Under these conditions second-class citizenship was a step forward. During medieval and early modern times, special charters were issued by rulers which endowed Jews with certain specific rights, almost always at a cash price. The right to milk the Jewish community was bought and sold on what might be called the civic market. Access to rulers in order to voice a community grievance was generally sought via an influential Jewish merchant or banker. Only in the late eighteenth and nineteenth centuries did the Jews begin to attain legal equality.

Manipulation of popular opinion, usually by government and church officials and commercial interests, gave rise to enduring myths. Perhaps most hoary was the allegation that Jews had "killed Christ," a charge that has lasted through the centuries until today. Another, slightly less aged, posits the existence of a recurrent worldwide conspiracy of Jews to accomplish ends that are redefined as the years pass and interests change. An American college student wrote recently: "When I edited the letters column for the *Los Angeles Examiner* last January [1981], one of my first discoveries was that roughly one out of every 25 letters in that paper's daily mailbag smacked of ardent antisemitism. Of those, nearly half seethed with maniacal claims about the national and international Jewish conspiracy."[1] Governments and military services have invested large sums of money in distributing printed materials embodying this myth. The twentieth century brought forward the self-contradictory tale of Jewish inventions of both capitalism and communism. (This was ridiculed mordantly by Nathanael West in his novel *A Cool Million*.)

Violence, backed by legal compulsion and civic exclusion and cemented by deadly myths, thus formed the core of anti-Jewish policies in the West. The precise combination varied among countries. Less clear is the process whereby these elements were joined. Indeed, can we speak of a "process" at all? Might it just have happened to happen? Did it all depend on the unraveling of historical events, peculiar to certain times and places?

Theorists have little help to offer us. Public opinion researchers tend to reduce antisemitism to a set of personal attitudes. People are ranked high or low on a scale of antisemitism depending on the configuration of responses to questions about their opinions. These scale positions are correlated with age, employment, schooling, and other variables. At best we are left with a collection of free-floating numbers, no two of which are necessarily linked. Nor is any inquiry made into a background or social context from which these individual attitudes presumably emerge.

Another perspective stresses the social contexts of periodic waves of antisemitism, paying little or no attention to individual responses. Again, the search is for correlations, only this time between the occurrence of antisemitic events and the type of social, economic, and political conditions that accompany the events. In many cases, antisemitism seems to rise during economic depressions. Resentment of the unemployed is said to lead to anti-Jewish behavior. Utterly missing, however, is a specification of the process whereby personal resentment is transformed into antisemitism.

The first approach gives us bits of reality in the shape of individual beliefs; the second leaves us with broad findings about the social context of the beliefs but omits individual behavior. Neither is able to explain why individuals at specific times and places participate in large-scale movements directed against Jews. Together, both approaches can tell us that specific attitudes and types of behavior are linked, but nothing more. Yet, we want to know the likelihood of the presence of antisemitism within certain populations at specific historical junctures. Answers of this breadth simply do not exist.

One reason for this absence is the failure of social researchers to consider the interrelationship of antisemitism with political power, economic problems, and social change. The widespread existence of antisemitism in a society is a declaration by those who control the society that real social problems are not going to be dealt with. It is not just Jews who are menaced by growing antisemitism. Anyone who seeks to reform a society will avoid antisemitism as a distraction from constructive change and as a warning signal.

Such failures create a cognitive vacuum, that is, a refusal or inability of government to remedy an admittedly deleterious social situation or even to offer an acceptable explanation of it. Such an intellectual abdication accentuates the popular demand for remedies and/or plans. There is nothing undemocratic about such demands. It is in these historical contexts that antisemitic "explanations" of depressions, unemployment, and natural disasters do their harm. In fourteenth-century

Europe, the black death killed one-third of the continent's population. A disproportionately smaller number of Jews were victimized, perhaps because of their relative isolation, food preparation practices, and more advanced medical techniques and sanitary procedures. Nevertheless, they were soon "blamed" for having brought on the general calamity, and widespread pogroms followed. Nazi leaders attributed many of their economic troubles during the early years of their rule to a worldwide Jewish plot to undermine the German economy. It was a towering exaggeration of a failed effort of Jews the world over to pressure the regime to ease its treatment of Jews. The attempted boycott was gravely weakened by internal conflicts within the Jewish community in a number of countries; one important group of Jews even entered into a commercial agreement with Nazi Germany for the ultimate easing of some German-Jewish emigration to Palestine—the agreement ran from 1933 to 1939. The German press was silent on the subject but voluble on the supposed Jewish conspiracy.

What role, besides that of victim, does the Jew play in antisemitism? Can it be said that Jews contribute in any way to the oncoming of antisemitism? During the eighteenth century, numerous social reformers—among them, Voltaire—held that Jews were hopelessly backward and peculiar in their worship and manners. The only hope to be held out for them was to cease being Jews. In effect, this view attributed antagonism toward Jews to the way Jews behaved. A more recent example can be found in the late 1930s in Paris where the Jewish establishment warned east European Jewish immigrants not to sit at sidewalk cafes and read Yiddish-language newspapers. Such a scene, it was cautioned, would surely arouse antisemitism. Still another finger pointed at the concentration of Jews in independent and professional employments as evidence of "clannishness" and antisocial sentiments. Unmentioned was the already existing anti-Jewish discrimination whereby Jews were not hired by non-Jewish employers, and thus working for oneself or other Jews was protection against discrimination.

In each of the three examples, the Jew is trying to be just that—a Jew. But antisemitism rejects this possibility: all men are free to be anything *but* Jews. No other people, to be treated as equal, is first required to pray or comport itself in a certain way, or improve its public presentability, or modify its employment pattern. Even the privilege of a white skin may be insufficient to protect an American Jew from antisemitism. Non-Jewish whites may lack the ability to read or to choose even the least-valued of careers, or they might be unable to engage in widely disapproved moral misadventures. They will not on any of these accounts be read out of the American polity by antisemites, but Jews may be.

In short, there is nothing Jews can change in their behavior that will still the doubts of antisemites other than to cease being Jews. To counsel Jews otherwise is to relieve gentile society of its fundamental responsibility for antisemitism. At most, Jews are innocent bystanders under antisemitism. The contemporary examples of Egypt and Poland, among others, show that antisemitism does not even require the presence of many Jews, as bystanders or otherwise. If we would understand antisemitism, we need first to comprehend the reasons why a dominant society adopts it. None of the reasons reside with shortcomings of Jews, at least in the dozen countries analyzed in this book.

Earlier, it was stressed that Jews have nearly always lived as a minority. Historian Salo Baron comments: "Diaspora Jewry almost invariably prospered most in heterogeneous empires, whereas ethnically and religiously homogeneous nations often proved extremely intolerant to it."[2] As will be made clear in the chapters on Egypt and France, Muslim rule over Christians and Jews was relatively evenhanded while Christian rule over Jews alone was highly oppressive and exploitative. Spain is an exception, having experienced both types of treatment with Muslim and Jewish minorities. In the United States of the nineteenth century Jewish immigrants shared a valuable economic advantage along with persons from other lands—they had white skins. While Jews and other Europeans faced social and other prejudices, they were spared legally based discrimination. Blacks were subjected to both kinds, serving as the principal object of social subordination. It would thus seem that blacks were buffers between the Jews and American society, and thereby the mistreatment of Jews was moderated. In Poland, on the other hand, where both Jews and Ukrainians were minorities, both were fully oppressed. It is doubtful that a plurality of minorities necessarily eases the treatment of any group or of the Jews in particular.

In recent years, "Never again!" has become a popular slogan, especially in Jewish circles. Referring to the events of the Holocaust, the slogan is intended to keep painful memories alive as a guarantee against the repetition of the Holocaust. The slogan, however, is not self-explanatory. It ignores the vast ignorance among the world's young of the Holocaust. After all, we cannot forget what we never knew. And we cannot know what we have failed to learn. In post–World War II public opinion polls, many non-Jewish respondents in the United States and Germany felt too much attention was being paid the Holocaust, which they tended to view as simply another special interest of Jews. This positively suggests a hostility to learning about the Holocaust. Late in 1984, representatives from teachers' organizations in six countries met at the International Committee of Educators to Combat Racism, Anti-Semitism and Apartheid. Judging from the official report of the conference, little was said explicitly about the need to study the Holocaust.[3]

The purpose of this book is to help answer a crucial question of our times: Never again—what?

NOTES

1. Bradley Campbell, Amherst College *Student*, October 7, 1982.
2. Salo W. Baron, *A Social and Religious History of the Jews*, 1, 2d ed. (New York: Columbia Univ. Press, 1952), p. 131.
3. See Clara van den Bosch et al., eds., *Educators against Discrimination* (Amsterdam: International Committee of Educators to Combat Racism, Anti-Semitism and Apartheid, May 1985).

Because
They Were Jews

1

A NOAH'S ARK OF BIGOTRY: ARGENTINA

A systematic record of known antisemitic incidents against Jewish people throughout the world shows that there are more reports of such incidents from Argentina than from any other country.
—Haim Avni, 1977

The historian Robert Weisbrot has called Argentina "something of a Noah's Ark of bigotry, preserving every major type and group of anti-semite in the world over the past century."[1] In fact, antisemitism in Argentina preceded the arrival of Jews in any numbers. As a Spanish colony Argentina was subject to the rules of the Inquisition, and Jews were excluded on religious grounds. While some entered nevertheless, not until the very end of the nineteenth century did many Jews begin to immigrate, especially from Russia. In 1889, no more than 2,000 lived in the country. By 1914, the number neared 100,000.

An unusually large number of Jews worked in agriculture on farm colonies financed by Baron De Hirsch, a European philanthropist. In this land of wheat and meat, such Jews were welcomed. Many others went directly to the cities where they worked in small shops and factories, alongside numerous proletarians from Spain and Italy. Exceedingly few Jews in those early years entered the business class except for numerous small shopkeepers.

The single most powerful political and economic force in the country was the so-called "oligarchy," composed principally of the large-scale owners of wheat fields and cattle ranches and, to a lesser extent, indus-trialists. A second group was the military, recruited from the same circles and accustomed to defend the oligarchy against internal and external attack. The Roman Catholic church, the third force, closely collaborated with the other two by defending the existing order, whatever its social injustices. The church was the custodian of antisemitic doctrine.

Racism was not part of the church's antisemitism. Jews were persons who practiced an illicit and misguided religion, not those who were "born" Jews or who had Jewish parents and grandparents. Conversion would cure them of their sin of Judaism. Catholicism had always been a de facto state religion but was declared so formally only in 1853, in the same measure that proclaimed the right of Argentines to practice any religion. Social power, political privilege, and religious doctrine were thus intertwined.

The earliest encounters of Jews with antisemitism arose out of class conflict as well as doctrines of ethnic hatred. In 1902, a general strike occurred in which socialists and anarchists took a prominent role. Many of these were immigrants. Russian Jews among them were singled out by authorities. Under the Residence Law of 1902 the central government was authorized to deport any foreigner who merited it under extremely vague regulations.[2] Police regularly used force to quell Socialist demonstrations as in 1909 "when cavalry . . . charged a protest march and left more than eighty wounded and fourteen dead; no police were hurt."[3] In the same year, a seventeen-year old Jewish immigrant killed the police chief of Buenos Aires with a bomb. Many Jews as a result were arrested and deported. On May 14 and 15, 1910, a full-scale pogrom was unleashed with "beating and raping [of] many in the Jewish quarter."[4] Another source describes some of the damage: "Mobs destroyed the offices of *La Protesta* and *La Vanguardia*, the anarchist and Socialist dailies. . . . The Russian Library, the most important working class cultural center in the Jewish community, was sacked."[5]

A new law was passed in 1910 barring the immigration of anarchists. Sentiment among middle-class Argentinians was strongly set against any further influx of "Russians," a codeword for Jews.

During the years 1914 to 1918, Argentina was cut off from many of its markets and sources of supply by World War I. High unemployment and soaring inflation generated much unrest among workers and the poor. Strikes and demonstrations spread at the end of the war. Conservatives, alarmed at the development of revolutions in Russia, Germany, Hungary, and elsewhere, demanded draconic measures be taken to head off any similar movements in Argentina. Catholic church attacks on the alleged radicalism of all Jews spread. In 1917, two new textbooks for use in Catholic schools incorporated much antisemitic material. Jews protested in vain.[6] Parish churches were the scenes of anti-Jewish preaching from the pulpit. In 1912, the church had organized Catholic Circles of Workers which physically attacked Jews and socialists on the streets.[7]

A period in January 1919 has become known in Argentina history as the "Tragic Week." The events grew out of what seemed an ordinary strike at the Vasena Iron Works. On January 7, police rushed the picket line and in the process killed five strikers. Revulsion struck many unionists and a citywide funeral was held two days later. Hundreds of thousands marched. Police shot at some demonstrators and there were exchanges of fire. Many other plants closed. Press reports the next day stated that from seventy to eighty had been killed with nearly 1,000 wounded. Most of these were workers or persons living near the Vasena factory. Preparations were made for a general strike.

The next day, January 10, soon was dubbed "Bloody Friday." To understand the course of the day's events it is necessary to realize what preparations were afoot in the government and among upper-class and industrial employer groups. President Hipólito Irigoyen announced a Communist plot to overthrow the government was underway and that the strikers were being pushed in that direction by foreigners, especially Russians. He all but used the word "Jews." Some 10,000 armed men, consisting of police and the military, were brought to Buenos Aires.[8] Two battle cruisers, with 600 marines, waited in the harbor. Bands of armed civilians were organized as civil police.

Historian Victor Mirelman begins his description: "A civilian group called *Guardia Blanca* (White Guard), joined by members of the Argentine 'elite', began active participation in the defense of the national institutions. They attacked anarchists and socialists, mostly foreign workers, who looked . . . 'Russian'. Carrying slogans such as 'Out with the foreigners' and 'Death to the Jews', the so-called *Caza de los Rusor* (chase of the Russians, as Jews were called) was started."[9] He continues: "The Jewish quarters . . . were attacked mainly by the civilian groups, with the acquiescence of the police and the army."[10] "All the while," adds Weisbrot, "the police stood by, in perfect order, completely impassive."[11] Mirelman recounts further: "Antisemitic groups were found in various schools at the University of Buenos Aires, notably at the School of Medicine, which was on the border of the Jewish quarter. Jewish students were repeatedly attacked by other students, most of them sons of the *porteno* elite."[12] A journalist, Juan Jose de Soiza Reilly, described "old men whose beards were torn out."[13] John Hebert adds: "As described by a contemporary, the reactionaries went into the Jewish quarters beating with rifles. Women and children were not spared."[14] Many of the attacks on Jews were coordinated by Rear Admiral Domecq Garcia.[15]

Nationalist fervor, antisemitism, and antiradical and antilabor sentiments could not be clearly demarcated. Out of the Tragic Week came a number of ultraconservative, nationalistic bodies. The Argentine Patriotic League tried to "stop union meetings, harassed laborers and was generally antilabor."[16] Members of the Civic Guard joined en masse, as did police and military people. Meetings were held in police stations. The provision to employers of scabs and mercenary guards was the function of the Association for Work, created by large businesses.[17] Another, named the Commission for Defense of Order, combined the military and big business. While all the private groups had attacked Jews during the week, apparently no single group was explicitly organized in the name of antisemitism.

Thousands of Jews (as well as Italian and Spanish radicals) had been arrested in the name of breaking a purported revolutionary plot. Not only was there a total failure to substantiate the widely repeated charge, not a single trial was given those arrested on the charge. Hebert refers to "the lack of proof of Irigoyen's later statement that foreign agitators had directed the revolt."[18]

The great mass of Jews "came to the rescue of the victims promptly."[19] In the heat of the events a centralized association of Jewish groups emerged to represent the community in dealings with the government. When a rabbi spoke to President Irigoyen about specific grievances, the latter complained that Jews should approach him as Argentinians, not Jews. In either capacity, however, none of the grievances was remedied. Some Jewish groups, especially the Zionist organization, distanced themselves from "hotheads" in the Jewish community. In the organized Jewish position on the events of the week, Mirelman stipulates: "There was no plea for justice, no assertion that the riots and assaults carried on by the police, the army, and some civilian reactionary groups were altogether out of place, nor was there a demand that justice should be administered."[20]

The events of the week constitute two tragedies instead of one. In this first pogrom of Argentine history, it had been demonstrated that the forces of law and order could be fully mobilized for anti-Jewish goals by the elite sections of Argentine society. They suffered no repudiation either within their own ranks nor from other countries. Their political enemy, Irigoyen, shared their objectives and means since he "used the ... red scare ... to justify the occurrence of the disorders and the particularly harsh treatment meted out by police and military forces against laborers and Jews."[21] The conservative nationalist heritage of political violence became rooted on the Argentine Right.

A second tragedy lay in the suddenness and the emotional depth of the attack on the Jews. They were not in a position to defend themselves from the fury of private power nor from the sweeping violence of formal military force. To many Jews, who had only recently come from the pogrom-ridden Russia of the tsars, it must have been overwhelming to meet the same treatment in the New World. Unfortunately, the Jewish community did not summon up an enduring unity with which to combat this menace. Communal organizations proliferated but defense associations were notable by their absence. The shock of the Tragic Week endured for decades beyond 1919. It helped install into Argentine Jewish affairs a presumption of destruction should the accumulated force of antisemitism be released. Dominant elements in the Jewish community therefore tended to avoid confrontation.

Agitation against further immigration of Jews continued during the 1920s. Nevertheless, the Jewish population grew significantly. During the same decade, Catholic antisemitism worsened. In church-connected intellectual journals, Jews were attacked as Christ-killers and as obstinate nonbelievers in Christianity.[22] Jews were charged with teaching anti-Argentinism in their Yiddish schools. (Before World War I, Jewish schools had been closed down temporarily on the same ground.) The national government both led and lagged in antisemitic matters. Administrative obstruction of Jewish immigration was an example of the former;[23] considerable anti-Jewish legislation or executive decrees in the provinces exemplified the latter. Frequently, the central government reversed a provincial step restricting the rights of Jews.

The 1930s were a fateful decade for Argentine Jewry. Along with the rest of the world, a severe economic depression struck the country. In 1930, the military seized control of the government in its first coup and the rise of Nazism profoundly influenced the fate of the Jews in Argentina.

In 1932, a year before Hitler's seizure of power, a group of German immigrants in Buenos Aires organized a branch of the Nazi party. According to one report, the development "was not taken seriously by the German population of the city."[24] Support in the German community, however, grew rapidly. By 1933, German diplomats in Argentina encouraged anti-Jewish activities as did the local Nazi party.[25] In part, this was aimed at counteracting organized efforts by Argentine Jews to conduct a boycott of German goods.[26] Members of the Argentine Legion, a fascist group, were arrested in March 1934 for having bombed a synagogue in Buenos Aires. The American Jewish Committee reported in the late 1930s that antisemitic propaganda was "most prevalent among the German colonies in those South and Central American countries where nationalistic dictatorships prevail."[27] By that time, Argentina belonged in this category.

The immigration policy of Argentina had always disfavored the influx of Jews. In colonial days, they had been excluded altogether. Haim Avni reports: "This policy of selection became more stringent during the 1930s and from 1938 onwards became a policy of almost completely closed doors, just when Jewish refugees from Central Europe were seeking a refuge in vain."[28] Between 1933 and 1941, some 25,000 Jews entered the country legally. During the Holocaust years, 1942–44, Argentina admitted only 2,225.[29]

By the late 1930s, the military administration had shown a hard fist to the Jews. "Under Uriburu [who headed the first military takeover in

1930] and his successors, the Special Section of elite police officers, designed to combat internal threats, turned so antisemitic that the German
population in Argentina, in sympathy with the Nazi movement in their
native land, contributed funds to the organization. The German embassy
also directly aided the Special Section."[30] In May 1938, teachers in eleven
Jewish schools were arrested and charged with teaching communism.
The schools were ordered closed. All the arrested denied the charges.
After a short time they were reinstated, the schools reopened, and books
and materials were returned.[31] On the other hand, the government
regularly refused, on the ground of defending freedom of expression,
to stop the circulation of printed materials advocating race hatred; such
materials were also classified by postal authorities as cultural works and
thus paid low postage rates.[32] In Santa Fe, a court turned aside complaints by Jews that they were being defamed and insulted collectively
by antisemitic propaganda which was held to be a permissible expression
of freedom of opinion.[33]

As part of a hypernationalist policy directed against minority languages, the use of all such languages in public meetings was banned;
this included Yiddish. Police frequently interfered at meetings conducted in the language. In other cases, special permission to use Yiddish
was granted with the provision that the subject of antisemitism not be
discussed. (In other words, the police wanted to be able to understand
what Jews thought of the policy of antisemitism.)

A number of organizations openly engaged in anti-Jewish activities.
These included Antisemitic Action, the Social Party of Restoration, the
Nationalist Youth Alliance, and two labor unions—the Federation of
Commercial Employees and the Union of Clothing Cutters, Measurers,
and Finishers. The appearance of the unions among the more middle-
and upper-class antisemites was unique in the country's history. There
is no evidence that the General Confederation of Labor shared these
sentiments. Father Virgilio Filipo, a Catholic priest, gave anti-Jewish
radio broadcasts every Sunday.

After repeated calls for government measures against Nazi and other
anti-Jewish agitation, the authorities responded reluctantly. In June
1938, Nazi schools were ordered closed and in September schools operated by any foreign organization were directed to cease teaching what
was regarded as foreign ideologies. The next month public meetings of
an anti-Jewish nature were forbidden and the Ministry of Posts and
Communication was ordered to censor Father Filipo's speeches to excise
antisemitic materials. In May 1939, the Nazi party was dissolved. All
groups directed by a foreign center were required to revise their bylaws
in line with democratic principles and register with the Ministry of the
Interior and the police. Donations or subsidies from abroad were

banned. Despite the legislation and decrees, in addition to those noted here, anti-Jewish activities did not subside.

The Jewish community was deeply concerned about fellow Jews in Germany. After *Kristallnacht*, on November 9–10, 1938, Argentine Jews called a week of mourning: "On November 22, Jewish shops closed in Buenos Aires; many Christians joined in this demonstration. A week later, a huge mass meeting, attended by over 30,000 persons, demonstrated in Buenos Aires against the persecution of the Jews in Germany, adopted a resolution to boycott German goods, and urged the Government to open the doors of Argentina to refugees."[34] Several weeks later a Socialist deputy, Americo Gioldi, asked the Chamber of Deputies to urge the government to ease restrictions against the immigration of refugee Jews. The government refused to yield on the issue.

Public authorities, however, invested much effort in protesting the government was free of antisemitism. In July 1939, a Buenos Aires court demonstrated such a concern on behalf of the government. A Jewish parent applied to change his son's name from Isaac to Inazio so that he would not be subjected to anti-Jewish taunts. The judge refused to grant the request on the ground that to do so would admit implicitly that Argentina was an antisemitic society.[35]

During the Tragic Week in 1919, community self-defense had not been possible. But it was otherwise in the 1930s. Defense was an obvious necessity in the face of incessant physical and verbal attacks, as well as discriminatory behavior toward Jews. In 1933, the People's Organization Against Anti-Semitism was started by Jewish Communists, and the Committee Against the Persecution of the Jews in Germany by other Jews. In 1934, the Committee Against Anti-Semitism and Racism was organized. Two years later it developed into the first truly umbrella national organization of Argentine Jewry, Delegación de Asociaciones Israelitas Argentinas (DAIA). Communists and anarchists were excluded. While DAIA restricted itself to public declarations and private conferences, some Jews took up arms to protect other Jews from physical attack: "Jewish defense volunteers won individual skirmishes against Nazi thugs who assaulted Jewish buildings and assemblies."[36] During the fall of 1940, Jews clashed with pro-Nazis in heavily German Misiones province and Rosario.[37]

From 1938 to mid-1943, the central government's policy on Nazi influence in the country consisted of sporadic crackdowns with virtually no follow-through. Thus, officials could point to specific formal actions that had been taken, but the prohibited behavior continued. In 1940, after the Senate voted to penalize antidemocratic parties, the editor of the pro-Nazi journal, *El Pampero*, was arrested but soon released. A month later, police arrested Karl Arnold, a Gestapo agent, and over twenty-five others, some of whom were deported along with Arnulf Fuhrmann, described by one source as the "prime antisemitic agitator in South America."[38] In 1942, the minister of the interior ordered the dissolution of a Nazi front group, the Federation of German Welfare and Cultural Clubs. In January 1943, following six weeks of pro-Nazi agitation among students at the University of Buenos Aires, the board of trustees authorized dismissal of all pro-Nazi faculty members.[39]

Yet, these trends were contradicted by other contemporary events. One source reports: "The May 1943 issue of *Clarinada* (Bugle Call), the violently anti-Jewish, anti-American and pro-Nazi Argentina magazine, reveals that it is again receiving support from the government through the advertisements of several government controlled national and municipal banks." It continued: "Henry Ford's [antisemitic publication] *The International Jew* was apparently enjoying increased popularity in Buenos Aries. It was common to see persons with a copy of Ford's book in one hand and *El Pampero* . . . in the other."[40] According to the Overseas News Agency, the number of foreign-language newspapers being subsidized by Nazi or other Axis-connected sources approached fifty. When a staff member of the liberal Buenos Aires newspaper *La Prensa* published a study of Nazi infiltration into Argentina, the book was banned by the government.

A turning point was reached in June 1943 when a group of army colonels—including Juan Perón—took control of the government. Thereafter, public policy became much more consistently anti-Jewish with fewer denials voiced by government representatives.

In October, publication of Yiddish newspapers was prohibited; the ban was soon retracted because of an appeal by U.S. President Franklin D. Roosevelt. Several days later the DAIA was compelled to declare publicly that no antisemitic discrimination existed in Argentina. Five days after this, however, all Jewish welfare and mutual-aid groups were dissolved.[41] In November, Jewish homes in Buenos Aires were raided by the political police; many Jews fled in fear to Uruguay and Chile. On two successive nights in Salta, during December, members of a Jewish theatrical troupe were attacked physically.

Jews living in Entre Rios province were menaced during this period: "Previously, the Federal Commissioner of Entre Rios had prohibited ritual slaughter, closed the Hebrew schools, revoked the corporate status of the *Chevra Kadisha,* discharged Jews in the civil service of the province and changed the Jewish names of towns and streets."[42] Although the measures were struck down on appeal, their vehemence spoke volumes about the deteriorating situation of the Jews. Further proof came in April 1944 when the governor of the province submitted a bill to the Jewish Colonization Association for $2.5 million on the novel theory that eleven Jewish colonies had not paid taxes for ten years. In the following months of May and June, 250 Jewish public school teachers were fired from their jobs. The pace of vandalization of Jewish shops and beatings of Jews quickened in Entre Rios.[43]

In June 1944, the military rulers decreed compulsory teaching of Roman Catholicism in the public schools. Upon registering in schools children were required to state their religious affiliation. Thereupon, Jewish children were separated from the others. They sat on separate benches and were often humiliated by non-Jewish schoolmates.[44] Some Jewish parents chose not to identify their children's religion; they then studied Catholicism but were spared physical separation.

Antisemitism in Entre Rios grew worse as signals of approval were received from the central government:

Jewish houses were marked with large red letters "J" or "Death to the Jews", or "Keep out of Jewish business". All Jewish school teachers, numbering 110, were dismissed from public schools largely on unfounded grounds of communism. On high holidays Jews had great difficulties in keeping stores closed because of threats of the local police; and only by appeal to higher authorities were they permitted to close.... In Jewish [agricultural] colonies, the gathering of more than three persons for other than religious meetings required special permission, thus causing serious youth problems.[45]

Some of these measures were too extreme for the military junta and these were revoked. As usual, authorities made misleading evaluations of the situation. In March 1945, vice-president Perón said, "There is no Jewish problem in our country, and we have nothing against the Jews."[46]

Yet, supporters of the same Perón, who was preparing to run for president in 1946, were among the most vicious antisemites. Toward the close of 1945: "Anti-Jewish demonstrations on the part of Perón supporters, previously sporadic in nature, assumed pogrom proportions. Antisemitic bands, apparently enjoying complete immunity, roamed through Jewish neighborhoods in Buenos Aires. Jews were beaten up, synagogues defiled, community buildings stoned. Several deaths occurred. For a time the Jewish community lived in a panic atmosphere of pogrom and threat of pogrom."[47] Government spokespersons called for peace in subdued tones. Destruction continued as synagogues in the capital city and a community center in Córdoba were attacked and defaced. Other structures suffered attacks. Armed defensive measures sometimes helped: "Jewish youth, aided by democratic elements, organized to repel the attacks of the Perónistas, affording a unique demonstration of courage and dignity."[48]

June 1946 saw the election of Perón to the presidency. He ruled for the next nine years. The scope and level of antisemitism narrowed. Outright anti-Jewish violence was restrained by the regime. Open gov-

ernmental approval for antisemitic aggression was apparently forbidden.
The principal element in Perón's support was a populist stream which,
in Mark Falcoff's words, "favored a style of government which combined
personalism, state capitalism, gangsterism, and bread and butter unionism with a rather haphazard showering of social-welfare benefits on the
'loyal', rather than a systematic restructuring of Argentina society along
more egalitarian lines."[49] In this array, antisemitism was secondary.

The Jewish community pressed Perón to open the doors to immigration by Jewish victims of Nazism, but this was rejected by the government:
"Though there were no formal restrictions against Jews as such, persistent reports indicated that the Argentine consuls in Europe were functioning on the basis of instructions from the central authorities in
Argentina not to issue visas to Jews, either permanent or transit. At the
same time, the entry of Italians and Spaniards was facilitated in every
possible way."[50]

Argentina, however, flung open its doors to the Nazis themselves. Even
before the war ended, some moved to Argentina. Before the first year
of the postwar period ended, thousands of Nazis had made the country
their new home. Perón was drawn ideologically to them but there were
other reasons as well: "He made lucrative deals with Gestapo officers
and other agents of Hitler's Reich. . . . [The process] involved the provision of forged identity passes to the Nazis and the transfer of much
of their wealth to Perón's own coffers."[51] These Nazis included Martin
Bormann, Adolf Eichmann, and Josef Mengele. Numerous Nazis entered the service of the Argentine government. Under Perón,

Argentina was the undisturbed center of the Nazi executive. The German-
language *Der Weg* [The Path] was published in Argentina as a central organ for
the world Nazi movement. . . . From Argentina the former Nazi Stuka bomber
wing commander Col. Hans Ulrich Rudel conducted neo-Nazi activities in Germany. . . . In his greeting to a large German conference in 1955, Perón paid his
respects to his comrades in arms, "the heroic German soldiers who had died
during the second World War for the cause of German freedom". The Alianza
Libertadora Nacionalista, an armed Fascist organization, openly maintained by
the Perón government, was intended to be the dictator's bodyguard. It consisted
for the most part of European Quislings.[52]

Perón was not himself an antisemite. He had frequently criticized
persons who participated in anti-Jewish demonstrations. At the same
time, when in May 1950 Jews protested the sale of the *Protocols of the
Elders of Zion* and Henry Ford's *The International Jew,* Perón defended
such sale as freedom of the press.[53] It was in the field of economic policy
that Perón, willy-nilly, succeeded in integrating the growing Jewish middle class into national affairs. Jews became far more involved in industry
as Perón strove to strengthen independent Argentine industry with ex-

tensive governmental financing.[54] New economic opportunities opened for Jewish youth in higher education and the professions.

The historian Weisbrot concludes that "with all his flaws, Perón still evolved into a president who was one of the most benevolent toward the Jewish community in modern Argentine history."[55] This fair-minded judgment may also be read as a bitter comment on the modern history of the country. Both the military and sections of the upper class were, in part, behind the ending of Perón's reign in 1955. Along with the church, both were in the forefront of antisemitism in past years. Their political resurgence gave a new impetus to antisemitism: "During the reign of President Pedro Aramburu from 1955 to 1958, virulent anti-Jewish magazines and books received continued immunity from government prosecution."[56] The remainder of the decade saw a rising trend of violence against Jews (and left-wing persons of any religious affiliation).

A principal organizer of this violence was the Catholic-fascist group Tacuara, formed in 1930 by "young men in their late teens and twenties, members of the Argentine landed aristocracy, the 'good' families, or oligarchy."[57] Its spiritual leader was Father Julio Meinveille, the author of *The Jew in the Mysteries of History,* in which he explained that Jews had invented both capitalism and socialism: "Capitalism to rob Christians of what they have, and socialism to poison the have nots, and thus establish a struggle of classes."[58] Tacuara tarried little over texts, however. It excelled in bombings and beatings. Because of their social and political connections, Tacuarans virtually never were arrested, let alone tried.

In 1960, Israel agents entered Argentina, captured the Nazi murderer of Jews, Adolf Eichmann, and brought him to Israel. He was tried, found guilty, and executed in 1962. These events ignited a tremendous explosion of anti-Jewish activities led by extreme right-wing nationalist and Nazi groups. In 1962, the army forced President Arturo Frondizi to resign and replaced him with Senator J. M. Guida whose regime "gave Tacuara and other groups complete liberty to wage their campaign against the Jews."[59] Perhaps the most reprehensible of the resulting deeds was the physical attack on a young Jewish woman Graciela N. Sirota in which the assailant used a knife to carve letters on her breast. So shocked were Jews and others that DAIA called a half-day national protest. All Jewish places of business closed and demonstrations of protest were held. Many non-Jews participated.

No more than a temporary abatement of attacks ensued. Israeli business installations were machine-gunned and Molotov cocktails were thrown at synagogues. Many attacks on Jews were not even reported. In May 1963, President Guida outlawed Tacuara and another Fascist group and closed down their offices. Tacuara failed, in fact, to disband but the government looked the other way. The Arab League, attacking both Jews and Zionists, became a central funding agent for antisemitic activities by the mid-1960s. In 1966, for the fifth time since 1930, a military coup unseated the legally elected government. The new head of government ruled by decree. Anti-Jewish activities continued their wretched course.[60]

It was in this climate that several social scientists chose to study the status of antisemitism in Argentina. In 1964, Pichon-Riviere asked a national sample of 500 persons how they would accept Jews in various social roles. Responses in percentages were as follows:[61]

Category of Social Acceptance (I would accept a Jew as a:)	All Civilians	Low-Income Persons	Members of the Military
Neighbor	80	85	43
Fellow worker	73	78	36
Teacher for my children	49	58	29
Lawyer	58	70	29
Doctor	72	74	22
Personal friend	68	78	29
Spouse of a close relative	52	54	14

Members of the same group were asked what qualities they attributed to Jews. In percentages, the responses were as follows:[62]

Mentioned by Civilians		Mentioned by the Military	
Industrious	45	Trading and dealing	83
Skillful	42	Avaricious	78
Trading and dealing	42	Hypocritical	44
Intelligent	39	Unscrupulous	44
Progressive	32		

In a separate survey, conducted by sociologist Gino Germani in 1962, the percentage of antisemites in relation to socioeconomic position was shown as follows:[63]

Upper class	6.9
Upper middle class	18.3
Middle middle class	18.7
Lower middle class	19.2
Upper lower class	27.7
Lower lower class	27.6

The sample comprised 2,078 persons in metropolitan Buenos Aires.

In Pichon-Riviere's study, the following persons were asked which immigrant groups they would bar. Their responses, in percentages, were as follows:[64]

Foreign group	Civilians	Low-Income Civilians	Military
Italians	7	11	11
Spaniards	4	7	11
Jews	26	23	72
Germans	8	8	6

Finally, in 1967 Joaquin Fischerman studied the incidence of anti-semitism among various social sections. Here are his findings, in percentages:[65]

	Percentage of Antisemites	
	Nonethnocentric	*Ethnocentric*
Upper class	33	66
Middle class	30	62
Lower class	19	50

Let us examine these findings closely. Basically, all three surveys involved opinions rather than actions in historical events. Typically, persons were asked what they preferred, hypothetically, rather than whether they had participated in an anti-Jewish occurrence in Buenos Aires or elsewhere. Conceivably, therefore, an active member of Tacuara was free to give "liberal" responses to hypothetical questions and thereby create a false impression.

We have seen earlier that much of Argentina's antisemitism was originated by upper-class persons during the past century. Yet, Germani found such respondents were the least antisemitic. He explained this by holding that there were two varieties of antisemitism rather than a single unified kind, traditional and ideological. The former rested on crude stereotypes and was strongest among the poor while the latter viewed Jews as conspirators and exploiters and was dominant among the rich. While this distinction has been widely accepted by writers in the field, it may be doubted that the distinction is really all that clear. So-called ideological antisemitism is also drenched with stereotypes, although these may be somewhat more sophisticated. In that event, the Germani distinction may come down to a measure of relative crudity of stereotypes.

The Fischerman findings clearly indicate that antisemites are more likely to be found among ethnocentric than non-ethnocentric persons. Also, the presence of antisemitic attitudes is much more likely to appear at the top than at the bottom of the social scale. An economic factor is also at work in Pichon-Riviere's findings. Low-income persons are somewhat less likely to favor barring Jews as immigrants. At the same time, they reproduce very closely the strong general tendency to bar Jews rather than Italians, Spaniards, or Germans.

The "sore thumb" in all the findings is the military's emphatic preference to bar Jews rather than the other three immigrant groups. This
stance is not an expression of simple anti-immigrant sentiment. Military
respondents match closely national views on further immigration of Italians, Spaniards, and Germans. Their zeal to exclude Jews, however, is
virtually triple that of the civilian population.

These polls, like most others, throw light only on individual dimen-
sions of antisemitism. They ignore institutional and historical antisemitism. As pointed out above, it is possible—even likely—that members
of antisemitic gangs could give replies that are socially acceptable even
though these do not reflect their actual views. The scourge of Argentine
Jewry has been the systematic discrimination built into the society with
the aid of the church, the armed services, and the economic oligarchy,
among others. The polls cannot, or at least do not, portray any of these
factors at work in the area of antisemitism. While individual opinions
may have a collective impact, the institutional avenues for this impact
must be studied.

The times themselves are a good test of this. During the years when
the above public opinion polls were taken (1962–67), Argentine antisemitism appeared to sweep everything before it. Anti-Jewish groups
had a free hand. In 1966, the military took over once more and antisemitism became an approved government activity if not one of its programs. There is no reason to believe individual opinions became more
hostile toward Jews and that this powered the sharp upturn of antisemitism. The reasons were institutional and political, both factors whose
visibility is strictly limited. Thus, on the eve of a great expansion of
antisemitic activities, a knowing observer of Argentine affairs was unable
to sense forthcoming events: "Organizationally, antisemitism is quite
weak, despite (or because) of its upper class exclusivity. Fringe groups
exist in various spheres of public life for the purpose of disseminating
antisemitic literature. None, however, are particularly potent."[66] Even
had the polls been available, their personal cast would have explained
few of the events to come.

Between the military coups of 1966 and 1973, the Argentine political
situation coasted downward. The Perónists divided into right and left
wings and still represented about one-third of the nation's voting
strength. Together with rightist nationalist circles, the military comprised
perhaps the leading element on the political scene. Both continued to
rely on the ready cooperation of the economic elite of the country.
Antisemitism fed on each group's support. In 1973, four different persons served as president, but the last one, Perón, served for only a little
more than a year. In 1974 he died and was succeeded by his (second)
wife Isabel. She served until 1976 when a military coup ejected her. That

junta, with changing membership, ruled until 1983 when it was replaced by a freely elected government.

During the years from 1973 to 1975, antisemitic forces drew ever nearer to the groups in power. They became involved in "the vital economic and political interests of the Argentine Republic."[67] Isabel Perón ruled with the advice and support of her late husband's one-time private secretary and extreme right-wing leader, Jose Lopez Rega: "Perón's death was followed by a period of complete insecurity and terror.... In November 1974 a state of siege was imposed; leftist guerrilla groups were outlawed... ultra-right paramilitary groups... killed hundreds of persons.... Right-wing groups openly incited towards the killing of Jews ... Professed antisemites were appointed to high positions in the universities."[68] Antisemites were given frequent access to government television stations.

From 1976 on, under the military, extralegal murders multiplied: "The military *junta*, in its zeal to eliminate left-wing dissidents, awarded Fascist groups free reign to prey upon 'undesirables'.... Jews rather than terrorists became the most vulnerable targets of this policy. Self-appointed 'death squads' were soon roaming the country with impunity, murdering prominent liberals, trade unionists, intellectuals, and Jews of every occupational and political background.... A wave of antisemitic incidents engulfed the nation."[69] Weisbrot notes that Jews "were not only brutally assaulted by freely operating extremist bands but were increasingly singled out for public slander by the government."[70] This was the era of political "disappearances" when persons were snatched from their homes without explanation or charge, never to be heard from again. Many were suspected of being involved in left-wing activities. While most of the imprisoned were not Jews, "Jewish political prisoners were subjected to particularly cruel torture."[71] In 1977, the Jewish publisher Jacobo Timerman was arrested and held for nearly two years without charges being specified. A reliable source reported, "Most liberal Argentines took it for granted that Timerman's continued arrest was attributable to antisemitism, and that the whole case started because *La Opinion*, the newspaper which he published, was regarded as too important to be in the hands of Jews and at the service of the Jewish community."[72]

In the military, especially after 1976, a certain turfism or even warlordism set in. Jurisdictions were established even within sections of separate services. Access to mass communication media was guarded jealously: "In Buenos Aires there are four TV channels. One belongs to the president of Argentina and directly depends on the government. That is channel 7. Channel 9 belongs to the army. Channel 11 to the air force and Channel 13 to the navy."[73] When Timerman was arrested, he was told: "You're a prisoner of the First Army Corps in action."[74] Some high governmental officials tried in vain to free him. Timerman wrote, "I was kidnapped by the extremist sector of the army."[75] Robert Cox, the editor-in-chief of the *Buenos Aires Herald,* made a similar characterization: "Argentina . . . is divided by the rivalries of the separate fiefdoms represented by the armed forces, with their various free-wheeling intelligence services and the beleaguered, powerless Presidency. . . . Central authority, and the responsibility that goes with it, has never been established by the moderates in the military who have held nominal power since the March 1976 coup."[76] This decentralization of semiofficial terror operated so as to protect antisemites who held any positions of authority, whether jailers or generals: "Lower-echelon officers and enlisted men in the police and military were notoriously antisemitic."[77] The numerous small formations created crevices and corners where such antisemites operated under color of the law. Of the military high command since 1976, James Nielson, assistant editor of the *Buenos Aires Herald,* wrote: "It has tried to rein in the autonomous commanders who committed what the government delicately describes as 'excesses' as quietly as possible, but it has been afraid that any head-on confrontation would lead to an uprising. Although some of the virtually independent units, led for the most part by majors or captains . . . have been dismantled, others are still operating."[78]

Evidence is overwhelming that the military regime knew exceedingly well the extent and character of Argentine antisemitism. It lent its own mass communication facilities to that purpose. It ignored when it did not encourage the circulation of anti-Jewish propaganda. It chose for political reasons to countenance the existence of semiofficial right-wing death squads. Many highly placed officers were themselves antisemites in action.

This is not to say that no national policy on Jews existed. In mid-1981, Timerman—freed from his unexplained incarceration and exiled to Israel—charged that the military junta had earlier accepted a plan drawn up by Gen. Carlos G. Suarez Mason to launch five anti-Jewish financial "scandals." He described the alleged plan: "The Anar affair . . . involved the powerful Madanes family, who were the first Jews to break into heavy industry—they control the aluminum industry. Then came the Bonner scandal—he was president of the National Association of Manufacturers, a leading position in Argentina, the first Jew to serve in that post. Then the Gelbard scandal—the first Jew to serve in the cabinet. And then the Timerman scandal—the first Jew who was editor of a national newspaper. And at the same time, the Graiver scandal—all five scandals together."[79] The staging of these scandals, according to Timerman, was aimed at discrediting the idea that Jews were acceptable as occupants of socially honored positions. According to Timerman, none of the five cases was tested in court.

How did the Jewish community respond to these torrents of anti-semitism? There are no public opinion polls nor other direct expressions of opinion by rank-and-file Jews. Occasional characterizations are available. Thus, Weisbrot wrote in 1978 that there was "a tendency among a substantial minority of Jews to deny or minimize the existence of antisemitism."[80] Judith Elkin, an American historian, summarizes the collective self-judgment of many Argentine Jews: "Most people were paralyzed with fear . . . ; the only real question [during 1976–83] was how to survive. . . . The most widespread verdict the Jews of Argentina render on themselves is, 'We were good Germans.' "[81] They knew of the horrors perpetrated by the engineers of disappearance, but they remained silent. Worse, all but a few separated themselves from the disappeared and the imprisoned. They did not wish to be identified with them. In addition, many felt that the charges of radicalism were true and thus not charge-able to antisemitism.[82] Elkin notes that while many rabbis expressed their intention to visit prisons to comfort Jewish prisoners, "it is widely agreed in the community that these visits were not made."[83] Two rabbis, Marshall T. Meyer and Roberto Graetz, visited and aided imprisoned Jews re-gardless of their political coloration.

In Catholic churches, relatives of the disappeared were also in effect ostracized. Since the church was so deeply involved in supporting the military junta, it was useless to expect church dignitaries to protest at the terror. Approval of the use of torture, in fact, was voiced by at least one bishop. Otherwise violent methods were explicitly defended by some priests and their superiors.[84]

DAIA largely abstained from public protests during the events. In 1984, the group published a book, *Special Information about the Incarcerated and the Disappeared Jews, 1976–1983*. As Elkin comments, "Noticeably absent from the book is any protest over the torture of prisoners or their being held without trial."[85] Rabbi Meyer stated the case in broad terms: "To my knowledge the Jewish leadership never spoke out directly on Jews who disappeared or the problem of disappearances in general. This was due basically to fear. This was due to the decision to maintain a low profile and not to do anything that might irritate the military dictatorship."[86]

While under house arrest in Buenos Aires after leaving prison, Tim-erman told a visitor, "I had not been humiliated by torture, by electric shocks on my genitals, but had been profoundly humiliated by the silent complicity of Jewish leaders."[87] In comparing Argentina with Nazi Ger-many it was the silence of Jewry in both places that struck him most.[88] Timerman contended that public and continued protest did not have to

await an Argentine Holocaust: "I never imagined... there would be
Jewish leaders who would utilize the horrors of the Holocaust to maintain
that the most advantageous response to certain antisemitic aggressions
of a much less brutal nature was silence."[89]

The conflict between the perspectives of DAIA and Timerman rested
largely on varying assessments of the place of antisemitism in Argentine
society. DAIA's leaders believed antisemitism had not affected the core
of the country's political institutions. In August 1980 its executive director, Bernardo Fain, said, "Jewish life here is normal. Our institutions
live normally, our religious life is normal, the Zionist movement is normal."[90] Yet, in the following two months, Rabbi Meyer later recalled,
"23 Hebrew day schools received bomb threats, four synagogues and
schools were actually bombed (there were no casualties) and a number
of tombstones vandalized." Nor, he added, was anyone arrested for any
of these events.[91] DAIA also believed there was no official antisemitism
as a deliberate government policy. This ignored the studied refusal of
the military junta to apprehend and punish well-known violent antisemites, many of them members of the government itself.

After publication in 1981 of his book, *Prisoner without a Name, Cell
without a Number,* Timerman raised another criticism of DAIA leaders:
their personal material stake in silence. He told one interviewer, "If I
had been pragmatic I would still be living in Argentina, very rich, as are
the Jewish leaders of Argentina, very rich."[92] He thus implied the silence
was motivated by desire for personal gain. Apparently, this issue was
not discussed publicly.[93] Timerman stated in another interview that Jewish leaders tended not to complain openly because they were politically
conservative and presumably favored government policies in subject
areas other than Jews.[94]

Argentina recognized Israel in 1948 and had entered into diplomatic
relations. How did Israel relate to anti-Jewish events in Argentina during
the nearly forty years after? According to one view: "The Israeli state
did business with the military. Consequently neither the Israel ambassador nor the Jewish establishment wanted to touch the issue of human
rights in the belief that it might harm trade with Israel. But other countries which traded with Argentina protested about the disappeared."[95]
It is quite true that some Israeli leaders went to considerable lengths in
such a direction. Arye Dulzin, Jewish Agency executive chairman, said
late in 1981 that the Argentine "government is 'not antisemitic' and the
conditions of Argentinian Jewry are 'not bad.' " He also said "the top
government leadership behaves 'normally' toward its Jewish citizens."[96]
This view corresponded closely with that of the DAIA.

On the other hand, there is ample evidence to demonstrate the involvement of Israeli officials, including the ambassador, in the matter
of individual disappearances. Writing late in 1981, Timerman declared,

"It is evident that the Israeli Embassy in Buenos Aires has made enormous efforts to help Jews who have been imprisoned or who have disappeared, and to rescue all those it can and bring them to Israel."[97] An item in an Israeli newspaper in 1978 is apropos: "After many inquiries by the Israel embassy in Buenos Aires, the authorities released the names of 100 Jewish prisoners. The junta was prepared to free these prisoners provided they left the country and were given asylum in Israel. Up to now, only 40 have been freed, and some of them are already in Israel."[98] In December 1982, Israeli foreign minister Yitzhak Shamir notified the Argentine president and foreign minister "that Israel is concerned about nearly 1,000 Jews who disappeared during the military regime's war on leftist terrorism from 1975 to 1979."[99]

Rabbi Meyer testifies along the same line as Timerman: "Under the military dictatorship [1976–83] to the best of my knowledge, the Israeli Embassy never ceased helping Jews who were threatened, or Jews who were in prison or attending the families of the disappeared. The Embassy was extraordinarily active and efficient in the work that it did. I spent hundreds and hundreds of hours with [Israeli] Ambassador Ram Nirgad during this period.... The state of Israel did everything in its power to help every one of the cases that I brought to their attention."[100] Nobody has contradicted Rabbi Meyer's testimony.

It was well-known that Israel had been supplying Argentina with arms and military equipment for some years. Since Israel was closely linked with U.S. foreign policy, American authorities did not criticize the trade. A question has arisen whether Israel was blackmailed into supplying Argentina with a threat of harm to that country's Jews. Patricia Derian, the Carter administration's assistant secretary of state for human rights during 1977–81, said as much in 1981: "Derian said that an Israeli official in Washington told her the Argentina government made it perfectly plain that if they don't get arms supplies [from Israel], Jews would suffer."[101] (In the event, they suffered even though supplies *were* sent.) Derian also stated that "the Israeli government refrained from criticizing Agentina [publicly] over antisemitic incidents in that country, and advised Jewish leaders in the U.S. to follow the same line."[102]

Thus, Israel worked hard behind the scenes to help imprisoned Jews and relatives of disappeared persons. It abstained, however, from criticizing publicly antisemitic activities in Argentina. Economic and diplomatic motives were uppermost with respect to the latter while communal motives were dominant in the former activity.

As a consequence of the disastrous war over the Falkland Islands in 1982 and a record inflation that peaked in 1983, the military junta agreed to abide by a free election in November of 1983. A month before the vote, Rabbi Meyer organized a demonstration against antisemitism as a first step toward creating a Jewish human rights movement. Thereupon

DAIA published a declaration in numerous newspapers denying it had anything to do with the demonstration. At the polls, voters placed in office an administration pledged to punish those responsible for the excesses of the military juntas. Upon taking up his post, President Raul Alfonsin retreated somewhat from this pledge but proceeded to investigate and ultimately try those charged with complicity. Little was said of the special fate of Jews under the dictatorship.

Acute antisemitism aggravated by a Jewish question had made the lot of Argentine Jews very difficult despite their upward social mobility and considerable cultural integration. Both intermittently and unrelentingly, waves of antisemitism swamped the Jewish community. The antisemites included those from reactionary Catholic circles, Nazi-style racists, and hypernationalists who could not abide any thought of pluralism or integration. Argentina was, indeed, a Noah's Ark of bigotry.

NOTES

1. Robert Weisbrot, *The Jews of Argentina from the Inquisition to Peron* (Philadelphia: Jewish Publication Society of America, 1979), p. 209.

2. Victor A. Mirelman, *The Jews in Argentina (1890–1930). Assimilation and Particularism* Ph.D. diss., Columbia Univ., 1973), University Microfilms Order No. 74–17,886, p. 74.

3. Eugene F. Sofer, *From Pale to Pampa. A Social History of the Jews of Buenos Aires* (New York: Holmes and Meier, 1982), p. 39.

4. Weisbrot, *The Jews of Argentina*, p. 200.

5. Sofer, *From Pale to Pampa*, p. 39.

6. Victor A. Mirelman, "The *Semana Tragica* of 1919 and the Jews in Argentina," *Jewish Social Studies*, 37 (January 1975), p. 67.

7. Ibid., p. 68.

8. John R. Hebert, *The Tragic Week of January, 1919 in Buenos Aires: Background, Events, Aftermath* (Ph.D. diss., Georgetown Univ., 1972), University Microfilms Order No. 73–4189, p. 155.

9. Mirelman, "The *Semana Tragica*," p. 62.

10. Ibid., p. 63.

11. Weisbrot, *The Jews of Argentina*, p. 201.

12. Mirelman, "The *Semana Tragica*," p. 66.

13. Sofer, *From Pale to Pampa*, p. 43.

14. Hebert, *The Tragic Week*, p. 190.

15. Ibid., p. 174.

16. Ibid., p. 177.

17. Ibid., p. 244.

18. Ibid., p. 264.

19. Mirelman, "The *Semana Tragica*," p. 73.

20. Ibid., p. 70.

21. Hebert, *The Tragic Week*, p. 263.

22. Mirelman, *The Jews in Argentina*, p. 118.

23. *Encyclopedia Judaica,* 3, col. 414.

24. *American Jewish Year Book,* 33, p. 61.

25. *Encyclopedia Judaica,* 3, col. 415.

26. *American Jewish Year Book,* 36, p. 199.

27. Ibid., 39, pp. 818–19.

28. Haim Avni, "Argentine Jewry: Its Socio-Political Status and Organizational Status," *Dispersion and Unity,* 12 (1971), p. 141. Curiously, by 1981 Jewish leaders in Argentina apparently transmogrified the fact into its opposite: "They point . . . to the fact that during the 1930s, Argentina openly received Jews fleeing German persecution" (*Time,* July 20, 1981, p. 39).

29. *American Jewish Year Book,* 47, p. 656.

30. Weisbrot, *The Jews of Argentina,* p. 67.

31. *American Jewish Year Book,* 39, pp. 488–89.

32. Ibid., 41, p. 361.

33. Ibid.

34. Ibid., p. 364.

35. Ibid., 42, p. 429.

36. Weisbrot, *The Jews of Argentina,* p. 67.

37. *American Jewish Year Book,* 43, p. 299.

38. Ibid., p. 298.

39. Ibid., 45, p. 347.

40. Ibid., pp. 346–47.

41. Ibid., 46, pp. 293–94.

42. Ibid., p. 295.

43. Ibid.

44. Ibid.

45. Ibid., 47, p. 477.

46. Ibid., p. 478.

47. Ibid., 48, p. 246.

48. Ibid.

49. Mark Falcoff, "The Timerman Case," *Commentary,* 72 (July 1981), p. 17.

50. *American Jewish Year Book,* 49, p. 551.

51. Weisbrot, *The Jews of Argentina,* p. 242.

52. *American Jewish Year Book,* 57, p. 522.

53. Weisbrot, *The Jews of Argentina,* p. 231.

54. Sofer, *From Pale to Pampa,* p. 130.

55. Weisbrot, *The Jews of Argentina,* p. 240.

56. Ibid., p. 245.

57. Victor A. Mirelman, "Attitudes towards Jews in Argentina," *Jewish Social Studies,* 37 (1975), p. 208.

58. Ibid., p. 209.

59. Weisbrot, *The Jews of Argentina,* p. 251.

60. See *American Jewish Year Book,* 66, p. 339; Weisbrot, *The Jews of Argentina,* p. 255; Mirelman, "Attitudes towards Jews in Argentina," p. 214.

61. Weisbrot, *The Jews of Argentina,* p. 211.

62. Ibid.

63. Ibid., p. 212.

64. Ibid., p. 215.

65. Ibid., p. 213.

66. Irving Louis Horowitz, "The Jewish Community of Buenos Aires," *Jewish Social Studies*, 24 (October 1962), pp. 216–17.

67. Haim Avni, "Anti-Semitism in Latin America after the Yom Kippur War—A New Departure?" in Moshe Davis, ed., *World Jewry and the State of Israel* (New York: Arno, 1977), p. 75.

68. *Encyclopedia Judaica Yearbook, 1975–1976*, p. 355.

69. Weisbrot, *The Jews of Argentina*, pp. 270–71.

70. Ibid., p. 272.

71. *American Jewish Year Book*, 80, p. 189.

72. Ibid.

73. Interview with Jacobo Timerman by Steve Wasserman, in *Los Angeles Times*, November 8, 1981.

74. Jacobo Timerman, *Prisoner without a Name, Cell without a Number*, trans. Toby Talbot (New York: Knopf, 1981), p. 11.

75. Ibid., p. 29.

76. Robert Cox, "Timerman Shows That 'Authoritarian Generals' Are Keepers, Captives of a 'Totalitarian Beast,' " *New York Times*, June 9, 1981.

77. *American Jewish Year Book*, 80, pp. 188–89.

78. James Nielson, "Newsman in Limbo," *Jerusalem Post Magazine*, November 24, 1978.

79. Louis Rapoport, "Crying for Argentina," *Jerusalem Post Magazine*, July 31, 1981. David Graiver, a co-investor in Timerman's newspaper, was charged by the military government with serving as an investment banker for the left-wing guerrilla group, the Monteneros. This was never proven.

80. Robert Weisbrot, "Anti-Semitism in Argentina," *Midstream*, May 1978, p. 21.

81. Judith L. Elkin, "We Knew but We Didn't Want to Know," *Jewish Frontier*, 52 (February 1985), pp. 9, 11.

82. An example of such reasoning is Seymour B. Liebman, "Argentine Jews and Their Institutions," *Jewish Social Studies*, 43 (Summer-Fall 1981), p. 323: "The Jews who have been victims [of disappearances] are primarily Leftists. If a Jew is active in any Left-wing movement, attacks against him should not be labelled antisemitism."

83. Elkin, "We Knew," p. 10.

84. See the comprehensive account by Penny Lernoux, "Blood Taints Church in Argentina," *National Catholic Reporter*, April 12, 1985, pp. 1, 4–10, 15. This account is based on a report by the government-appointed National Commission on the Disappearance of Persons. Fifteen priests are listed as having participated in the repression.

85. Elkin, "We Knew," p. 10.

86. Uri Timerman, "Jews and the New Argentina," *Jewish Frontier*, April 1984, p. 11. This is an interview with Rabbi Meyer.)

87. Timerman, *Prisoner without a Name*, p. 78.

88. See Jacobo Timerman, "The Silence of the Jews," *Harper's*, November 1981, pp. 20–23.

89. Timerman, *Prisoner without a Name*, p. 141.

90. *Los Angeles Times*, August 25, 1980.

91. *Washington Post,* February 28, 1981.

92. Louis Rapoport, "Crying for Argentina," *Jerusalem Post Magazine,* July 31, 1981.

93. Agreement with this view, voiced anonymously, can be found in the *Chicago Sun-Times,* August 11, 1981.

94. *Los Angeles Times,* November 8, 1981.

95. Santiago Mellibovsky, in Penny Lernoux, "Report Asserts Jews Also Silent," *National Catholic Reporter,* April 12, 1985, p. 9. Mr. Mellibovsky's daughter was one of the disappeared.

96. *Jerusalem Post,* December 22, 1981.

97. Timerman, "The Silence of the Jews," p. 22. This statement directly contradicts Penny Lernoux's statement in the April 12, 1985, *National Catholic Reporter* about Timerman's view of Israel's supposed inactivity in this field.

98. *Jerusalem Post,* May 17, 1978.

99. *New York Times,* December 15, 1982.

100. Uri Timerman, "Jews and the New Argentina," pp. 11–12. Referring to the year 1978, another source stated that Nirgad "maintained very privileged relations with leading figures in the Argentine military and political establishment"; *American Jewish Year Book,* 80, p. 189.

101. *Jerusalem Post,* June 7, 1981.

102. Ibid.

2

A TRADITION OF TOLERANCE: BULGARIA

> If there ever was a people without any antisemitic tendencies, the Bulgarians are a prime example. They never locked the Jews in ghettos, never discriminated against them, defended them whole-heartedly in times of need, and never interfered with their way of life.
>
> —Wolf Oschlies, 1984

Of all Jews in Balkan countries, Bulgaria's were freest to live as Jews. While antisemitic sentiments were not unknown, in the great crunch of the Holocaust the Bulgarian political system rallied against the severest measures.

From the ancient Near East, over a 600-year period, Jews emigrated to the Balkans. By the first century A.D., Jews from Persia, Egypt, and Palestine had arrived. Not until 500 years later did the first Slavic people begin to settle the present area of Bulgaria. Conquered by the Ottoman Empire in the fourteenth century, Bulgaria did not become a fully independent country until 1908. Even during the earliest days of the Bulgarian state, in the ninth century and after, "a curious affinity for Judaism"[1] prevailed among Bulgarians, even after conversion to Christianity. Five centuries of Muslim Ottoman rule were congenial to this relationship.

During the sixteenth century a small group of Jews engaged in financial services including banking and moneylending. Jews were also found in nearly every other occupation. They could count on the protection of the central government. During the nineteenth century, with the decline of the central power came provincial outbursts against Jews. Some were led by local administrators. There were even scattered cases of ritual murder charges against Jews. While Jews did not oppose the

Bulgarian nationalist movement somewhat after the mid-nineteenth century, the rise of a native middle class, anchored in trade, led to greater Bulgarian-Jewish tensions. Antisemitic riots occurred throughout the country during 1877–78 but, asserts Vicki Tamir, "not a single mention ...can be found in history textbooks."[2] In 1880, a bitter struggle occurred over market days on Sabbath. During the decade of the 1880s antisemitic literature began to circulate in Bulgaria. Jews successfully defeated a proposal to withhold public funds from all but Turkish parochial schools.

By the beginning of the twentieth century, Jews were virtually barred from positions in government and the armed forces. Yet, such exclusion was rare in the private economy. In few cases did Jews compete for jobs with non-Jews. The presence of Turks and Greeks, traditional enemies, distracted from the possible use of Jews as scapegoats. Further, as Frederick Chary points out, "all minorities, even nationals of countries at odds with Bulgaria, were normally well-treated."[3]

During the 1920s, Communists twice attempted to overthrow the government which denounced Jews as being avaricious capitalists and evil Reds. The depression of the 1930s stimulated further antisemitism. In the cities, Nazi-linked groups emerged. A full-scale pogrom occurred in September 1939. With the outbreak of World War II, Bulgaria allied itself with Germany and Nazi influence in Bulgaria expanded. Government-operated radio broadcasts began to reflect antisemitic attitudes. In 1940, the government introduced a far-reaching antisemitic bill, entitled "Law for the Defense of the Nation." It required the registration of all Jews and restricted Jewish participation in governmental and economic affairs. Opposing it were many workers, students, physicians, lawyers, and the Christian churches. In support of it were business groups, some students, right-wing organizations, veterans' groups, and others. The measure passed and took effect in January 1941. While quotas were installed by the law, they were not enforced very stringently.

Chary stresses, however, that "the Bulgarians pursued with ardor one feature of their Jewish policy—confiscation."[4] Jewish property was registered with government authorities and a capital levy of from 20 to 25 percent placed on all Jews. A decree issued in August 1942 expropriated all Jewish property holdings and ended all exemptions under anti-Jewish laws and regulations. Tamir declares that "the pivotal force behind all anti-Jewish measures was Bulgarian greed for Jewish property. No wonder, then, that the big Jewish capitalists of Bulgaria were high on the lists of 'undesirables.' "[5] Confiscation was enforced by the Commissariat for Jewish Questions (KEV), created in 1942.

Jews were assigned to compulsory labor. Foreign Jewish males, aged twenty to forty-five, were drafted into labor battalions. The next month native Jews joined them. Violators of anti-Jewish laws were placed in concentration camps. Jews in Sofia, over half the country's total, were redistributed among twenty other cities. This aroused the Orthodox church, many of whose leaders publicly opposed the action. The Nazi espionage chief Schellenberg complained in 1942 that the metropolitan of the Orthodox church gave a sermon in September "castigating the government for its anti-Semitic program."[6]

On February 22, 1943, Germany and Bulgaria signed an agreement whereby the latter would send up to 20,000 Jews from the newly acquired territories—part of Bulgaria's war booty—to death camps in Poland. Shortly thereafter, the Bulgarian cabinet secretly issued warrants to implement the agreement. The KEV immediately began preparations to carry it out. To create an illusion of popular support for the action, the KEV arranged for orders "to send expressions of thanks from the citizens, mayors, benevolent associations, and others to the cabinet and the KEV after the Jews left their cities."[7]

In March, when police began detaining Jews in Plovdiv, "Kiril, the bishop of Plovdiv (who later became the patriarch of Bulgaria), sent a telegram to the king threatening a campaign of civil disobedience, including personally lying down on the railroad tracks before the deportation trains, if the planned operation was carried out."[8] Metropolitan Stefan warned King Boris III that his soul would be placed in mortal danger. (The future Pope John XXIII, Angelo Roncalli, apostolic visitor to Bulgaria for a decade in the past, urged Boris to protect the Jews, while "Rome advised Roncalli not to concern himself with such political matters).[9] Also in March a well-known politician, V. P. Peshev, put together a petition signed by forty-three members of the national legislature (the *Subranie*) protesting the anti-Jewish policy of the government. After a bitter, prolonged debate, the petition was rejected, Peshev was censured, and finally he was deprived of his seat in the *Subranie*.

Nevertheless, the protest movement—for this is what it had become—brought about the exclusion of Jews living in Bulgaria proper from the deportation order. Of the 11,840 Jews living in the newly acquired territories in Greece and Yugoslavia, however, fully 11,393 were shipped to the Treblinka death camp.[10] Yet, it was not so much protests as Allied military victories that were decisive in saving the remainder of Bulgaria's Jews. As German defeat became more likely, Bulgarian resistance to Nazi demands stiffened. As the Red Army approached Bulgaria, government leaders started to unravel the skein of racist legislation enacted during the war. On August 31, 1944, all anti-Jewish measures were abrogated and promises were made to return confiscated property. Five days later the USSR declared war on Bulgaria; on September 8 the Red Army entered the country. The next day, a new government, the Fatherland Front, took over with Soviet blessings. On October 28, an armistice was signed. It required, among other things, the release of all persons imprisoned "for religious or social reasons." Many wartime leaders were arrested, tried, and executed.

On the eve of World War II, some 50,000 Jews lived in Bulgaria. Approximately the same number lived there at war's end. Jews had welcomed Soviet troops since they knew their entry foreclosed any Nazi-linked policies. During 1944–47, the Jewish community of Bulgaria was represented by numerous organizations, all operating with the approval and/or financial assistance of the Patriotic Front (the former Fatherland Front). Communist and non-Communist groups abounded. Jewish children could be sent to public schools in which they learned Hebrew and studied Jewish history. Research on Jewish life and history was carried out in the Jewish Scientific Institute. Groups that were Zionist in perspective were permitted and even encouraged.

In 1947, however, this calm was shattered by political reverberations of the split in the Communist camp between the Soviet Union and Yugoslavia. Stalin set off a hunt for "Titoites"; he called it "searching for their enemy in one's own ranks." Arrests and trials occurred in what Wolf Oschlies calls "a dangerously antisemitic atmosphere."[11] In Czechoslovakia and Hungary, veteran communists seemed more likely to become "enemies" if they were Jewish. A code word for them was "Zionist." (This label was not meant to describe an agent of the new nation of Israel.)

Bulgarian Jews, alarmed at the new plight of Jews in other communist countries, decided not to await a crisis. In just two years, 1948 and 1949, 33,362 Jews, or two-thirds of all the Jews in the country, left for Israel. Between 1946 and 1956, 88.9 percent left for Palestine and Israel. They were not only permitted to leave; they could also take all their belongings with them, a rare convenience in Eastern Europe. One reason for this comparative freedom was the influence of Bulgaria's world-renowned Communist leader, Georgi Dimitrov. During much of the war, he had broadcast to Bulgaria from a radio station in Haifa and had attacked Bulgarian leaders for their antisemitic actions.[12]

By 1965, only 5,108 Jews lived in a Bulgaria of 8,227,868 total population. Numerous Jewish institutions were dissolved, including schools, cultural centers, and Zionist and other organizations. Three synagogues were kept open as "cultural monuments" and used for religious worship. "Basically," wrote Oschlies in 1984, "one cannot speak of a Jewish life in Bulgaria in the last twenty years. The few Jews who are still living there are fully integrated, prosperous and almost totally assimilated."[13]

NOTES

1. Vicki Tamir, *Bulgaria and Her Jews. The History of a Dubious Symbiosis* (New York: Sepher-Hermon Press, 1979), p. vii.

2. Ibid., p. 96.

3. Frederick B. Chary, *The Bulgarian Jews and the Final Solution 1940–1944* (Pittsburgh, Pa.: Univ. of Pittsburgh Press, 1972), p. 33.

4. Ibid., p. 43.

5. Tamir, *Bulgaria and Her Jews,* p. 206.

6. Chary, *The Bulgarian Jews and the Final Solution,* p. 74.

7. Ibid., p. 89.

8. Ibid., p. 90.

9. Ibid., p. 188 n. 7.

10. Ibid., p. 127.

11. Wolf Oschlies, "Bulgarian Jewry since 1944," *Soviet Jewish Affairs,* trans. Ann Adler, 14 (May 1984), p. 46.

12. Chary, *The Bulgarian Jews and the Final Solution,* p. 193.

13. Oschlies, "Bulgarian Jewry since 1944," p. 52.

3

A CYCLE OF CENTURIES: EGYPT

> In the Arab lands antisemitism is not, as in Europe, exploited by politicians, but is created by them. It has, so to speak, been switched on; it could as easily be switched off.
>
> —Bernard Lewis, 1971

Antisemitism in Egypt is not quite as old as the Jewish community in that ancient country. After Alexander the Great's conquest of Egypt in 332 B.C., Jews were invited to settle in Alexandria and they did in large numbers. Within a century the community was well-established and Jews worked as merchants, tradespersons, and artisans. According to Bell, "There is no trace of any strictly racial or religious antagonism under the Ptolemies."[1] In 47 B.C. when Roman armies conquered the country, Jewish forces helped the invaders and Caesar thereafter favored the Jews. By attacking the Jews, Alexandrians were, in a safer, roundabout way, also criticizing the Romans. While Jews were not full citizens either under the Romans or their predecessors, they regulated their own religious and communal affairs.[2] Jews and Greeks were bitter competitors in economic life, especially in trade.

Under later Roman rulers, the lot of Jews became especially difficult. When Caligula ordered the Jews as well as others to worship his image, Jews refused. Greeks called for punishment which soon followed. A formal ghetto was established and in A.D. 38 a full-scale pogrom—perhaps the first one in history—occurred. Many Jews were killed and plundering was widespread.

Not least of the forces behind the hatred was a formal antisemitic literature that had emerged in Egypt. Leon Poliakov writes of a third century B.C. historian and priest, Manetho, who contended that the Jews spread leprosy and that they were exceedingly unsociable.[3] Others held that Jews were atheists, as their temples were bare of adornments. Alexandrian writers led the pack, with the grammarian Apion the best known. In one of his books "he declared that leprosy was a disease indigenous to the Jews, that the Jews were devoid of any gift for government or the arts, that their laws were abominable and full of hatred for others, that they annually sacrificed a foreigner, and that they worshiped the golden head of an ass."[4] A revolt by Jews in A.D. 115–117 was put down with great force in Alexandria and led to the near-disappearance of an organized Jewish community until about A.D. 300.

Antisemitism was revived when, late in the fourth century, Christianity became the state religion of Egypt. "There followed severe persecutions of the Jews by the clergy and by fanatical mobs. These persecutions persisted until the middle of the 7th century."[5] Bell describes events in A.D. 415 when the patriarch Cyril led mobs against the Jews in Alexandria: "The synagogues were all captured and turned into churches, the houses of the Jews pillaged, and the Jews themselves expelled *en masse* from the city."[6]

The place of Jews in Egypt changed markedly—"in most places indeed for the better"[7]—after the Arab conquest in A.D. 640. They ceased being considered an alien, threatening, and evil civic element, fair game for physical attack and extortion. During the first century or so of Muslim rule in the Arab empire, non-Muslims with a religion "of the book"—primarily Christians, Jews, and Zoroastrians—were assigned a second-rate civil status. They were known collectively as *dhimmi*, protected people. In return for paying a special tax—*jizya*—they could practice their religion and organize their community as long as these practices did not offend Islam. Muslim attitudes toward *dhimmi* combined contempt with forebearance. "The position of the non-Muslims under Arab Islam," writes S. D. F. Goitein, "was far better than that of the Jews in medieval Christian Europe."[8]

None of the highly restrictive legislation of Christian Europe could be found in Muslim countries. All economic pursuits were open to Jews; none was restricted. Jews were neither confined to ghettos nor forbidden to live among non-Jews. Neighborliness was not outlawed and social relations of mutual trust were common. Jews could and did testify against Muslims in Muslim courts.[9] On the other hand, discrimination against *dhimmis* was far-reaching. They were required to wear distinctive clothing articles such as hats of a certain color, they could not ride a horse, and Jewish-built structures could not be higher than Muslim mosques or other buildings. Nor did any law protect them from oppressive exactions levied by occupants of high offices. More often than not, neither the discriminatory nor the oppressive practices held sway for long. The rights of *dhimmi* were most secure when the central government exercised effective control over the entire country. Never were the rights equal to those enjoyed by Muslims.

There was no ideological or doctrinal antisemitism under Islam. Nor could there have been since Jews did not suffer any disabilities because they were Jews. If anything, they seem to have been somewhat favored over the Christians.[10] To a limited extent, however, antisemitism did exist during the tenth to the thirteenth centuries. Goitein, after reviewing evidence collected in Cairo during those years—the Genizah manuscripts—found that Egyptian Jews had a word for antisemitism, *sin' uth*, "hatred," with the exponent being known as *sone*, "hater." Goitein writes, "The phenomenon is nowhere referred to as general; it is mentioned throughout in conection with certain groups, towns or persons."[11] He notes that very many of the references were to Alexandria, as one might expect from historical evidence.

Under the Fatimid and Ayyubid dynasties (969–1270), Jews became integrated into Egyptian society with little difficulty. The rulers chose not to enforce most of the discriminatory decrees adopted earlier. Early in the eleventh century, al-Hakim, a Fatimid caliph, suddenly struck out against *dhimmis* in an extreme manner, giving new life to the decrees. In time, he repented and allowed *dhimmis* who had converted to Islam for protection to resume their original religion. During the years 1250 to 1517, under the Mamluks, however, life for the *dhimmis* became difficult, especially for the Copts, the native-born Christians of Egypt. The Jews did not escape similar treatment. Old and new discriminatory laws were enforced. Churches and synagogues were sometimes closed down, as in 1301. In 1354 "there were attacks on non-Muslims in the streets of Cairo."[12] During many of these violent episodes, the communal integrity of *dhimmi* groups remained intact.

A new era in Jewish life began in 1517, when the Mamluks were ejected from the country and Egypt became part of the Turkish Ottoman Empire. The new rulers opened trade to *dhimmi* participation and all but ignored traditional discriminations. Jews were appointed to government positions involving financial affairs. "Jewish reports on Turkish behavior and Turkish attitudes are almost uniformly favorable."[13] On the Turkish side, the feeling was mutual: "Jews were seen as a useful and productive element and were used as an instrument of imperial policy."[14]

This rather cozy relationship began to crumble during the seventeenth and eighteenth centuries when one after another administration used its political authority principally to loot the most readily available sources of income—the *dhimmis* involved in trade. Ali Bey, who served as governor of Cairo from 1760 to 1772, "allowed only himself the right of extortion. . . . [For another official] to extort Europeans was equivalent to stealing state funds."[15] At the same time, the Jewish and Christian

merchants themselves earned exceedingly high profits without the necessity to leave much in Egypt. In no sense was this interplay part of a
policy of religious persecution.

During a three-year interlude, 1798–1801, a French army commanded
by Napoléon Bonaparte invaded and occupied Egypt. Jews and Christians were proclaimed equal citizens. It seemed a new day had dawned.
Within a short time, however, external considerations dictated a French
withdrawal. The momentarily equal Jews and Copts were attacked by
Egyptian Muslims for their aid to the enemy.[16] Soon they resumed their
accustomed status as inferiors.

Egypt was transformed during the nineteenth century and along with
it the Jewish community. The country changed from a subsistence economy, in which a great mass of farmers and peasants aimed to raise just
enough to live on, to an export economy, based almost wholly on raising
and selling a single crop—cotton—on the world market. Land, which
was owned solely by the state at the beginning of the nineteenth century,
began to become privately owned. The Egyptian village crumbled as its
one-time common purpose was split into a relative few landholders and
numerous landless peasants and small holders. Craft guilds in the cities
fell under competition of European manufactured goods. Many of the
Ottoman Turks who ruled now awarded each other land and they thus
became important landowners. In government they were replaced increasingly by Egyptians.[17]

An industrial working class had begun to develop by the beginning
of the twentieth century. As Turkish bureaucrats became large landowners, smaller landowners joined the civil service. Wealthy merchants
bought landed estates. One could almost say the Egyptian social structure
was becoming "modernized" but, as Gabriel Baer observes, "there was
no social class of Egyptians whose principal interest [was] concentrated
in the towns and in the promotion of urban economy."[18] This burden
was carried by others, that is, foreigners.

At the end of the eighteenth century, no more than a few hundred
foreigners lived in Egypt, most in Alexandria. By the end of Mohammad
Ali's caliphate (1805–49), some 10,000 foreigners lived in the country.
The number grew to more than 150,000 by 1907. During the 1860s,
when the world cotton supply was disrupted by the American Civil War,
Egyptian production greatly expanded. In 1869 the Suez Canal was
completed and the world came to Egypt. Thirteen years later, the British
took Egypt and managed it as an economic colony. "By the late 1870s,"
writes Marius Deeb, "the foreign domination of commerce in Egypt was
complete, leaving for the Egyptians some petty trade and some traditional sections of commerce.... During the period from 1882 to 1918
foreign domination of finance, banking, trade, and various joint stock
companies was almost complete."[19]

It was in connection with this foreignization of the economy that the country's non-Egyptian population expanded. Virtually every major position in the economy was occupied by a foreigner. The Greeks, for example, played the broadest economic role of any foreign element between Mohammad Ali's rule and World War II: "More than any other community, they operated at every level of Egyptian society except the government bureaucracy, from high finance and large-scale cotton exporting to village grocers, petty traders and moneylenders, and industrial workers."[20] In addition, foreign residents could obtain the protection of a foreign government or outright citizenship and thus be exempted from the jurisdiction of Egyptian courts. Foreign companies were exempted from certain Egyptian taxes. Legislation considered harmful to the economic interests of foreign powers—such as a tariff on imported goods—was prohibited by treaty.

Conflicts among the foreign minorities arose from clashes of economic, political, and religious interests. During the latter half of the nineteenth century, many accusations of ritual murder—charges that Jews killed Christian children so as to use their blood in religious ceremonies—were brought by Greeks against Jews. Greeks hoped to deflect from themselves antiforeigner sentiment arising from resentment at economic privileges enjoyed by foreigners: "It is likely that precisely for this reason the Greeks wanted the Jews to be their scapegoat for the mob's hatred of foreigners and thus save their own position."[21] This was especially true in larger cities. Port Said was an example: "The numbers of Jews in Port Said and their business rivalry with the Greeks, Syrian Christians, and local Muslims, incited religious antagonism. The Christians, for example, were in the habit, each Easter, of preparing a straw effigy wearing Jewish dress, which they burned. Sometimes this provocation was accompanied by rioting (as in 1883), blood libels [another term for ritual murders], or the desecration of the synagogue (1902)."[22]

Occasionally, the government stepped in to punish instigators of anti-Jewish excesses. In 1877, Muslims in Mansura charged Jews with the ritual murder of a child. Upon government investigation the child was found alive. Leading Muslims were arrested and fined heavily. In 1902, a newspaper editor in Tanta was imprisoned for four months after having attacked Jews violently in his publication.[23] Generally, Jews had neither political power nor influence during the nineteenth and early twentieth centuries and so could not do much more than petition the government for redress of grievances. Yet, as Jacob M. Landau notes, "while the style of the earlier petition was submissive and even imploring, this changed during the British occupation to a more assertive, sometimes aggressive tone."[24] In 1882 it had pleased Britain's imperial purpose to grant Jews equal rights before the law.

The rights came none too soon. From the 1860s on, doctrines of antisemitism began to make their appearance in the Middle East. They were imports from western Europe, especially France, and were spread almost wholly by Christian Arabs. "Significantly," writes Bernard Lewis, "the appearance of antisemitic slogans and accusations was almost always accompanied by attacks on Jewish shops and workshops and calls for boycotts."[25] Economic competition lay at the core of the movement. Lewis also points to the role of European consuls and traders who cooperated with local Christian minorities in ousting Jews and replacing them with local Christians: "They were also active in the spread of certain classical themes of European antisemitism—for example, in the introduction of the blood libel, and in conjuring up fantasies of Jewish plots to gain world domination."[26] Arabic translations and adaptations of European antisemitic works were published in the Middle East in the late nineteenth century.

At the beginning of the twentieth century, however, Muslims did not generally join with Christian Arabs in propounding antisemitic doctrines. To the contrary, as Sylvia G. Haim shows in a study of Muslim publications, at this time: "The most influential of them denounced the racialism manifest in Europe.... [In] *al Manar,* perhaps in its day the most widely-read Arabic publication in Moslem lands ... one can clearly discern a steady and large-minded spirit of tolerance in its editor."[27]

With the issuance of the Balfour Declaration of 1917, in which Britain pledged the creation of a Jewish national home in Palestine, an issue arose whose potential for anti-Jewish movements was extraordinarily large. In fact, however, little of this emerged during the following decade or so. Egyptian nationalists during the 1920s were most deeply involved in freeing their country from British rule and paid little attention to the Palestinian issue. James Jankowski writes: "Considerable sympathy was shown by some Egyptian publicists and politicians for the Jewish National Home emerging in Palestine. Articles of analysis sympathetic to the Zionist movement as well as contributions written by Zionist leaders or by spokesmen inclined to Zionism appeared in the Egyptian press."[28] Another source reports that the same decade witnessed "at public rallies, Jewish and Muslim personalities [who] stood side by side beneath a portrait of Herzl surrounded by Egyptian and Jewish flags."[29] In Cairo on April 26, 1920, when news came that the Balfour Declaration had been made part of the Allied peace treaty with Turkey, "groups of Muslims cried: 'Long live the Jewish Nation!' and the Jews reciprocated with: 'Long live Free Egypt!' "[30]

Outright anti-Jewish behavior was rare in the Egypt of the 1920s. Such an event nevertheless occurred in 1925. A Catholic priest in Alexandria cautioned children to watch out for Jews who sought to commit ritual murder. Inflammatory leaflets were distributed. Nearly 2,000 Christians and Muslims paraded in support of the priest.[31] In 1929, the Palestine issue erupted over Arab and Jewish access to the Wailing Wall–Dome of the Rock area.[32] Rioting, led principally by Arabs, broke out in several cities and led to many deaths among Jews. In Egypt, however, the religious element became foremost. Islamic groups attacked "Jews" and not "Zionists" for the events. Protest meetings were held by Syrian and Palestinian émigré groups along with religious Muslim groups. Public opinion was not moved and the Egyptian government refused to intervene, though it was not asked to do so by the protestors. Secularized groups spoke of "Zionists" and "Arabs" rather than "Jews" and "Muslims."

Egyptian nationalism took several directions during the 1930s, all of which affected Jews. Renewed efforts were made to overcome foreign control of the economy. Religion became more politicized. And a xenophobic trend, verging on racism and antisemitism, set in.

With the aid of government financing, a number of new industries took root. A basic factor in their favor was the first enactment of a tariff which, in part, shielded these industries from foreign competition. (In 1937, Egypt ended the Capitulations which had forbidden devices like tariffs.) Egyptian banks, though weaker than those of Britain, were far more interested in financing manufacturing. Many educated Egyptians resented the lack of places in the old European-owned industry. The new enterprises could more easily provide such jobs. One group which gained little from new industry was the growing working class. During the years between both world wars real wages fell in Egypt. Social legislation was rudimentary and remained largely unenforced. The drift of economic affairs was unmistakably away from the traditional dependence on foreign capital. All the foreign minorities, Jews as well as others, understood the changes this trend portended.

The growing involvement of Islam with politics can be seen in the changing reception of the Palestine issue in Egypt during the 1930s. In literature of the Muslim Brotherhood, Jews were denounced as exploiters of the people and as sympathetic to the Zionists.[33] In Port Said in 1936, after a visit by the president of the Islamic Youth Organization of Palestine, the first anti-Jewish slogans were painted on walls of Jewish houses. Muslim theologians, however, refused to allow their sympathy with Arabs in Palestine to become accepting of racial antisemitism which they regarded as antithetical to Islam. Nevertheless, Jewishness as such was made into a political issue: "An antagonism to Jews *qua* Jews can be seen in Egypt in the late 1930s."[34]

Full-blown antisemitic ideologies became familiar to Egyptians in the 1930s. Anti-Jewish stereotypes rife in Nazi literature now appeared in Egyptian political literature. Jews were described in terms of "decay,

cowardice, obscenity, destructiveness, depravity."[35] Jews were identified
with high finance and as allegedly dominating economic affairs both in
the Middle East and the world at large.

Nazi influences were very powerful in pre–World War II Egypt. Already in 1926 and 1927, a local unit of the Nazi party had been organized
in Cairo.[36] By the mid-1930s, some 1,200 Germans, mostly businessmen,
lived in Egypt. (With the advent of Hitler, Jews organized an Egyptian
branch of the League Against German Antisemitism and began a boycott
against German-made goods.) German diplomatic personnel arranged
for anti-Jewish articles to appear in the Egyptian press. In 1933, Germans
organized an Arab-language press service and two years later opened a
Cairo branch of DNB, the German wire agency. In 1936, with aid from
both the Nazis and the French embassy in Egypt, the Arabic-Palestinian
Information Bureau was formed. It published a daily bulletin and distributed antisemitic material even in French North Africa.[37] Two years
later, in Cairo, there was convened the Parliamentary World Congress
for the Protection of Palestine. Delegates were offered Arabic translations of Adolf Hitler's *Mein Kampf* and *The Protocols of the Elders of Zion*.[38]
At times, Egyptian authorities banned a German antisemitic news
service.[39] According to one source, the government also confiscated writings attacking German anti-Jewish policies that were published by the
Jewish-Egyptian League. Meanwhile, the *Protocols* continued to circulate
without government ban.[40]

Two Egyptian organizations were heavily influenced by Nazi and Italian doctrine: Young Egypt and the Muslim Brotherhood. The former
began in Cairo as a society in 1933. Its program was nationalist, stressing
an antiforeign tone couched in patriotic terms. The Green Shirts was its
paramilitary formation. Young Egypt was pro-monarchy and anti-
British. During 1933–36, only a few hundred members joined. Early in
1936, however, its fortunes improved as the royal palace began financing
it. At that time "the society was able to hold large public meetings and
marches by its Green Shirts without any police interference or harassment."[41] That same year the society became a party.

In 1938, Ahmad Husayn, the party's leader, visited Germany after
having described it in writing as "absolutely the greatest state in Europe."
He hoped "one day to achieve in its meetings what the Nazis have
achieved in theirs." In mid-1938, upon completing his visit, he wrote
Hitler admiringly: "How much have you accomplished, oh leader."[42] Il
Duce's country he described as "the greatest state in the Mediterranean,
a model and an example to be imitated."

About the same time, the party abruptly switched tactics and started
heated campaigns against various immoralities such as prostitution and
liquor consumption. Shortly thereafter, it began a new line of policy.

Articles defending the causes of the Palestinian Arabs and attacking Zionist intentions and British policy in Palestine had been published in Young Egypt journals since at least 1938, but in mid-1939 the party turned to attack Egypt's native Jewish population through organizing a boycott of Jewish merchants in Egypt. A "Committee for the Boycott of Jewish Commerce" was formed by Young Egypt in July 1939. It established local boycott committees. . . . By the end of August 1939, this Boycott Committee had published three lists of Jewish merchants in Cairo who should be boycotted, with further lists promised. The agitation surrounding the boycott soon had effects beyond mere boycott: In Asyut, a cache of bombs was found by the police along with pamphlets advocating the boycott.[43]

With the outbreak of World War II on September 1, censorship was clamped on the press and strict governmental controls were now exercised over groups like Young Egypt.

Young Egypt tended to attract educated Arab youth of middle-class backgrounds with more of a secular than a religious viewpoint. A larger group, the Muslim Brotherhood, drew on the same social sources, in addition to many small traders, professionals, and lower and middle officials. Both these organizations fed on a profound and growing conviction that foreign control was not only objectionable on patriotic grounds but resulted also in denying jobs and economic shares to their members and others like them. Antisemitism gave them a chance to blame a single group for these difficulties even though responsibility for the system they attacked went far beyond that group. It also, they hoped, distracted attention from radical critics who did not point to this or that religious group as much as calling for revolutionary changes in Egyptian society to set the country on a new path.

Amid rising currents of antisemitism in 1938–39, the most influential leaders of the Jewish community were able to convince Egyptian governments to control organized antisemites; there were, in fact, few other kinds. Antisemitic literature was confiscated and demonstrations were banned. The rector of Cairo's Muslim Al-Azhar University forbade the circulation of antisemitic material on campus. The Arab press called for an end to attacks on Jews. The government itself was of two minds. Ideologically, the royal palace was pro-Axis. King Farouk desired a German victory in the war, as did many high military officers. On the other hand, the government felt obliged to avoid civil strife if only to permit the wartime economy to prosper.

Egypt broke diplomatic relations with Germany two days after the war broke out in 1939 but it failed to declare war until February 1945, when Germany was clearly about to be defeated. Thus, numerous German agents were at liberty during most of the war; they expanded greatly their anti-Jewish and anti-British propaganda. When, in the spring of

1940, Nazi armies swept over the Low Countries and France, expectations of a final German victory spread throughout the Middle East. In 1941, German armies occupied North African territory and approached Egypt. "Farouk," writes Lukasz Hirszowicz, "maintained contact with the Germans during the whole of 1941."[44] In April 1941, he sent a personal emissary to meet a German envoy in Tehran. The emissary "expressed Farouk's sympathy and respect for Hitler and Germany, as well as his best wishes for victory over England."[45]

Near the end of January 1942, Nazi forces under Marshal Rommel began a counter-offensive and young demonstrators in Cairo shouted "Forward Rommel!" while linking the British with the Jews. When German forces neared the borders of Egypt Jews started to leave their homes. The chief rabbi met with the prime minister who pledged that the government would never adopt Nazi-style legislation against the Jews. British forces, however, defeated the Germans at El Alamein and ended the Nazi menace to Egyptian (and Palestinian) Jewry. With the defeat, "the Royal Palace . . . ceased preparations, as did the Muslim clergy . . . to greet Rommel."[46] A year later, the Red Army victory at Stalingrad permanently ended the prospects of German triumphs anywhere. Anti-Jewish sentiment continued to be expressed, nevertheless, when, weeks later, students at Azhar University and national legislators publicly objected to the admission of Jewish refugees to Egypt.

While Egypt was not a battleground in the war, its economy was significantly affected. Industry expanded and profits rose sharply. Wartime inflation, however, swamped any wage gains workers had achieved; real wages fell. Per capita national income also declined during wartime. On the countryside in this rural country, the royal house and a small number of private landowners held much of the arable land. Three out of five rural dwellers were landless, and their numbers were increasing. Altogether, poverty in Egypt was growing. Insistent calls for change arose both in cities and rural areas. The urban Muslim middle class heightened its demands for economic advancement. This was the background for the postwar history of antisemitism in Egypt.

By 1945, Palestine had become a major political issue in Egypt. The Muslim Brotherhood and a number of Islamic groups—including the Islamic Nationalist party, formerly Young Egypt—interchanged "Jew" and "Zionist" in their everyday agitation. Increasingly, they pointed to Jews in Egypt as a major cause of the country's severe economic problems. Three elements were joined together: Palestine, Jews, and foreign control of economic affairs.

Jews traditionally celebrated November 2 as Balfour Day. In 1945, the Muslim Brotherhood and its allies chose that occasion to launch the first mass action against Jews in modern Egyptian history. On that day an organized mob of 20,000 invaded the Jewish quarter of Cairo and plundered both Jewish- and non-Jewish-owned businesses. A synagogue was burned down and houses were attacked. Non-Jewish businesses had been warned beforehand to close. Ten Jews were killed and 350 wounded. Smaller demonstrations occurred in other places. In Cairo police had been ordered not to shoot demonstrators. On the next day, police did prevent new demonstrations from being mounted. Jewish youths formed a defense organization: "Soldiers from Palestine instructed young Egyptian Jews in the techniques of self-defense and the use of firearms."[47]

By 1946, writes Gudrun Krämer, the Islamic and left-national press in Egypt regularly described all Jews as Zionists and represented them as "Communists, Capitalists, bloodsuckers, merchants of death, peddlers of women or in general a 'disturbing element' in all states and societies."[48] In February, a series of demonstrations by the Muslim Brotherhood and Islamic students called for total British evacuation from the country, for "Egyptianization and Islamization of the economy and society, struggle against foreigners and local minorities as dominant powers in the economy and culture, and for better living and working conditions in industry and agriculture."[49] Although the Arab League, formed a year earlier, was making Palestine a supreme issue, it was still not that important in Egypt, even among Islamic groups.

The political oligarchy of the country still refused to undertake wholesale changes. But in 1947 they began to yield on the matter of foreign control. Jews were deeply affected by the change, as was every other category of person not a citizen of Egypt. Robert Tignor summarizes the requirements of Company Law No. 138 which stipulated "that at least 40 percent of the board members of companies be Egyptian, 51 percent of the stock of new companies be held by Nationals, 75 percent of the white-collar employees be Egyptian and receive 65 percent of the salaries, and 90 percent of the workers be Egyptian and receive 80 percent of the wages."[50] The measure was not antisemitic—since it aimed at unseating foreigners and not Jews alone—but it probably harmed Jews more than any other goup. As one of those observed: "thousands of Jews found themselves jobless."[51] In 1929 a nationality law was enacted to offer citizenship rights to all, including Jews. Bureaucrats, however, interpreted the legislation restrictively and many Jewish applicants were turned away. (It should be noted that probably most Jewish noncitizens were born in Egypt and lived out their lives as "foreigners.") However severe the impact, few Jews were struck so negatively as to leave the country. Nearly ten years before, members of B'nai B'rith had spoken out in favor of Egyptianization and Arabization.[52]

The Palestine issue came to a head when, in November 1947, the United Nations debated a motion to partition the area between Jews and Arabs. Five days before the vote, Haykal Pasha, the Egyptian delegate to the U.N. General Assembly, stated: "The Arab Government will do everything in their power to protect Jewish citizens in their lands. But we are all aware that mob fury is often stronger than the police. Unconsciously you are on the verge of lighting a flame of antisemitism in the Middle East which would be more difficult to extinguish than it was in Germany."[53]

The motion passed on November 29 and four days later mass demonstrations opposing the measure broke out all over Egypt and lasted two days. Mobs attacked and partly destroyed institutions belonging to Jews, Zionists, the British, Copts, and Greeks. The events resembled those of Balfour Day in 1945. Krämer contends that the Muslim Brotherhood bore at least the moral responsibility for these events.[54] In January 1948, the government rejected a proposal by a legislator to ban Zionism by law.

Late spring 1948 brought a crisis as the State of Israel was proclaimed on May 15. A number of Arab countries, including Egypt, responded by invading Israel. On the same day, a state of emergency was declared in Egypt. Ten days later, the Egyptian government announced that persons who wanted to leave the country needed a special exit visa. Numerous Jews were arrested. On May 30, according to Siegfried Landshut, Proclamation No. 2 "provided for the sequestration of the property of any persons interned or placed under surveillance and of anyone, even though living outside Egypt, whose activities were considered prejudicial to the security of the state. Likewise, sequestration could be ordered against any company in which such a person had substantial interests."[55] Many of the persons arrested were charged with being Communists or Zionists.

For five weeks the combined Arab armies fought Israel. Egyptians were given little or no accurate news about the war. Official commentators repeatedly forecast victory. A British diplomatic report, written on June 2, stated: "The Jewish community in Egypt lives without molestation by the Egyptian authorities, and Jews, both rich and poor carry on their normal activities in satisfactory conditions. . . . No drastic measures have been taken against them."[56] This observation understated the shock of arrests and sequestrations. Nevertheless, the war with Israel had not disturbed the basic integration of Jews in Egyptian society.

On June 20, the calm was shattered as a bomb exploded in the Jewish quarter of Cairo and killed over twenty Jews. There was a vain effort by authorities to blame it on the Jews themselves. Meanwhile, Jews and Europeans were beaten in the streets. In July an Israeli plane dropped a bomb by error in the Jewish quarter. When an air-raid alert was sounded later in the month, a round of antiforeign rioting began. Two days later, an explosion in Cairo partly destroyed two Jewish-owned department stores. In August, there were no bombings but they were resumed the next month and again in November. Jewish families living near militarily sensitive areas in Cairo and Alexandria were moved elsewhere in September.[57] It was an open secret that the Muslim Brotherhood was responsible for the bombings.[58]

Thus, the second half of 1948 saw a reversal of the security under which Jews lived in Egypt. While private parties and associations undoubtedly set off the explosions, government stood by quietly. Landshut explains the shift to a conscious decision of public authorities: "The riots were not due to a [popular] grudge against the Jews as such. They were deliberately fostered by the Government; and even the Government was unable to prevent them turning into outbreaks against every kind of Western foreigner."[59]

For whatever reason, the Egyptian government modified its policy on Jews during 1949–50. Many detainees were released from jails, sequestered properties were returned to owners, and emigrants were no longer required to have special exit permits. Locked in a political struggle with the Muslim Brotherhood, the government tended to moderate its Jewish policy, a realm to which the Brotherhood attached the highest priority. Meanwhile, Jews left the country in growing numbers as the government avoided passing anti-Jewish laws and enacted instead measures aimed at Zionists and Communists. Most of the Jews who left in these years were from the middle and lower strata of society, especially public officials and merchants.[60] By 1951, all Jews but Communists had been released from prisons, Jewish schools were reopened, and a Jewish newspaper resumed publication.

The next year, army officers overthrew King Farouk and established a military dictatorship; in 1953 a republic was proclaimed. The military regime was headed by Gen. Mohammed Naguib who opposed any antisemitic programs. Others in the ruling group, however, felt differently. In 1952, after the coup, for example, the United Nations Mission for Egypt invited Gerald L. K. Smith, leading American Fascist and antisemite, to address them.[61] During 1953, Gen. Naguib made several goodwill excursions to the Jewish community, but these stopped early in 1954, perhaps because of internal differences in the ruling group. Written attacks on Jews reappeared in the extreme nationalist press, led by the Muslim Brotherhood. Numerous Jewish youths were arrested on charges of Zionism or communism although few were either Zionists or Communists.[62] In 1954, Gen. Naguib was compelled to resign and he was replaced by Col. Abdel Nasser who represented a stringent anti-Jewish program. During 1954 and 1955 anti-Jewish propaganda was centralized in the Ministry of National Guidance and in the general secretariat of the Muslim Congress, headed by Lt. Anwar Sadat, a pro-Nazi of long standing. In the Ministry of Interior, a special department dealing with Jews was organized.

The Nasser wing of the military rulers was deeply involved with ex-Nazi officers. Former SS general Oskar Dirlewanger was employed as the head of Nasser's personal guard.[63] One of his officers, Battalion Commander Eugen Eichberger, became a major in the Egyptian army. Leopold Gleim, a former SS colonel and chief of the Gestapo in Poland, became chief of the Egyptian secret police. Former SS general Alois Moser, who presided over massacres of Jews in the Ukraine, advised the Egyptian Information Department which also employed another Nazi leader Johann von Leers, as its political adviser.[64]

In 1951 an Israeli intelligence officer came to Cairo under an assumed name and contacted a group of Egyptian Jews who began training secretly. By 1954, they were ready to go into action. The British government had agreed with Egyptian authorities to pull out of Suez soon. The Israeli government opposed this and contrived a plan to "dynamite a number of American and British buildings in Egypt, thus seeming to demonstrate the 'irresponsibility' of the Nasserist regime and it was hoped, persuading the British to remain on."[65] Operations began in Cairo and Alexandria. "Throughout July of 1954, as a result, homemade bombs exploded in post office buildings, public checkrooms, movie theaters, and United States information centers and consulates in Cairo and Alexandria."[66] Many arrests were made and thirteen Israeli spies were tried in a spectacular trial in Cairo between December 11, 1954, and January 5, 1955. By the latter date, "one of the accused had committed suicide, two others had been sentenced to death and were later hanged, and all but two of the remaining defendants had received sentences varying from seven years to life imprisonment."[67]

During the summer of 1956, Egypt nationalized the Suez Canal. Several months later, France and Israel attacked Egypt and were soon joined by England. Sweeping arrests of Jews were made. A source sympathetic to the Egyptians charged that Jews in Port Said had "collaborated" with the invaders and, fearing reprisals, later fled.[68] It became a crime for anyone to advocate Zionism. Thousands of Jews were given a few days to leave the country under compulsion. They could not sell their property or take their capital with them. During the remainder of the 1950s and the following decade, the numbers of Jews—and "foreigners" in general—fell sharply. From 75,000 in 1945, there were only some 3,000 left in 1967. The 1967 war between Israel and Egypt brought widespread arrests of the remaining Jews. Unlike previous occasions, "they were beaten, tortured, and abused."[69] During the 1970s, only some 400 Jews could be found in Egypt. By the mid-1980s, that number was halved.

In the three or so decades since the accession of Nasser, a new generation of Egyptians has grown up amid two unique circumstances: (1) there are virtually no Jews with whom to interact, and (2) the central government has become the major organizer of a sustained anti-Jewish propaganda campaign.

During the 1920s, as we have seen, opprobrium was not attached to advocacy of Zionism by Jews. Indeed, some Egyptian officials and public figures were also advocates. Other than Islamic groups, during the 1930s the picture was not greatly different as Egyptian officials frequently offered to mediate between warring sides in Palestine, thus lending legitimacy to the Zionist position. With the end of World War II, in 1945, extreme nationalist Muslim groups successfully singled out Jews for attack. Even then, neither popular opinion nor the government supported this new turn in the road. While government policies did begin to change with the 1948 war and especially the conflicts of 1956 and 1967, there is little reason to think Egyptian public opinion became antisemitic. "It is wrong to speak of any deeply-rooted anti-Jewish feeling in Egypt," wrote Landshut in 1950.[70] Little information is available to gauge the inroads three decades of official antisemitism have made on public opinion.

In 1956, the Ministry of National Guidance published a complete Arabic edition of *The Protocols of the Elders of Zion.* In urging the veracity of the document, the ministry cited Nazi philosopher Alfred Rosenberg in support.[71] Nasser, at one point, denied the reality of the Holocaust: "No-one, even the simplest of men, takes seriously the lie about six million Jews who were murdered."[72] Government-sponsored publications frequently quoted the *Protocols* as an authority. A pamphlet published in 1964 in Cairo charged that Jews killed President John F. Kennedy. It continued: "In France the French people have no property whatsoever left; everything has gone to the Jews."[73] In 1955, Sadat, who was then minister of state, declared: "It is our duty to fight the Jews in the name of Allah and in the name of our religion, and it is our duty to finish the war which Muhammad began."[74] As president, seventeen years later, he said Jews were "a nation of liars and traitors, plotters, a people born for deeds of treachery."[75]

Egypt—as well as some other Arab countries—delved deeply into the reservoir of European antisemitism. In a new edition of an 1890 book, *Talmudic Sacrifices,* published in 1962 by the Ministry of Education, the editor said the work was "an explicit documentation of indictment, based upon clear-cut evidence that the Jewish people permitted the shedding of blood as a religious duty enjoined in the Talmud."[76] Similarly, in 1975, the Egyptian minister of state, a Copt, Albert Salamah, stated: "The new Israel...has carried out the most terrible crimes in history and...bears the responsibility for the crucifixion of the Messiah; its hands will remain stained with his blood for eternity."[77] In 1977, *October,* "a government-owned weekly magazine...published a serialized Arabic version of an old French book called *The Evil Found in the Talmud*, complete with graphic descriptions of Jewish blood rituals and grotesque drawings of evil-eyed characters wielding long daggers."[78]

Has Egypt's government-sponsored antisemitism abated any since the Sadat initiative of November 1977 toward Israel and the Egyptian-Israeli Peace Treaty of 1979? One source reports the Egyptian press "has slightly veered toward a more realistic evaluation of Israel and of its chances of survival."[79] Also noticeable during the early 1980s, according to the same source: "While public opinion as reflected in the Arab media in general has remained rather persistent in its violent hatred of Jews and Israel, the Egyptian press has shown neither the same consistency nor the same relentlessness as the rest."[80] Still another source found the flow of antisemitic books unabated in Egypt. It proceeded as well to raise the issue of governmental responsibility for undoing anti-Jewish attitudes that had been engendered by the government: "It is critical to... insist that Egyptian officials begin to make serious efforts to discourage antisemitic outbursts and to educate Egyptians to live on equal terms with Israel and the Jews."[81] The 2,000-year history of Jews in Egypt had to begin all over again.

NOTES

1. H. I. Bell, "Anti-Semitism in Alexandria," *Journal of Roman Studies*, 31 (1941), p. 3.

2. See H. I. Bell, *Jews and Christians in Egypt. The Jewish Troubles in Alexandria and the Athanasian Controversy* (Westport, Conn.: Greenwood Press, 1972, orig. 1924).

3. Leon Poliakov, *The History of Anti-Semitism*, 1, trans. Richard Howard (New York: Vanguard Press, 1965), p. 9.

4. "Apion," *Universal Jewish Encyclopedia*, 1, p. 415.

5. "Egypt," *Universal Jewish Encyclopedia*, 4, p. 11.

6. Bell, "Anti-Semitism in Alexandria," p. 17. There is some doubt whether the expulsion order was completely carried out; see *Encyclopedia Judaica*, 6, col. 491.

7. Bernard Lewis, *The Jews of Islam* (Princeton, N.J.: Princeton Univ. Press, 1984), p. 18. See also Merlin Swartz, "The Position of Jews in Arab Lands Following the Rise of Islam," *Muslim World*, 60 (1970), pp. 6–24.

8. S. D. F. Goitein, *Jews and Arabs. Their Contacts through the Ages*, rev. ed. (New York: Schocken, 1974), p. 84.

9. Amnon Cohen, *Jewish Life under Islam. Jerusalem in the Sixteenth Century* (Cambridge, Mass.: Harvard Univ. Press, 1984), pp. 110–26.

10. Lewis, *The Jews of Islam*, p. 60.

11. S. D. F. Goitein, *A Mediterranean Society*, 2 (Berkeley: Univ. of California Press, 1967–83), p. 278.

12. "Egypt," *Encyclopedia Judaica*, 6, col. 495.

13. Lewis, *The Jews of Islam*, p. 235.

14. Ibid., p. 138.

15. John W. Livingston, "Ali Bey Al-Kabir and the Jews," *Middle Eastern Studies*, 7 (1971), p. 223.

16. For a discussion of how Muslims retaliated against the Copts, see Benjamin Braude and Bernard Lewis, eds., *Christians and Jews in the Ottoman Empire. The Functioning of a Plural Society*, 2 (New York: Holmes and Meier, p. 189.

17. Gabriel Baer, *Studies in the Social History of Modern Egypt* (Chicago: Univ. of Chicago Press, 1969).

18. Ibid., p. 225.

19. Marius Deeb, "The Socioeconomic Role of the Local Foreign Minorities in Modern Egypt, 1805–1961," *International Journal of Middle Eastern Studies*, 9 (1978), pp. 15–16.

20. Braude and Lewis, eds., *Christians and Jews*, 1, p. 266.

21. Jacob M. Landau, "Ritual Murder Accusations in Nineteenth-Century Egypt," in Jacob M. Landau, *Middle Eastern Themes. Papers in History and Politics* (London: Frank Cass, 1973), p. 107.

22. Jacob M. Landau, *Jews in Nineteenth-Century Egypt* (New York: New York Univ. Press, 1969), p. 35. For later references to anti-Jewish disturbances at Port Said, see *American Jewish Year Book*, 5, pp. 217–18; 9, p. 546; and 11, p. 70.

23. Ibid., pp. 39, 41.

24. Landau, "Ritual Murder," p. 151.

25. Bernard Lewis, "The Decline and Fall of Islamic Jewry," *Commentary*, 77 (June 1984), p. 46. See also Norman Stillman, *The Jews of Arab Lands. A History and Source Book* (Philadelphia: Jewish Publication Society of America, 1979), p. 107.

26. Lewis, *The Jews of Islam*, p. 185.

27. Sylvia G. Haim, "Arabic Antisemitic Literature. Some Preliminary Notes," *Jewish Social Studies*, 17 (1955), p. 309.

28. James Jankowski, "Egyptian Responses to the Palestine Problem in the Interwar Period," *International Journal of Middle Eastern Studies*, 12 (1980), p. 4.

29. Bat Ye'or, "Zionism in Islamic Lands: The Case of Egypt," *Wiener Library Bulletin*, 30 (1977), p. 21.

30. Ibid., p. 20.

31. Gudrun Krämer, *Minderheit, Millet, Nation? Die Juden in Ägypten 1914–1952* (Wiesbaden: Verlag Otto Jarrassowitz, 1982), p. 231.

32. See Howard M. Sachar, *A History of Israel from the Rise of Zionism to Our Time*, (New York: Knopf, 1976) pp. 173–75.

33. Krämer, *Minderheit*, p. 292.

34. Jankowski, "Egyptian Responses," p. 15.

35. James Jankowski, "Zionism and the Jews in Egyptian Nationalist Opinion, 1920–1939," in Amnon Cohen and Gabriel Baer, eds., *Egypt and Palestine. A Millennium of Association (868–1948)* (New York: St. Martin's Press, 1984), p. 325.

36. Krämer, *Minderheit*, p. 260.

37. Ibid., pp. 263, 276, 291.

38. Ibid., p. 295.

39. *American Jewish Year Book*, 41, p. 374.

40. Ye'or, "Zionism in Islamic Lands," p. 26.

41. James P. Jankowski, *Egypt's Young Rebels. Young Egypt: 1933–1952* (Stanford, Calif.: Hoover Institution Press, 1975), p. 23.

42. Ibid., p. 60.

43. Ibid., p. 248.

44. Lukasz Hirszowicz, *The Third Reich and the Arab East* (London: Routledge and Kegan Paul, 1966), p. 233.

45. Ibid., p. 232.

46. Ibid., p. 248.

47. Ye'or, "Zionism in Islamic Lands," p. 29. See also Krämer, *Minderheit,* p. 320.

48. Krämer, *Minderheit,* p. 408.

49. Ibid., p. 323.

50. Robert L. Tignor, *State, Private Enterprise, and Economic Change in Egypt, 1918–1952* (Princeton, N.J.: Princeton Univ. Press, 1984), p. 180.

51. Victor D. Sanua, "A Jewish Childhood in Cairo," in Sanua, ed., *Fields of Offerings. Studies in Honor of Raphael Patai* (Rutherford, N.J.: Fairleigh Dickinson Univ. Press, 1983), p. 292.

52. Krämer, *Minderheit,* p. 331 n. 2.

53. Siegfried Landshut, *Jewish Communities in the Muslim Countries of the Middle East* (London: Jewish Chronicle, 1950; Westport, Conn.: Hyperion Press, 1976), p. 33.

54. Krämer, *Minderheit,* p. 411.

55. Landshut, *Jewish Communities,* p. 34.

56. Quoted in Krämer, *Minderheit,* pp. 418–19.

57. See Richard P. Mitchell, *The Society of the Muslim Brothers* (London: Oxford Univ. Press, 1969), pp. 63–64; Krämer, *Minderheit,* pp. 420–21.

58. The Brotherhood was later tried on watered-down charges and found guilty; mild sentences were handed down. See Mitchell, *The Society,* p. 78.

59. Landshut, *Jewish Communities,* p. 40.

60. Krämer, *Minderheit,* p. 424.

61. Gerald L. K. Smith, *Besieged Patriot. Autobiographical Episodes Exposing Communism, Traitorism, and Zionism from the Life of Gerald L. K. Smith* (Eureka Springs, Ark.: Elna M. Smith Foundation, 1978), pp. 244–45.

62. *American Jewish Year Book,* 56, p. 491.

63. For material relating to Dirlewanger's possible involvement in making soap of Jews, see Raul Hilberg, *The Destruction of the European Jews,* 3, rev. and def. ed. (New York: Holmes and Meier, 1985), p. 966.

64. Dafna Alon, *Arab Racialism* (Jerusalem: The Israel Economist, September 1969), pp. 15–25 passim.

65. Howard M. Sachar, *A History of Israel from the Rise of Zionism to Our Time* (New York: Knopf, 1976), p. 480.

66. Ibid.

67. Ibid.

68. Ali Ibrahim Abdo and Khaireh Kasmieh, *Jews of the Arab Countries* (Beirut: Palestine Liberation Organization, May 1971), p. 71.

69. *Encyclopedia Judaica,* 6, col. 501.

70. Landshut, *Jewish Communities,* p. 40.

71. Y. Harkabi, *Arab Attitudes to Israel*, trans. Misha Louvish (Jerusalem: Israel Univ. Press, 1972), pp. 231–32.

72. Ibid., p. 277.

73. "Arab Antisemitic Propaganda: The Spirit of Streicher," *Wiener Library Bulletin*, 19 (Autumn 1965), p. 16.

74. Moshe Ma'oz, "The Image of the Jew in Official Arab Literature and Communications Media," in Moshe Davis, ed., *World Jewry and the State of Israel* (New York: Arno, 1977), p. 40.

75. Ibid., pp. 36–37.

76. Ibid., p. 45.

77. Ibid., p. 46.

78. Howard Adelman, "Egyptian Anti-Semitism," *Judaism*, 28 (Winter 1979), p. 71.

79. Raphael Israeli, "Anti-Jewish Attitudes in the Arabic Media, 1975–1981," *Research Report* (Institute of Jewish Affairs), 15 (September 1983), p. 13.

80. Ibid., p. 17.

81. Abraham H. Foxman and Kenneth Jacobson, "Egyptian Poison," *ADL Bulletin*, May 1985, p. 3.

4

ISOLATED FIDELITY: ETHIOPIA

From the time of the introduction of Christianity into [Ethiopia]
...the history of this country has been stained with Jewish blood.
—Jacques Faitlovitch, 1920

Jews have been an integral part of Ethiopia's history for the last 2,000 or more years. The national myth holds that in ancient times King Solomon and the Queen of Sheba mated and a son, Menelik, was born. Menelik later became emperor of Ethiopia as the ruler of a Jewish dynasty. In A.D. 350, his descendant converted to Christianity. The Beta Israel (House of Israel), a large tribe of black Jews, continued to honor this religion. For the following 1,300 years the ruling house of Ethiopia waged war on the Jews, reducing their numbers by wholesale slaughter and forced conversions. Wars against the Jews reached a peak during the thirteenth to the seventeenth centuries.

In this violent era, the Beta Israel was reduced from a self-ruling agricultural kingdom to a wholly subordinated handicraft caste, subject entirely to Christian domination. Extermination, however, was not part of the royal design. Instead, in the seventeenth century, the Beta Israel was forever forbidden to own any land. Jews could work on others' land as sharecroppers or for wages. The Ethiopian rulers hoped thereby to destroy the economic—and thereby the religious communal—basis of Beta Israel unity. The effort failed, however, when Beta Israel succeeded in making a transition to handicraft and continued an agricultural economy under difficult circumstances.

Jews became the nation's only artisans, especially blacksmiths, potters, and weavers; in the late sixteenth century they began to practice the crafts of masonry and carpentry. They were employed by the royal palace as armorers and helped build stone buildings for royal occupation. While

Jews continued to live principally in the northwestern part of the country, fairly near present-day Sudan, almost nowhere did they occupy entire villages. Instead, they lived by themselves within or alongside Christians.

Transformation of the Beta Israel resulted from a combination of political and economic changes. Religion, however, did not remain undisturbed. As Jews suffered political and economic deterioration they also developed means of gathering their spiritual forces together. Religious leaders borrowed from the Christians the institution of monasticism; monks became highly authoritative religious figures. And the Beta Israel liturgy was more closely adapted to the Christian liturgy. At the same time, detailed rules were worked out to ensure that the Beta Israel community would be kept clear of any Christian presence. Christians were not allowed to step inside a Jewish home; if a Jew touched a Christian, the Jew hurried to wash his or her hands.

The lower the Jew sank in status within the larger community, the more restrictive the Christian community became. During the period of the mid-eighteenth to mid-nineteenth centuries, for example, Christians perfected the old doctrine that Jews, especially because of their control of fire in the process of blacksmithing and iron-making, were contaminated by evil spirits. Jews were accused of having *buda,* or an evil eye, for which they were blamed for a broad range of illnesses and mishaps. When traditional Christian society was riven by power conflicts, cries of *buda* served as a unifying factor among the majority. Jews served as a scapegoat.[1]

By the mid-nineteenth century, then, the people of Beta Israel had become an occupational caste of low social status and were prohibited from close social interaction with Christians by their own religious proscriptions as well as by detailed regulations of the larger society. Jews did not suffer from active religious persecution but their Jewishness was a signal for treatment as inferiors. Christian missionaries from western Europe began arriving at about this time but they met with little success.[2] Religious differences also produced attacks upon the Jews from outside the country. In 1888, for example, an invasion from neighboring Sudan by Muslim forces destroyed Beta Israel schools so completely that they were never rebuilt.[3]

Based on firsthand observation over many years, the French scholar-activist Jacques Faitlovitch reported in 1920: "The masses of the people are in perfect harmony with the Jews whom they hold in esteem because of their own spirit and their industry. It is only the [Christian] priests who, from time to time, hurl execrations against the descendants of the 'Deicides' of their Savior, and the Falashas have often experienced the consequences of the venomous sermons of these apostles of the religion of love."[4]

The 1920s saw an upsurge in work among Beta Israel, principally because of the intense endeavors of Faitlovitch. In 1928 the Ethiopian crown prince, Ras Tafari Mekonnen—the future emperor—gave $5,000 to Faitlovitch to honor his contribution. It was used to expand a school formed by Faitlovitch in Addis Ababa five years earlier.[5] Very occasionally, anti-Jewish incidents arose, such as charges of ritual murder of Christian children in Asmara, during 1913.[6] In 1925, a dispute developed over the requirement that Jews work on the Sabbath but it was resolved in their favor by the crown prince.[7]

In 1935, Italy invaded Ethiopia and the next year began what turned out to be a five-year occupation. At first, occupation authorities allowed Italian Jews to aid the Jews of Ethiopia. The Union of Jewish Communities of Italy sent a representative to contact Beta Israel as well as establish communal organizations in two cities. Oaths of allegiance to Italy were said to be made by Jews who were promised their freedom to worship. In 1937, the Italian government announced it had made land grants and established agricultural and handicraft schools for Beta Israel.[8]

The year 1938 saw an end to these promises of beneficence. With the promulgation of Mussolini's anti-Jewish regulations, the Jews of Beta Israel felt the full weight of Fascist suppression. A contemporary source reported: "Since Mussolini's swing to racial antisemitism, the situation of the Falashas has grown worse; in view of the strong hand used by the authorities in Ethiopia, they were threatened with severe persecution. The Jewish communities in Addis Ababa and Diredawa were dissolved."[9] (Ethiopian Jews rejected the label of "Falasha," that is, stranger.) A Jewish school in Addis Ababa, nurtured since the 1920s by Faitlovitch and others, was closed by the Fascists who proceeded to harass the Jews. Understandably, members of Beta Israel joined the underground and fought as guerrillas.[10] In 1941, Italian forces were ejected by the British. Three years later, in a symbolic gesture, Emperor Haile Selassie appointed Faitlovitch as an advisor in the Ethiopian embassy in Cairo. The end of the war in 1945, however, brought no change in the situation of the Jews. The emperor continued to ignore his pledge of 1922 to Faitlovitch that persecutors of Jews would be punished. "In general," wrote an American scholar, "the Ethiopians think of [Beta Israel] . . . as a group apart, using the Ethiopic word *attenkugn* which means 'do not touch me', to describe them."[11]

A more desperate picture was sketched by the Jews themselves. Three times during 1958–59, they submitted petitions to Haile Selassie: "They listed the names of thirteen of their number who had been murdered, accused of sorcery, three instances of arson, including the school at Wuzaba, eight attacks on cemeteries, innumerable examples of eviction and details of outrageous rents and tithes."[12] They complained, too, of exceedingly large shares of crops paid landlords, of extra charges levied on them, and even that they were being compelled to pay a tithe of their income to the Christian church. The emperor refused to discuss these matters with the Jews when he visited Gondar in 1959. In an open letter to world Jewry, published the next year, the Ethiopian Jews declared that "world Jewry has cast us forth from the fold of Judaism and is far from willing to help us in this last stand against overwhelming factors."[13] Except for glorious but scarce examples like Faitlovitch, few Jews elsewhere seemed interested in helping Beta Israel.

A century before, the Christian missionary Henry Stern—himself a converted Jew—wrote: "We believe that Jerusalem will again be rebuilt is the answer on the lip of every Falasha, when questioned as to the future destiny of his nation."[14] When, in fact, the State of Israel came into existence, in 1948, it did not bring the Ethiopian Jews any nearer to Jerusalem. For one thing, they were not acknowledged as genuine Jews by rabbinical and, for that matter, civil authorities. Ethiopian Jewish liturgy and religious practice varied considerably from those of Jews in the State of Israel. Consequently, Ethiopian Jews could not qualify under the Israeli Law of Return under which all Jews have the right to apply for citizenship in that country. Another reason for the reluctance of Israel to welcome Ethiopian Jews was a desire not to ruffle Ethiopian-Israeli relations. Israel wanted to retain access for its ships through the Red Sea and feared that if the Eritrean revolt for independence from Ethiopia succeeded, Arab forces would be able to cut off that access. Thus, it supported the central government and refused to heed the call for a large-scale transfer to Israel. Haile Selassie opposed all such movements.

Nevertheless, occasional aid was sent by Israel. Between 1954 and 1956, the Jewish Agency from Israel opened schools in thirty-three Ethiopian villages; by 1956 all but one had closed. The next year, the agency spent a total of $5,400 on the school. Leaders of the Labor government strongly opposed the immigration into Israel of Ethiopian Jews. This included prime minister Golda Meir. In 1959, Yisrael Yesayahu, longtime Labor speaker of the Knesset, the Israeli national legislature, visited Ethiopia and advised the Jews to convert to Christianity: "The government and the Christian community would be very happy and the Falashas would only stand to benefit from such a move; e.g., they would receive their own region."[15] Within Israel itself the Jewish orthodox religious community was most antagonistic to affirming the Jewishness of Beta Israel. There was more than a suspicion that racism was contributing to the general reluctance. "If our skin would be only a little lighter," wrote Yona Bogale, a leader of the Ethiopian Jews during the early 1970s, "I am sure World Jewry would take a greater interest."[16]

In fact, in 1972, the chief Sephardi rabbi of Israel ruled that Beta Israel was authentically Jewish. However, his Ashkenazi counterpart stalled and did not agree until 1975. In April 1975, the Israeli government proclaimed Ethiopian Jews as eligible immigrants under the Law of Return.

During the years from 1973 to 1975 Ethiopia had changed greatly. Haile Selassie was forced to abdicate in 1974 by a revolutionary government headed by army officers. The next year, one of the world's most radical land reforms was announced.[17] The government confiscated all privately owned land and awarded all farmers the right to work a minimal amount of land. Outlawed were the practices of wage employment on farms and sharecropping. Peasant associations were formed to protect the newly won rights. Even Jews were entitled to work an equal share of the land. As Asa Azariah explained: "This land reform angered the Christian aristocrats of the old regions who still had private armies. They hated the Falashas, who had for long been their servants. . . . The new government of Ethiopia didn't have enough power in the area where the Falashas are living; and the number of massacres kept growing in 1977 and especially 1978. Many villages were totally destroyed. Jewish people were killed in big numbers, sold [as slaves] in marketplaces in different regions in Ethiopia and sold in Sudan."[18]

Relations between Ethiopia and Israel had begun to change even before the revolution. Under Haile Selassie, Israelis trained the Ethiopians' elite counterinsurgency force, provided instructors in military academies, and performed a wide range of public health, educational, and agricultural tasks. In 1973, during the Yom Kippur War, Ethiopia broke diplomatic relations with Israel in exchange for an Arab-bloc pledge that in return Arab secessionists in Eritrea would be compelled to restrain their efforts.[19] After the revolution, Israel very quietly continued to supply some arms to Ethiopia and a few technicians serviced Ethiopian jets. Perhaps the seeming calm encouraged Prime Minister Menachim Begin to pledge in 1977 that Israel would welcome Ethiopian Jews. This was the first such declaration by a high Israeli official, let alone the head of state. A trickle of Ethiopian Jews left for Israel over the next several years.

In February 1978, however, a crisis in this course of events occurred when Gen. Moshe Dayan, foreign minister of Israel, speaking in Geneva, Switzerland, let "slip" the news that Israel was supplying arms to Ethiopia. The Ethiopian government immediately stopped the trickle of emigrants. (Ethiopian Jews in Israel tended to believe the slip was deliberate. Two of them asked three years later: "Why has no voice in Israel been raised against Dayan's monstrous act to this day?")[20]

Far worse was the widespread pogrom inside Ethiopia that was set off by the "slip."

[The revelation] sparked a bloody rightist pogrom. . . . The landlord-led EDU [Ethiopian Democratic Union] rebels, infuriated that Israeli arms were being used [by the government] against their forces, went on a rampage against the Beta-Israel "Zionists" and destroyed whole villages. Babies were bludgeoned to death, children's feet were hacked off, men were killed or castrated, women were raped and mutilated.... Captives were sold in the slave trade.... Slave raids were directed against the Falashas...[in] a region the Ethiopian Democratic Union had occupied for several months. One Falasha blacksmith fetched... about $350.[21]

The remnants of a far-left group which had been decimated by the government, the Ethiopian Peoples Revolutionary party, attacked Jews as Zionists. An Israeli official reported in January 1979 that 2,000 Jews had been killed in Ethiopia during the past three years;[22] he noted they had not been killed *because* they were Jews.

Associations of private citizens were formed that called upon the Israeli government to arrange for large-scale immigration from Ethiopia. The most energetic of these were located in Canada and the United States. The head of the Association of Ethiopian Jews in Israel, Avraham Yardai, called the Israeli government racist for not rescuing his countrymen. "While the entire world is called to protest the jailing of one Russian Jew not a word is said about the murder, rape, and destruction of the Ethiopian Jews," Yardai charged.[23]

Sometime after the pogrom of 1978, the small-scale exodus from Ethiopia was resumed quietly under the direction of Israeli authorities. In 1980, it was expanded. The route was by land to Sudan and from there by air to a third country and then to Israel. Because the Israeli government feared a repetition of the 1978 pogrom, no public acknowledgment of the still modest-sized rescue mission was made. Nobody wanted another "slip."

It was about this time that Major Melaku Teffera became governor of Gondar Province, the home of most Ethiopian Jews. According to one report, "in his campaign of terror, Falashas have been arrested and tortured to make them confess that they are 'Zionist and CIA agents.' "[24] In September 1981, Melaku shut down a large-scale project financed by ORT, the worldwide Jewish aid organization. As a result, there were no more Jewish schools in Gondar and no more teaching in Hebrew. For a few months, Jewish children who formerly attended ORT schools were excluded from public schools.[25] Under Melaku's rule, Christian landlord violence against Jews continued while land reform prohibitions of sharecropping seemed to mean little. Outside observers frequently confused Melaku's policies with those of the central revolutionary government. This was true only with respect to a verbal animus against Zionism.

In 1981, an American correspondent wrote from Ethiopia: "Numerous reliable sources...assured me that the Ethiopian government was fully aware of organized efforts to rescue Falashas from refugee camps in other countries to take them to Israel."[26] Sudan was the unmentioned other country. In March 1984, another story reported that 2,500 Ethiopian Jews had arrived in Israel during the past year. (As of 1974, only 200 lived there.) The same story stated plainly that 500 Ethiopian Jews had recently arrived "despite an official exit ban by the Marxist government" and that they had arrived via Sudan.[27] Another correspondent-activist wrote in September 1984 that a total of 7,000 Ethiopian Jews lived in Israel, another 8,000 were still in Ethiopia, and 11,000 more were in camps, primarily located in Sudan. "What is needed . . . is a mass rescue airlift from the camps and from Ethiopia."[28]

This is precisely what was in the making secretly between Ethiopia, Sudan, and Israel. In December 1982, an Ethiopian government official invited Israeli envoys to visit the Ethiopian Jews.[29] This was a reversal of previous policy. The next month members of a delegation representing the Israeli branch of the World Jewish Congress returned from a ten-day inspection tour of four towns in Ethiopia. They reported: "We were permitted to meet freely with the Falashas. We found no signs of hunger or extreme poverty, no manifestations of antisemitism, and we heard nothing about indiscriminate torture or mass murders."[30]

Another year passed until the spirit activated diplomatic discussions. In June 1984, the Ethiopian government sent a single representative to Jerusalem on a secret mission. Early in August, a statement was released on the occasion of a meeting between Ethiopian ministers and a minister of state of the British Foreign Office. In the statement, the Ethiopians "admitted there had been problems in the past but assured . . . that there was now no impediment in the way of members of the [Jewish] community emigrating to Israel."[31] In September, the Ethiopian Foreign Ministry confirmed this commitment.[32] On November twenty-four, the first flight in "Operation Moses" began. It did not remain secret for long, except in Israel where military censors blocked the story. The first story in the United States appeared in the *Jewish World* and the *Washington Jewish Week* two weeks after the operation began. It reported that "the rescue of a substantial number of Ethiopian Jews is under way" and that the U.S. government would pay part of the transportation and medical expenses. It also informed readers that only a week earlier the Ethiopian government had given the American Jewish Joint Distribution Committee permission to locate feeding stations in the Gondar area.[33] Four days later the *New York Times* added that an airlift was involved and that third countries were involved.[34] The next day, the *Boston Globe* mentioned refugee camps in Sudan: "Unmarked planes landing at night at Khartoum and boats pulling in surreptitiously along the Red Sea coast near Port Sudan."[35] The Sudanese government warned Israel it would stop the airlift if further disclosures were made.[36]

Military censorship of the story was lifted in Israel on January 2, 1985, and Operation Moses ended three days later. According to the Absorption Ministry, over 9,500 Ethiopian Jews had come to Israel, 2,213 in 1983 and 7,354 in 1984.[37] Altogether, according to Prime Minister Peres, 12,000 had been brought to Israel.[38] He said 6,000 to 8,000 remained in Ethiopia while 4,000 more were still in various camps. While Ethiopian Jews rejoiced at their arrival, they were deeply concerned about their family and relatives who were now unable to be airlifted.

Operation Moses used the services of the Trans-European Airlines, a charter carrier. Ethiopians in Sudanese camps were driven to planes which flew to Brussels in order to preserve the myth that there was no contact directly with Israel. From Brussels the planes flew to Israeli airfields.[39] Once the airlift was an open secret, both Ethiopia and Sudan denied they had cooperated with Israel. Sudan, a member of the Arab League, released a statement in London: "The Sudan need not reckon its unswerving positions and policies toward the Israeli enemy, which is still occupying Palestinian and other Arab territories. Ethiopia has always been using Ethiopian Jews as a bargaining card with Israel for obtaining arms and money." According to the statement, an Israeli firm, the Amiral Trading Company, with offices in Ethiopia, channeled the arms and money to the Ethiopian government.[40]

Sudan itself came under question when, after an April 1985 coup which overthrew the Niemiery regime, critics charged that "Niemiery and his vice president received $10,000 for each Ethiopian Jew smuggled from Sudan to Israel in . . . Operation Moses. The claims of bribes . . . came from sources in the military government who suggested that Zionist organizations had paid a total of $56 million to the Khartoum regime during the 18-month operation."[41] Ethiopia charged that the airlift was due to "anti-Ethiopian and counterrevolutionary elements operating from within the Sudan [which] have for a long time been forcing and enticing the inhabitants of the region to illegally cross over into the Sudan." The Foreign Ministry claimed Ethiopia's Jews "have for centuries lived side by side with their Ethiopian compatriots without any discrimination."[42]

Nearly three months after the end of Operation Moses, the remaining Jews in Sudan and the camps were evacuated to Israel by another airlift. This time, with the cooperation of the CIA, the State Department, and the U.S. Air Force, some 800 Jews were picked up and flown directly to Israel. C–130 Hercules transports were used and the operation took three days to complete.[43] Little publicity was given these flights. In January 1985, Prime Minister Peres had said some 4,000 Jews were still in Sudan; as it turned out, the number was only one-fifth that number. The discrepancy was not explained.

Ethiopia and Sudan were willing partners in a deception that failed to deceive. Very likely arms and/or money had flowed to both countries.

The Jews were no great moment to Ethiopia; at peak, there were only 28,000 out of a population of 30 million. The revolutionary government had never adopted consciously antisemitic programs; discouragement of religion applied to all faiths. To Sudan the Jews were hardly more than a temporary earning asset. Israel's communal conscience, tardy by decades, was finally joined to political advantage and Ethiopia's long-suffering Jews benefited.

Their rescue was a historical irony. In 1959, Jews petitioned Emperor Haile Selassie: "If through their own fault, our forefathers were removed from their lands, surely it is within the power of the king to revoke the order of his predecessors, and we, your servants, prostrate ourselves before the flag of Ethiopia and the throne of your exalted Majesty."[44] In the end it was not the emperor but his enemies who were in a position to grant the petitioners' request. Under the 1975 land reform, Jews had, for the first time in three and a half centuries, an equal right to work the land. Some began to be employed in government offices. While the governor of Gondar province oppressed the Jews fiercely, in October 1983 the central government replaced him with a far friendlier administrator. One delegation after another of foreign visitors reported those positive developments along with a few negative ones. However, once the Ethiopian Jews learned a move to Israel was practicable, they began streaming out. A close observer in that country described their arrival: "They are in shock—they believe their rescue is a miracle, a chapter in the story of redemption. . . . 'Are we really in Jerusalem, in Zion?' is a common question. When they are told they are, they fall to the ground and kiss it."[45] Thus did the Ethiopian Jews realize their age-old dream of Zion just when their earthly existence was starting to become more tolerable.

NOTES

1. See James A. Quirin, *The Beta Israel (Falasha) in Ethiopian History: Caste Formation and Cultural Change, 1270–1868* (Ph.D. diss., Univ. of Minnesota, 1977), University Microfilms Order No. 78–2709; James A. Quirin, "The Process of Caste Formation in Ethiopia: A Study of the Beta Israel (Falasha), 1270–1868," *International Journal of African Historical Studies,* 12 (1979), pp. 235–58.

2. For examples of reports written by two of these missionaries, see Henry A. Stern, *Wanderings among the Falashas in Abyssinia,* 2d ed. (London: Cass, 1968); J. M. Flad, *The Falashas (Jews) of Abyssinia,* trans. S. P. Goodhart (London: Macintosh, 1869). A third, written a century later, is Eric Payne, *Ethiopian Jews. The Story of a Mission* (London: Olive Press, 1972).

3. Jacques Faitlovitch, "The Falashas," *American Jewish Year Book,* 22 (Philadelphia: Jewish Publication Society of America, 1920), pp. 94–95.

4. Ibid., pp. 98–99.

5. "American Pro-Falasha Committee," *Universal Jewish Encyclopedia,* 1,

p. 271. Rapoport writes that Faitlovitch "is honored by the Falashas more than anyone in their modern history"; Louis Rapoport, *The Last Jews. Last of the Ethiopian Falashas* (New York: Stein and Day, 1979), p. 178.

6. *American Jewish Year Book,* 16, p. 167.

7. Ibid., 27, p. 28.

8. Ibid., 39, pp. 373–74. See also ibid., 40, p. 235.

9. "Ethiopia," *Universal Jewish Encyclopedia,* 4, p. 185.

10. David Kessler, *The Falashas. The Forgotten Jews of Ethiopia* (London: George Allen and Unwin, 1982), p. 148.

11. Wolf Leslau, "The Black Jews of Ethiopia. An Expedition to the Falashas," *Commentary,* March 1949, p. 223.

12. Kessler, *The Falashas,* p. 151.

13. Ibid., p. 152.

14. Stern, *Wanderings,* p. 193.

15. Rapoport, *The Lost Jews,* p. 196.

16. Kessler, *The Falashas,* p. 157.

17. See Fred Halliday and Maxine Molyneux, *The Ethiopian Revolution* (London: Verso, 1981), pp. 104–10; David B. Ottoway, "Ethiopia Nationalizes Rural Lands," *Washington Post,* March 5, 1975.

18. Rapoport, *The Lost Jews,* p. 5.

19. Howard M. Sachar, *A History of Israel from the Rise of Zionism to Our Time* (New York: Knopf, 1976), p. 789.

20. Letter by Yeshiahu Ben-Baruch, chairman, and Abraham Yeshiahu, secretary, Union for Saving Ethiopian Jewish Families, *Jerusalem Post,* April 16, 1981.

21. Rapoport, *The Lost Jews,* p. 9.

22. *Jerusalem Post,* January 12, 1979. The official was Yehuda Dominitz, director-general of the Jewish Agency's aliya and absorption department.

23. *Jerusalem Post,* October 29, 1979.

24. Steven B. Kaplan, "An Eye Witness—A Second Version," *Present Tense,* 9 (Summer 1982), pp. 43–44. See also *Jerusalem Post,* February 10, 1984 (AP story).

25. Abraham Karlikow, "An Eye Witness—One Version," *Present Tense,* 9 (Summer 1982), p. 42.

26. Michael Winn, "Falashas: Doomed to Extinction?" *National Jewish Monthly,* May 1981, p. 44.

27. *Boston Globe,* March 31, 1984.

28. Simcha Jacobovici, "Ethiopian Jews Die, Israel Fiddles," *New York Times,* September 15, 1984.

29. *Jerusalem Post,* December 14, 1982.

30. *Jerusalem Post,* January 21, 1983. See also David Kessler, "The Falashas—the Jews of Ethiopia. An Almost Forgotten Community," *Research Report* (Institute of Jewish Affairs, February 1983), p. 9.

31. Jacobovici, "Ethiopian Jews Die, Israel Fiddles," *New York Times,* September 15, 1984.

32. Judith Miller, "The Birth of a New Ethiopia: From Feudalism to Marxism," *New York Times,* October 8, 1984.

33. Michael Berenbaum, "Efforts Underway to Rescue, Help Resettle Ethiopian Jews," *Jewish World,* December 7, 1984.

34. *New York Times,* December 11, 1984.

35. *Boston Globe,* December 12, 1984.

36. Larry Cohler, "Ethiopian Rescue May Be Able to Resume Quietly," *Jewish World,* January 11, 1985. This report was attributed to Israeli absorption minister Yascov Tsur.

37. *Jerusalem Post,* January 7, 1985.

38. *Boston Globe,* January 9, 1985.

39. *New York Times,* January 9, 1985.

40. *New York Times,* January 8, 1985.

41. *Boston Globe,* April 29, 1985. Operation Moses seems to have lasted six weeks. On the other hand, a much smaller air operation was organized in 1980. The eighteen-month figure does not fit either one.

42. *New York Times,* January 5, 1985.

43. *New York Times,* March 24, 1985.

44. Kessler, *The Falashas,* p. 152.

45. Judy Siegel and Louis Rapoport, *Jerusalem Post,* January 4, 1985.

5

FROM JEW TO CITIZEN: FRANCE

> When the Germans began their systematic deportation and extermination of Jews in 1942, Vichy's rival antisemitism offered them more substantial help than they received anywhere else in western Europe, and more even than they received from such allies as Hungary and Rumania.
> —Michael R. Marrus and Robert O. Paxton, 1983

Jews in France suffered the typical afflictions of non-Christians in late medieval Europe. Added to the zeal of religious doctrinaires, the rapacity of secular rulers moved one government after another to hound the Jews. After some six centuries, French Jews began their historic transformation into equal citizens, the first in Europe. The nineteenth and twentieth centuries gave many of them pause about this pursuit of civic status.

During the ninth and tenth centuries, Jews in France acquired legal equality. Early in the ninth century, Charlemagne's son Ludovic (824–840) became "the first Christian monarch to place the Jews under his direct tutelage."[1] Jewish merchants were valued assets to the growing kingdom. Jews owned land and participated extensively in agriculture and viticulture. Countryside competitors with these Jews and church prelates pressed in vain for royal outlawry of the ownership of non-Jewish slaves by Jews. The competitors' motives were strictly economic, that is they knew slaves were still essential to farm production, while church prelates feared these slaves would be converted to Judaism, as indeed many were. Church councils were unsuccessful in gaining state approval for their restrictive measures.

According to Leon Poliakov, during the ninth century the Roman Catholic liturgy started treating the Jew as a being apart. At the same time, he notes, emphasis was on the Jew's beliefs rather than on his alleged killing of Jesus. In fact, at this time, writes Poliakov, "there was no trace of a specific, popular anti-Semitism."[2] During the ninth and tenth centuries, no French chronicle records any popular movement against Jews.

Early in the eleventh century began a series of anti-Jewish events set off by clergymen. After numerous Jews were forced to convert to Christianity—a gross violation of church rules—appeals to popes brought relief. Generally, lower clergy were in the forefront of these anti-Jewish actions.

The Crusades, which affected Jews all over Europe, were aimed at reconquering the Holy Land from the Muslims. Before crusaders set off, however, they turned against Jews in their home countries. In the First Crusade (1096–99), "Jewish suffering was widespread in France, and at the hands of Frenchmen."[3] In Germany, the losses were even greater; synagogues were burned down; homes were plundered; and Jews were massacred at will. The succeeding Crusades extended this trail of destruction and poured over into the political realm. As Simon Dubnov writes: "The carnage in Middle Europe during the Crusades brought about the complete dependence of the Jews upon the emperor, monarchs, and feudal princes, who protected the Jewish tributaries to the extent that it was advantageous to their treasuries."[4] During the worst excesses of the Crusades in France, bishops and nobles had attempted to protect Jews. The Jews' greatest enemies were traveling friars who egged on demonstrators to commit vile attacks on Jews. In some areas, such as the Rhone Valley, Jews organized an effective resistance.

During the twelfth century, moneylending by Jews expanded. Borrowers came from every social level of France. As an incentive to expansion of the trade in money, the government guaranteed many loans, thus ensuring their ultimate collection. (A century later, moneylending had become the chief employment of Jews in France but the bulk of the business was always conducted by Christians.) Toward the close of the twelfth century, a rising urban Christian bourgeoisie more readily replaced Jews in the trade and thus Jews became less useful to the monarchs. Further, authorities, for their own political and religious reasons, gave way increasingly to church demands for more restrictive measures on Jews. In 1223, King Louis IX, the Pious (1176–1226), issued an ordinance against usury, the first "such royal order in medieval Europe."[5]

Alongside the declining economic role of Jews occurred an upsurge in violent actions against Jews in the thirteenth century. In 1242, under papal encouragement, copies of the Talmud and other sacred volumes were burned in Paris and elsewhere. In 1288 and 1290, Jews were tried by the church, found guilty, and burned at the stake. Around the same time, calls were heard for the expulsion of the Jews from France. Robert

Chazan comments on the thirteenth century: "The religious zeal evoked by the mid-century Crusades, by royal enthusiasm for these expeditions, and by royal despoiling of the Jews encouraged the growth of anti-Jewish sentiment and perhaps fostered the feeling that violence could be committed with relative impunity."[6]

Under Philip the Fair (1285–1314) the rapacity of the French throne reached its peak. In mid-1306, many Jews were arrested. This was a prelude to a royal policy of expelling Jews from the entire country. (Expulsions from specific localities had occurred more than a century earlier.) The property of incarcerated Jews was then confiscated by the king. Jewish moneylenders were required to deliver all their records of loans outstanding. By late summer only a handful of Jews remained in France. Meanwhile, Philip sold the Jewish goods and land he had seized and gained an immense profit. He was careful not to flood the market and drive down prices; sales of the formerly Jewish property were phased in over several years. Loans extended by Jews to Christians were then called in by Philip. He took the capital amount—that is, the sum that had actually been lent—and did not require payment of interest. Some Jews were permitted to remain only to help collect the debts they had originated. Philip and many barons fought not over the principle of expulsion but over the division of the spoils. From time to time, Jews were given rights of residence for short periods and then ejected. In 1394, a "final" expulsion occurred.

During the following four centuries Jews were all but absent from France. Yet antisemitism came of age during this long period. Poliakov points out that anti-Jewish stereotypes became part of the national vocabulary as Roman Catholic catechism instructed French children in hatred of Jews. Abbé Fleury's, which went through 172 editions in two centuries, read: "Did Jesus have enemies?—Yes, the carnal Jews.—To what point did the hatred of Jesus' enemies go?—To the point of causing his death." Jacques Bossuet described the Jews as "a monstrous people ... the evil spirit and the detestation of the world."[7] Rare was a dissenting voice such as that of the humanist Jean Bodin.

The century and a half of the Enlightenment preceding the French Revolution of 1789 laid the basis for a new antisemitism. Its chief spokesman was Voltaire who detested Jews but not on religious grounds. Instead, he combined race and culture, a new deadly amalgam. Arthur Hertzberg has characterized that view comprehensively: "There is a cultural, philosophical, and ethnic tradition of Europe which descended, through the human stock of that continent, from the intellectual values that were taught by the Greeks. Those were in turn carried to all the reaches of the European world by the Romans." Voltaire regarded this culture as normative. The Jews, however, are the product of a different origin and tradition and thus alien to the European tradition. Hertzberg's summary of Voltaire continued: "The case of the Jews is radically different. Being born a Jew and the obnoxiousness of the Jewish outlook are indissoluble; it is most unlikely that 'enlightened' Jews can escape their innate character. The Jews are subversive of the European tradition by their very presence, for they are the radically other, the hopeless alien. Cure them of their religion and their inborn character remains."[8]

In 1771, Voltaire wrote of the Jews: "They are, all of them born with raging fanaticism in their hearts, just as the Bretons and the Germans are born with blond hair. I would not be in the least bit surprised if these people would not some day become deadly to the human race."[9] He accused them of hating all other people, repeatedly citing their refusal to eat at the same table with non-Jews.

During Voltaire's lifetime (1694–1778), however, Jews became more useful to the state as it strove to expand foreign trade and its colonies. Only about 5,000 Jews lived in the France of 1700. Many were concentrated in Bordeaux, a leading colonial port. The French crown cared more for the condition of their capital than for the state of their religious conscience. By 1776, Louis XVI was granting Sephardic Jewish merchants in Bordeaux and elsewhere the right to trade anywhere in France. This meant little for the roughly half of French Jewry that lived along the German frontier, in Alsace. These Yiddish- and German-speaking Jews were exceedingly poor and in the 1770s, according to Hertzberg, confronted "pogroms and threat[s] of pogroms."[10]

Enlightened commentary on the problem of the Jews tended to agree that they suffered from discrimination and persecution and that they should be accorded equal civil rights, including wider economic opportunities and access to secular western education. Just below the surface of the discussion dwelt an assumption that these advances would remedy certain imperfections in existing Jewish culture, primarily by being replaced. Jews were to be improved by becoming less Jewish. Clermont-Tonnerre, in a debate on the issue in the National Assembly during late 1789, declared: "Jews, as a *nation*, deserve nothing, but Jews, as a *people*, deserve everything." He continued: "A nation within a nation is inconceivable."[11] Two months later, in February 1790, a body of elders declared an end to the "Jewish nation" and the next year the National Assembly proclaimed the emancipation of French Jewry. French Jews were transformed into Frenchmen of the Mosaic persuasion as their Jewish heritage continued to be suspect in the Voltairian scheme.

During the summer and fall of 1805, physical attacks upon Jews increased. Widespread questioning of Jewish intentions to measure up to the requirements of citizenship was heard. The next year Napoleon himself declared: "Jews are to be regarded as a nation, not a sect; it is a nation within a nation."[12] An Assembly of Notables was convened by the government to meet in 1806. "The deputies," writes Frances Malino, "were united in their attempts to make Judaism and the Jews completely compatible with France."[13] The actual course of the conference, however, is suggested by Dubnov: "After starting out by compromise and servility, the assembly kept on sliding downhill."[14] It resolved, for example, that rabbis possessed no judicial powers and that no Jewish nation any longer existed. In 1807, Napoleon arranged for the convening of the Great Sanhedrin, a council of Jewish leaders.

The next year, Napoleon issued decrees that set up Jewish consistories in each department of the country—Dubnov says in order to spy on Jews—which could authorize new synagogues. In addition, three separate actions were directed: (1) certain loans made by Jews were annulled, postponed, or reduced; (2) before entering a trade, Jews had to obtain a patent from the prefect; and (3) freedom of movement and of residence was limited. Jews of Bordeaux were exempted. By these measures, asserts Malino, "the majority of Jews of France had been reduced to second class citizens, emasculated economically and discriminated against socially and politically."[15]

Between 1815 and 1870, the number of Jews in France more than doubled, from 47,000 to 100,000. In the half-century after 1811, their representation in the entire population rose merely from .16 to .26 percent; four-fifths of the Jews lived in Alsace-Lorraine or Paris, with an increasing part in Paris. Post-Napoleonic France saw these Jews integrated into the national economy. Phyllis Cohen Albert sums up the main lines of development: "There was an increasing participation in liberal professions and skilled labor, a greater diversification of such occupations, a rise in 'productive' occupations, an improvement in socioeconomic status within the various groups, and a decrease of activity at the lowest levels of commerce."[16] In the largest concentrations of Jews, both wealth and poverty coexisted. An estimate in 1840 held that 20 percent of Jews in Paris lived in poverty, a somewhat greater number than among the general population.

Social integration lagged, however. As Albert observes, "Except for the very richest class, Jews were still restricted to socializing within the Jewish milieu."[17] Within the consistories and synagogues, wealthier Jews tended to dominate internal affairs as well as regular contacts with governing authorities.

While the years 1815 to 1870 saw no organized antisemitic movement, anti-Jewish goals actuated many localized government decisions. By 1829, there were sixty-two Jewish public schools. Their number expanded significantly in the next decade. Local authorities, who were bound by law to support such schools, lagged agonizingly in supplying resources. School authorities in Strasbourg protested to the Ministry of Education against providing public schools for Jews because they were "a foreign, ignorant and dishonest colony among the educated and productive population of Alsace."[18] A major reason for organizing Jewish public schools lay with exclusory and discriminatory treatment of Jewish children. Many Christian schools refused to accept Jewish children while in the earlier grades Jewish children were often subjected to proselytism. "In 1853," writes Albert, "the community of Macon (Bas Rhin) prohibited Jewish children from entering the *lycee*. When the government applied pressure, they were finally admitted but were forced to attend Catholic religious lessons with everyone else."[19] Jews found it especially difficult to teach in higher education.

Antisemitism could be found in areas other than education. Outright violence against Jews was by no means unknown. In 1848 and in the 1850s, anti-Jewish riots occurred in Alsace; Albert says violence was limited to Alsace. When anti-Jewish pamphlets were protested, the government refused to suppress such publications. Jews in prisons also experienced discrimination. Municipal funds for charitable purposes were sometimes denied to the Jews. Newspaper stories reporting arrests in criminal cases noted "Jew" after the arrestee's name.

During the 1870s and 1880s, antisemites conducted forays rather than sustained campaigns against Jews. Many of the encounters were literary. Robert Byrnes reports that for over 200 years the Jew had appeared in plays as "an odious and grotesque person."[20] In 1870, Henri Gougenot des Mousseaux wrote a book which, in Byrnes' words, "presented the theme that the Jews were utilizing eighteenth-century liberal ideas and the secret force of Freemasonry to overthrow Christianity and to obtain rule over the entire world."[21] *Les Juives, nos maitres,* written by Father Chabauty in 1882, contended that "secret Jewish chiefs led the Jewish nation and all secret societies against Christianity and the Christian nations with the aim of obtaining rule of the world for the Jews."[22] In 1886, Sydney Vigneaux, in his novel *Baron Jehovah,* "found the source of Jewish financial power in a planned program for world rule through the establishment of a 'central gold council.' "[23] Indeed, summarizes Byrnes, "custom provided that the Jew in the French novel be foreign, capitalist, and anticlerical."[24]

Until 1870 or so, socialists were the prime source of antisemitism in France. In time, however, it became clear that very few capitalist employers were Jewish, regardless of what the literary antisemites alleged. At the 1891 Brussels Conference of the Socialist International Organization, antisemitism was denounced as "a natural enemy of social progress."[25] French socialists shared this view; after 1870 their support of antisemitism had diminished sharply.

French Catholics, and especially the clergy, became the soul of French antisemitism. They published antisemitic newspapers and financed others. In the army, especially the officer corps, hatred of Jews was very strong. Byrnes notes that "students from Jesuit schools, which had practically a monopoly over entrance into the military schools and which resented the success of Jewish scholars, were especially bitter enemies of the Jews."[26] Small merchants and minor bureaucrats were the strongest supporters of the anti-Jewish movement. Support was also to be found among an intellectual proletariat of professionals who could always point to a Jewish competitor who was more successful than they. This sometimes extended to graduate students in the universities. A number of writers and journalists became among the most enduring of antisemites.

Edouard Drumont's *La France Juive* (Jewish France), published in 1886, argued that Jews all but controlled France and attributed to them central responsibility for many major social problems. Little was in fact demonstrated in the book but its lurid tone attracted many readers. Six years later, he founded a daily newspaper, *La Libre Parole;* it was financed by Jesuits. Drumont attacked, among others, Jewish army officers for allegedly selling defense secrets to other countries.

Ten years later, in 1894, Captain Alfred Dreyfus, a Jew, was arrested on charges of being a German spy. Soon, the matter was transformed from the Dreyfus case to the Dreyfus affair. The former involved only the captain's personal innocence or guilt; the latter encompassed antisemitism, French democracy, and the political role of the Catholic church. Although Dreyfus was found guilty and imprisoned, severe doubts were raised about the evidence and a conviction grew that he had been railroaded for his Jewish ancestry. Much of the country took sides on the matter. The Dreyfus affair uncovered a deep reservoir of antisemitism in French society.

Stephen Wilson points to the formation of antisemitism as a coherent ideology by the 1890s as a basic factor in the affair. The contemporary emergence of antisemitic organizations helped translate the ideology into social action. During 1898, the peak year of the affair, antisemitic riots erupted in sixty-nine places in France; in Algeria, reports Wilson, "a full-scale pogrom took place under the complaisant eye of the military."[27] In large cities, persons from all social groups participated. The political parties stayed away from antisemitism although some marginal ones embraced it successfully during a momentary enthusiasm.

In part, the affair expressed economic grievances of shopkeepers and petty traders who felt increasingly pressed by the competition of department stores, consumer cooperatives, and other varieties of mass distribution. While only a few Jews were involved in department stores, they were frequently thought to be extensive owners. "French workers," notes Wilson, "were not very prone to antisemitism."[28] This was despite the fact that they were affected directly by large-scale economic changes. Between 1850 and 1910, "employment in craft work fell from 2.5 million to 900,000, while the numbers for industrial companies rose from 1.2 million to 4.5 million."[29] Yet, this transformation of the workplace was accompanied by a decline in antisemitism among the working class. During the Dreyfus affair, worker antisemitism was a secondary issue.

The rise of socialism and trade unions frightened the propertied classes of France who feared the outcome of open class conflict. Wilson observes that in this context, antisemitism functioned as a conservative social doctrine, operating so as to "mask class conflict and to divert resentments into a channel that did not threaten the existing social system."[30] To the bourgeois antisemite, according to Wilson, the traditional world in which one took an accustomed place rather than earning it by competitive striving was felt to be slipping away. The Jew could be imagined as symbolizing this unwelcome transition which endangered the elevated status of bourgeois antisemites.

At the time of the Dreyfus affair, antisemitism prevailed among French Catholics. The clergy was strongly anti-Jewish and had for centuries guided the French toward Jew-hate. The church never accepted the French Revolution's secular ideals nor could it forget the loss of land and political power it had suffered in the 1790s. It could not resist the opportunity to use antisemitism as a means of recovering its status if not its property. In some other countries, protest against the modern industrial world did not employ antisemitism. In France, it was at the heart of the protest.

By the outbreak of World War I, in 1914, French Jewry consisted of two sharply divided groups: a bourgeoisie made up of almost all so-called native Jews and a working class nearly all of which was composed of east and central European immigrants. The latter were overwhelmingly artisans rather than factory workers and were concentrated in Paris. There they lived in closely packed quarters which gave rise to de facto segregated schools attended overwhelmingly by Jewish immigrant children. The Left called for desegregation of such schools which closed on Saturdays rather than the customary Thursdays. Zosa Szajkowski writes that "such protests by the liberals and leftists against separate Jewish schools did not contain even a trace of antisemitism."[31] Instead, they feared setting a precedent that Catholic schools might adopt.

A ghetto life emerged from such circumstances. Between 1918 and 1939, for example, 133 Yiddish periodicals were established. Jewish merchants and storekeepers did most of their business with other Jews instead of the public at large. Jewish workers joined Jewish unions. (In part, this resulted from momentary expressions of antisemitism during 1910–11 by the general labor movement.) Jewish clothing workers frequently labored at home, under exceedingly poor conditions in the needle trades. Such home workers were not permitted to join general unions in their trade since many worked for substandard wages and sometimes acted as strikebreakers. During the 1920s and 1930s, the

Jewish labor movement in Paris was heavily Communist, another factor that alienated it from native, bourgeois Jews.

Native Jewish leaders aimed to "remake immigrant Jews in their own image and to use their institutions as agents of assimilation."[32] Unemployment in the 1930s arose out of the world depression and from the refugee stream from Germany and eastern and central Europe. Condescension was the dominant stance of native Jewish leaders toward immigrant Jews. They tried to regulate the slightest details of immigrant life. Thus, in mid-1939, just weeks before the first battles of World War II, the central Jewish welfare organization declared publicly that aid would not be given to "those indigent [who] go to cafes where they ... ostentatiously read Hebrew [i.e., Yiddish] newspapers, [an act] which is likely to provoke or develop antisemitism."[33] These same circles "found it most comforting to attribute the spread of antisemitism in France to the presence of unassimilated immigrant Jews who offended the sensibilities of native Frenchmen."[34]

French Fascist groups proliferated in the 1930s; most were openly antisemitic. Their prime target was the large Jewish immigrant population. The native Jewish leadership ignored the worst of these during the early 1930s. Indeed, one of the most dangerous of the Fascist groups, the Croix de Feu, participated in some synagogue ceremonies. A representative of the chief rabbi of Paris attended meetings of the group and endorsed their cause. "There were many [Jewish] natives," David H. Weinberg writes, "who felt a strong attachment to right-wing ideology."[35] Weinberg writes of the central Jewish organization, the Consistoire, that "the religious organization was often closely aligned with a number of right-wing movements in France."[36] Many such Jewish leaders convinced themselves that antisemitism in France was an import from Nazi Germany rather than a native growth. "The overriding fear of the association of Judaism with Bolshevism," Weinberg observes, "was the major factor that shaped French Jewish attitudes toward the question of the appropriate response to antisemitism."[37]

The leading group that opposed antisemitism was the Ligue International contre l'Antisemitisme (LICA). It conducted mass demonstrations and fought fascists in the streets; many immigrant Jews belonged to it. As Paula Hyman puts it: "Mass demonstrations and protest meetings, self-defense against anti-Semitic gangs in Jewish neighborhoods, and left-leaning politics were part of the accepted political legacy of a large segment of Eastern European immigrant Jews."[38] By 1936, even the native Jewish press was calling for formation of armed defense groups. The Jewish establishment as a whole, however, failed to cut its ties with the Right.

Two international crises during 1938—the *Anschluss* with Austria and the Munich appeasement conference—delineated ever more clearly for many Jews in France the menace of Nazi Germany. Throughout the Jewish communities of France, a silent sentiment in favor of war took shape. "Indeed," writes Weinberg, "there was a noticeable upsurge in antisemitism in Paris directly after the *Anschluss,* attributable in large part to the rumor that Jews had tried to force the French government to declare war on Germany for their own interests."[39] Until the very eve of the war, Jews continued to be regarded as warmongers, even in left-wing circles. The Right, of course, made the most of such charges. In 1939, Pope Pius XII dropped the interdict on fascist Action Française which had been in effect since 1926.

The French government did not for long separate itself from measures striking at immigrant refugee Jews. In 1935, more than 3,000 foreigners were expelled because their papers were not in order. Three years later, a series of decrees was issued. "Among the provisions of the new decrees," writes Weinberg, "were limitations on the number of foreign merchants and artisans in specific trades, restrictions on aliens opening up new businesses, repatriation of refugees who failed to register with government authorities, and expulsion of foreigners who could not produce valid work permits."[40] Those provisions hit especially hard at refugees from Germany and Austria. Later in 1938, a decree announced that naturalized Frenchmen could be stripped of their nationality if they were found "unworthy of the title of French citizen."[41] Concentration camps were established for foreigners improperly present in France. Spanish refugees from the Franco regime were placed in the camps as were many Jews. Of the 40,000 persons who remained interned in late 1940, about 28,000 were Jews.

In April 1939, the army was opened up to immigrant volunteers. Jews flooded the offices. Weinberg describes the outcome: "By late April, the recruitment program had reached such a fever pitch that the Ministry of National Defense was forced to issue a declaration criticizing Jewish organizations for their overzealousness and demanding the suspension of further registration."[42] (Many of these volunteers were later sent to Auschwitz with the cooperation of the French while others were used by the French as virtual slave labor in Algeria.)

While World War II began with a Nazi attack on Poland in September 1939, the war in France occupied some six weeks during May–June 1940. The armistice split the country into two areas: the north, including Paris, called the Occupied Zone; and the south, called the Unoccupied Zone. The former was held by Germans, the latter by the French government located in Vichy and headed by Marshal Pétain. In the absence of any pressure by the Nazis, the Vichy region adopted a broad program of measures aimed directly at Jews.

In August 1940, the *loi Marchandeau* was repealed. Decreed a year earlier, it had outlawed press attacks by newspapers or magazines on the basis of race or religion. The *loi* had worked well. In October, a *Statut des juifs* was passed, the first law in modern French history that singled Jews out for explicit legal disadvantages. Jews were given an inferior civic position. None could occupy leading jobs in the civil service, army, mass communications, teaching, theater, or films. About 6,000 Jews lost their citizenship under the 1938 statute described above. Another measure, requiring lawyers and physicians to have had a French father, affected Jews especially hard. Still another law, adopted in October, authorized prefects to intern foreign Jews in camps or place them under surveillance in remote villages. Several days later the Cremieux Decree was revoked; issued in 1870, it had made Jews in Algeria French citizens. French colonists in Algeria and/or antisemites had long urged revocation of the decree. In mid-1941, legislation tightened the restrictions on Jews in the professions and literary positions.

A second *Statut des juifs* was passed in June 1941. In many professions, the law established a ceiling of 2 percent for Jews. In higher educational institutions the quota was placed at 3 percent. Lower-level public service positions were made available to Jewish veterans. A census of Jews in the Unoccupied Zone was taken, with data collected on property owned, income, and debts. The following month an Aryanization Law was adopted that provided for government confiscation of Jewish property. This measure aimed to eliminate "all Jewish influence from the national economy."

Between mid-1940 and mid-1942, a far-reaching body of anti-Jewish legislation had been constructed. Michael Marrus and Robert Paxton write: "Vichy's anti-Jewish program . . . met with the indifference of most French people, with the approval of a growing number, the doubts of some, and the open opposition of very few."[43] An aura of legality surrounded the program. Special governmental mechanisms were created to implement the measures. In March 1941, France had created a Commissariat-General of Jewish Affairs (CGJA) to oversee the program; Germany had urged the creation of the office. Also in response to German pressure, there was organized a *Judenrat*—a Jewish council called the Union Generale des Israelites de France (UGIF). Its role was to transmit governmental directives concerning Jews to the Jewish population. One council existed in each zone. When the Germans levied a collective fine of one billion francs on Jews in December 1941 because the Resistance had killed several German soldiers, the UGIF was charged with collecting the money. Jews were treated exceptionally in one respect: no ghetto was created and even in the Occupied Zone Jews continued to walk about into 1944.

During 1940–42, no center of non-Jewish opposition to the anti-Jewish program emerged. Neither the De Gaulle Resistance forces nor the Com-

munist party made the program a critical political issue. The Catholic
church was perhaps the strongest supporter of the Vichy government
but avoided dealing with the Jewish issue. After the passage of the *Statut
des juifs*, the Bishop of Marseille declared: "Already we see the face of
a more beautiful France, healed of her sores which were often the work
of . . . foreigners."[44] The French ambassador to the Vatican reported back
home that "an authorized source at the Vatican told me, they don't intend
to get into a fight over the *Statut des juifs*."[45]

In June 1942, Adolf Eichmann, the principal engineer of the Final
Solution, brought a directive from SS chief Heinrich Himmler to deport
all Jews in France to death camps. Earlier in the month, Jews in the
Occupied Zone were ordered to wear a Jewish cloth star on their outer
garment. Vichy refused to follow the order, the first time it did so. In
July, some 9,000 French policemen set out to arrest the first large contingent of Jews to be shipped to the death camps. When Jews answered
a knock on the door, they "were often reassured by the French uniform,
the instructions in French, and the 'correct' deportment of the arresting
officer."[46] Nearly 13,000 Jews were arrested and sent to the main French
concentration camp at Drancy. From there all but a few went on to
Auschwitz.

Such events, necessarily perpetrated in public, brought about a sudden
change in public opinion. The scene of children being separated forcibly
from their parents deeply disturbed many of the French. The sight of
French police openly functioning as surrogates of the Nazis helped create
a "public nausea." So revolting were these events that establishment
figures began to protest openly. The annual assembly of cardinals and
archbishops sent an unpublished protest to Pétain. The Archbishop of
Toulouse wrote in a pastoral letter: "The Jews are real men and women.
. . . They are part of the human species. They are our brothers like so
many others."[47] The Bishop of Montauban declared in another pastoral
letter: "I proclaim that all men, Aryans or non-Aryans, are brothers."[48]
Altogether, note Marrus and Paxton of the church prelates in the Unoccupied Zone, fewer than half made critical statements from the pulpit
while none did so in the Occupied Zone.

Unfortunately, when the next round of shipments to Auschwitz came,
in February 1943, the church was silent. In the interim, the church and
the Vichy state had negotiated successfully over the long-term problem
of state funds for church use.

Meanwhile, the legal structure of France continued to implement anti-
Jewish legislation. "There is no doubt," write Marrus and Paxton, "that
the judicial system facilitated legal persecution, permitting it to go on
forward relatively smoothly."[49] Endorsements of the legislation were
given by well-known jurists; learned law journals and commentators
interpreted coolly the laws that brought ruin to thousands. Even after

Allied troops had landed on French soil, in 1944, the courts continued their assigned task.

French police cooperation in enforcing anti-Jewish laws was critical as the Germans were extremely short of personnel. In the absence of such cooperation, much less harm would have come to the Jews in France. The some 70,000 Jews who were brought to the Drancy concentration camp and then sent off to Auschwitz were arrested by French police. Germany found French police to be highly cooperative. From 1942 onward, when Germans were designing the first large-scale shipments to death camps, they were helped enormously by the 150,000-card file of Jews in the Seine department put at their disposal by the Jewish section of the Paris police. The cards were alphabetically arranged by street, profession, and nationality. Jews were arrested by police for trying to escape to other countries and for not having their identification papers— after December 1942, stamped "Jew"—in order. A decline in cooperation began only in 1943, after Frenchmen were sent to work in German factories. However, a separate force, the Police for Jewish Affairs, operated from its inception in the autumn of 1941 until the Liberation in Paris, nearly three years later.

The Aryanization Law of 1941 laid the basis for expropriating Jewish property. Legally appointed trustees judged whether to sell businesses under their authority or simply close them down. Corruption was rife. By May 1, 1944, more than 42,000 Jewish-owned enterprises were under trusteeship. Influential Germans simply picked and chose whatever properties they wanted. Organized business interests eliminated Jewish competitors in the name of the national or "racial" interest. When certain Jewish-owned factories were to be sold, non-Jewish owners in that industry helped decide who would be permitted to purchase them. Outright bribes to trustees and their staffs were common.

In eight departments in southeastern France, Italian occupation forces were vigilant in protecting the rights of Jews. They forbade the stamping of "Jew" in ration books and identification cards. In February 1943, when French police were busy arresting Jews to be sent to their deaths, the Italians forbade prefects from arresting any foreign Jews. The next month, both native French as well as foreign Jews were placed under Italian protection. *Carbinieri* in Nice guarded the synagogues. Jews there were authorized by Italian authorities to issue their own identity cards. Marrus and Paxton note: "The *carbinieri* commander, Captain Salvi, told the local prefect he would personally order the arrest of any French policeman who interfered."[50] After Mussolini was overthrown, in July 1943, Italian forces withdrew to Nice; in September they signed an armistice with the Allies. Thereupon, Nazis moved in to the eight departments, arrested all the Jews, and sent them to Auschwitz.

Between 300,000 and 350,000 Jews lived in France in 1940. About 30 percent, or around 100,000, lost their lives during the war. Nearly three-quarters of these perished in Auschwitz. Immigrants, who comprised about half of all Jews, made up over two-thirds of those who ended up in Auschwitz.

"Every Jew who survived in France during 1942 to 1944," observed Marrus and Paxton, "owed his or her life to some French man or woman who helped, or at least kept a secret."[51] But every Jew who did not survive owed his or her death in part to the German and Vichy governments. France was the only western country that created its own body of anti-Jewish laws. It built this shameful edifice on top of a decade of hostility and suspicion directed at foreign Jews but, ultimately, at native-born Jews as well. Vichy-France outstripped all other countries in aiding the Nazis in implementing the Final Solution, although its leaders seemed to distance themselves from identifying with the goal.

"For about twenty years after the war," wrote Raymond Aron, "for obvious reasons, there was general silence on the Jewish issue."[52] A certain degree of antisemitism, however, persisted. In a poll of 208 respondents taken in Paris and its suburbs during 1954, persons were asked: "Do you think the Israelites are Frenchmen like any others?" Nearly half of those identifying themselves as belonging to the Right answered "no"; only about one-eighth of those on the Left replied in the negative.[53]

In 1966, the Institut Français de l'Opinion Publique reported that about one-fifth of the French "held seriously antisemitic opinions."[54] Several years later, the *Encyclopedia Judaica* summarized a number of postwar polls: "Approximately 10 percent of Frenchmen were openly antisemitic and another 20 percent exhibited definite indications of antisemitism. From 1969 to 1971, the number of anti-Semites did not increase, but the inhibitions that made themselves felt after World War II were fading away."[55] One event commonly regarded as having aroused latent antisemitism is a statement made by General Charles de Gaulle in 1967. In a press conference he referred to Jews as "an elite people, sure of itself, and domineering."

In 1980, a bomb killed four persons outside a Paris synagogue located on the Rue Copernic. Responsibility for the bombing was asserted by the Fascieux Nationalistes European, a neo-Nazi group. Critics of the government claimed that many neo-Nazis were members of the French police and this was why few perpetrators of earlier bombings and other outrages had not been arrested. During the preceding eighteen months or so, anti-Jewish actions included machine-gun attacks on Jewish cultural buildings, schools, and synagogues. In 1979, a Molotov cocktail was thrown at a Paris synagogue; thirty-two persons were injured. From July to September 1980, according to one report, "there have been 40 attacks in France by groups whom the police consider neo-Nazis. They follow a mounting campaign of graffiti with swastikas and anti-Jewish slogans, antisemitic tracts, and threatening letters sent to Jews."[56] Another report refers to "an inordinate number of extreme right-wing activists in both French and Italian [neo-Nazi] groups are serving [as] members of the police force."[57]

A Harris poll taken after the Rue Copernic bombing produced mixed results. On the one hand, one-eighth of the respondents thought there were too many Jews in France while a tenth felt Jews were not "as French" as other citizens. Over half (55 percent) felt there was "widespread" antisemitic feeling in France.[58] At the same time, 1980 responses were compared with those of 1977 to the same questions:

"Are there too many Jews in France?"

    1977: 17 percent "yes"
    1980: 12 percent "yes"

"Is a Jew as 'French' as other citizens?"

    1977: 65 percent "yes"
    1980: 87 percent "yes"

Thus, a decline in antisemitism could be detected over a three-year period.[59] While the Left was named as the "most responsive" to Jewish fears, voters for the Communist Party were more antisemitic than voters for other parties.[60]

René Shmuel Sirat, chief rabbi of France, told an interviewer of the reality of antisemitism in his country. While Jews met with no discrimination in employment or elsewhere, they and their community were subject to violent attacks.

The search for equal citizenship was unending for French Jews. Most of them had only recently arrived from North Africa and were all too familiar with the historical reality of antisemitism there. The lesser number of older French Jews had experienced the shock of Vichy-Nazi racial policies. Both groups, however, were unprepared for the latest outburst of anti-Jewish violence and sentiment. Their puzzlement was in the French tradition.

NOTES

1. Simon Dubnov, *History of the Jews,* 2, trans. Moshe Spiegel (South Brunswick, N.J.: Thomas Yoseloff, 1968), p. 547.

2. Leon Poliakov, *The History of Anti-Semitism,* 1, trans. Richard Howard (New York: Vanguard Press, 1965), p. 33.

3. Norman Golb, "New Light on the Persecution of French Jews at the Time of the First Crusade," *Journal of Jewish Studies,* 16 (1965) p. 35.

4. Dubnov, *History of the Jews,* 2, p. 668.

5. Robert Chazan, *Medieval Jewry in Northern France. A Political and Social History* (Baltimore, Md.: Johns Hopkins Univ. Press, 1973), p. 112.

6. Ibid., p. 137.

7. Poliakov, *The History of Anti-Semitism*, 1, pp. 180, 184.

8. Arthur Hertzberg, *The French Enlightenment and the Jews* (New York: Columbia Univ. Press, 1968), pp. 306–7.

9. Ibid., p. 300.

10. Ibid., p. 121.

11. Dubnov, *History of the Jews*, 4, pp. 513, 514.

12. Ibid., p. 546.

13. Frances Malino, "From Patriot to Israelite: Abraham Furtado in Revolutionary France," in Jehuda Reinharz and Daniel Swetschinski, with Kalman P. Bland, eds., *Mystics, Philosophers, and Politicians* (Durham, N.C.: Duke Univ. Press, 1982), p. 237.

14. Dubnov, *History of the Jews*, 4, p. 552.

15. Malino, "From Patriot to Israelite," p. 246.

16. Phyllis Cohen Albert, *The Modernization of French Jewry: Consistory and Community in the Nineteenth Century* (Waltham, Mass.: Brandeis Univ. Press, 1977), pp. 29–30.

17. Ibid., p. 39.

18. Zosa Szajkowski, *Jewish Education in France 1789–1939* (New York: Conference on Jewish Social Studies, 1980), p. 4.

19. Albert, *The Modernization of French Jewry*, p. 155.

20. Robert F. Byrnes, *Antisemitism in Modern France* (New York: Howard Fertig, 1969), p. 104.

21. Ibid., p. 107.

22. Ibid., p. 129.

23. Ibid., p. 105.

24. Ibid., p. 107.

25. Ibid., p. 168 (the quoted words are those of Byrnes).

26. Ibid., p. 264.

27. Stephen Wilson, *Ideology and Experience. Anti-Semitism in France at the Time of the Dreyfus Affair* (Rutherford, N.J.: Farleigh Dickinson Univ. Press, 1982), p. 13.

28. Ibid., p. 294.

29. Michel Beaud, *A History of Capitalism 1500–1980*, trans. Tom Dickman and Anny Lefebvre (New York: Monthly Review Press, 1983), p. 127.

30. Wilson, *Ideology and Experience*, p. 319.

31. Szajkowski, *Jewish Education in France*, p. 32.

32. Paula Hyman, *From Dreyfus to Vichy. The Remaking of French Jewry, 1906–1939* (New York: Columbia Univ. Press, 1979), p. 116.

33. Ibid., p. 132.

34. Ibid., p. 203.

35. David H. Weinberg, *A Community on Trial. The Jews of Paris in the 1930s* (Chicago: Univ. of Chicago Press, 1977), p. 80.

36. Ibid., p. 77.

37. Ibid., p. 76.

38. Hyman, *From Dreyfus to Vichy*, p. 217.

39. Weinberg, *A Community on Trial*, p. 175.

40. Ibid., p. 176.

41. Michael R. Marrus and Robert O. Paxton, *Vichy France and the Jews* (New York: Schocken, 1983), p. 56.

42. Weinberg, *A Community on Trial*, p. 201.

43. Marrus and Paxton, *Vichy France and the Jews*, p. 214.

44. Ibid., pp. 198–99.

45. Ibid., p. 201.

46. Ibid., p. 251.

47. Ibid., p. 271.

48. Ibid., p. 272.

49. Ibid., p. 143.

50. Ibid., p. 319.

51. Ibid., p. xiv.

52. Raymond Aron, "The Paris Synagogue Bombing," *American Spectator*, December 1980, p. 28 (trans. Roger Kaplan from *L'Express*, October 18, 1980).

53. Marrus and Paxton, *Vichy France and the Jews*, p. 180.

54. *Encyclopedia Judaica*, 7, col. 39.

55. *Encyclopedia Judaica Yearbook*, 1972, col. 203.

56. Flora Lewis, "Now Swastikas in French," *New York Times*, October 7, 1980.

57. Walter Schwarz, "Nation in the Shadow of the Swastika," *Weekly Guardian*, October 12, 1980.

58. Yadin Kaufman, "French Jewry's Well-Grounded Fear," *New York Times*, October 30, 1980.

59. Andre Baeyens, "A Drive to Split French Jews from Non-Jews," *New York Times*, November 4, 1980 (letter).

60. "France," *Jewish Currents*, January 1981.

6

THE CLASSIC CATASTROPHE: GERMANY

> The history of modern antisemitism in Germany is a part of the
> history of the difficulties obstructing the achievement of social and
> economic stability and political democracy in Germany.
> —Hans-Joachim Bieber, 1979

Contemporary study of the history of antisemitism in Germany is made difficult by our knowledge of events between 1933 and 1945. Much of the pre-Nazi history was more or less repeated in other countries, as the present volume attests. What occurred in Germany to combine in so deadly a way these almost conventional developments with the unprecedented barbarities of the Nazi period still puzzles many. It is insufficient merely to seek for unusual events as such. We need to discover unique ties between the seemingly innocent and the blatantly guilty.

Jews lived in Germany since Roman times and in the tenth and eleventh centuries began to move into the cities. During the First Crusade, which began in 1096, Jewish communities were plundered and massacred by crusaders; synagogues were sacked. During the Second Crusade (1146–47), writes Simon Dubnov, "the agitation...and the flaming fanaticism that had engulfed all strata of Christian society placed the Jews as though on a volcano."[1] Seeking a refuge, they drifted under formal protection of rulers who could protect them from these periodic ravages. By the early thirteenth century, a body of German law—"Jewry law"— guarded their status as equals in courts of law.

Jews could and did bear arms, using them for protection against attacks; they fought some Crusaders but lost the battles. Jews were subject to common legal requirements and punishments. Moneylending by Jews and others was allowed but usury was condemned. The practice of religion by the Jews was not tampered with and Germany witnessed no burning of Jewish sacred books as occurred in thirteenth-century France. Sexual relations between Jew and Christian were prohibited although by the fifteenth century a death penalty was no longer applied. Jews, until late in the Middle Ages, were permitted to own land. Because of Jewish involvement in trade and moneylending, an extensive body of law existed to regulate the rights of Jewish practitioners in these fields.

Jews generally, but not exclusively, lived in concentrated fashion. At first, this semisegregation was voluntary in order to utilize more readily the community institutions of the Jews. But in time the practice tended to become compulsory in order to facilitate the levying of special municipal taxes on Jews. Also, in medieval towns, persons engaged in the same trade or craft often lived in common neighborhoods.

Jewish males could be easily discerned by their beards and horned hats that they wore by choice. While the wearing of distinctive badges by Jews was prescribed by the Fourth Latern Council in 1215 and a decade earlier by Pope Innocent III, Guido Kisch reported that "in Germany...no explicit mention of the yellow or red wheel as a Jew badge is found [in German law books] prior to the fifteenth century."[2] From the mid-thirteenth century, however, wearing of the special hat by Jews was made compulsory as was the yellow badge during the fifteenth and sixteenth centuries.

Social relations between Christians and Jews were ordinarily cordial until the thirteenth century. Church leaders, however, greatly feared that Jews would use such relations in order to gain converts to Judaism. As a result, church legislation restricting social contacts greatly expanded. Nevertheless, Kisch stresses, "The Jew was not regarded as belonging to a different or alien nation...nor [is there any]...trace of a conscious national antipathy or opposition toward them as an alien element or group."[3]

Yet, the mid-fourteenth century witnessed a severe reversal with widespread persecution of Jews in nearly every German city. Many communities expelled entire Jewish communities, a number of which migrated to Poland. What factors accounted for such changes?

Many Jews, traditionally involved in trade, were displaced by Christians as post-Crusade European cities became centers of long-distance trade. Jews lost status as a result. During the same time, merchant guilds in the same cities refused to admit Jews and expelled those already members. The guilds, whose members generally formed a privileged group in towns, thereby further excluded Jews from the circle of political power. Christians began more openly to enter moneylending, directly competing with and ultimately displacing Jews. These economic and political motives for exclusion of Jews were joined by another, and most compelling of all, the religious motive.

Under heightened church tutelage, Christians were increasingly exposed to a "conception of the Jew as a deliberate unbeliever, as a creature of a different (not human) nature, inspired and instigated by Satan's own majesty, to a concretely apprehended image in the medieval mind."[4] In the fourteenth and fifteenth centuries, complaints of usury against Jewish moneylenders multiplied. A merging of church and civil doctrine further lowered Jewish status. Thus, in 1237 the Holy Roman Empire adopted the doctrine of *servitus Judeorum*, according to which Jews were serfs as punishment for their allegedly anti-Christian acts and beliefs. (It had been laid down by Pope Gregory IX three years earlier.) In 1342, a poll tax was levied on Jews, thus again expressing the legal inferiority of Jews.

Under the now-outdated doctrine of legal equality, Jews possessed "basic rights of their own and . . . at least in some measure, a status of legal security."[5] The new church doctrines, however, "erected an insurmountable wall between the Christian and the Jewish elements in the city population."[6] From the eleventh to the fourteenth centuries, the adoption of Roman law in Germany furthered this trend since the anti-Jewish laws of Christian Rome (after A.D. 325) formed a significant part of the importation. "On the basis of Roman law," observes Kisch, "German legal doctrine and legislation in the later Middle Ages thus participated in the general trend to deprive the Jews not only of their legally recognized status but also of the recognition of their human dignity."[7]

One thing did not change: the cash-value of Jews to their rulers. In 1343, Emperor Louis IV declared to the Jews of Nuremberg: "You belong to us, body and belongings, and we can dispose of them and do with you as we please."[8] Jews were subject to special levies, taxes, and fines; they could be expelled without a right to move their property and could be called upon to provide services and commodities of value to the crown without charge. When their co-religionists were enslaved, only the payment of money could ransom them. A bribe paid to church or court circles often purchased relief from oppressive regulations of religious practice. For all these reasons, money came to have a special meaning to the medieval Jew. As Leon Poliakov explains: "The right to life, which Christian society granted the merest yokel, had to be *bought* by the Jew at regular intervals. . . . Money became more important to him than his daily bread—as necessary to him as the air he breathed."[9]

During the black death (1347–50) over one-third of all Europeans died. Relatively few Jews did, however; they were frequently attacked out of anger; some even accused the Jews of having, somehow, caused the plague.

Four years before the outbreak of the plague, Jews had been deprived of their citizenship in the Holy Roman Empire. Poliakov writes, "We can confidently date from this period, [the plague] the crystallization of antisemitism in its classic form."[10] The armory of the German antisemites was raided frequently for whatever weapons were at hand. Charges of "ritual murder"—referring to the supposed mixing of Christian blood into matzohs made for Passover celebrations—representations of the Jew as the Devil, and, in 1493, the earliest-known caricature of the Jew as a long-nosed creature made frequent appearances. "Passion plays" that dramatized the trial and crucifixion of Jesus often led to mob attacks on Jews.

The advent of the Protestant Reformation left the Catholic church's anti-Jewish doctrines unreformed. If anything, Martin Luther appropriated them wholesale and even provided a more embittered justification for them. Luther's anti-Jewish views developed over a twenty-year period, 1523–42. In 1523 he published a pamphlet, *Jesus Christ Was Born a Jew,* which defended Jews against the "Papists," that is, the Roman Catholic church. The latter, he charged, had "treated the Jews as if they were dogs and not men.... We must welcome them in friendship, let them live and work with us, and they will be of one heart with us."[11] The statement hinted not so much at the acceptability of Judaism as at the prospects for conversion to Christianity. Yet, this did not happen. In 1539 he complained to a friend: "I cannot convert the Jews. Our Lord Christ did not succeed in doing so; but I can close their mouths so that there will be nothing for them to do but lie upon the ground."[12]

Against the Jews and Their Lies, an embittered pamphlet written in 1542 by Luther, attacked Jews without reserve: "In truth, the Jews, being foreigners, should possess nothing, and what they do possess should be ours.... They... have become our masters in our own country.... No one wants them.... They are a heavy burden on us, a scourge, a pestilence and misfortune for our country.... They steal and pillage every day."[13] He continued: "Know, O adored Christ, and make no mistake, that aside from the Devil, you have no enemy more venomous, more desperate, more bitter, than a true Jew who truly seeks to be a Jew."[14]

In calling Jews foreigners, Luther conveniently forgot that Jews had lived in Germany since Roman times. Also, the basic laws of the country did not single out Jews as a nationality different from other Germans.[15] More than two centuries before Luther the most authoritative law code of Germany, the *Sachsenspiegel* (1221–24), treated Jews as equals before the law. Luther was not a racist; he did not condemn Jews for having been born of Jewish parents. Rather, he condemned them for following Judaism. Thus, in seeking to punish Jews for their Jewishness, he was profoundly antisemitic. When he cried that Jews were "children of the Devil, condemned to the flames of hell," it was their religious fidelity more than their supposed moral shortcomings that truly irked him.

But Luther's hatred of Jews went far beyond writing heated pamphlets. He advised that Christians burn synagogues and confiscate the Judaic holy books. He appealed successfully to the German princes to expel Jews from their jurisdictions. Expulsions took place in Saxony, Brandenburg, and Silesia. One piece of Luther's advice was rejected: he called for the Jews to be compelled to labor with their hands. But since such a step presupposed that craft guilds would be opened to Jewish members and that farm land could be freely bought by Jews—both of which the Jews welcomed—Luther's call could only succeed in arousing doubts about the propriety of ordinary Jewish economic activities.

Luther's anti-Jewish writings continued over the years to be reprinted in editions of his complete works. It must therefore be assumed that they formed part of the theological curriculum of Lutheran seminaries. Large-scale popular printings of Luther's antisemitica had to await the advent of the Nazi regime.

During the century following Martin Luther's death in 1546 German Jewry continued its customary employments at the margins of local economy. Small-scale trade, peddling, and pawnbrokering occupied the great majority of Jews in the country. Whatever prosperity prevailed for the economy as a whole was seriously disrupted by the Thirty Years' War (1618–48). Widespread destruction of productive property and an unparalleled demand for military goods and services pressed rulers to seek out new sources of economic support. To finance the repair of facilities and to build new armies in the German states, the rulers turned to wealthy Jews. "This situation," writes F. L. Carsten, "proved the great opportunity for those Jews who provided the armies with food and fodder, bought the soldiers' booty at advantageous prices and traded in the wake of armies."[16] Known later as Court Jews, a tiny group, they were able to use their wealth as a shield against antisemitic attacks during the Thirty Years' War and after. As Carsten notes: "Already during the ... war many princes and generals ... had protected the Jewish ghettos against looting and requisitioning because they needed the money of the Jews for the conduct of the war."[17]

In France and England, well-developed business classes provided bankers and merchants to aid the state in achieving national power. Bureaucracies there were recruited from native-born groups. In Germany, however, in the absence of a thriving bourgeoisie during the seventeenth and eighteenth centuries, some few jurisdictions recruited Court Jews who were granted an unaccustomed degree of legal rights in exchange for financial services provided to rulers. In 1671, well-to-do Jews were first permitted to settle in Prussia while poor Jews were barred. The former were granted monopolies in trading and producing certain selected products. In Prussia, Court Jews were heavily represented in manufacturing. Tradesmen and artisans resented the competition and repaid Jews with heightened hostility.

Numerous special levies and taxes were laid upon Jewish communities—charges which ended up in a princely purse rather than in municipal treasuries. In 1750, Prussia enacted a Revised General Privilege or Regulation which restricted Jews to certain economic fields. They could, for example, buy and sell secondhand clothing, engage in pawn-broking, and peddle from door to door. These fields were regarded with disdain and contempt by non-Jews. Obviously, the day of the Court Jew had all but passed and Prussia reluctantly housed a growing population of poorer Jews. Stefi Jersch-Wenzel observes: "The image of the Jews received by the non-literate majority of the Prussian population and passed on from generation to generation . . . was that of a contemptible alien group that must be kept outside the pale of domestic society."[18] Residential ghettos where Jews were compelled to live existed through-out Germany. At night the gates were locked.

Meanwhile, early in the eighteenth century printed antisemitic tracts circulated in the country. (More than 1,000 titles are listed in one bib-liography.) Antisemites of that time and afterward found most useful a two-volume tract by A. I. Eisenmenger, *Judaism Unmasked, a True and Accurate Report*. This literature as a whole portrayed the Jews' purported "secret vices and crimes, their shameful diseases, bizarre sexual attri-butes, and above all, their special relationship with the Devil."[19] The century no longer witnessed open mob attacks on Jews. One reason for their rarity was the opposition to them expressed by government au-thorities. It was not a sudden tenderness but a rage for order that brought the government to this point. Considerations of usefulness triumphed over those of strangeness. Jews began to be viewed as po-tential members of the polity and as possible contributors in a more central way to the national economy.

Those publicists and writers who now discussed the possible emanci-pation of Jews agreed on only two items: (1) German society would gain if Jews became equal citizens, but (2) they must be transformed into a more acceptable kind of person. This latter point arose from a very widespread view that the "typical" Jew lived an unwholesome life which bred a viewpoint antithetical to the needs of modern society. Thus, it was not the Court Jews, polished and prosperous, who constituted the nub of the problem but rather "the masses of poor petty traders, hawkers, vagabonds, and money lenders [who] constituted the true issue of Jewish emancipation."[20] By far most German Jews lived in villages and small country towns and were thus neither urban nor industrial. In this sense they were not very different from non-Jews. Nevertheless, emancipation was opposed by most Germans.

Early in the nineteenth century, a business class started to mature and many Jews became part of it. As in other countries, businessmen emerged as a new center of economic power. In Germany, however, feudal ele-ments such as great landowners in the eastern part of the country did not give way but only reluctantly assigned subsidiary political power to the business class. A traditional bureaucracy gave its first loyalty to this arrangement, rarely if ever challenging it. It was the bureaucracy that studied endlessly the topic of emancipation and established its ground rules.

Reinhard Rürup has pointed out three weaknesses in the German approach to the emancipation of Jews.[21] First was the gradual, phased nature of the process. A new phase was not authorized until state governments approved of the progress already made. Gradualism governed the entire process. This feature was criticized by a most enlightened bureaucrat, Wilhelm von Humboldt, who, in 1809, wrote, "For as a result of gradual abolition the very segregation that it sets out to liquidate is confirmed in all the spheres in which it has not yet been abolished and the new greater freedom [for Jews] redoubles the attention focused on the remaining restrictions so that the gradual abolition militates against itself."[22] (A century and a half later the same issue would be involved in the desegregation of white and black schools in the United States.)

Related to this point was another that faced the problem of ending discriminatory attitudes against Jews. Humboldt stressed the positive obligation of government in this task: "It is not that the State ought to teach respect for the Jews. What it ought to do is to eradicate the inhumane and prejudiced mentality that judges a human being not by his specific qualities but by his descent and religion, and treats him not as an individual but as a member of a race with which he is considered to share certain characteristics of necessity. This the State can only do by saying loud and clear that it no longer recognizes any difference between Jews and Christians."[23] Little heed was paid this advice.

A second weakness of emancipation was the absence of a unified policy for all Germany. With no national government, the states were supreme and implemented emancipation as they wished, if at all. Inevitably, then, a great profusion of stages and phases coexisted among the German states. Jews and their allies might want the most advanced example to serve as a model. The bureaucracy and its chiefs proceeded otherwise. They drifted toward the lowest common denominator. Thus, demands for greater liberties in one state could be put off by finding another state that was even worse off. Projected policies could be justified by pointing to places where they worked, however badly.

Managing Jewish emancipation in a non-emancipated society was a third weakness. As Rürup noted: "The emancipation and integration of a minority with ethnic, religious and social characteristics within a society that is itself not or only partly emancipated presented a nearly insoluble problem."[24] German society was in many respects a closed society, inhospitable to innovation and fearful that traditional structures would be changed too quickly. Its rulers were unaccustomed to declarations of universal principles of freedom and pluralism. Organizationally, Germany was ill-prepared to implement emancipation as everywhere laws and regulations clashed. And the newer values of national liberty had made slow headway. The emancipation of any one required the emancipation of all. Few elements in the nation could be said to live a self-determined existence, least of all the Jews.

When the armies of Napoleon occupied German territory, emancipation of Jews followed, as it did within France, Italy, and other countries. An 1812 Prussian law accorded Jews many important rights but these remained theoretical only. Some states extended rights to Jews while yet others cut back after the defeat of Napoleon. In 1819, in Frankfurt and other cities, severe rioting against Jews broke out. Known as the "Hep, Hep" riots, they originated from non-Jewish businessmen who feared more effective competition from the Jews who had recently begun to enter once-monopolized lines of trade. They viewed the drive for Jewish political equality as a prelude to heightened business competition.[25] That the riots were serious is evidenced by Rürup's assertion that they consisted "of persecutions of the Jews on a scale not witnessed for centuries."[26] This was especially true of the cities in which the issue of Jewish rights was still to be settled.

In Posen, an eastern province of Prussia that was acquired in 1815, the government adopted a law in 1833 that created two classes of Jews, the naturalized and the tolerated. As Julian Bartys writes, "the naturalized Jews had the right to live not only in any of the towns of the province but also in the country, as well as to buy farmland, and to choose their occupation without restriction, but in accordance with official regulations."[27] By 1842, only 5.5 percent of the Jews of Posen were naturalized. These generally bore Germanized names, were merchants and craftsmen, and joined with the government in denying the claims of Polish nationalism, especially with regard to language and school policies. The remainder of the Jews were desperately poor peddlers and day laborers, orthodox in religion, who were viewed with "deep contempt and prejudice" by Prussian authorities.[28]

In other parts of Prussia, anti-Jewish discrimination was rife. Higher education was a prime example. At the universities of Berlin and Breslau in 1847 there was no religious test for teachers, but in fact no Jews were hired. While that year the law was changed to encourage the employment of Jews, nothing else altered. In a poll that asked the faculty of seven institutions if they would accept Jews as colleagues, 243 responded; 141 voted affirmatively, 102 negatively. Again, this had no practical effect. Fear of competition from Jews as clearest in the case of the medical faculty at Breslau. As Ismar Schorsch writes, "In the medical faculty... Jews constituted some 60 percent of the student population and Jews dominated the medical profession in Breslau."[29] Repeatedly, the Prussian government pledged no discrimination but, in Schorsch's words, "duplicity became normative."[30]

At the outset of the nineteenth century, Jews almost universally spoke Yiddish. In non-Jewish circles the language was regarded as a great social handicap. As a writer asserted in 1844, "The greatest obstacle to the prospering of the Jewish artisan and worker is his peculiar speech."[31] Eager to integrate and to partake of the growing economic modernization of the country, Jews hastened to adopt standard German as their everyday tongue. By century's end, the transition was largely completed. Yet, as Peter Freimark points out, "changes in language behavior postulated by educationists and language reformers in the first half of the nineteenth century had failed to secure the hoped-for social integration. Socioeconomic and religious factors as well as age-old mental stereotypes and prejudices had proved stronger."[32] Toward the end of the nineteenth and early in the twentieth centuries, it was all but impossible for a Jew to be employed as a university professor of the German language, no matter how skilled his mastery of the subject.

During the 1830s and 1840s, capitalist development went on apace in Germany. Production of iron, cotton textiles, railroad rails, and other manufactures doubled and tripled. In 1844, the Silesian handweavers fought bitterly against replacement by machines. Movements for liberalization of government culminated in the revolution of 1848–49. While Jews strongly supported such movements, they themselves sometimes suffered attacks by revolutionists. These attacks were described by Rürup as "far more violent even than had been the outrages of 1819."[33] They originated in resentments of rural people to crop failures and changing rural life occasioned by new governmental regulations. They did not characterize the age of revolution, however. In December 1848, the short-lived German Parliament at Frankfurt adopted a declaration of fundamental rights. Article V read: "The enjoyment of civil and political rights is neither dependent upon nor restricted by religious creed."[34]

After defeat of the revolution in 1849, one German state after another backtracked from the recent pledges of freedom. Yet the movement for Jewish emancipation endured. It had become part and parcel of the striving of the German middle classes for political equality. So integrated economically did the Jewish middle classes become by the 1860s that it was becoming exceedingly difficult to treat them differently from non-Jews. In this sense they backed into emancipation.

German liberals favored emancipation but they were not its warm devotees. Conceivably, liberalization of oppressive rule should be favored by all who felt victimized by it. In Germany, however, too many Germans were able to moderate their sense of oppression by oppressing Jews. Friedrich Hecker, a prominent revolutionary leader in south Germany, wrote penetratingly in 1846: "In states where no true liberty reigns, where we feel crushed every day by the burden of the police state, it makes a man feel good to see someone even worse off than himself, someone he may despise and bully and mistreat, thereby gaining some slight relief from the daily oppression and stifling atmosphere of the police state. It is because of the lack of freedom in our states, because of the pressure and bitterness that we did not want to emancipate the Jews. By bullying the Jews, we fancied ourselves more free and higher up."[35]

During the Napoleonic period the issue of Jewish rights had spurted forward and then all but receded. The gains of 1848–49 also proved insecure, but they persisted, more or less. In 1869, the North German Federation—soon to become the Second German Empire—completed the legal voyage. Two years earlier the federation ruled: "No subject of the Federation is to be prohibited—because of religious motives—in his right of domicile and sojourn, and engaging in any pursuit and in acquiring real estate."[36] In 1869, it was legislated that "we command the abolition of all existing restrictions in civic and political rights, that stem from various religions; in particular, everyone is to enjoy the right to participate in municipal and agricultural self-administration, and to hold public office, regardless of religion."[37] In 1871, the latter measure was applied to all the territories of the German empire.

Formal political equality was the culmination of a long political, social, and economic process which made emancipation meaningful. It also complicated emancipation and influenced new forms of antisemitism. During the first seventy years of the nineteenth century, capitalism developed in Germany.[38] Jews played a minor role in the process. Most capitalists by far were Germans, not Jews. However, as we have seen, Jews became integrated into the national economy just at the time when capitalism was triumphing. Thus, their economic successes were associated in the popular mind with that system.

There were many successes to point to. About the years 1800–1870, Heinz Holeczek writes:

Whereas at the outset only an insignificant minority of 2 percent of all Jews enjoyed the standards of the haute bourgeoisie, and only 7 percent had a secure middle-class livelihood, with well over two-thirds of the Jewish population living in poverty, by the time the Second *Reich* came into being nearly two-thirds of the Jewish population were classed among the prosperous middle stratum, and only a declining residual group (consisting in the main of recently arrived East European immigrants) was classed in the lowest income bracket. Thus, within a few generations the great majority of German Jews had succeeded in joining the ranks of the bourgeoisie.[39]

Jews played an insignificant role in the sweeping development of German industry and coal mining. Instead, they entered fields of activity that were basically an extension of traditional areas of employment. Thus, a number of Jews became prominent in banking; wholesale and retail trade became centers of Jewish business operation. Many Jews were employed in these enterprises. After 1870, law, medicine, and engineering attracted more Jews. While the entire country was becoming urbanized, Jewish urbanization grew more rapidly.

After the Franco-Prussian war, which led to the unification of Germany and creation of the Second Reich, France was obliged to pay a large indemnity in gold. This inflow created considerable inflation and led to speculation on the stock market. In 1873, the stock market crashed and a deep economic depression followed. (A depression following speculative movements occurred in a number of western countries.) Although both Jews and non-Jews had fed the speculative fever, popular attention fixed on the former. Antisemitic writers interpreted the events as the outcome of a Jewish conspiracy. In 1878, five years into the depression, Adolf Stöcker formed the Christian Socialist Workers' party to woo workers from the burgeoning Socialist party. When workers proved uninterested, he shifted emphasis to antisemitic doctrine. Now, however, he selected a new audience—small businessmen, shopkeepers, and artisans along with a few lesser public officials. Stöcker, who dropped the word "workers" from his party's name, preached that Jewish capitalists increasingly controlled the press and the economy. He attacked them as alien elements, an ancient theme in German antisemitic doctrine. Other leading antisemites emerged, such as Wilhelm Marr who, not a racist, strongly advocated that Jews assimilate into Christian German society. Also in 1879, the historian Heinrich Treitschke published a bitter, extended attack on Jewry for its allegedly foreign nature. Supposed character traits of Jews were ridiculed.

As historian Jacob Katz has written: "The year 1879 is a turning point in modern Jewish history: it marks the beginning of modern antisemitism."[40] Going far beyond simple antipathy or individual prejudice, hatred of Jews was incorporated into an antisemitic press, political parties, and full-blown ideology. Nor was modern antisemitism a self-contained movement. Its essentials were welcomed in more conventional circles such as conservative and nationalistic political parties. Its ideology accorded all too well with basic patterns of social and political discrimination against Jews in Imperial Germany. Conservatives and antisemites alike deeply resented the persistence of the Jewish community. The presence of stability among great social changes aroused emotions of fear and envy. How did Jews manage to persist in their ways when tradition and custom elsewhere in the general society seemed in the

process of dissolution? And what were the sources of such persistence?
Was it being achieved at the expense of non-Jews?

Antisemitic doctrine provided answers of a sort to each query. The
unity of the Jewish community was transmogrified into a conspiracy of
Jews. A desire to rule Germany and the world was said to lie behind the
plot. Accumulation of wealth in Jewish hands through exploitation of
ordinary Christians was represented as the means of effecting the conspiracy. Where gaps in logic separated one element of the argument
from another, linkages were provided. Jews, for example, were said to
be peculiarly immoral and thus somehow capable of the vilest deeds.
While some of this was new, much was consonant with the older anti-
Jewish doctrine propagated so assiduously in the past by the Christian
churches.

During the Second Reich (1870–1918), anti-Jewish discrimination was
the rule. Jews were virtually excluded from public office. Although the
laws of various German states were liberalized in 1848 and after, discrimination continued through the early 1860s. Jews were barred from
federal service in the Foreign Office and the military departments. In
various states Jews could not find jobs in public education, police, courts,
railways, and the postal service. During the first half of the nineteenth
century, some few municipal offices were open to Jews. For some years,
Jews could become officers in the Prussian Reserve Corps but this
stopped in 1885. Service on the higher levels of the judiciary was infre-
quently open to Jews. In fact, it declined with time. As Peter Pulzer
writes: "Although the number of Prussian judicial posts had increased
by almost fifty percent between the mid-1870s and mid-1890s, the number of Jewish judges had almost halved."[41] Until 1870, Jews as judges
were unknown. After that date, some Jews were given these posts, but
they continued to be barred from the more honored positions.

Around 1900, some 200 Jews taught in German universities, half of
them in medical faculties. Since all the institutions were governmentally
operated, personnel of professorial rank were appointed by the government. In 1909, Jews comprised the following percentages of each of the
three ranks:[42]

Privatdozent	10 percent
Assistant professor	7 percent
Full professor	2 percent

Privatdozenten were unpaid lecturers whose untenured appointment was
based on high-quality research they had produced. Normally, they could
look forward to a regular appointment as time went on. Jewish *Privatdozenten,* however, sometimes attained an assistant professorship but almost never a full professorship. Rarest of all was a Jewish full professor

who had not yet been baptized. Even then, notes Ernest Hamburger, "non-baptized scholars were never appointed to a chair of German language and literature or of classical philology."[43]

In all the Prussian public high schools, no more than a dozen Jews were teachers; during 1910–16, only six taught. Bavaria and Baden were somewhat more open to Jewish teachers. In public elementary schools, there were practically no Jewish teachers. Jews were more readily employed in publicly sponsored technical services, especially in the field of public health. The Prussian army continued to exclude Jews from the ranks of reserve officers, despite repeated protests by Jews and other critics of government policy. Only when World War I broke out in 1914 were Jews "allowed to fight and die as reserve officers."[44]

Before the rise of organized antisemitism in the late 1870s Jews were elected as members of legislative bodies. Afterward, however, even the Liberal party supported most avidly by Jews became reluctant to continue doing so. Only one party ignored the attacks on Jews and continued to run Jews for legislative bodies including the Reichstag. This was the German Social Democratic party, or simply Socialists. Most Jews, securely settled in the bourgeoisie, shared the anti-Socialist sentiments of their class brethren. The Socialists were not in any sense "pro-Jewish"; indeed, they scorned Judaism as they did all other organized religions. As Hamburger explains: "Only the Socialists remained unaffected by the ups and downs of the antisemitic movement.... They interpreted antisemitism as an abhorrent by-product of the capitalist order and bound to disappear with it. Consequently they did not shun the nomination of Jews."[45] While the rank and file of the Socialists was overwhelmingly non-Jewish, a number of Socialist intellectuals were Jews. Werner Angress points out that "the party followed an unwritten rule by which roughly ten percent of its Reichstag deputies could consist of Jews."[46] (At this time Jews made up about 1 percent of the total population.) The Socialists' nomination of Jews was as much an act of defiance as it was of doctrine.

In earlier centuries Jews in many cities were compelled to live in specially designated areas, so-called ghettos. In time, such restrictions were lifted, but a number of municipalities passed legislation that achieved the same end. Until 1870, for example, Jews in Frankfurt still had to live inside the walled ghetto. "In Hamburg," writes Steven Lowenstein, "Jews were restricted to a number of streets."[47] Early in the nineteenth century, both in Berlin and Frankfurt, the concentration of residence for Jews reached such a point that over three out of five Jews would have needed to be moved in order to eliminate any disproportionality of location. Late in the century, the development of new residential areas for wealthier Jews removed more than one-third of the degree of concentration in older Jewish areas of Berlin. "In Berlin," according to Lowenstein, "Jews were seven times more concentrated than the Catholic minority."[48] Gershom Scholem recalls that "only in 1861 was the so-called *'Matrikelzwang'* abolished in Bavaria; according to this rule the oldest son of every Jewish family was granted the right of residence, so that all the other children were more or less compelled to emigrate."[49] To an undetermined degree, Jews also preferred to live near their religious and community institutions. It is not clear what relative proportions choice and compulsion played. The heritage of compulsion, however, endured.

Segregation also characterized social interaction between Jew and non-Jew. Scholem refers to "this rather far-reaching social ostracism of the Jews."[50] At an early age he realized that only other Jews made friendly visits to his home while his parents in turn visited only Jews. Lamar Cecil makes a similar point when he observes that Prussian "aristocrats went to Jewish houses, but few Jews received invitations to noble drawing rooms."[51] The matter was different, however, when a marriage across religious lines was contemplated. One aristocratic Prussian general who married a wealthy Jewish woman referred to her as his "change purse."[52]

A special target of antisemitism was the large number of Jews who came from Poland, Russia, and the Galician areas of Austria-Hungary. Most remained aliens and only a few became citizens. They were, in a sense, the proletarians of German Jewry. In the parts of Prussia bordering on Poland, Jews from the latter were not allowed to live. Naturalization was usually permitted only if children had been born in Germany. Residence permits were temporary and when these expired, mass expulsions were ordered. While native German Jews defended the easterners, including aliens, Jack Wertheimer notes the "deep ambivalence" of the former.[53] The antagonism to the easterners was not extended to all immigrants. Industrialists and large-scale farmers who wanted to employ Polish seasonal labor in mines, factories, and farms avidly recruited such labor. Jews, however, were regarded as unsuitable for such jobs. During World War I, a labor shortage led to the entrance of many Jewish workers, but in April 1918 Prussia was declared closed to further Jewish immigration. Many German Jews resented these measures for they regarded them as attacks upon themselves and as evidence of a new, more virulent antisemitism.

A special eastern population that suffered from antisemitism was the growing contingent of Russian and Polish Jewish students attending universities and technical institutes in Germany. Excluded from secondary and college institutions in their own countries by an arbitrarily low quota, they streamed to Germany. Many were radicals and supported efforts to overthrow the Russian government. During 1912–13, some 2,500 were in Germany. They were, in general, excellent students who tended to go to the best universities. The German government, responding to requests by its Russian counterparts, supervised and harassed the students. Tsarist agents were allowed to follow the students wherever they wished. Efforts were made by the Germans to police the political activities of students. Russian (i.e., Jewish) students were not permitted to subscribe to *Vorwärts*, the newspaper of the Social Democratic party. In response to agitation by German students and associations of German professionals, German universities required the Russian Jews to pay double or triple the regular tuition, gave Germans priority rights in attending, required high levels of fluency in German, and established quotas. Professors and administrators generally defended the Russians but were overruled by government authorities.[54]

The same government that actively discriminated against Jews was not averse to using them for its own political advantage. At the outset of World War I in August 1914, Germany set up a Department of Jewish Affairs in the Foreign Office and called upon Polish (i.e., Russian) Jews to support German troops. Upon occupying Polish territory, German authorities ended quotas in secondary and higher education and opened elementary schools to all, regardless of creed.[55] Yiddish was permitted in schools and newspapers printed in Yiddish or Hebrew were allowed, something the Russians had forbidden. "Not only did there come into existence in those days a ramified network of free kitchens, free loan societies and many other relief agencies, but political parties were also formed and many other cultural Jewish institutions established."[56]

How did German Jews combat the broad range of largely officially sponsored discrimination? Until the 1890s, Jews had been very reluctant to defend publicly the interests of their group. They feared such an action would diminish their identification as Germans and present themselves as a special group. Yet, small protest groups had been formed even earlier. In 1869, the German-Israelite Community League defended the right of Jews to marry outside their religious group and worked to diminish the flow of Russian Jews to Prussia. Leaders of the league greatly feared the image of poor eastern Jews making their way through the countryside by begging. In 1873, the league also opposed the anti-Jewish attacks launched by the Prussian Evangelical church on the occasion of several conversions to Judaism.

During 1873–81, while antisemitism grew as a national movement, Jews were perplexed as to the most effective ways to fight it. In 1881, when rioting against Jews occurred mainly in eastern Germany, the imperial government intervened. As Ismar Schorsch describes it: "The Ministry of Interior forbade all antisemitic speeches in Pomerania and W. Prussia. Rioters were arrested and punished, and the municipalities were ordered to compensate their Jewish residents for damages suffered."[57] Yet, in other respects governments refused to protect the rights of Jews. Thus, when Jews appealed to public prosecutors to enforce the law against defamation of religious groups, the officials held that the deriding of Jews was not the same as defaming them. After a number of such encounters, the league advised no more public protests by Jews. It took a complementary approach by organizing historians to write works that showed the historical contribution of Jews to German history. Schorsch writes of this period that "German Jewry did not organize to defend its interests" and refers to "the deep aversion of German Jewry to open resistance."[58] He contends that "the aversion to any public display of Jewishness" was profound.[59] Additionally, Jews were accustomed to accommodate to differences and even discord; traditionally, contacts with powerful Christians had served to protect Jews at critical junctures. But such avenues were inadequate against continuing political antisemitism.

In 1890, there was formed the Union for Defense Against Anti-semitism. The following year it made its political debut with release of a declaration of principle signed by some 500 "Christian gentlemen of repute." Barbara Suchy characterizes its orientation and techniques as "fighting the antisemites with 'enlightenment', logical arguments, reason and the appeal to 'free, fine and true humanity' and 'genuine *Deutschtum*' [Germanity]."[60] Its leadership linked discrimination against Jews with that against other minorities, thereby broadening the movement into one of equal opportunity for all. Arguments against antisemites most frequently dealt with the factual dimension. As Suchy puts it: "Attention was fixed too much on the behavior of the Jews. . . . Neither an increase in the number of Jews tilling the soil nor a drop in the number of Jewish lawyers, physicians and students to the level of their 'proportionate share' of the population would have had any appreciable effect on antisemites. . . . [Its publications] produce[d] all too many statistics about the military prowess of Jews, the number of Jews killed in the wars and of those with military decorations."[61] With respect to Germanity, the union was happiest with Jewish minorities in Posen and Austro-Hungary when they represented Germanization rather than supporting the Polish and the Czechs in those two places.

The tide of antisemitism failed to turn. In 1892, the Conservative party became "the first major German party to adopt an antisemitic plank in its . . . platform.[62] A sizable bloc in the Reichstag was openly antisemitic. In 1893, three national groups significantly heightened the antisemitic fever. Two were organized and a third was reorganized that year. One of the two, the Agrarian League, succeeded in blending antisemitism with racism and a touch of anticapitalism. The other, the German Federation of Commercial Employees, "was founded . . . to combat the danger of its members' sinking into the proletariat."[63] Antisemites often connected Jews with large-scale changes in distribution of products that sometimes tended to undercut traditional modes of employment. The third group was the reorganized Pan German League, which formulated expansionist foreign-policy objectives and whose hypernationalism customarily found no room for Jews.

Also in 1893, Jews formed the Central Union of German Citizens of the Jewish Faith. Its principal method was to file lawsuits on behalf of Jews who were defamed or deprived of equal rights. Within a decade, more than 100 cases a year were being filed. By that time, also, the Central Union had begun to participate in politics by announcing that Jews should prefer Socialist over antisemitic candidates. (The Socialists, it will be recalled, were almost the sole party to run Jewish candidates for national office.) Within another decade, campaign contributions to Socialist candidates were being made by the organization. This matter was not made public. Schorsch concludes that "it is extremely doubtful that the legal policy of the *Centralverein* affected the course of anti-semitism in the Second *Reich*."[64]

The Central Union confronted a great deal more than a momentary change in public mood. During the late nineteenth century and until 1914, the beginning of World War I, anti-Jewish actions proliferated. Schorsch summarizes the developments:

Social intercourse between Jewish and Christian families had substantially diminished over the last few decades. At high schools and universities Jewish students were excluded from fraternal organizations. In legal and medical organizations, Jewish lawyers and doctors were rarely elected to office. . . . Discrimination also began to appear in economic life. Christian merchants hesitated to hire Jewish help. . . . Some Christian stores advertised that they did not welcome Jewish patronage. Jewish engineers and chemists faced increasing difficulties in finding employment. In small towns Christians often boycotted Jewish lawyers and doctors, driving them into the cities where the concentration of Jews in these professions steadily rose.[65]

Another organization, the Federation of German Jews, was founded in 1904. It dealt particularly with the Prussian bureaucracy. In Posen, where earlier Jews had been an acknowledged force for Germanization, after the turn of the century this role was rejected by the Prussian government. "In fact," writes Schorsch, "the government drove Jews off the land, denied citizenship to any Jewish alien, refused to award contracts to Jews in proportion to their numbers, and appointed no Jew to the bureaucracy governing the area."[66] As a result, many moved to Berlin.

Historians disagree over the success of Jewish efforts at collective self-defense. Schorsch contrasts Jewry in Germany and France: "Unlike its German counterpart, French Jewry could not bring itself to admit and combat the existence of an internal and indigenous antisemitic enemy."[67] Further, "measured against the former silence of German Jewry and the continued passivity of French Jewry, the *Centralverein* [Central

Union] represents a watershed in the history of emancipated Jewry."[68]
Ideologically, however, the Central Union occupied an ambiguous position on the central issue of German nationalism. Peter Pulzer points
out that the union's leaders hovered uneasily between the earlier orthodoxy of "we are Germans like everyone else" and a frank recognition
that there could and should be only one kind of German."[69] By 1913,
German Jewry was wealthy enough to reward its few political friends
but not powerful enough to punish its more numerous enemies. Defense
organizations contributed some to the rectification of this imbalance.

Pulzer contends that antisemitism in Imperial Germany became a
unique menace because, unlike in other Western countries, it was also
accompanied by a revival of the Jewish question. A society that thought
it legitimate to question whether Jews had a proper place as equals of
others could all the less defend itself against antisemitism; and all the
more difficult was it for Jews to fend off such sweeping, profound attacks.
Such questions did not arise in the modern history of Italy or France.
In Germany they had become endemic by 1914 and had led to what
Lamar Cecil calls "the debased citizenship which all Jews were forced to
endure in the Second *Reich*."[70]

Many Jews fought in the German armed forces during World War I.
Of a total of 100,000 Jewish soldiers, some 2,000 became commissioned
officers; of these, 1,200 were officials and medical officers. Yet, antisemitism took on a new life. The basis for it had been laid during the
last prewar years. Angress describes the process:

What happened after the 1912 election was the systematization of antisemitism,
a process which signified a transformation from its random manifestations in
the past and as such was closely tied in with the changes that occurred within
the political Right during the decade preceding the war. Never before had a
serious attempt been made to orchestrate antisemitism, to use it consistently as
a political tactic and to make it the one common denominator of a still precarious
alliance of right-wing forces.... It was this cross-fertilization of bigotry, consciously fostered by a new breed of professional antisemites and aided by the
re-grouping within the Empire's right-wing forces that was as novel as it was
effective.[71]

As far back as the early 1880s, Chancellor Otto Bismarck had secretly
encouraged organized antisemites for the government's advantage. He
had also suddenly ended the practice, for the same reason. Small antisemitic parties had existed during the last two decades of the century
but they had met only with sporadic, uneven success. The process that
Werner Angress described, however, involved the building of a large-
scale coalition around antisemitism, including right-wing traditional parties. By war's opening, in 1914, there was in formation "a movement

that was racist, chauvinistic, right-radical and with a strong populist appeal."[72]

The war years, 1914–18, saw increasing economic concentration, with large corporations growing at the expense of smaller firms, and a growth in the number of industrial workers. Many artisan shops and small plants were closed down. Hans-Joachim Bieber stresses how such developments stirred feelings of insecurity among middle-class Germans who feared that their class positions were threatened.[73] A wartime drop in real income tended to produce a similar sentiment.

Military events also played a part in the emergence of a new antisemitism. Jews had long been excluded from the war establishment. Antisemitism was rife in the upper reaches of the officer group, as was the case in the relevant government ministries. The Fatherland party, a wartime right-wing political coalition, was "ardently antisemitic." As victory continued to elude Germany and its allies, disappointment and impatience gave a special tone to the rising antisemitism. In August 1916, a change in the high command occurred when Paul von Hindenburg and Erich Ludendorff shared the high office. The latter was notoriously chauvinistic and antisemitic. Within days the Ministry of War conducted a census of Jews in the war efforts, presumably to discover whether popular charges that Jews were evading frontline duty were correct. The issue of such a census had been approved by the Reichstag; only the Progressives and the Social Democrats opposed it. The mere taking of such a census seemed to many evidence that the charges were true. In fact, however, the government never released the findings. Nevertheless, suspicions had been aroused and antisemites played on them. Hamburger, in reviewing the Reichstag approval, declared that "the majority of the Reichstag . . . surrendered abjectly to the ruthless antisemitic tendencies of the military, on the one hand, and those rife amongst the populace, on the other."[74]

Foreign Jewish laborers who had been imported from Poland were, as we saw above, made an issue by antisemites during the war. Many native Jews knew they were the prime target of that agitation. Here was a way that antisemites could keep alive the age-old question of whether or not Jews could also be Germans.

The discredited Imperial government was overthrown only two days before the signing of an armistice in November 1918. In 1919, the Weimar Republic was proclaimed. Its principal support rested on the Socialists and liberal middle-class parties. A liberal constitution proclaimed the end of religious exclusion from public office. For the first time in German history, Jews filled high-ranking positions in every major department of government. This fact alone moved antisemites to protest against the "Jew Republic." Extreme right-wing organizations sprang up throughout Germany. One such, the League for Defense and Defiance, formed in 1919 and financed by industrialists, claimed over 200,000 members by 1922. Bands of armed ultranationalists, some antisemitic and some not, attacked supporters of the new government. Embittered by loss of the war and German territory, they spoke of the anti-Christian values of Weimar. The German Nationalist People's party adopted in 1920 a platform plank declaring that "we emphatically reject the predominance of Jewry in government and public life, which since the revolution [of 1918] has become increasingly ominous."[75]

In 1920, a new party, the National Socialist Workers party of Germany—the Nazis—adopted a platform part of which dealt with Jews. The document called for an end to civil rights for Jews, the deportation of Jewish aliens, revocation of citizenship for all Jews, and exclusion from public office. In 1931, two planks were added: no intermarriage between Jews and non-Jews and barring of Jews from national economic and cultural life. In 1923, Adolf Hitler and followers, including General Ludendorff, attempted a beer-hall *Putsch* or coup d' etat in Munich.

Organized antisemites were able to play on the traditional antisemitism nurtured for centuries by the Christian churches of Germany. When numbers of so-called German Christians in the Protestant Evangelical church openly worked for a Nazi victory, the hierarchy did not even remonstrate with them. The Catholic church was somewhat more spirited in its opposition. Yet, when in 1930 Bishop Hugo of Mainz denied the sacraments to Nazi party members, he remained the only Catholic bishop to do so. Opponents of antisemitism were numerous in both Protestant and Catholic churches. Donald Niewyk notes, however, "Far more critical . . . were the great masses of ordinary Christians of both persuasions who were either indifferent to the Jews or influenced to varying degrees by the criticisms of Jews as bearers of secularism. Those criticisms, more than any other single consideration, neutralized much Christian opposition to antisemitism and helped open the way to Christian support for National Socialism."[76]

In the universities could be found the most antisemitic of all groups— the students. Besides viewing Jews as future competitors in the professions and business, they imbibed many a mystic *völkisch* doctrine about the "un-German character of German Jews." "With few exceptions," writes Niewyk, "the faculty-elected rectors of German universities took their stand against antisemitism."[77] In 1930 the faculty at the University of Jena refused to offer a Nazi-oriented luminary a professorship in anthropology; the next year, at the University of Munich, the faculty defended a Jewish professor of constitutional law from an antisemitic attack. During Weimar, virtually never did antagonistic students molest Jewish faculty members.

On the other hand, a milder variety of antisemitism was widespread in the universities. A Jewish applicant for a full professorship at the

University of Berlin in 1924 later recalled: "No Jew had ever been granted a full professorship in Philosophy at the University of Berlin. . . . At the time of the Weimar Republic, even outside the field of Philosophy only a few full professorships had been given to Jews in the nation's capital."[78] This was a continuation of the prewar situation.

Fritz Ringer points to "the orthodox majority" of the German professoriate as preaching "the unquestioning submission of the individual to the 'national community' as the only alternative to modern egotism and materialism."[79] Such sentiments were usually aimed at leftists and liberals, reflecting the rightist orientation of academics. According to Ringer, the core of these sentiments was a revulsion against that with which Jews were identified: social change, political liberalization, rational clarification, and enlightenment.[80] His conclusion is that "the orthodox majority within the German academic community of the Weimar period . . . seriously weakened what safeguards can ever provide against unreason and brutality."[81]

The common schools of Germany also reflected during Weimar the religious prejudices of the Christian churches. Geoffrey Field indicates the strong confessional nature of the public elementary and high schools before the war: "The Catholic and Protestant churches examined prospective religion teachers for their orthodoxy, clerics served as local school inspectors in most of the Reich and played a leading role on school boards and in poorer, rural areas schoolteachers were often obliged to perform a variety of menial duties at the local church."[82] Little changed after the war. Four out of five children attended confessional public schools and exceedingly few secondary-school students were children of workers. Generally, Jewish schools were not financed as the others but depended upon private funds. Jewish teachers were all but excluded from the Christian public schools. In Prussia, governmental authorities even refused to grant public school funds to Jewish communities too poor to support their own schools. In 1922, Jewish teachers in the same state were informed they could not teach in certain alternative schools if no Jewish students were in attendance.

The courts of Weimar Germany, according to Niewyk, protected Jewish rights evenhandedly. Heavy penalties were levied on persons found guilty of overt actions against Jews and their property. Court actions against Jews were examined carefully: "Every known case brought to harass Jews or to cripple their self-defense activities was thrown out of court."[83] Apparently, neither the police nor the army could be regarded as riddled by Nazis.

Fending off expected and actual attacks was a task assigned to the National League of Jewish Frontline Veterans, organized after World War I; in 1932, it had some 30,000 members. Niewyk tells the story this way:

Early on, league members established clandestine arms caches and formed defensive detachments in Berlin, Munich, Königsberg, Kassel, and Breslau against the possibility of pogroms or of a racist *Putsch*. These they used to good purpose in defending Eastern Jews during the 1923 Berlin riots [when mobs of 30,000 persons attacked Jews and looted Jewish stores for two days], during which a veteran shot and mortally wounded one of the racists. . . . After the courts acquitted them of using their weapons illegally and, in effect, recognized their right to bear arms for defensive purpose, they began openly to patrol the neighborhoods around synagogues. In 1927, following a Nazi attack on Jews in the streets of downtown Berlin, the league joined with the Jewish Boxing Club "Maccabi" and the Zionist Sports Association "Bar Kochba" to found a Jewish Defense Service. . . . [In 1932] the league stood arm-in-arm with the republican paramilitary defense organization, the Reichsbanner, to counteract an expected Nazi coup.[84]

German Jewry did not organize a Jewish party during Weimar but expanded its program of helping to finance political parties that stood up against antisemitism generally and the Nazis in particular. The Socialist party was the most steadfast in these regards: "Antisemites who raised their heads in the party either resigned or were expelled."[85] The Communist party, on the other hand, while not antisemitic, appealed to rightists by agreeing with the latter's attacks on Jewish capitalists. Until 1930, the Democratic party, a middle-class liberal organization, could be counted on to oppose most anti-Jewish measures; in that year it changed its name and abruptly embraced an antisemitic group as part of its augmented membership. The Catholic Center party usually opposed antisemitic actions while the People's party remained silent in the face of anti-Jewish attacks.

The Central Union begun in 1893 continued its work into the 1930s and recorded modest successes. Most Jews, while appreciative of the Socialists' position on antisemitism, resisted the anticapitalism and antireligion of the same group. Niewyk speculates that the predilection of a number of Italian Jews for fascism might have suggested in Germany "potential Jewish support for a fascism without antisemitism."[86] Little concrete evidence for the existence of such a movement has been presented.

During the waning years of the Weimar Republic, Germany was enveloped by a profound economic depression. Unemployment reached unheard-of heights. Between 1929 and 1933, the Nazis attracted record support by making two appeals: (1) they pledged to eliminate unemployment, and (2) they declared they would save Germany from a communist revolution. Antisemitism was not made a central appeal during these years. Niewyk notes: "As case studies of specific groups of Nazis have shown, antisemitism rarely played an important part in bringing new converts to National Socialism."[87] Nothing was retracted, to be sure.

Nor were physical attacks on and boycotts of Jews muted. All this re-assured antisemites that the Nazi party was their true home. Meanwhile, Germans who might have been repelled by a major appeal on anti-semitism could still their doubts and go on to join with the Nazis.

Among the main recruiting sources of Nazism were low- and middle-level civil servants, white-collar employees, skilled artisans, and small shopowners. Hans Morgenthau calls these the "proletarized middle classes with a fascist psychology and a fascist philosophy."[88] As a half-century earlier, such groups now saw Jews as their mortal competitors, as evil-doers of a new form of government, and of an economy unac-countably idled.

Jews, for their part, were deeply uncertain about what awaited them. The Nazis introduced no program for Jews which had not been heard many times before. Nor did any new social groups join the Nazi move-ment that had not been antisemitic in earlier decades. The most unset-tling—and novel—factor was the obvious catapulting electoral support that the Nazis were attracting. In the last quarter of the nineteenth century, antisemitic parties had not been notably successful. Failure to rally voter support for antisemitism occurred in 1912 despite the united effort of a broadly based coalition of conservatives. Yet Jews also reflected on the Nazi decision not to make antisemitism one of the electoral issues of the early 1930s. In Hitler's speeches made during the election cam-paigns of 1928, 1930, and 1932, no discussion of Jews appears. Bieber writes of Germany's Jews that "until the end of the 1920s, they took antisemitism no more seriously than they had in the Empire."[89] Relatively few had experienced personal violence. Many were immune from hostile demonstrations since they lived in middle- and upper-class areas distant from the centers of cities. Antisemitism thus presented itself as an ab-stract threat. By the opening of 1933, the danger had become far more palpable, if still indistinct in its contours.

When Hitler became chancellor on January 30, 1933, the Nazis lacked a plan for government policy on Jews. Their party program contained six planks relating to Jews which in one degree or another were imple-mented by 1939. Beyond that, policies were developed in response to immediate political pressures, intraparty conflicts, national economic needs as interpreted by government ministries with contradictory advice, foreign policy concerns, and the ever-present personal authority of Adolf Hitler.

Few Germans of any political persuasion thought the Hitler regime would last long. This very tentativeness made somewhat more bearable the worst anti-Jewish excesses of early Nazi rule. During these days initiatives were in the hands of the Brown Shirts or SA (from *Sturm Abteilung*), hardly more than uniformed gangs who marauded against Jews and their property without fear of punishment. Jews were, for example, abducted for ransom. The SA organized boycotts of Jewish-owned stores on a hit-and-miss basis. On April 1, Hitler proclaimed a nationwide boycott but it was largely unsuccessful. Non-Jews continued to patronize Jewish stores.

That same month the first four antisemitic laws were decreed. Civil servants appointed from the fall of Imperial Germany in 1918 could be discharged if they were Jews, socialists, or communists. Veterans were exempted from this rule. Limitations were placed upon Jews becoming judges and public prosecutors. Persons who used Jewish physicians could not have their expenses repaid under the national health service. A quota of 1.5 percent was established for Jews in secondary and higher educational institutions. These were only the first of some 400 pieces of legislation aimed at Jews between 1933 and 1939.

All Jews who had become naturalized citizens after November 1918 were deprived of their citizenship. They were denied the right to own farmland or engage in farming. Another law provided for organizing Chambers of Culture under the Propaganda Ministry; these covered films, theater, music, fine arts, literature, broadcasting, and the press. Jews were excluded from all these employments. On the other hand, larger Jewish businesses were not molested, either by law or in fact. The Nazis needed the production of these businesses to supply jobs and goods. More important, because many of these businesses either had foreign markets or branches overseas, they attracted foreign currency to Germany. This money then could be used to purchase necessary raw materials from other countries.

During 1934–35, therefore, a certain illusion of security set in among Jews. No new measures were passed. Some 10,000 Jews who had escaped from Germany now returned, convinced the danger had passed. Another reassuring factor was a seeming intensification of Jewish community life arising from a turning inward. Almost purely a defensive reaction, it nevertheless comforted many. Between 1936 and 1938 most Jewish children attended Jewish schools, an unheard-of fact. A Zionist leader, Robert Weltsch, recalled: "In a religious vacuum every collective Jewish activity, however pedestrian, assumed an emotional dignity which gave ample satisfaction to its promoters.... It was, alas, a kind of euphoria before the end."[90]

In 1933, German Jewish leaders signed a public statement solicited by Nazi leader Hermann Göring condemning the "atrocity propaganda" against Germany.[91] That same year, the National League of Jewish Frontline Veterans, which had armed itself in the 1920s and early 1930s to protect Jews from physical attack, "sent a declaration to the new government, affirming their stand with the German fatherland, for Germany's *Lebensraum* and honor were at stake."[92] In February, a young right-wing Jewish historian, Hans Joachim Schoeps, when excluded from activity in the Hitler Youth, formed his own group, Deutscher Vortrupp. He "wanted to prove...that young Jews were still prepared to defend their fatherland despite the severe restrictions placed on the Jewish community by the Hitler regime."[93] In early 1934, at least one other Jewish leader thought it realistic to hope that an agreement could be reached between Jews and a "left" faction of the Nazi party. This possibility, if such it was, ended in June when the faction's leader, Ernst Roehm, was executed by Hitler's order.[94] All these incidents exemplified a persisting belief in the political normality of German public life. Undoubtedly, they served more of a psychological than a political purpose.

Early in 1935, public opinion monitoring services permitted an impression to form about the pressure of a "growing mood of indifference, disillusion and disgruntlement among the population at large and even within the National Socialist movement itself, seeming to be turning into a crisis of confidence in the regime."[95] During July, the Hitler Youth and the SA engaged in "pogrom-like mass attacks" on Jews in the fashionable neighborhood of the Berlin Kurfürstendamm.[96] Hitler stopped the actions; he held consistently that such an approach was largely ineffective and disliked the fact that the events were out of control. He preferred orderly action. In addition, monitoring reports indicated the unpopularity of physical attacks on Jews and of boycotts on the ground, however, of inappropriate methods rather than moral reasons.

These events were introduced and followed by two laws that struck at the civic status of Jews. In May 1935 a military service law stipulated that Jews could no longer serve in the armed forces. In September, the infamous Nuremberg Laws were passed. The chief one was entitled "Law for the Protection of German Blood and Honor" illegalizing intermarriage of Jew and non-Jew as well as any sexual relations between the two. Jews were also deprived of their citizenship. Jews were excluded from civil service jobs and from universities; a quota was established for Jewish lawyers and physicians. Passage of these laws set off an exodus of Jews from Germany. Not only did the measures affix a racial definition on them, but they "resolved" the age-old Jewish question so as to close off any possibility of equal treatment. The Jew in Germany was to be a racial outcast and a civic eunuch. Nevertheless, the body representing all German Jews accepted the measures: "In late September, the *Reichsvertretung der Juden in Deutschland*...issued a statement expressing its willingness to work for a *modus vivendi* with the National Socialists. The *Reichsvertretung* was willing to view the Nuremberg Laws as the beginning to such a 'tolerable arrangement.'"[97]

By passing the Nuremberg Laws, the Nazi party came to terms with its party program. Elements in the party that favored permanent pogroms were appeased, in part, and at the same time antisemitism was institutionalized and thereby stabilized. Preparations for the 1936 Olympics moderated open attacks on Jews. During that year and most of 1937, what Herbert A. Strauss calls "creeping persecution" transpired: Jews were excluded from the semipublic sphere, including accounting, pharmacies, and publishing.

The economic sphere of Jewish life was the final area of Nazi action. Many pre-1933 followers of the Nazis had been attracted by the prospects of helping relieve "Jewish capital" of its bounties. Small businessmen waited to be freed of the "chains of interest-slavery." Nothing much occurred for, as we saw earlier, Jewish ownership of larger businesses was undisturbed. Yet the Nazi party had for years pledged to expel Jews from national economic life. Despite that, even as late as 1937, Jewish-owned firms were still being awarded public contracts. Small businesses owned by Jews were another matter; especially in small towns they suffered much informal harassment.

Party pressures for "Aryanization" increased in 1936 and 1937. In some cases this meant that a Jewish-owned firm was closed altogether. In others, owners were compelled to sell to "Aryans," usually for only a small fraction of the commercial value of the business. Two of the largest publishing firms in the country were sold for only 10 percent of their value. Late in 1937 and through 1938 economic recovery was complete; production of armaments no longer required Jewish firms; and so Aryanization of large, Jewish companies proceeded. Now, however, smaller-sized non-Jewish businessmen were pushed aside: "Aryanization served to concentrate wealth and industry into even fewer hands."[98]

Legally, the process was perfected in 1938. Jews were forbidden to receive any more government contracts and it became illegal to hide the fact of Jewish ownership of any business. In April, all Jewish property holdings worth more than 5,000 Reichsmarks were required to be registered with the government. In July, Jews were barred from working in any commercial enterprise; that same summer some 30,000 Jewish salesmen were discharged. Nazis now moved with great dispatch. As Karl Schleunes points out: "About 80 percent of the Jewish businesses which had managed to hold out until April 1938 had fallen into the Nazi clutches during the following year."[99] During the spring of 1938, a law abolished the legal status of Jewish congregations; thereafter, these institutions could no longer collect any money from their members. All Russian Jews who had lived in Germany since the Russian Revolution of 1917 were expelled. And in June the Gestapo arrested some 1,500 "antisocial" Jews, a puzzling rubric since about 500 were merely guilty of traffic violations.

Clearly, an atmosphere of crisis was being created: "At the unofficial level, party functionaries ... were calling for sterner measures and organizing their own anti-Jewish campaigns.... The summer of 1938 was a period of unparalleled persecution. Boycotts, beatings, expropriation,

and arrests. . . . The terror which party and SA officials excited introduced the confusion of early 1933."[100] In early November, under the
initiative of Joseph Goebbels, a vast, coordinated pogrom broke out all
over Germany. Windows of Jewish-owned stores were smashed, synagogues burnt down, houses and offices sacked and looted by Nazi demonstrators. The *Kristallnacht*—the night of crystals or glass splinters—
behind them, Jews were terrified and sensed a beginning of the end of
things after November 9, 1938. It was a special Goebbels touch to mark
the twentieth anniversary of the overthrow of the Kaiser in World War I
by a national pogrom.

Five weeks later, Göring became coordinator of all Jewish affairs. He
ordered the disbandment of remaining Jewish civil and other groups.
All Jewish newspapers except one were closed. Pensions received by Jews
were reduced, and they were no longer allowed to use railroad dining
and sleeping cars. During the following three years or so, writes, Sarah
Gordon, "no indignity appeared too trivial to legislate."[101] Jews were
forbidden to buy books or sell their own. Nor could Jewish women
patronize non-Jewish hairdressers. Increasingly, Jews were sent to concentration camps where, until 1941, they were mistreated but not yet as
in death camps.

The regulations flowed on. Jews were ordered to live in certain houses
only the better to concentrate them as in a ghetto. A special income tax
was levied on Jews. In September 1941 they were required to wear a
yellow star as a badge. A few weeks later, a Gestapo order forbade any
friendly relations between Jews and non-Jews. Only during certain hours
of the day could Jews shop in stores. Houses with Jewish occupants were
marked on their exteriors. Noteworthy about these and other measures
since early 1939 were their profusion and breadth rather than their
immediate purpose. This activity presaged a deadly reformulation of
policy against the Jews.

On the sixth anniversary of the Nazi seizure of power, January 30,
1939, Hitler declared: "If international-finance Jewry inside and outside
Europe should succeed once more in plunging nations into another
world war, the consequence will not be the Bolshevization of the earth
and thereby the victory of Jewry, but the annihilation of the Jewish race
in Europe."[102] Seven months and two days later, Germany attacked Poland and World War II began. Sometime during the spring of 1941—
just before the Nazis' June attack on the Soviet Union—a decision seems
to have been reached in the high German governmental circles to destroy
the Jewish people as a whole. Nazi armed victories had added millions
of Jews to the German realm and this ghoulish goal seemed practical.
On July 31, 1941, a secret message from Göring was delivered to Reinhardt Heydrich, head of the Reich Security Main Office: "I request that
you send me before long an overall plan concerning the organization,

factual, and material measures necessary for the accomplishment of the desired solution of the Jewish question."[103] After preliminary planning transpired, Heydrich convened a high-level, very secret meeting in a Berlin suburb, Wannsee, on January 20, 1942; the person keeping minutes of the meeting was Adolf Eichmann, Heydrich's designee to organize what was called the "final solution" to the Jewish problem. Two more meetings were held in the spring and fall. During the spring, it was decided to use gassing as the principal technique of killing Jews on a large scale.

On September 30, 1942, Hitler addressed the country as a whole, declaring, "In my Reichstag speech of September 1, 1939, I have... [said] that if Jewry should plot another world war in order to exterminate the Aryan peoples of Europe, it would not be the Aryan peoples which would be exterminated, but Jewry."[104] He repeated his prediction. The mass killings took place in six death camps built in Poland. When the war began in 1939, there were some 150,000 Jews left in Germany. During 1941–42, over 100,000 were sent to their deaths. The rest were killed before the end of 1944. Altogether, Germans executed between 5.1 and 5.9 million Jews.[105]

Viewing Nazi policy on Jews in the perspective of 1933–45, two landmarks appear: around 1938 when anti-Jewish policy took a marked lurch forward and late 1941–early 1942 when the extermination policy set in. Both were probably more the product of external than internal forces. The year 1938 saw Germany acquire Austria and press the Western powers into an appeasement mode. From that moment it had the initiative in world affairs and could act without great concern about adverse world opinion. During the first years of the Nazi regime, Jews gained from their ability to arouse moderate protests against anti-Jewish affairs in Germany. By the end of 1938 the outside world was bored and uninterested. In 1941–42, the Nazis occupied much of Western Europe and were riding high in the USSR. With a dominion of nearly 9 million Jews—three-fifths of the world's Jews—Nazis saw extermination as achievable. Thereupon, that became one of the prime aims of Nazi war policy.

How did Jews and non-Jews react to the various twists and turns in Nazi policy on Jews? Just over half of all German Jews emigrated, some 300,000 out of 550,000. During the years 1933–39, the Nazis were pleased to see them go. No laws prevented their going, although special exit taxes were levied on emigrant Jews. It was considerably more difficult to find places where they were welcome than to gain permission to depart. German Zionists were favored over other Jews as an aspect of German immigration policy. Their work in publicizing immigration was encouraged by the Nazis. Early in 1933, an agreement was signed between the government and Zionist organizations whereby facilitation of Jewish immigration to Palestine would be linked with expanded sale of German goods overseas. Although such aid was critical to the young Hitler government, German Zionists supported the arrangement; one part of the agreement provided that German Jews would be allowed by the Nazis to transfer investment funds to Palestine.[106] After passage of the Nuremberg Laws of 1935, Jewish organizations in Germany began working for emigration on a large scale. *Kristallnacht* in November 1938 set off an avalanche of emigrants. The Gestapo, especially, now worked toward the "goal of the mass expulsion of Jews at any price."[107] Outbreak of the war slowed the outflow. In October 1941, Himmler ordered an end to Jewish emigration from Germany and German-occupied areas of Europe.

Following is a table summarizing the trend of Jewish population in Germany from 1933 to 1945:[108]

January 1933	525,000 (est.)
June 1933	499,682
May 1939	213,390
September 1939	185,000
October 1941	164,000
1942	139,000
January 1943	51,257
April 1943	31,910
September 1944	14,574
Mid-1945	25,000 (est.)

Until October 1941 most of the decline reflected emigration. During 1942–44, the decline directly resulted from murderous Nazi policy.

Nazi anti-Jewish policy was also met by protests, especially in the early years. As Konrad Kwiet points out:

In telegrams, letters and memoranda addressed to the Nazi authorities, German Jews and German-Jewish organizations protested against moral defamation and social ostracism. . . . Speeches and sermons, publications and cultural events are evidence here. German Jews refused to obey Nazi directives. The attempts to oppose the "designation directive" of September 1941 by not wearing or by concealing the Yellow Star are an example of this. Rebellion and indignation was quite publicly expressed. . . . This protest exploded in verbal utterances, insults and acts of violence.[109]

Until the Final Solution was implemented, oppositional pamphlets by Jews continued to be distributed.

Kwiet estimates that there were as many as 2,000 Jews working in the underground. Most were part of the Communist movement. The best-known was the Baum Group in Berlin, composed of thirty-two Jewish

Communists and Zionists; the greater part consisted of youngsters eleven to fourteen years old; four were as old as nineteen. Baum worked as a forced laborer at the Siemens electrical works in Berlin. Group members posted bills on walls and painted anti-Nazi slogans on buildings. All were finally caught and executed.[110] Meanwhile, these groups could usually find a place to meet in the houses of Jewish sympathizers in Berlin. Since opposition groups were restricted to large cities, where Jews tended to live, there are no records of the kind of partisan fighting groups found on the Russian, French, or Yugoslavian countryside during the war. (The non-Jewish underground in Germany was subject to the same limitation.)

How did non-Jewish Germans view the results of Nazi policy on Jews? Three major historical researches into this question have been made recently. The works are by Sarah Gordon, Ian Kershaw, and Otto Dov Kulka.

Gordon found, she reports, "only around three thousand cases of Germans—out of a population of around sixty million—who aided Jews or who were arrested for violating Nazi laws regarding Jews."[111] (This can be compared with Kwiet's finding that "about 10,000 German Jews found a hiding place, 5,000 of them in Berlin alone."[112] Since most hiding probably involved single persons, perhaps as many as 10,000 Germans helped Jews hide.) The Nazis took great care not to publicize specific outrages against Jews for fear that Germans would reject such methods. At the same time, the press was instructed, in detail, how to keep up its campaign against Jews. As Gordon writes, "Had the majority of Germans regarded Jews as enemies, the Nazis would have had limited need for their endless antisemitic propaganda."[113]

A special news service sent weekly directives concerning Jews to the German press. On May 31, 1941, the press was told to stress Germany was waging war to save Europe from the Jewish menace. On January 9, 1942, it put forward "the Jews are guilty" as a slogan. In February 1943, when German reverses at Stalingrad were multiplying, the press was instructed to discuss the plans the Jews had for Europe if their side triumphed. How to arouse antisemitism in other countries was specified on May 21, 1943. Even as late as December 22, 1944, when the German army was losing crucial battles, the press service exhorted: "The task of the German press [is] never to let this theme sleep."[114]

The Propaganda Ministry did not allow printed discussions of Nazi party responsibility for anti-Jewish measures, including specific occurrences in concentration camps. According to Gordon, "After 1939 a general ban was placed on publishing any information on anti-Jewish measures, and arrests of Jews were not to be reported during the war. ... Hitler himself gave a blackout order on further publication of measures against Jews on February 7, 1942.... The Propaganda Ministry blacked out all events and facts both great and small that would have allowed Germans to form an accurate picture of racial persecution and to arrive at an independent judgment of it."[115] On the other hand, this did not mean that Germans were unaware of what was going on. Gordon insists "it would...be a gross inaccuracy to conclude that Goebbels's [news] blackouts and camouflage of racial persecution prevented the general public from perceiving that Jews were being tormented with ever-increasing cruelty."[116]

Gordon reports that numerous Germans helped Jews during the first months of the regime. From 1933 to 1935, while most people remained indifferent to the persecution, the number of both supporters and opponents grew. The Nuremberg Laws of 1935 were generally supported, according to Gordon, and between 1935 and 1938 "it appears that antisemitic measures and propaganda received increased support, certainly more than between 1933 and 1935."[117] *Kristallnacht*, in late 1938, was very unpopular among wide circles of Germans: "During and after *Kristallnacht*, many Germans aided Jews by forewarning them of Nazi attacks, hiding their possessions, hiding Jews in their homes, providing medical care, and giving food. For this assistance a large number of Germans were arrested in a Nazi attempt to root out criticism of their racial policies."[118] Further, this temper of criticism spilled over into the next two years, during 1939 and 1940: "murder, destruction of property, and violence were condemned by the minority that had earlier opposed persecution, but also by large segments of the previously indifferent population. Public opposition to rabid antisemitism was at a peak after *Kristallnacht*."[119]

Late in 1941, Jews began to be sent to death camps. Most Germans, writes Gordon, did not know of these camps. "At least a minority of Germans approved of draconian measures against Jews, although there were no indications that gassing in death camps was widely known or accepted."[120] All in all, however, "opponents of antisemitic persecution ...[consisted of] a small minority of Germans."[121]

Most institutions failed to oppose anti-Jewish oppression during the Nazi years. With reference to church leaders, "even though they fought with the Nazis to retain their prerogatives on other issues, they did not seriously attempt to intercede in Hitler's war against the Jews."[122] The Catholic church did not even protest against *Kristallnacht*. Protestants were, if possible, more silent. Gordon reserves the word "disgrace" for two institutions: the churches and the army. The former refused to lend their moral authority to any movement against the killing of Jews. And "the majority of the German military leaders bear a great responsibility for the murder of Jews (and others) in Europe. They were the only group that could feasibly have deposed Hitler or refused to tolerate genocide, simply because they were the only genuine counterweight to the armed power of the SS."[123] The German universities were corrupted by Nazi purpose early in the Hitler regime and fueled the flames of antisemitism. (Hans Ebert writes that "there is certainly no room for doubt as to the political reliability—in the Nazi sense—of all scholars and scientists appointed to university posts in Germany between 1934–1944.")[124] Gordon does not discuss two other institutions of high prestige in German life—big industry and banking—which hastened to use slave labor provided by Jewish (and other) prisoners. None was known to have opposed the persecution or slaughter of the Jews.

While a relative few Germans helped Jews, probably many more betrayed them. One historian, after examining a large sample of arrest records, reported that "the overwhelming majority of the personal files of German Jews examined show entries and other proofs of denunciations."[125] Gordon studied the arrest records of a sample of 452 violators of laws against befriending Jews and race defilement (sexual relations between Jew and non-Jew). All were from Düsseldorf. Both groups of violators were classified as opponents of Nazi persecution of Jews although there may well not have been any political implications in the illicit sexual relations. Nevertheless, on the basis of her classification Gordon found that middle-class persons were far likelier than blue-collar workers to be violators and therefore opponents of persecution. In the country at large, however, it was more common by far for blue-collar workers than middle-class persons to be active in general anti-Nazi activities, without reference to Jews.

Kershaw reviewed much of the same kind of evidence used by Gordon. "The relative indifference of most Germans towards the 'Jewish Question' before 1933," he writes, "meant that the Nazis had a job on their hands after the takeover of power to persuade them of the need for active discrimination and persecution of the Jews."[126] During anti-Jewish boycotts and attacks on Jews during 1933–35, few gentile citizens joined in. Customers in Jewish stores continued to buy there; workers in Jewish-owned businesses did not wish to close down their source of employment; tourist areas wanted all to feel welcome. This combination of material considerations and self-interest meant "that while there was no broad swell of opinion actively supporting Nazi measures, nor was there any notable sign of support for the Jews as Jews in the conflict."[127]

After nearly two years of unrelenting attacks on Jews the terror started making headway among some Germans. Business in Jewish stores began to drop. While criticisms of the violence of Nazi methods were heard frequently, people nevertheless were taking sides. During the first ten months of 1935, the circulation of *Der Stürmer*, a notorious Nazi sheet edited by Julius Streicher that specialized in baiting Jews, quadrupled. At the same time, a secret socialist report informed its readers that there was "an almost uniform rejection of the *Rassenwahn* [race-hate campaign] of Hitler and Streicher among the working class."[128] From 1935 to 1938,

Germans seemed little interested in Jewish issues, including the Nuremberg Laws. Yet Kershaw observes that by the end of the period "the Jew-baiting had not been without influence on popular opinion, and attitudes had filtered through which earlier would have been rejected."[129]

The *Kristallnacht* pogroms met with numerous dissents by non-Jews. Many helped Jews, as Gordon pointed out. In Catholic rural areas sympathy and aid were more frequent than elsewhere. While the hierarchy held its tongue, ordinary parishioners took concrete steps. Especially in Catholic regions, according to Kershaw, peasants rejected the pogroms, both on grounds of Christian charity and common humanity and also through outrage at the senseless destruction of goods and property. "Materialistic reasons for condemnation could also be heard in workers' circles ... [which] responded negatively to the pogrom from less materialistic motives."[130]

Yet muttered dissent did not deter the main line of march. Jews became less a concern of ordinary Germans as they were shoved out of the people's line of sight. After *Kristallnacht*, the pace of Jewish emigration quickened and measures were adopted to segregate Jews from the general population. As Jews faded from view, wider and wider circles of Germans found less to criticize in terms of violent methods.

During the war, writes Kershaw, "the 'Jewish Question' was of no more than minimal interest to the vast majority of Germans ... [while] the mass slaughter of Jews was taking place in the Occupied Territories of the East.... The depersonalization of the Jew had been the real success of Nazi propaganda and policy."[131] The Nazi attack on the USSR in June 1941 hurried the process. In September came the yellow star, followed by a wave of new restrictions. The next month all Jewish emigration was stopped. By November systematic murder of the German Jews began in the death camps. By December 1942, over 100,000 Jews had been annihilated. "Knowledge of atrocities and mass shootings of Jews in the East," according to Kershaw, "mostly in the nature of rumor brought home by soldiers on leave, was fairly widespread."[132] The Final Solution, he concludes, "would not have been possible ... without the silence of the church hierarchies and consent-complicity of bureaucracy, industry, and armed forces."[133] This was despite aid to Jews by some members of the bourgeoisie, a connection that was denounced by Goebbels.

Kulka reviewed German public opinion on the Nuremberg Laws, *Kristallnacht*, and the death camps. The Nuremberg Laws found general acceptance although, more or less accurately, a Nazi report stated that "lack of proper understanding [of the laws] is prominent mainly among the members of the so-called upper and better-educated classes."[134] The Communist party in Berlin distributed leaflets attacking the sharp turn toward official racism. One declared, "We hate no race. We hate the capitalist base ... Workers! Open your eyes! The agitation against the

Jews is meant to divert your attention from all the broken promises."[135] The Department of Warfare Against Jewry, a unit of the security office within the SS, recommended to superiors "the deliberate and controlled exploitation of 'popular rage that expresses itself in violent outbursts' as a psychological instrument for honing the Jews' historical sensitivity to 'a hostile atmosphere that could spontaneously turn against [them] at any moment.' "[136] In other words, deliberately terrorize Jews by organizing violent attacks upon them. This is precisely what happened.

Kulka points to four different types of reaction to passage of the Nuremberg Laws. First, some regarded them as a clarification and settlement of the Jewish question. This group included those who hoped cruder, more violent attacks on Jews would cease. Second, a very few openly opposed the laws and criticized them. Some did so out of fear that the laws would move some countries to retaliate by invoking economic reprisals against Germany. Third, a rather large group saw the laws facilitating the acceptance of the antisemitic movement as a fully legitimate alignment with public policy. Anti-Jewish actions were interpreted by this group as an extension of the spirit of the laws. Fourth, a very large group was simply indifferent.

Kristallnacht, as we saw earlier, was not an isolated episode but simply the largest-scale pogrom in a series of violent episodes during the first ten months of 1938. The Left, which had been comparatively silent at the time of the Nuremberg Laws, now attacked the government for leading *Kristallnacht.* Intellectuals, isolated clergymen, and some traditionalists also were critical. Kulka observes that much of the criticism avoided any attack on the immorality of the violence against Jews but dwelled instead on the economic wastage that resulted. "The tendency exhibited here," he comments, "is that of a growing depersonalization in the attitude towards the Jews and the Jewish problem."[137] Kershaw and Kulka agree on this point.

Between November–December 1941 and June 1943 Nazis massmurdered over 100,000 German Jews in the death camps. No reaction by the German population was observable. Internal Nazi party and government reports "indicate the public's knowledge of details, including the fact that the deportees were being massacred."[138] After the murders of German Jews ended, the reports began "to mention remarks [by Germans] about the fate of the deportees and the possible consequences for the German public."[139] Kulka stresses his impression "that the population of Germany was generally aware of what became of the Jews deported to the East.... Of this there can hardly be any doubt."[140] During the war, dissent disappeared on the subject of Jews and was replaced by seeming inattention to the issue. Kulka holds there was an "almost total absence of any reference to the existence, persecution and the extermination of the Jews—a kind of national conspiracy of silence."

Apparently, he judges, "the 'Jewish question' and the entire process of its 'solution' in the Third Reich reached the point of almost complete depersonalization."[141] The extermination of moral persons sank from view, only to be replaced first by regret over waste of material resources and second by simple ignoring and thus a kind of manufactured ignorance.

Most Germans, Kulka writes, seem to have agreed with the Nazi view on the need to eliminate the Jews, whatever the method used to this end. Whether it was to be "emigration or segregation within Germany, deportation to ghettos and camps or systematic mass murder whose objective was the extermination of a whole people—genocide—did not constitute a problem for them."[142]

Kulka and Gordon disagree on several important points. Most significant is how much ordinary Germans knew about the death camps. Gordon portrays a state of affairs in which relatively few knew the details, while Kulka stresses the widespread knowledge of the general character of what was happening there. Gordon also regards the number of Germans who helped Jews as surprisingly large while to Kulka the topic is so insignificant he does not even mention it. Kulka assigns considerable responsibility for the Final Solution to most Germans, who, he insists, refused to reject it. All three authors are agreed on the moral default of the Christian churches and the rarity with which individual clergymen took a principled position on the treatment of Jews. Both Kershaw and Kulka underscore how many or most Germans came to regard Jews as depersonalized beings rather than as equal human beings. Gordon does not discuss this in any detail.

In two successive postwar decades, 1947–66, various national samples of the German people were polled by the Institute for Public Opinion on a number of public issues, including Jews.[143] Only 30,000 Jews lived in both parts of the country during these years.

Direct attitudes on Jews. Asked whether Jews "belong to a different race than ourselves," 73 percent responded in the affirmative. Only 10 percent thought similarly of the British. At two different times, samples responded that they had been closely acquainted with Jews (33 percent) or had a Jewish acquaintance (1961). Seventy-three percent had seen Jews wearing yellow stars in 1941; half in 1961 made disapproving remarks about the star, and 7 percent made approving ones. Fifty-three percent thought antisemitism was caused by characteristics of Jewish groups rather than by antisemitic propaganda or by differences of the Jewish religion. In 1949, 23 percent were antisemitic; in 1952, 34 percent were. Sixty-five percent felt the Nazis had succeeded in spreading aversion to Jews while 13 percent felt they had an opposite effect. Thirty-two percent had heard about the mass extermination of Jews before the end of the war; 88 percent felt no personal responsibility for mass extermination while only 6 percent did. The following percentages represent those who felt it better for Germany not to have any Jews: 37 percent in December 1952, 29 percent in April 1956, 22 percent in May 1958, 18 percent in May 1963, 19 percent in May 1965.[144]

Antisemitism. With reference to alleged characteristics of Jews, 45 percent believed Jews avoided manual labor; 25 percent thought they were often exploiters, living off the work of others. Twenty percent felt that Jews often stir up hatred among nations; 15 percent felt that most Jews are cowards; and 14 percent felt that many Jews were arrogant and insolent. Asked whether they would marry a Jew, in August 1949, 70 percent answered negatively, compared with 54 percent in April 1961. The frequency of negative responses rose directly with age but inversely with education. When queried whether antisemitic activities should be punishable by law, the following percentages represent those who answered affirmatively: 41 percent in 1949, 46 percent in 1958, and 78 percent in 1960. Thirty percent replied affirmatively when asked if there were still many Germans in the country who had killed Jews and others during 1933–45.[145]

Denazification. On the process of denazification, 40 percent thought it was wrong, both in 1948 and 1953. Asked whether former Nazis still had influence, the percentages of those replying "none" were 16 percent in 1954 and 24 percent in 1960. In January 1960, 24 percent agreed that high-ranking former Nazis were active in politics. Thirty-five percent agreed that "there are still many judges . . . who were guilty of maladministration of justice during the Third Reich." Only 6 and 7 percent thought in 1952 that a named high Nazi general and a high Nazi admiral were justly imprisoned. In the same year 32 percent evaluated Hitler positively.[146]

Teaching children. As for teaching the young, 21 percent of adults over twenty-five with at least one child had discussed Nazi persecution of Jews with their children. Eighteen percent of persons under twenty-five said a parent had discussed the subject with them. Forty-one percent thought children at school learned too little about Hitler, while 36 percent said they did not know whether that was true.[147]

Personal. In October 1948, 41 percent said they had approved of the Nazi seizure of power in 1933. Forty-nine percent of the men owned medals or war decorations of the Third Reich. And the following percentages of all respondents replied they would oppose a Nazi party should one again assume power:[148]

November 1953	54	May 1959	53
June 1956	52	August 1962	63
August 1957	56	June 1966	65
June 1958	53		

When persons were asked whether the Nazi state had been an unjust and criminal regime, 38 percent in 1964 and 24 percent in 1978 said "no."[149]

In 1975, 1977, and 1978, the institute plumbed overall attitudes on the Third Reich. Responses were as follows, by percentage:[150]

Item	April 1975	September 1977	November 1978
The Third Reich was not all that bad	35	38	37
It was bad in every way	42	40	40
Undecided, no opinion	23	22	23

Respondents who in 1978 chose the first option—"not all that bad"—identified their political orientations as follows: Left, 25 percent; Center, 32 percent; and Right, 47 percent.[151] Frequencies in which different age groups chose this same option in 1978 varied greatly, by percentage:[152]

16–29 years	21
30–44 years	31
45–59 years	48
60 years and over	52

In other words, the older the person, the less objectionable the Nazi regime was.

Let us review the preceding material on public opinion to ascertain whether the conclusions of Gordon, Kershaw, and Kulka are supported by the postwar poll data based on retrospective responses of Germans. All three historians, for example, had observed that exceedingly few Germans were anti-Nazi to the extent of helping Jews or opposing the government. This is largely supported by the postwar data. Three years after the war more than two out of five Germans admitted they had approved of the Nazi seizure of power. Seven years after the end of the war, nearly one-third still evaluated Hitler positively. Nearly 80 percent of adults over twenty-five with at least one child could not say they had discussed Nazi persecution of Jews with their children. Nearly three-quarters thought Jews belonged to a different race than they tehmselves did, thereby attesting to the success of Nazi propaganda, as did the conviction of 53 percent that antisemitism was a product of Jews' characteristics rather than of propaganda. Only two out of five Germans thirty-three years after the war rejected every Nazi policy; nearly another quarter could not decide their view of the matter, and those feeling the Third Reich was not all that bad nearly equaled those totally rejecting it.

Both the historical analyses and the public opinion data portray a population that accepted without major demur the Nazi view of Germany's destiny and the place of Jews in that future.

During 1979–80, the Sinus Institute of Heidelberg conducted a poll of nearly 7,000 persons; it was sponsored by the Federal Chancellory. Some 13 percent were found to have a right-extremist world outlook. One out of four thought that in some degree "Jews and Freemasons still have a great influence in our country." One out of five agreed with engaging in "protest with like-minded people against the anti-German reports on concentration camps." Nearly twice that proportion of right extremists agreed.[153]

In November 1977, sociologist Badi Panahi of Nuremberg investigated antisemitism in Germany, among other topics. He found a generally positive attitude toward Jews except on the subjects of business affairs and economic power; even then, however, a majority rejected a negative view. With reference to racial attitudes, over 60 percent of the respondents agreed that "even if people really had equal opportunity, members of one race will have more success than others." Attitudes of antisemitism and racism are importantly interrelated. He demonstrates "that while only 9.4 percent of the total sample felt strongly that Jews should keep to themselves, 51 percent of those who believe in the immorality of some races want the Jew to segregate; while only 3.6 percent feel strongly that Jews have a harmful influence on Christian culture; among those who think blood and race determine human behavior the believers in harmful Jewish influence rise to 21 percent, and among those who consider some races more immoral than others they rise to 60 percent."[154]

Another study, made by sociologist Klaus Sochatzky of Frankfurt University, investigated attitudes of 867 youths, most of them between thirteen and eighteen years of age. It was conducted in 1979 in the greater Frankfurt region. Just over a quarter (26.1 percent) were classified by Sochatzky as right-extremist. A sixth (17 percent) were antisemitic. Strong proponents of both views were quite a bit smaller in number.

The Sinus study was apparently withheld from publication by the federal government for six months after completion. Steven J. Roth observes that these four public opinion studies—one of which was reported above—show that "at present there is a large potential for the spread of right extremism."[155]

While the studies just reviewed tend to show a fairly direct relationship between age and antisemitism, knowledge of recent German history by youths is very slight. In 1977, Dieter Bossman, a teacher in Flensburg, collected 2,070 student compositions on "what I have heard about Adolf Hitler," mostly written by students aged fourteen to sixteen. He classified only four of them as adequate, suggesting that teachers were steering clear of the Hitler period.[156] Characteristic of many complaints about teachers was one by a Jewish student born in Bonn in 1946: "For them history books ended in 1933. In history class we would spend half a year treating the Weimar Republic in detail only to end up racing through the 'modern' history from 1933–1945 with a kind of vague nostalgia in the last class before the summer vacation."[157]

During the latter half of World War II, the principal allies pledged to eradicate Nazism from public life in Germany and to punish all those guilty of mass murders and atrocities. Both measures became known, somewhat inaccurately, as denazification. On November 1, 1943, the governments of the United States, Britain, and the Soviet Union declared in Moscow that after the war persons responsible for atrocities and massacres would "be sent back to the countries in which their abominable deeds were done in order that they may be judged and punished according to the laws of those liberated countries." The governments affirmed that they would "pursue them to the outermost ends of the earth and . . . deliver them to the accusers in order that justice may be done." At the war crimes trials at Nuremberg during 1945–46, high-ranking Nazis such as Göring and Hess were found guilty. Some were executed while others were sentenced to prison terms. In general, however, both denazification and punishment of war criminals lagged.

In the British and American zones of Germany, many former Nazis were employed by the military government and German generals who had been responsible for mass slaughter were honored. Prelates of the Christian churches were highly protective of former Nazi party members and in some cases forbade church members from testifying in denazification trials. Anti-Nazis were not encouraged to participate; indeed, they were frequently barred from partaking in these proceedings. More than a year after the close of the war, at the end of September 1946, a report to the commander of American forces in Europe informed him that "of the 41,782 cases completed by the German denazification tribunals . . . only 116 Germans were held to be major offenders, while 29,582 were classed as just 'followers', which implied no punishment."[158] Throughout higher education, academics who had a long Nazi record continued to be employed. The police force and law profession were drenched with former Nazis. German judges who had enforced Nazi law by and large retained their positions.

Nazi officers who had been responsible for notorious mass murders of civilians were excused or even employed in the Western zones of Germany. These included the "Butcher of Warsaw," SS General Heinz Reinefarth. He later became a major, then a high official in the West German Ministry of the Interior. SS *Obergruppenführer* Karl Wolff, personal adjutant to Himmler, was sentenced to life in prison for the murder of 300,000 Jews; after seven years he was freed.[159] He has served one day for every 117 Jews or twelve minutes for each Jew he was responsible for killing. Almost the entire top rung of Nazi SS officers who had

commanded the murder of over 400,000 Hungarian Jews retired from
the scene unpunished; most lived peacefully on pensions from the West
German government.[160] They suffered no handicap in later careers in
government and business.

At bottom, the refusal to convict and punish—or even try—Nazis increasingly characterized American and British policy. By 1946 and 1947,
writes Hilberg, "the Western coalition . . . began to look upon the West
German industrial complex as a potential bulwark against the Soviet
Union."[161] Late in 1947, top American and British occupation authorities
had begun to discuss with German authorities an eventual independent
government. In April 1948, Army Secretary Kenneth Royall, in secret
testimony before a House of Representatives committee, "told congressmen that he wanted to end the war crimes program much earlier because
it was weakening the government's prime objective of building up a
strong Germany."[162] By 1948, in fact, the war crimes program was already in tatters: "Just under six percent of all sentences were over one
year. . . . Although the maximum sentence was ten years, the highest
sentence passed in all the trials was five years, against a single defendant.
. . . Both judges and prosecutors were refusing to implement the law."[163]

Restoration rather than denazification became the reality. Industrial
and banking groups that prospered under the Nazis had even freer rein
now that they did not need to share power with Hitler. Much the same
leadership continued at the head of the largest corporations. The national government was highly responsive to these leading groups. Neither the churches nor the universities stood in the way as a new order
was installed. It was presided over by many of the same institutional
forces that had wielded more or less power during the preceding half-
century. None had ever demonstrated a concern about antisemitism
except when they used it to their advantage. "The Allies," writes Tom
Bower, "had settled for a Germany in which power, influence and
wealth remained in the hands of those who had held them under the
Third Reich."[164]

The old order left an obvious trail whose evidences were all too obvious. Beginning in the late 1950s, the Ilman Lake Travel Club started
holding annual meetings in various resort towns in West Germany. In
1984, however, in the Hesse town of Oberaula, the meeting was exposed
as in fact a reunion of Hitler's Waffen SS 3rd Panzer "Death's Head"
formation. During the war about 900,000 men fought in the formation.
According to the Union of Jewish Students in Germany, the division
supplied more than one out of three of the "special assignment" troops
whose job was to kill Jews and others in Russia by shooting. By 1942,
according to the student group, about 15,000 served in concentration
camps. In 1943, the division allegedly helped put down the Warsaw
ghetto revolt. The division's commander, SS general Theodore Eicke,

was known by his troops as "Papa Eicke."[165] In 1983, another veteran officer of the Waffen SS, Theo Maria Loch, was forced to resign as chief editor of West German Broadcasting Service after his record became known. Numerous other such cases had come to light. One, Werner Vogel, nominated by the reform Greens, resigned when his record as a former Brown Shirt officer became known.

During 1977–78, a "Hitler Wave" swept over Germany in the form of publication and manufacture of so-called memorabilia of the Nazi period. These ranged from yellow stars to swastikas to Nazi uniforms. Books of reminiscences were published and sold in large numbers. Even several years later, 1981–83, some of the same continued to happen. A best-seller in the former year, by the vice chief editor of the Bavarian state television and radio station, extolled the Waffen SS.[166] In May 1982, a book was banned by a Stuttgart court entitled *The Auschwitz Myth— Legend or Reality?* A retired judge, the author contends there is no evidence that gas chambers were used to kill Jews at Auschwitz. In 1983, neo-Nazis sold a macabre game called *Jew, Don't Get Angry* in which dice are thrown to try to advance players to the end-space designating extermination of 6 million Jews. Issued by "Viking Youth," a neo-Nazi group, the game resembles a traditional German family game called *Man, Don't Get Angry.* The game first appeared in Bonn schools and discotheques, according to a leader of the Bonn Jewish community.[167]

The honorary archivist of the town of Moringen, site of an early concentration camp in 1933, wrote a 368-page history of the town in which he stated that Jews provoked Nazi attacks. He charged *Kristallnacht* in 1938 was a retaliation for damage by American Jews to stores owned by German-Americans. The concentration camp in Moringen is called a "protective custody camp" in the book. In World War II, according to the volume, Germany was fighting a war of self-defense.[168]

Such seemingly "extreme" events were not, in fact, separable from the general political environment of the Federal Republic of Germany. With SS members generously pensioned and a number of their former officers now high officials in government, let alone in business and other pursuits, the continuity of the old order was assured. So, too, were many of its myths. Rampant, organized antisemitism, however, the surest reminder of the most destructive of the myths, was not permitted to revive. The generally conservative governments of postwar Germany sought constantly to reassure themselves and their well-wishers that in this respect Germany had indeed changed. In 1979, a television dramatic series, "Holocaust," gave them an unexpected opportunity to do so.

The program director of a Cologne television station pushed for acquisition of the series from its American producers and urged that it be shown on regional West German television and radio. He stressed "the fact the most important ally of the Federal Republic has been exposed to this show and to its enormous impact compels the Germans not to close their eyes to it."[169] It was expected in trade circles that, at most, some 15 percent of the potential audience would watch. Usually, the regional network attracted up to 3 percent. (The series was not to be shown on the main national network where the audience might be far greater.)

Shown on four successive evenings, without the American-originated commercials and dubbed in German, the series proved to be an extra-ordinary "hit." The programs became a national event with audience reaction. Viewers phoned their stations, asked questions, wept, expressed their sense of horror at the "revelations," and asked for further infor-mation. In all, some 15 million adults watched the eight-hour series; this represented half the potential audience. A poll conducted by Western German TV and the federal Office for Political Education explored reactions to the programs as well as political attitudes.[170] Seventy-three percent of viewers found it valuable; two-thirds of teenagers wanted it shown again. Unchanged from their opinions before seeing the series, about 30 percent of viewers thought "Nazism was a basically good idea that was only carried out badly."

Audience response was enormous. *Variety* reported there were "30,000 telephone calls, 4,395 letters plus 1,099 telegrams and telexes from view-ers, and there were 450,000 requests for printed material offered by the German TV stations to explain the shows and the Nazi horrors."[171] Perhaps attributable to the series, certain political attitudes changed siz-ably: "The number of people who felt that the 1944 plot by German officers to kill Hitler was justified rose from 49 to 63 percent. The group favoring legislation that would block the statute of limitations from stop-ping prosecution of Nazis rose from 15 to 39 percent; and the group wanting to halt trials of Nazis dropped from 51 to 35 percent."[172] The state of Hesse purchased copies of the tapes to show in schools when the Nazi period is studied.

While younger viewers tended to be the most enthusiastic about "Hol-ocaust," questions on racial attitudes produced disturbing responses. A psychologist for the Office for Political Education reported the poll's findings demonstrate that younger Germans, "although they seldom reveal antisemitic tendencies, and although they know few Jews or none at all, nonetheless have taken over certain prejudices to a shockingly high degree."[173]

While the event received almost no attention in other countries, the "Holocaust" series was replayed in November 1982, nearly four years later. About double the original audience—29 million rather than 15 million—saw it the second time. (It was shown on a national network.) Three thousand phone calls were received, many of them quite negative. The press officer of the television network reported: "In contrast to the 1979 transmission, the brunt of the calls no longer asked for information or said, 'We learned about this for the first time.' Rather, the focus was on the demand to drop the theme at long last and let the past alone. There were statements of approval, radical rejection of the film and criticism of its aesthetics."[174]

In East Germany, denazification took a very different course. There was no restoration of the old ruling groups there. Between 1945 and 1949 a thorough land reform was completed whereby the old Junker class was expropriated. It had been a standby of national conservative rule for many decades. Similarly, by 1948 the largest industrial firms had been expropriated under Soviet rule "on the grounds of participation in the wartime economy and its concomitant crimes (employment of concentration camp prisoners, forced labor, pro-Aryan discrimination, etc.)."[175] War criminals were arrested, tried, and sentenced promptly, often with the death penalty. (Hitler had allowed over 3 million Soviet soldiers to die of starvation and the Soviets were in no mood to dally.)

Active supporters of Nazi rule were generally barred from public office. "In Thuringia and in Saxony, in 1945, over 90 percent of all teachers in schools were dismissed overnight for having been members of the Nazi Party. After two or three years in manual labor, the bulk of them were granted reinstatement or even invited to return."[176] In the universities of East Germany the first concerns were "to remove National Socialists amongst the teaching staff from their posts and to retain a sufficient number of those who were bourgeois and 'anti-Fascist' to get the work of the universities going again."[177]

Positions of public responsibility were closed to any who had been active members of the Nazi party. Specialists in science, economics, and other technical fields, even if they had a Nazi record, were allowed to hold jobs in their fields but were kept out of any leading post. Former Nazis who were not war criminals were admitted into public life. Hans Werner Schwarze reports, for example, that "about ten percent of the People's Chamber *(Volkskammer)* representatives are former NSDAP members." Even the cabinet and executive group of the ruling party contained some ex-Nazis.

Depersonalization of Jews led ultimately to their dehumanization. A widespread sense that Jews were being exterminated failed to interrupt the fateful circuit. After World War II, political circumstances permitted open confessions by considerable numbers of support of the Nazi order in past years. In time, however, uneasy consciences were quieted all too readily by a general lassitude toward perpetrators of the Final Solution.

NOTES

1. Simon Dubnov, *History of the Jews*, 2, trans. Moshe Spiegel (South Brunswick, N.J.: Thomas Yoseloff, 1968), p. 683.

2. Guido Kisch, *The Jews in Medieval Germany. A Study of Their Legal and Social Status* (Chicago: Univ. of Chicago Press, 1949), p. 293.

3. Ibid., pp. 310–11.

4. Ibid., p. 324.

5. Ibid., p. 355.

6. Ibid.

7. Ibid., p. 362.

8. Leon Poliakov, *The History of Anti-Semitism,* 1, trans. Richard Howard (New York: Vanguard Press, 1965), p. 118.

9. Ibid., p. 76 (emphasis in original). See also Werner E. Mosse, "Judaism, Jews and Capitalism. Weber, Sombart and Beyond," *Leo Baeck Institute Year Book* (hereafter this source will be designated *LBI Year Book*), 24 (London: Secker and Warburg, 1979), p. 9

10. Poliakov, *The History of Anti-Semitism,* 1 p. 123.

11. Quoted in ibid., p. 222.

12. Ibid., p. 223.

13. Ibid., p. 217.

14. Ibid., p. 218.

15. Kisch, *The Jews in Medieval Germany,* pp. 5, 310–11.

16. F. L. Carsten, "The Court Jews. A Prelude to Emancipation," *LBI Year Book, 3,* pp. 142–43.

17. Ibid., p. 143.

18. Stefi Jersch-Wenzel, "The Jews as a 'Classic' Minority in Eighteenth- and Nineteenth-Century Prussia," *LBI Year Book,* 27 (1982), p. 43.

19. Poliakov, *The History of Anti-Semitism,* 1, pp. 241–42.

20. H. D. Schmidt, "The Terms of Emancipation 1781–1812. The Public Debate in Germany and Its Effect on the Mentality and Ideas of German Jewry," *LBI Year Book,* 1 (1956), p. 29.

21. Reinhard Rürup, "Jewish Emancipation and Bourgeois Society," *LBI Year Book,* 14 (1969), p. 86.

22. Ibid.

23. Ibid.

24. Ibid., p. 91.

25. See Jacob Katz, *From Prejudice to Destruction. Anti-Semitism, 1700–1933* (Cambridge, Mass.: Harvard Univ. Press, 1980), p. 102; Jacob Katz, "Misreadings of Anti-Semitism," *Commentary,* 76 (July 1983), p. 40.

26. Rürup, "Jewish Emancipation and Bourgeois Society," p. 77.

27. Julian Bartys, "Grand Duchy of Poznan under Prussian Rule. Changes in the Economic Position of the Jewish Population 1815–1848," *LBI Year Book,* 17 (1972), p. 197.

28. Ibid., p. 196.

29. Ismar Schorsch, "The Religious Parameters of Wissenschaft. Jewish Academics at Prussian Universities," *LBI Year Book,* 25 (1980), p. 16.

30. Ibid., p. 19.

31. Peter Freimark, "Language Behaviour and Assimilation. The Situation of the Jews in Northern Germany in the First Half of the Nineteenth Century," *LBI Year Book,* 24 (1979), p. 170.

32. Ibid., p. 177.

33. Rürup, "Jewish Emancipation and Bourgeois Society," p. 83.

34. Ibid.

35. Quoted in ibid., p. 64 n. 18.

36. Dubnov, *History of the Jews*, 5, p. 270.

37. Ibid., p. 271.

38. See Michel Beaud, *A History of Capitalism, 1500–1980*, trans. Tom Dickman and Anny Lefebvre (New York: Monthly Review Press, 1983).

39. Heinz Holeczek, "The Jews and the German Liberals," *LBI Year Book*, 28 (1983), p. 79.

40. Katz, *From Prejudice to Destruction*, p. 245.

41. Peter Pulzer, "Religion and Judicial Appointments in Germany, 1869–1918," *LBI Year Book*, 28 (1983), p. 185.

42. Ernest Hamburger, "Jews in Public Service under the German Monarchy," *LBI Year Book*, 9 (1964), p. 230.

43. Ibid.

44. Werner T. Angress, "Prussia's Army and the Jewish Reserve Officer Controversy before World War I," *LBI Year Book*, 17 (1972), p. 40. See also ibid., p. 236.

45. Ernest Hamburger, "One Hundred Years of Emancipation," *LBI Year Book*, 14 (1969), p. 21.

46. Werner T. Angress, "The Impact of the 'Judenwahlen' of 1912 on the Jewish Question. A Synthesis," *LBI Year Book*, 28 (1983), p. 385.

47. Steven M. Lowenstein, "Jewish Residential Concentration in Post-Emancipation Germany," *LBI Year Book*, 28 (1983), p. 473. n. 6.

48. Ibid., p. 490.

49. Gershom Scholem, "On the Social Psychology of the Jews in Germany: 1900–1933," in David Bronsen, ed., *Jews and Germans from 1860 to 1933: The Problematic Symbiosis* (Heidelberg: Carl Winter, 1979), p. 11.

50. Ibid., p. 19.

51. Lamar Cecil, "Jew and Junker in Imperial Berlin," *LBI Year Book*, 20 (1975), p. 53.

52. Ibid., p. 49.

53. Jack Wertheimer, " 'The Unwanted Element.' East European Jews in Imperial Germany," *LBI Year Book*, 26 (1981), p. 39.

54. See ibid. and two other articles by Wertheimer: "The 'Ausländerfrage' at Institutions of Higher Germany. A Controversy over Russian-Jewish Students in Imperial Germany," *LBI Year Book*, 27 (1982); "Between Tsar and Kaiser. The Radicalization of Russian-Jewish University Students in Germany," *LBI Year Book*, 28 (1983).

55. Steven E. Aschheim, "Eastern Jews, German Jews and Germany's Ostpolitik in the First World War," *LBI Year Book*, 28 (1983), p. 362.

56. Zosa Szajkowski, "The Struggle for Yiddish during World War I. The Attitude of German Jewry," *LBI Year Book*, 9 (1964), p. 143.

57. Ismar Schorsch, *Jewish Reactions to German Anti-Semitism, 1870–1914* (New York: Columbia Univ. Press, 1972), p. 39.

58. Ibid., p. 65.

59. Ibid., p. 67.

60. Barbara Suchy, "The Verein zur Abwehr des Antisemitismus (I). From Its Beginnings to the First World War," *LBI Year Book*, 23 (1983), p. 215.

61. Ibid., pp. 237–38.

62. Schorsch, *Jewish Reactions to German Anti-Semitism*, p. 104.

63. Ibid., p. 118.

64. Ibid., p. 131. See also Gordon Mork, "Out of the Ghetto: German Jews and American Blacks," *Integrateducation*, 12 (May–June 1974), p. 48.

65. Ibid., p. 137.

66. Ibid., p. 164.

67. Ibid., p. 205.

68. Ibid.

69. Peter Pulzer, "Why Was There a Jewish Question in Imperial Germany?" *LBI Year Book*, 25 (1980), p. 142.

70. Cecil, "Jew and Junker in Imperial Berlin," p. 57.

71. Angress, "The Impact of the 'Judenwahlen' of 1912 on the Jewish Question," p. 409.

72. Ibid., p. 410.

73. Hans-Joachim Bieber, "Antisemitism as a Reflection of Social, Economic and Political Tension in Germany: 1880–1933," p. 52 in David Bronsen, ed., *Jews and Germans from 1860 to 1933: The Problematic Symbiosis* (Heidelberg: Carl Winter, 1979).

74. Hamburger, "One Hundred Years of Emancipation," p. 28.

75. Donald L. Niewyk, *The Jews in Weimar Germany* (Baton Rouge: Louisiana State Univ. Press, 1980), p. 49.

76. Ibid., p. 61.

77. Ibid., p. 67.

78. David Baumgardt, "Looking Back on a German University Career," *LBI Year Book*, 10 (1965), p. 246.

79. Fritz K. Ringer, "Inflation, Antisemitism and the German Academic Community of the Weimar Period," *LBI Year Book*, 28 (1983), p. 5.

80. Ibid., p. 8.

81. Ibid., p. 9.

82. Geoffrey G. Field, "Religion in the German Volkschule, 1890–1928," *LBI Year Book*, 25 (1980), p. 46.

83. Niewyk, *The Jews in Weimar Germany*, p. 75.

84. Ibid., p. 91.

85. Ibid., p. 69.

86. Ibid., p. 198.

87. Ibid., p. 80.

88. Hans J. Morgenthau, "The Tragedy of German-Jewish Liberalism," in Max Kreutzberger, ed., *Studies of the Leo Baeck Institute* (New York: Ungar, 1967), p. 51.

89. Bieber, "Antisemitism as a Reflection of Social, Economic and Political Tension in Germany," p. 59.

90. Robert Weltsch, "Introduction," *LBI Year Book*, 1 (1956), pp. xxvii, xxxi.

91. Herbert A. Strauss, "Jewish Emigration from Germany. Nazi Policies and Jewish Responses (II)," *LBI Year Book*, 26 (1981), p. 354.

92. George L. Mosse, "The Influence of the Volkisch Idea on German Jewry," in Kreutzberger, ed., *Studies of the Leo Baeck Institute*, p. 107.

93. Carl J. Rheins, "Deutscher Vortrupp, Gefolgschaft Deutscher Juden, 1933–1935," *LBI Year Book*, 26 (1981), p. 223. (The organization was closed down in 1935 and three years later Schoeps fled to Sweden.)

94. See Mosse, "The Influence of the Volkisch Idea on German Jewry," pp. 104–5.

95. Otto Dov Kulka, "Public Opinion in Nazi Germany and the 'Jewish Question,'" *Jerusalem Quarterly*, 25 (Fall 1982), p. 132.

96. Strauss, "Jewish Emigration from Germany. Nazi Policies and Jewish Responses (I)," *LBI Year Book*, 25 (1980), p. 331.

97. Karl A. Schleuncs, *The Twisted Road to Auschwitz. Nazi Policy toward German Jews, 1933–1939* (Urbana: Univ. of Illinois Press, 1970), p. 126.

98. Ibid., p. 164.

99. Ibid., p. 221.

100. Ibid., pp. 234–35.

101. Sarah Gordon, *Hitler, Germans, and the "Jewish Question"* (Princeton, N.J.: Princeton Univ. Press, 1984), p. 125.

102. Quoted in Raul Hilberg, *The Destruction of the European Jews* (Chicago: Quadrangle, 1961), p. 257.

103. Ibid., p. 262.

104. Ibid., p. 266.

105. The figures underlying both estimates can be found in ibid., p. 767, and Lucy S. Davidowicz, *The War Against the Jews, 1933–1945* (New York: Bantam, 1975), p. 544.

106. See Strauss, "Jewish Emigration from Germany. Nazi Policies and Jewish Responses (II)," pp. 349–50.

107. Ibid., p. 364.

108. Ibid., p. 317.

109. Konrad Kwiet, "Problems of Jewish Resistance Historiography," *LBI Year Book*, 24 (1979), p. 54.

110. See Helmut Eschwege, "Resistance of German Jews against the Nazi Regime," *LBI Year Book*, 15 (1970), pp. 169–71.

111. Gordon, *Hitler, Germans, and the "Jewish Question,"* p. 302.

112. Kwiet, "Problems of Jewish Resistance Historiography," p. 56.

113. Gordon, *Hitler, Germans, and the "Jewish Question,"* p. 152.

114. See G. Bording Mathieu, "The Secret Anti-Juden Sondernummer of 21st May 1943," *LBI Year Book*, 26 (1981), pp. 293–98.

115. Gordon, *Hitler, Germans, and the "Jewish Question,"* pp. 157–58.

116. Ibid., p. 163.

117. Ibid., p. 171.

118. Ibid., p. 178.

119. Ibid., p. 180.

120. Ibid., p. 197.

121. Ibid., p. 195.

122. Ibid., p. 246.

123. Ibid., p. 282.

124. Hans Ebert, "The Expulsion of the Jews from the Berlin-Charlottenburg

Technische Hochschule," *LBI Year Book,* 19 (1974), p. 167. See also Max Pinl and Lux Furtmuller, "Mathematicians under Hitler," *LBI Year Book,* 18 (1973); Max Weinreich, *Hitler's Professors. The Part of Scholarship in Germany's Crimes Against the Jewish People* (New York: Yiddish Scientific Institute—YIVO, 1946).

125. Kwiet, "Problems of Jewish Resistance Historiography," p. 45.

126. Ian Kershaw, "The Persecution of the Jews and German Popular Opinion in the Third Reich," *LBI Year Book,* 26 (1981), p. 264.

127. Ibid., p. 268.

128. Ibid., p. 272.

129. Ibid., p. 274.

130. Ibid., p. 279.

131. Ibid., p. 281.

132. Ibid., p. 284.

133. Ibid., p. 289.

134. Kulka, " 'Public Opinion' in Nazi Germany," p. 126.

135. Ibid., p. 127.

136. Ibid., p. 129.

137. Ibid., p. 144.

138. Otto Dov Kulka, " 'Public Opinion' in Nazi Germany: The Final Solution," *Jerusalem Quarterly,* 26 (Winter 1983), p. 37.

139. Ibid., p. 38.

140. Ibid., p. 43.

141. Ibid., p. 44.

142. Ibid., p. 45.

143. See Elizabeth Noelle and Erich Peter Neumann, eds., *The Germans. Public Opinion Polls 1947–1966,* trans. Gerard Finan and John Fosberry (Westport, Conn.: Greenwood Press, 1981). These surveys were conducted by the Institut für Demoskopie Allensbach.

144. Ibid., pp. 127, 185, 186, 187, 189.

145. Ibid., pp. 189, 190, 192, 316.

146. Ibid., pp. 219, 206, 311, 202.

147. Ibid., pp. 77, 333.

148. Ibid., pp. 197, 176, 432.

149. Frederick Weil, "The Imperfectly Mastered Past: Anti-Semitism in West Germany since the Holocaust," *New German Critique,* 19 (Winter 1980), p. 139.

150. Institut für Demoskopie Allensbach, *Demokratie-Verankerung in der Bundesrepublik Deutschland* (n.p., n.d.), p. 102.

151. Ibid., p. 103.

152. Ibid.

153. "How Popular Is Neo-Nazism in Germany?" *Research Report* (Institute of Jewish Affairs), 6 (May 1981), pp. 2–4.

154. Ibid., p. 7.

155. Ibid., p. 12.

156. Ellen Lentz, "West German Youth Found to be Ignorant about Hitler Period," *New York Times,* April 7, 1977.

157. Yudit Yago-jung, "Growing up in Germany: After the War after Hitler 'Afterwards,' " *New German Critique,* 19 (Winter 1980), p. 75.

158. Tom Bower, *The Pledge Betrayed. America and Britain and the Denazification of Postwar Germany* (Garden City, N.Y.: Doubleday, 1982), pp. 164–65.

159. Ibid., pp. 229–30.

160. See Randolph L. Braham, *The Politics of Genocide. The Holocaust in Hungary,* 2 (New York: Columbia Univ. Press, 1981), pp. 1174–75.

161. Hilberg, *The Destruction of the European Jews,* p. 738.

162. Bower, *The Pledge Betrayed,* p. 256.

163. Ibid., p. 285.

164. Ibid., p. 379.

165. See Tyler Marshall, "Reunion of Nazi SS Unit Protected," *Los Angeles Times,* April 1, 1984; James M. Markham, "4,000 Germans Protest Reunion of SS troops," *New York Times,* April 1, 1984; "Clashes in W. Germany as SS Veterans Hold Reunion," *Jerusalem Post,* May 22, 1983. This last item describes another reunion of the same group, held in Bad Hersfeld in May 1983. Veterans were from the Adolf Hitler Personal Guard and the Hitler Youth Division.

166. Jewish Telegraph Agency, "Nazi Work a Best Seller," *Southern Struggle,* December 1981.

167. "Anti-Jewish Game Circulates in Germany," *Jerusalem Post,* June 19, 1983; "2 'Neo-Nazis' to Be Charged for an Anti-Semitic Game," *Worcester Telegram,* June 21, 1983. Charges were being brought by authorities of Zweibrücken.

168. "German Book Says Jews Provoked Attacks by Nazis," *Jerusalem Post,* July 18, 1983.

169. Michel Gordey, " 'Holocaust' on German TV?" *Los Angeles Times,* June 13, 1978 (reprinted from *Newsday*).

170. John Vinocur, "Germans Surveyed on TV 'Holocaust,' " *New York Times,* May 9, 1979.

171. Hazel Guild, "Germany and the TV 'Holocaust,' " *Variety,* May 23, 1979.

172. Vinocur, "Germans Surveyed on TV 'Holocaust.' "

173. Ibid.

174. "W. German TV Viewers Want Nazi Horrors off the Screen," *Jerusalem Post,* November 23, 1982.

175. Hanns Werner Schwarze, *The GDR Today. Life in the 'Other' Germany,* trans. John M. Mitchell (London: Oswald Wolff, 1973), p. 49. See also Welles Hangen, *The Muted Revolution. East Germany's Challenge to Russia and the West* (New York: Knopf, 1966), p. 177, for an unsuccessful attempt to belittle the denazification program in East Germany.

176. Ibid., p. 25.

177. Kurt Southeimer and Wilhelm Bleek, *The Government and Politics of East Germany,* trans. Ursula Price (New York: St. Martin's Press, 1975), p. 134.

7

ON BEING USED AND BEING USEFUL: HUNGARY

In no other country did the Germans receive such enthusiastic support for the implementation of the Final Solution as they did in Hungary.

—Randolph L. Braham, 1981

Those whose position in society depends on their usefulness to others usually do not reckon with what will happen when their help is no longer needed. At that point usefulness becomes simply being used. From apparent partnership to straightforward "usefulness" was the fate of Jews in Hungary. Surprisingly, complete annihilation nevertheless was averted.

From the mid-fourteenth to mid-fifteenth centuries, the legal position of Jews in Hungary deteriorated as the king declared them his property, deigning to protect them in return for a special tax. In 1360 another king expelled them from the country. Jews found safety during the next four centuries only by serving as managers on the agricultural estates of Hungarian aristocrats. During the Turkish occupation of the land (1526–1718), Jews hewed to the Ottoman standard as under Islam they were treated far better than under Christian rule in the German areas of Hungary where they were persecuted almost without pause. The Turkish departure, however, set off a long period of economic expansion in connection with which large-scale immigration was encouraged by the country's rulers.

From 1700 to 1910, the Jewish population of Hungary grew as follows:[1]

1700	4,071
1735	11,621
1787	80,775
1825	185,075
1869	542,279
1910	911,227

Also, Hungarian Jewry became less of a geographically marginal people over this same period by moving from the border areas into the heart of the country. In 1840, Jews were granted the right to live anywhere they chose. The next twenty-nine years saw "the period of most rapid urban development for Hungarian Jewry."[2] It was during these years, too, that capitalism developed rapidly. A number of Jews benefited from the new opportunities and became principal factors in Hungarian financial and industrial development. The great majority of them, however, were poor; most "spent their lives tediously eking out pennies to survive."[3] A sizable minority was quite rich, however. Jews were legally emancipated by measures adopted in 1849, 1867, and 1895.

In 1867, Hungary became an autonomous unit within the Austro-Hungarian empire. A heavily agricultural-rural society, it was dominated by a landowning gentry class that ethnically was Magyar. The majority of the country was non-Magyar and consisted of Rumanians, Slovaks, Ruthenians, Serbs, and Croat-Slovenes, most of whom lived in eastern rural provinces. An unrelenting program of Magyarization was undertaken in schools and elsewhere that denigrated the cultures of non-Magyars. In the eastern provinces, Jews as a whole served as advance agents of Magyarization and were regarded as such by the national minorities. Antisemitism was a problem in those areas.

So was it, however, at the national level during the last quarter of the nineteenth century. Here, two classes sustained anti-Jewish sentiments: the lesser nobility whose economic fortunes suffered in the period of industrial development and change in world markets for agricultural products, and the German-speaking bourgeoisie who saw the Jewish business class as their competitors. Between 1882 and 1884, charges of ritual murder were lodged against some Jews, antisemitic demonstrations and riots occurred, and a newly organized antisemitic political party won seventeen seats in Parliament. During the next decade, the Catholic People's party became the principal defender of antisemitism. The party, writes Nathaniel Katzburg, "concentrated its attacks mainly against what it regarded as destructive ideas introduced and disseminated by Jews, such as liberalism, socialism, cosmopolitanism and similar currents of thought, regarded as anti-Christian, unpatriotic and alien to the deep-rooted Magyar tradition."[4]

To help industrialize the country, the government called upon Jewish capitalists who succeeded beyond expectations. Around 1900, "the Jews, though they comprised only some five percent of the population, occupied almost all the key positions in the leading financial sector of the country's economy. They held also about 60 percent of the important posts in a burgeoning industrial establishment and constituted some 50 percent of all persons engaged in trade in the booming capitalist city, Budapest. Even those Jews who lived in villages were the capitalists of the area."[5]

Jews thus served the regime loyally in ethnic and economic affairs and were rewarded by a state policy that stilled rare antisemitic outbursts and opened wide avenues to upward social mobility by Jews. Just before World War I, for example, half the students in the medical school of the University of Budapest were Jews.[6] Assimilation of Jews proceeded apace.

World War I (1914–18) upset this arrangement. Hungary became altogether independent but it lost 64 percent of its area and 60 percent of its population. Aside from a small German minority, the country became almost wholly Magyar, a homogeneity it had never before experienced. With the loss of the eastern lands, Jews were no longer needed as Magyarizers. And with the drastically shrunken economy, both impoverished Magyar nobles as well as a rising Magyar middle class sought to replace Jewish jobholders. A short-lived Communist regime was suppressed in 1919. Because most of its cabinet ministers were Jews, it was denounced as "Jewish" and severe antisemitic riots ensued. Less than a year later, in 1920, a law was passed establishing a quota on Jewish students in universities, although it was not rigidly enforced. In 1928, nevertheless, a new, somewhat moderated measure was passed.

During the 1920s, the aristocratic gentry resumed its rule which had become more antisemitic. Jews saw no alternative to supporting such rule. As Ezra Mendelsohn explains: "All minorities need allies, and in Hungary, which lacked a strong left [after the 1919 events] and which possessed no strategically national minorities, the only possible allies of the Jews who possessed some influence were precisely the moderate antisemites."[7]

Revision of the Trianon peace treaty of 1920 that had carved up Hungary was the most enduring political issue of the various administrations that held office in the 1920s and 1930s. The issue was useful in dampening economic and other internal concerns as well as awakening hope by numerous large landholders that they might some day regain their estates lost in 1920. On the world scene, Hungary sought allies that would help regain the lost territories. Fatefully for the Jews, Nazi Germany proved to be the most reliable of these.

The depression of the 1930s struck Hungary with force and laid a basis for rising antisemitism. Extreme rightists came to the fore. One such, Gyula Gömbös, served as prime minister from 1932 to 1936, being supported by "impoverished lower middle classes, the unemployed academicians and intellectuals, the 'humiliated' officer corps, and the army of civil servants and patriotic refugees from the territories ceded to the Successor States [such as Czechoslovakia and Yugoslavia]."[8] In 1933, close ties with Germany were established. Trade between both countries increased as did German investments in Hungary.

Most menacing to the Jews, however, were the activities of the Nazis inside Hungary. They financed a number of newspapers and successfully organized parties and associations. The Nazi cause bolted forward in 1938 when, after Germans occupied Austria and achieved an Allied diplomatic surrender at Munich, parts of Czechoslovakia's Slovakia and Subcarpathian Rus were returned to Hungary.

Almost at the same time, and not coincidentally, the Hungarian government passed the first of three laws against Jews. The overall goal of the 1938 measure was to reduce Jewish participation in industry and commerce to a one-to-five ratio; the same was to apply in the professions of law, medicine, and engineering, all with large Jewish components. While Jews protested vigorously, the Christian churches publicly supported the measure. (Composer Béla Bartók, not a Jew, attacked the law.) Jews were now defined legally by religion; not since the university quota law of 1920 had such a formal distinction been drawn.

The second law was passed in May 1939. Jews were excluded from all government employment; Jewish teachers were to retire by 1943. A 6 percent Jewish quota was to prevail in the professions and universities. No Jews would be permitted to work as editors, publishers, or directors of plays and movies. Four months later, World War II erupted. In August 1941, the third law was signed. It embodied the Nazi definition of a Jew: a person was Jewish by birth rather than by religion. Intermarriage between Jews and non-Jews was prohibited as were extramarital sexual relations between the two. Passage of the anti-Jewish laws was widely regarded as being, in part, a gift of gratitude to Germany for the returned territories. (In April 1941, Hungary had regained its one-time territory in Yugoslavia.) As Randolph Braham puts it, "The traditional antisemitism of the Christian middle classes was exacerbated by the commensurate increase in their sympathy with the admiration for Nazi Germany, an attitude which was increasingly shared by ever large numbers of industrial workers and peasants."[9]

By mid-1941, Hungarian armed forces were engaged in Yugoslavia and in the Soviet Union where they fought alongside Nazi troops. In July and August, both Hungarian and Soviet Jews in the Ukraine were about to be massacred by local militias when Hungarian soldiers intervened to stop the killing. In other cases, however, both Jews and Serbians in Yugoslavia were massacred by Hungarian troops. (Some Jews were in the Hungarian army while many others served at the front as members of labor-service details. In 1942, call-ups to labor service concentrated on Jews denounced by Christians as "objectionable.") Reports from the front detailed some Hungarian-German conflict over treatment of Jews in the labor service; some of the latter escaped to the Soviet Union and joined partisan groups. Raoul Wallenberg, a Swedish diplomat, helped save thousands of Hungarian Jews by endowing them with emergency passports.

In January 1943, the Red Army destroyed the Second Hungarian Army in Voronezh. The next month Nazi forces were defeated in the titanic Battle of Stalingrad. The eventual end of the war came into sight. Enemies of the Reich took heart while among its supporters disarray began to set in. Hungarian authorities sent out peace feelers and started maneuvering to withdraw their forces from the Russian front. In March 1944, Nazi Germany, fearful that Hungary was about to withdraw from the war, invaded the country without encountering a single shot of resistance.

No military operations were carried out inside Hungary. Instead, preparations began for the transportation of thousands of Jews to the ovens of Auschwitz. Under the direction of Adolf Eichmann some 450,000 Hungarian Jews were shipped there between May 15 and July 8, 1944. This ghastly enterprise was staffed not by Nazi soldiers but by Hungarian personnel acting on order of their own superiors: "The overwhelming majority of the local, district, and county officials, including the civil servants, police, and gendarmerie officers, collaborated fully."[10] Braham explains that "the Hungarians...were basically passive and many of them, intoxicated by the vicious antisemitic propaganda of the past two decades, were eager to share in the wealth expropriated from the Jews."[11] Nowhere else in Europe had the local population cooperated so slavishly. Some Christian churchmen objected but only privately.

For whatever reason, all the Jews sent to Auschwitz came from areas other than Budapest. That city's 250,000 Jews were scheduled to be sent to their deaths on July 10. Three days earlier, however, the Hungarian ruler, Admiral Horthy, ordered the action stopped. In part, he yielded to the deteriorating military situation of the Nazis and their allies and to domestic and foreign opposition to the planned deaths of Budapest Jews. Messages of protest and warning were received from President Franklin D. Roosevelt and the kings of England and Sweden, as well as Pope Pius XII. On July 2 Americans bombed Budapest heavily.

Death was the only indignity spared these Jews. During the summer, book burnings continued. On June 16, 1944, alone, 447,627 books, or the equivalent of twenty-two freight carloads, were burned. Jews were excluded altogether from universities. A number of Jews converted hastily to one or another Christian church.

Late in September, Hungary asked the Soviet Union for an armistice. On October 11, Soviet terms were accepted by Hungary. Four days later Admiral Horthy announced the acceptance publicly and criticized the Nazis while doing so. Immediately, a coup overthrew the Horthy regime. Gangs of thugs roamed the streets slaughtering Jews. Little if anything was done to stop such actions by the new government. Only when Soviet troops entered Budapest on January 17, 1945, were the city's remaining Jews safe. Braham writes straightforwardly: "The Red Army played a determinative role in saving the [250,000] Jews of Budapest and thousands of Jews in the labor service companies.... The liberation of Jews was the consequence of the military operations of the Soviet forces against the Axis rather than the result of a conscious policy of rescue or considerations of humanitarianism."[12]

During World War II, a total of 564,507 Hungarian Jews were killed. Still alive at the end of 1945 were 255,500 Jews. Sharing central responsibility for this slaughter were Hungarian public authorities and Nazi Germany. Not far behind, however, were the Christian churches of Hungary. Churchmen had been at the apex of the antisemitic movement since before 1900. Their unceasing agitation "not only fostered the climate of antisemitism that determined the passivity if not open hostility of the masses, but also shaped the reaction to the Nazis' Final Solution."[13] Church newspapers kept the political atmosphere heated. Many church leaders had acclaimed the advent of Nazi rule in Germany. Churches also favored passage of the first two anti-Jewish laws (1938 and 1939) and opposed the third one (1941) only until Jewish converts were exempted from its provisions. Most bishops, on the other hand, tried to help ease the situation of Jews in the localities. Only three, however, preached publicly against antisemitic outrages. The Vatican, which was fully informed of the Final Solution, intervened privately to stop the killing of Hungarian Jews late in June 1944, only after hundreds of thousands had already been murdered. A number of Catholic priests were later declared war criminals for agitating against the Jews during the war.[14]

A few foreign countries also helped. Some Jews were able to flee the country with the cooperation of Switzerland, Sweden, Portugal, and Turkey. The International Red Cross was tardy in entering rescue work.

The traditional leadership of the Jewish community in Hungary was exceedingly slow to recognize changing conditions and revise its tactics and strategy. During the 1920s, it opposed the world Jewish community making anti-Jewish legislation in Hungary an international issue. Into

the next decade the leadership failed to develop any independent political power and continued to depend on friendly protective action by
the traditional aristocratic gentry. The great mass of Jews was kept in
ignorance by leaders as to the seriousness of the Final Solution and was
thus fatally unprepared to defend itself when the attacks came. German-
appointed Jewish councils administered the machinery of genocide and
were able to ease burdens in only a few cases. Poor Jews were least able
to defend themselves by buying favors and exceptions from German
and Hungarian officials.

After the war, when Hungary's economy was socialized under domestic
Communist leadership and Soviet troops, many Jews—as well as non-
Jews—lost their businesses. A number entered public service, in the party
and other public enterprises such as trade unions and police departments. All anti-Jewish laws were repealed and antidiscriminatory legislation passed. While the peace treaty required the government to provide
"fair compensation" to Jews for their property that had been confiscated
during wartime, this was never carried out. Antisemitic pogroms occurred in 1946 in supposed protest against black marketing and payment
of reparations to Jews who had suffered losses. These protest movements
were also powered by elements of the former governing class whose
property had been nationalized. They identified the new order with the
rising prominence of Jews in public life. At the same time, the Communist party leadership, itself heavily Jewish, failed to condemn pogroms
in Kunmadaras and Miskolc.

In 1948, agreements were concluded between the government and
the Jewish community in which was affirmed the full freedom of worship,
including synagogues, religious books, and seminaries. Jewish organizations were recognized. In 1950, church and state were separated, thus
making Judaism equal to other religions for the first time in Hungarian
history. Jewish cultural life thrived in the form of newspapers, libraries,
and museums as well as in scholarly research on the life and history of
Jews.

In neighboring Poland, antisemitism entered prominently into the
deadly factional struggles within the Communist party but in Hungary
this did not happen. In 1956, when many Hungarians took up arms for
thirteen days against their unpopular government, some Jews feared
the uprising would ignite the flames of antisemitism. This did not happen, not even in Budapest.

Hungary became the least antisemitic country in eastern Europe. Jews
had, and continue to have, the Communist world's only rabbinical sem-
inary, facilities for producing matzohs and selling kosher meat, and
community institutions. According to Paul Lendvai, Jews may enter a
very broad range of employments: "There is no ceiling to their advance-

ment in government service of any kind."[15] Yet, according to Dr. Laszlo Salgo, chief rabbi of Hungary, Jews are not permitted to work as teachers, a prohibition he felt was unexceptionable.[16]

The number of Jews in Hungary fell from 800,000 to 100,000 during the period from 1940 to 1977, from over 5 percent to less than 2 percent of the total population. Jews held many senior positions in the government and the Communist party and so were far more prominent than before the war. Yet antisemitism declined sharply in the same years. It did not, however, disappear. Based on limited public opinion surveys in villages and cities during the late 1960s and early 1970s, Andras Kovacs generalized: "Anti-Jewish prejudices are strongest in the lowest occupational strata and among those with little education; they diminish as one moves up in social level."[17] The intensity of the prejudice—Kovacs says it is no more than this—is quite modest. Writing about a 1967 poll of people in three villages, Lendvai reports that "13 percent would not 'willingly accept' a Jew as a neighbor, 16.3 percent would not like to have a Jewish friend, and 36.3 percent would not accept a Jewish spouse."[18] "Jews," Kovacs comments, "are not afflicted by systematic disadvantages compared to other social groups."[19] It is this sense that post-1945 Hungary departs sharply from its historical traditions.

NOTES

1. Erno Morton, "The Family Tree of Hungarian Jewry. Outline of the History of the Jewish Settlement in Hungary," in Randolph L. Braham, ed., *Hungarian-Jewish Studies* (New York: World Federation of Hungarian Jews, 1966), p. 38.

2. Nathaniel Katzburg, "Hungarian Jewry in Modern Times. Political and Social Aspects," in Braham, ed., *Hungarian-Jewish Studies,* p. 139.

3. W. O. McCagg, Jr., "Jews in Revolutions: The Hungarian Experience," *Journal of Social History,* 6 (Fall 1972), p. 119.

4. Katzberg, "Hungarian Jewry in Modern Times," p. 148.

5. McCagg, "Jews in Revolutions," pp. 80–81.

6. Ezra Mendelsohn, *The Jews of East Central Europe between the World Wars* (Bloomington: Indiana Univ. Press, 1983), p. 92.

7. Ibid., p. 110.

8. Randolph L. Braham, *The Politics of Genocide. The Holocaust in Hungary,* 1 (New York: Columbia Univ. Press, 1981), p. 52.

9. Ibid., p. 199.

10. Ibid., p. 414.

11. Ibid., p. 431.

12. Ibid., p. 1118.

13. Ibid., p. 1027.

14. Bela Vago, "The Destruction of the Jews of Transylvania," in Braham, ed., *Hungarian-Jewish Studies,* p. 193.

15. Paul Lendvai, *Anti-Semitism without Jews. Communist Eastern Europe* (Garden City, N.Y.: Doubleday, 1971), p. 321.

16. *Chicago Sun-Times*, November 3, 1977 (reprinted from the *Manchester Guardian*).

17. Andras Kovacs, "The Jewish Question in Contemporary Hungary," *Telos*, 58 (Winter 1983–84), p. 70.

18. Lendvai, *Anti-Semitism without Jews*, p. 322.

19. Kovacs, "The Jewish Question in Contemporary Hungary," p. 67.

8

TWO DESTINIES IN ONE LAND: ITALY

> As late as 1848, there was hardly a country in Europe where the restrictions placed upon the Jews were more galling [than in Italy]; twenty-two years later there was no part of the world where religious freedom was more real, or religious prejudice so small.
>
> —Meir Michaelis, 1978

Italy has been two homes for Jews: a troublesome place where, despite residence since the early days of the Roman Republic, they were frequently subjected to terror and oppression; and a modern country in which their civil status was exemplary and antisemitism all but absent. No simple dividing line separates the two.

In post-Roman Italy most Jews lived in Rome, the center of the Catholic church, and in Sicily which was conquered by the Muslims in the ninth century. In the late twelfth century there were no more than 40,000 Jews in a country of about 8 million inhabitants. In Sicily they lived largely without the insecurity Jews felt in other Western countries. Many were involved in trade. After the Muslims were ejected, Jews continued their customary pursuits. In the thirteenth century Jews were brought from Africa by the Sicilian crown and given land on which they raised indigo and henna, plants that yielded dyes that were in great demand in the growing textile industry. Most Sicilian Jews, poor laborers and artisans, were not the economic envy of their Christian neighbors. Under Spanish rule, occasional violence against Jews broke out in the late fifteenth century. In 1492–93, the Spanish banished all Jews from Sicily. Roman Jews were, in the main, exceedingly poor and played a very minor role in economic and political affairs.

Until the fifteenth century, Italian Jews were not subjected to general antisemitic onslaughts such as characterized other European countries.

They generally were treated as citizens and their place in the social structure was not exceptional: "The upper classes ... tended to be consistently friendly; the bourgeoisie considered their economic interests to be threatened by Jewish competition, and were correspondingly stern; while the populace swayed uncertainly between the two extremes in accordance with the prevailing mood."[1]

Fanatical friars preached hatred of Jews with increasing success. In 1475, the church sanctioned a blood libel in Trent, that is, it accepted as true a charge that Jews had used Christian blood to prepare Passover matzoh. Pope Sixtus IV eased restrictions on Jews and reined in some of the preaching friars. Localized and short-term disorders against Jews continued in the early sixteenth century. In 1516, Venice created a ghetto, that is, a segregated residential area for Jews which was closed off from the rest of the city by an iron gate.

The Protestant Reformation effected a fundamental change in the treatment of Jews in Italy. In 1542 Pope Paul III, founder of the Jesuit order, authorized the Inquisition which shortly became the scourge of Jewry in the Western world. In 1555, Pope Paul IV issued a papal bull that Roth characterizes as "one of the landmarks in the history of human persecution."[2] It was to apply in Italy and the rest of western Europe.

The bull required segregation by street or by a quarter that had a single entrance and a single exit. There could be only one synagogue in each city; all others had to be destroyed. Jews could own no real estate; any that they had had to be sold to Christians. Jews were to wear a badge and could not employ Christian wetnurses or servants. They were not to associate with Christians on familiar terms nor could they bear any title of civil honor. Jewish physicians could not attend Christians. Loan banks operated by Jews would be regulated. They could not buy or sell wheat or any necessity of life. They were, however, specifically permitted to deal in used clothing.

The bull was implemented fully in the Papal States. Marranos, or converted Jews who secretly continued to observe their original faith, were burned alive. Printed books in Hebrew were made illegal: "In the spring of 1559, more than 10,000 volumes were committed to the flames in Cremona alone."[3] Some of the bull's prohibitions were retracted by Pius IV, Paul's successor. But his successor, Pius V, restored some provisions and added many more. Jews were expelled from most Papal States and hounded from place to place. Lending at interest by Jews was outlawed but such lending by Christians, though also illegal, continued. After heavy bribes paid by wealthy Jews, in 1586, Pope Sixtus V issued a bull on Christian piety under which Jews were allowed to return to the Papal States. They could, in fact, live anywhere, they could employ Christian servants, and they could practice medicine freely.

Since half of Italy's Jews lived in Rome and another one-quarter to one-third in the Papal States, papal declarations of policy were exceedingly important to them and to Jews in other parts of the country. As Cecil Roth summarizes: "By the end of the first quarter of the seventeenth century, the Ghetto and all the accompanying degradation had been introduced into nearly all the cities of those parts of Italy where Jews were now allowed to live—complete segregation, the red or yellow badge, exclusion from honorable callings, the forced sermon, the censorship of literature, the House of Catechumens, and all the rest."[4] Jewish shops were confined to the ghetto, retailers could sell only to other Jews, who were forbidden to enter any organized craft or manufacturing; nor could they employ Christian labor. Tailoring became a prime Jewish employment.

Jews were almost powerless against abuses. Pope Benedict XIV ruled that baptism of abducted Jewish children was binding. Jews were compelled to attend sermons by churchmen. In university towns Christian students could, on the first snowfall, bombard Jews with snowballs. Systematic, outright pogroms, however, seldom occurred. Italian Christians seemed not to take papal prohibitions on day-to-day interaction with Jews too seriously.

The low point in treatment of the Jews came with the issuance of a forty-four-clause bull by Pope Pius VI in 1775. It resurrected all the oppressive enactments by previous pontiffs. Roth writes of "this appalling code, which has been termed one of the most inhuman acts in the history of man."[5] Within the Papal States, at least, the prohibitions were enforced with exactitude. Six years later, the enlightened despot Austrian King Joseph II lightened the burdens on Jews living in Italian cities under his rule. It was not until fifteen more years passed that a basic change was wrought all over the land.

In 1796, Napoleon Bonaparte's armies invaded Italy. They ordered the ghetto walls torn down and religious discrimination was abolished. Jews for the first time could run for public office and serve in the Civil Guard. The declaration creating the Napoleonic Cisalpine Republic proclaimed: "The Jews are citizens, and must be recognized as such in society." In Mantua and Venice, the next year, Jews and Christians demolished ghetto gates. Between 1798 and 1800, while the Napoleonic armies were in Egypt, however, there were widespread physical attacks on Jews in an effort to reverse the tide. The intensity of their fury was without precedent. After Napoleon returned, in 1800, the attacks ceased and for the next fourteen years Jews were integrated into civic and social life. Discriminatory laws passed during the two-year interim were allowed to expire.

Jews bought land, entered the professions, and sent their children to public schools, open to them for the first time. Public authorities protected Jews from physical attacks. A representative body of Jews was created. All this disappeared during the reaction that followed Napoleon's defeat in 1814. Throughout Italy Jews were flung back to the status of unequal subject rather than equal citizen. Conditions were worst in the Papal States where the Inquisition was revitalized. In 1826, Pope Leo XII reinstated the provisions of the 1775 bull that had oppressed the Jews so severely. Jewish students were excluded from public schools and universities.

Despite this abrupt diminution of rights, Jews from the 1820s through the 1840s played a prominent role in the nationalist movement which sought to unify Italy's numerous states and to become independent of foreign, especially Austrian, domination. The liberal movement, dedicated to equality for all Italians, became a de facto advocate of Jewish equality. In 1846, even Pope Pius IX was moved to moderate the anti-Jewish regulations a predecessor had proclaimed two decades earlier. During the nationalist revolution of 1848–49, once more ghetto gates were pulled down by popular mobs. While the revolution failed in its primary aims of unity and independence, certain enduring gains were made toward Jewish emancipation.

In 1848, for example, the government of Piedmont proclaimed an "Edict of Emancipation" which granted civil rights to Jews and other non-Catholics and abrogated anti-Jewish laws. Jews were now allowed to attend universities in that state. After the revolution of 1848, Piedmont retained its enlightened laws. In 1859, Austrian rule was overthrown and Jewish rights were established. Two years later the Kingdom of Italy was proclaimed under the advanced Piedmontese constitution. Elsewhere in the country, however, reaction ruled. Not until 1870 was Rome occupied and declared part of a united Italy. Within days, all religious disabilities were abolished. "The liberation of Italy and of Italian Jewry were completed by the same stroke," writes Roth.[6] Thus, Italian Jews did not bear a label of "foreigner." They shared everything but religion with their fellow Italians. According to Roth, "there was no part of the world where religious freedom was more real, or religious prejudice so small."[7]

In the years 1870 to 1918, Jews as a whole prospered. They participated across a wide political spectrum. In economic life they became more middle class than ever. A Jew served as prime minister in 1909. The cultural contribution of Jews was immense, given their small numbers. In 1861, Jewish illiteracy was only one-tenth that of the rest of the country. (In 1930, when Jews made up one-tenth of 1 percent of the population, one-twelfth of all university professors were Jewish.) Jewishness seemed to have become a social irrelevancy.

The rise of Italian fascism under Benito Mussolini immediately after World War I attracted support from a number of Jews. In 1922, 750 Jews belonged to the Fascist party, 1,770 more by 1928, and an additional

4,800 by 1933. Among honored Fascist martyrs and pioneers were prominent Jews including Aldo Finzi. Michael Ledeen gives further particulars: "As time passed, Jewish participation in the Fascist state continued to be quite active, from the highest rungs of the Army and Navy to the Ministry of Finance. Outside the Government, such figures as Gino Olivetti at the head of the *Cofindustria* added to the impressive list of Jewish figures in Fascism's elite circles."[8]

There was nothing "Jewish" about fascism. Jewish anti-Fascists quite likely outnumbered Jewish Fascists. Roth mentions the nationalism of fascism as one attraction for Jews. But he also adds that the Fascist party "was anti-socialist, and the Italian Jews were now pre-eminently members of the bourgeoisie."[9] Class was a powerful factor in political affiliation both for Jews and non-Jews.

Mussolini had used antisemitic arguments against Russian Communists during 1917–18 but dropped these upon complaints by Jewish Fascists. During the ensuing years, he failed to bring up the issue, sensing its lack of general appeal. As a result, Italy remained unusually free of open antisemitism. Jewish students in Hungary, Rumania, and Poland who were increasingly barred from universities in their homelands were welcomed in Italy. Indeed, they were offered scholarships, lowered fees, and reduced fares.

Mussolini, however, was playing a double game. Publicly, he continued to avoid any expression of antisemitism. Privately, however, he promoted antisemitism in two ways. First, he wrote anonymous articles in which, according to Meir Michaelis, "he gave repeated vent to his irritation against the Jews."[10] Second, he privately encouraged rabidly antisemitic Fascist publicists such as Giovanni Preziosi and directed the Fascist press into antisemitic forays. In addition, Mussolini saw to it that Jews were kept out of controlling positions in the party and government. On the other hand, "under Fascism the number of Jewish university teachers continued to be disproportionately high, and so did the number of Jewish generals and admirals."[11]

In 1934, police arrested sixteen anti-Fascists, fourteen of whom were Jewish. The press dwelt on the latter point. In a controlled press, this action was ominous. The same year, Italian delegates to an international Fascist conference signed a declaration tinged with antisemitism. Yet in 1935, when Nazi troops occupied the Saar, Mussolini arranged for Jews there to leave safely.

Mussolini's plans for the conquest of Ethiopia required peace in Europe, but Hitler's foreign policy campaign tended to destabilize the European scene. Antisemitic tirades in the Italian press were toned down. The attack on Ethiopia was launched in 1935. As the League of Nations voted sanctions—however sweepingly they were evaded—Mussolini was driven to seek German support which was freely given. During 1936–

37, antisemitic campaigns in Italy took on a new virulence. In 1937 Mussolini apparently was converted to the Nazi theory of racial anti-semitism as embodied in the Nuremberg Laws of 1935.

In 1938, Mussolini released his "Manifesto of the Race" in which Italians were proclaimed Aryans and Jews as not part of the Italian "race." Pope Pius XI publicly attacked the declaration. Just preceding issuance of the "Manifesto" some Jews had been fired from the civil service and higher education and the Fascist militia discharged some high-ranking Jewish officers.

After the "Manifesto," however, all this was done systematically. A Jew was defined as an issue of Jewish parents. All Jews were excluded from teaching and none could enter officially recognized schools or colleges. Exemptions from racial laws were granted to honored Fascists and decorated veterans. Jewish organizations, including schools, were permitted to operate. Jewish converts to Catholicism could send their children to Catholic schools.

When World War II began in 1939, antisemitic measures were strengthened. In 1940, needy Jewish couples were ruled ineligible for marriage loans. Jewish scholars were excluded from libraries and archives. When the Vatican made some of these scholars welcome, Fascist thugs attacked persons peddling Vatican newspapers. Italian entry into the war in June 1940 unleashed a full-scale attack on Jews. All Jewish bank accounts were blocked. Foreign Jews and "dangerous" Jews were interned. All Jews in Sicily and Sardinia were expelled. Roman Jewry, many of whom were peddlers, were seriously harmed when their licenses were withdrawn. (Later, they were reinstated.) By the end of 1940, writes Michaelis, "it was estimated that no less than half of Italy's Jews had lost their means of earning a livelihood."[12]

When, at the end of 1940, Italian forces suffered setbacks in Libya, anti-British riots broke out in three large Italian cities; shortly, they became antisemitic riots. During 1941–42 antisemitic incidents broke out in Trieste. In mid-1942 all Jews aged eighteen to fifty-five were mobilized for forced labor. Jews in Turin, Milan, and Genoa were deported to South Tyrol and their possessions were confiscated. Many similar indignities were suffered by Jews. They were not, however, altogether abandoned.

The Fascist party expelled more than 1,000 *pietisti* for compassion with oppressed Jews. And the mayors of Florence and Padua were deposed for implementing the racial decrees too slowly. Sympathetic non-Jews sometimes demonstrated at railway stations when Jews were sent to work as forced labor. Jewish internees were not maltreated in camps and prisons.

During 1942, when Axis military reverses started to mount, Italians more freely criticized the alliance with Germany; some top Italian Fascists also grew restive. The Jews were direct beneficiaries of these changes. When Italian troops occupied new areas, Jews in those places were left alone. In Michaelis's words: "Not content with protecting the Jews in their own zone of occupation, the Italians did their best to help those in the German-occupied areas.... In addition to intervening on behalf of their own Jewish nationals, the Italian diplomatic and consular representatives in Eastern Europe tried to aid and protect non-Italian Jews until they themselves were arrested or expelled."[13]

Leon Poliakov, the future historian of European antisemitism, described the situation in occupied France during 1942–1943: "During this period the 'Italian Zone' became for the Jews of all of France an oasis of peace and security. Not only did the Italian authorities not indulge in any kind of anti-Jewish activity, but they prevented by force the attempts of the Vichy administration to carry out the arrests and internments prescribed by Vichy.... It is the imperishable glory of Italy that in all circles and in all administrative divisions there was evident, from the start, a tenacious resistance to the racial policy and its consequences."[14]

Near the end of July 1943, the king dismissed Mussolini and arrested him. In September the Nazis occupied the country and remained in the north—the main area of Jewish residence—until June 1944 when American forces liberated Rome. Mussolini, who had been freed by the Nazis, became the puppet ruler over the Nazi-created Salo Republic. In November, the Salo government ordered the arrest and interning of all Jews; in the next month certain exemptions were made. In January 1944 all Jews' wealth was sequestered; some Jews were sent to the death camps. By March it had become exceedingly difficult for Jews to earn a living. Meanwhile, the SS, in June 1943, had slaughtered Jews in the summer resorts of Lago Maggiore. During the summer and fall of 1943 preparations were made for the Final Solution in Italy. Nazi leaders concocted a scheme, instead, to collect a gold ransom for the Jews who contributed enough to buy 50 kilograms worth of gold. Payment was made late in September. In about two weeks, nevertheless, thousands of Jews were arrested by the Nazis and sent to Auschwitz.

The Catholic church, as we have seen, had opposed Mussolini's racist policy of antisemitism. When, in 1943, the Nazis occupied Rome, they decided not to take over the Vatican. Thereupon Pope Pius XII directed that Jews be given refuge. Nearly 5,000 were saved by this means. Many more owed their lives to their Christian neighbors who made them welcome in a moment of supreme need. As Michaelis writes, the Jews "could count on the sympathy of the Italian masses."[15] Catholic clergy would generally help, too. Many Fascist officials aided. Most surprising, "there were quite a few Germans in the...[Salo] Republic—diplomats and scholars, soldiers and policemen—who joined with the Italians in sabotaging the anti-Jewish policy."[16]

After the creation of the State of Israel in 1948, the Italian government adopted a strongly pro-Israel policy. It was, however, over that same country that the most serious postwar crisis of antisemitism arose in Italy. When Israeli forces invaded Lebanon in June 1982, left-wing groups led by the Communist party severely criticized the action. That same month, in connection with a general strike in Rome, about 200,000 striking workers paraded through the city. When they came abreast the Great Synagogue marchers dropped a coffin and shouted, "Murderous Jews, Jews to the ovens!" After the massacre of Muslims by Christian militia in the Sabra and Shatila camps of Lebanon, organized workers in Italy refused to handle El Al planes and Israeli ships. In September 1982 the pope granted PLO (Palestine Liberation Organization) leader Yasser Arafat a special audience, despite angry protests by Italian Jews. The next month, three bombs exploded at the Great Synagogue, killing an infant and injuring thirty-four persons. Jews conducted a three-day protest. Twenty-thousand persons attended the funeral of the dead infant. Elio Toaff, chief rabbi of Rome, described the event: "Not a voice was heard during the entire procession, from the hospital to the synagogue." In retrospect, Toaff observed: "The dignified stand of the Jews of Rome caused a complete cessation of antisemitic propaganda in Italy. There are no longer articles in the papers against the State of Israel, and no longer does one hear on radio or see on TV terrible reports directed against us."[17]

Somewhat after this, persons described as "radical leftist youths" threw Molotov cocktails at the Tripolitanian synagogue; two were arrested. Rabbi Toaff described one consequence: "As a result, heads of the workers' organizations, the mayor and the regional leader visited the congregation. They asked to speak with me in order to discuss measures to prevent the danger of antisemitism in all areas of life in Italy."[18] Luciano Lama, secretary-general of the principal labor federation and a leading Communist, denied Rabbi Toaff's charge that the Communist party had become antisemitic. He, however, invited the rabbi to conduct a study day on the subject; it went on for over nine hours.

During the past 150 years or so, popular antisemitism has been almost unknown in Italy. This was true under constitutional monarchy, liberal democracy, and fascism. The small number of Jews could not explain it as they had also constituted a tiny minority in the horrendous eighteenth century and earlier. More impressive was the success of Italians in resisting church-inspired antisemitism, especially before World War I. The momentary eruption of antisemitism in the early 1980s profoundly embarrassed the nation.

NOTES

1. Cecil Roth, *The History of the Jews in Italy* (Philadelphia: Jewish Publication Society of America, 1946), p. 155.

2. Ibid., p. 295.

3. Ibid., p. 304.

4. Ibid., p. 328.

5. Ibid., p. 415.

6. Ibid., p. 473.

7. Ibid., p. 475.

8. Michael A. Ledeen, "The Evolution of Italian Fascist Antisemitism," *Jewish Social Studies,* 37/38 (1975), p. 4.

9. Roth, *History of the Jews in Italy,* p. 509.

10. Meir Michaelis, *Mussolini and the Jews. German-Italian Relations and the Jewish Question in Italy, 1922–1945* (Oxford: Clarendon Press, 1978), p. 30.

11. Ibid., p. 52.

12. Ibid., p. 292.

13. Ibid., pp. 313, 321.

14. Leon Poliakov, "Mussolini and the Extermination of the Jews," *Jewish Social Studies,* 11/12 (1949–50), p. 250.

15. Ibid., p. 387.

16. Ibid., pp. 386–87.

17. *Forum on the Jewish People, Zionism and Israel,* 49 (Summer 1983), p. 47.

18. Ibid., p. 47.

9

THE CONTINUITY OF OPPRESSION: POLAND

Towards the end of the nineteenth century, parallel with the growth of nationalism, Polish antisemitism became vehement, reaching in the 1930s, and even after the catastrophic experience of the Second World War, psychopathic proportions and an intensity which, except in Nazi Germany, is probably without precedent in the history of the Jewish people.

—Joseph Marcus, 1983

Despite the general virulence of Polish antisemitism the country's traditions were broad enough to contain elements encouraging to Jews. Welcomed, indeed invited, by various authorities, initial relations of Pole and Jew were cooperative. In time, Europe's largest Jewish population developed the most elaborate set of Jewish community institutions and practices. The Nazi death camps all but erased this heritage from the face of the earth.

Poland was Christianized in 966, at a time when Jews already lived there. The first ones came from the Khazar state of Russia and Kievan Rus. Late in the eleventh century, Jews fleeing from persecution in southern and western Europe arrived. Not, however, until the fifteenth century did large numbers of Jews begin to live in Poland. During these years, Polish rulers invited German merchants to locate in the country, there to live principally in the few cities. The Germans brought along with them their severely anti-Jewish sentiments, not unrelated to commercial competition between German and Jewish merchants.

Before 966, no legal distinctions existed between Jews and non-Jews. Only 300 years later did the Polish state begin to enact such measures. On the protective side, in 1264, King Boleslaw the Pious issued the country's first charter establishing the rights of Jews. With an eye toward outrages against Jews in the West, Boleslaw's charter addressed the issue of Christians charging Jews with ritual murder of Christian children. Six witnesses, half Jews, were required to prove such charges. In the absence of such evidence, the accuser could be put to death. Jewish moneylenders were protected in vindicating financial claims. And the charter set up many protections for the personal security of Jews.

Three years later, on the negative side, a synod of the Polish Roman Catholic church, under the guidance of papal legate Cardinal Presbyter Guido, ordered that Christians stop having any close social relations with Jews. They were not to eat meals together nor dance at Jewish weddings. Residential segregation was also decreed, with fences to surround the Jewish quarters. Jews were excluded from Christian bath houses and they were required to wear distinctive headgear. Before adoption of the measure, writes Simon Dubnov acerbically, "the native population, which medieval culture, with its religious intolerance and class prejudice, had not yet had time to 'train' properly, lived at peace with the Jews."[1] Similarly, as Adam Vetulani points out, the introduction to the declaration "stressed that Poland was a country recently conquered by Christianity and it was especially important to instil this awareness in the faithful."[2]

Antagonism toward Jews was thus regarded as a vital part of the Christian heritage. The Polish clergy, trained principally in France and northern Italy, tended to import the system of religious antisemitism as part of the legal and doctrinal structure of the Church. According to Vetulani, however, "the anti-Jewish provisions remained dead letters in Poland up to the 15th century...[and] found no echo in the Polish provincial statutes in the 13th and 14th centuries."[3]

The fifteenth century brought success to the efforts by churchmen. In 1399, fifteen Jews in Posen were burned at the stake, an early if not the first recorded instance of religious persecution in the country. They were charged with desecration of the host. Dubnov explains the onslaught as emanating from Christian city dwellers who envied the prosperity of some Jews in Posen and wanted to dispose of these competitors. In 1454, the Church convinced the king to revoke the grant of rights to Jews and to reactivate the restrictive anti-Jewish proscriptions of 1267. Attacks on Jews were recorded in Cracow during 1463 and 1494.

A great many Jews expelled from Spain in 1492 emigrated to Poland. While their treatment there was far better, the oppressive institutions of Catholicism gradually took root in Poland, as they had in Italy during the sixteenth century as part of the Counter-Reformation. In the new schools founded by the Jesuit order antisemitism was a prime subject of instruction. Pogroms were often led by students from these schools. "Based on malicious fabrications," writes Dubnov, "ritual murder trials become endemic during this period, and assume an ominous, inquisitorial character."[4] Many earlier Jewish immigrants from Germany and central Europe generally came from urban places where they had business and financial experience. These, especially, were the targets of commercial countermeasures disguised as religious conflicts.

Jews, however, continued to flock to Poland where they performed highly useful economic services for noble and royal circles. In return they gained a secure civic status more or less as equals of other immigrants and as freemen rather than mere subjects in the west European style. The Polish gentry, or *Szlachta,* and church prelates employed Jews as estate managers and as toll farmers, that is, collectors of feudal dues and taxes. Neither role endeared the Jew to the peasants. Little antisemitism lay behind such attitudes, however. (In contemporary France, for example, where all tax collectors were Christians, peasants were known to attack those who tried too zealously to collect charges of one kind or another.) Some Jews also lent money to their lords. The absence of a native-born business class underscored the role of estate Jews who made up nearly three-quarters of all Polish Jews by the mid-eighteenth century.

The Polish state and church during the fifteenth through eighteenth centuries were more eager to suppress minority Christian churches than to eliminate Judaism. Attacks were not uncommon against Protestants, Orthodox, and dissenting Catholics. Intermixed with these issues were those of subject nationalities, especially of the Ukrainians. Because Jews were identified with the Polish landowners and oppressors, minorities tended to consider them enemies.

The mid-seventeenth century brought an unparalled disaster to the Jews of Poland. It might, with justice, be called a pre-Holocaust. Nearly half the country's Jews—and one-fifth of the world's total—were killed as were many Poles; both groups fought as allies against unrestrained attacks by Cossacks, Ukrainians, and Crimean Tatars. Bernard Weinryb describes the events as "a war of extermination."[5]

In 1648, Cossacks led a movement that became a revolt for independence from Poland by Ukrainian peasants headed by Bogdan Chmielnicki. At times, Russia became an ally. Dubnov characterized the "unbridled bestiality" and "frightful tortures" used on Poles and Jews.[6] These included skinning persons alive. Many Jews converted to Christianity and thus escaped death. Soon after the fighting stopped, most if not all such converts reverted to Judaism. During the first half of the eighteenth century Cossacks led repeated attacks on Jews and punished by death the hiding of Jews by peasants or Greek Orthodox priests.

Around the same time a general heightening of antisemitism was apparent. Local officials of the central government, pledged to protect Jewish rights, became instead extorters of Jews, levying heavy fines and other collective charges on them. A closer alliance than ever developed between the Catholic clergy and Christian merchants and artisans.

Church synods grew more malignant toward Jews. Numerous trials were staged in which Jews were accused of various evil deeds, often involving the killing of Christian children. Dubnov refers to "the clerical party, which sometimes even took a direct hand in arranging the settings of the crime, by throwing dead bodies in the yard of Jews."[7] The *Szlachta* became ever more opportunistic toward estate Jews and degraded their status to the point that the latter little resembled Jewish freemen of the sixteenth century.

Within their own religious communities, Jews lived under increasingly difficult circumstances of their own making: "The Jewish plutocracy followed the example of the Polish pans [lords] in exploiting the poor laboring masses," writes Dubnov. "The rabbinate, like the Polish clergy, catered to the rich. The secular and the ecclesiastic oligarchy, which controlled the Kahal [Jewish self-government], victimized the community by a shockingly disproportionate assessment of state and communal taxes, throwing the main burden on the impecunious classes, and thus bringing them to the verge of ruin."[8]

In 1772 the process of dismantling the Polish state began, continuing in 1793, and concluding two years later. Most Jews belonged to the part of Poland that was acquired by Russia. This remained the case until 1918 when Poland was reconstituted as an independent state. (For events during 1795–1918, see chapter 11.)

Independent Poland between the world wars (1918–39) was the scene of a sweeping growth of antisemitism. Fanned by government and political forces, the flames of Jew-hatred were ignited by a broad range of Poles who drew on deep sources.

The years right after World War I and during the war with Soviet Russia (1918–21) saw widespread pogroms. As Ezra Mendelsohn reports, "during the Polish-Soviet war the Polish government went so far as to intern in a concentration camp Jewish officers serving as volunteers in the Polish army, thus demonstrating to the public at large that it regarded all Jews as potential traitors."[9] In 1919, the Polish government signed a Minorities Treaty which obliged it to establish public elementary schools taught in a language other than Polish if a language-minority group of Polish residents requested it. This was in fact done, but not for the Jews who requested it repeatedly in vain. The League of Nations was unable to remedy this.

No level of government employed Jews in the official bureaucracy. They could teach in private Jewish secondary schools and a few worked in public elementary schools. In the mid-1930s, when the central government took over a number of industries, one of the first actions was to discharge all Jewish employees. This happened, for example, in the tobacco industry.

Jews were all but excluded from employment in non-Jewish-owned private industry. Jewish manufacturers also hired few Jews; they disliked the greater tendency of Jewish workers to unionize. Two out of five Jews lived in economically backward eastern Poland where they shared extreme poverty with their Christian neighbors. In the country as a whole Jews could be found disproportionately in petty trade, including peddling. In 1929, more than one-fourth of all Jews were so employed. Over half of these employed no one. Because Jewish workers were shut out of industry, they tended to labor in small shops which were not covered by unemployment insurance or other social benefits. Worse yet, in 1929 Jews were four times more likely to be unemployed than non-Jews. As a last resort, many unemployed Jewish workers became homeworkers, opening "shops" in their houses, employing even poorer employees, and exploiting them to the hilt. These homeworkers were, in turn, squeezed by contractors in search of the lowest production costs.

The class structure of Polish Jewry grew more lopsided during the interwar years. Joseph Marcus reports: "0.1 of Jewish income recipients, or about 1,000 families, received about 5.5 percent of the Jewish population's total income . . . and most of this accrued to about 1,000 families. . . . There was a deep gulf between a small minority at the top, and a large mass of people at the bottom."[10]

The upper reaches of the Jewish community were occupied by bankers and bank managers, industrialists, large-scale merchants, and physicians, lawyers, and other professionals. Non-Jewish Poles who aspired to these positions formed the core of the urban antisemitic trend. During the 1930s, the national government joined these Poles in assaults on the business stratum of Jewish society.

Jews were excluded from bidding on public contracts. A Sunday-rest law was passed to compel Jewish businesses to close on Sunday even if they had done so on Saturday to observe their Sabbath. Under government guidance, numerous cartels were formed after 1918. These monopolistic alliances of many formerly competing firms threatened smaller competitors in industry in commerce. Jews were excluded from membership in the cartels. After 1933, especially, Jewish-owned firms felt the competition. Taxes on commerce affected Jews heavily because petty traders were licensed by the state. In time, Jewish licensees were forbidden to trade in commodities produced by state-owned firms. Examinations for renewal of licenses in 1927 began to be offered only in Polish; a number of elderly Jewish traders were unable to read Polish and thus lost their licenses. In 1936, the Ministry of Commerce ordered "that signs on stores and establishments carry the name of the owners (as they appeared on birth certificates). . . . It made it easier for customers to avoid Jewish enterprises."[11]

Antisemitism swept over higher education. Already in 1923, universities adopted a *numerus clausus* or quota on Jewish enrollment. From

1921–22 to 1938–39, the number of Jewish university students fell by more than half while the number of non-Jewish students rose by three-quarters.[12] Constituting 9.8 percent of the entire population, Jews' proportion of university enrollment over these years fell from roughly one-fourth to one-twelfth. In 1935, some universities started requiring Jewish students to sit in a separate section of classrooms on so-called "ghetto benches." Virtually all refused to do so and chose to stand along a wall. Two years later, ghetto benches were required by the rectors of nearly every university.

Jewish students were subjected to other indignities. During the mid-1930s, they were forbidden to dissect non-Jewish corpses in university laboratories. Celia Heller provides graphic details: "Jewish students were heckled, humiliated, and attacked by some of their Polish fellow students and helpers from anti-Jewish terrorist groups outside the university.... Toughs invaded the classrooms and laboratories and forcibly removed Jewish students."[13]

During the 1930s, full-scale pogroms broke out in Poland. In June 1935 a pogrom, the first since 1920, erupted in Grodno. Soon, another one occurred in Odrzywol. According to Marcus, "there were hundreds of violent attacks on Jews in the second half of 1935."[14] In March 1936, a pogrom occurred in Przytyk. The Jews who were attacked were found guilty and punished severely. Open attacks on the streets became ordinary events. As Jacob Lestschinsky remarks, "Polish antisemites avoided the Russian model of a concentrated attack, limited in time," preferring the use of "sporadic murders, of assaults with knife, blackjack and bomb on Jewish businesses, of picketing of Jewish stores, spreading terror in the market and panic in the village and establishing ghettos at the fairs.... The Polish form was intended to induce emigration, to force Jews to abandon their stores, market stalls, workshops and medical and law practices."[15] Nevertheless, during 1936–38, a number of pogroms were recorded.

Jews resisted, alone where necessary and in league with allies whenever possible. The courts were asked to order the enforcement of protective statutes but they responded weakly. The Bund, a Jewish socialist group, organized two militias. As Heller described their work: "They patrolled parks and streets where Jews were being attacked by the nationalist hooligans. When terror reached the universities, members of youth militia waited nearby to teach the hooligans a lesson."[16] While private militias were illegal, their existence buoyed the spirits of Jews. In addition to the Bund, the Zionist-Socialists, the Pioneering Youth organizations, and the Communists had armed defense squads whose members were trained. So-called "physical fitness" courses which secretly drilled such squads were organized by the Movement for Labor Palestine.[17] A Jewish woman recalled that in Tarnow, during the mid-1920s, "The Jewish youth organized itself into groups for self-protection. My uncles would often come home with bloody noses and torn clothes but they always boasted that the attackers did not get away easily either."[18]

The only political parties that attacked antisemitism were those of the Left, principally the Polish Socialist party and the Communist party. Socialist workers often joined in with Jewish militias and armed groups to protect Jews from physical attack. Isolated Polish intellectuals also defended Jews against their detractors. As a consequence, in the last years before World War II, Jews moved to the left in politics. Marcus suggests the scale of this shift: "It seems likely . . . that in Warsaw and Lodz, at the end of 1938, the proportion of Jews who voted for socialist parties was as high as 80 percent—a higher percentage than socialists had ever received at free elections in any large town in the world."[19] Socialism seemed a constructive alternative to fascism.

The advent of the world depression of the 1930s and the coming to power of the Nazis in 1933 moved Polish politics sharply to the right. In 1934, Poland and Nazi Germany signed a ten-year nonaggression treaty and a trade agreement. The same year Poland denounced its Minority Treaty, signed in 1919. The pact had been a dead letter for years as far as Jews were concerned. Rightist forces were failing to lead the country toward solutions to problems of unemployment in the cities and land reform in the countryside. The attractiveness of antisemitism grew in proportion as their governing effectively shrank. One government after another moved closer to Nazi Germany as each found new ways to deprive Jews of their dignity and livelihood, let alone their safety.

The Catholic church was in the front ranks of antisemitism. When attacks on Jews were at their height, during the 1930s, church officials chimed in. Catholic worshippers received pastoral letters calling on them to join anti-Jewish boycotts. A pastoral letter by Cardinal Hlond endorsed the campaign to isolate Jews economically but warned against violence. A more resounding endorsement was issued by the archbishop of Cracow, later cardinal, Adam Sapieha. Heller writes of "the vehement antisemitic preaching of the Polish clergy."[20]

Franciscan monk Maximilian Maria Kolbe, canonized in 1982 as St. Maximilian, edited several church-sponsored newspapers during the 1920s and 1930s. In 1926 he wrote that Freemasons were "an organized clique of fanatical Jews, who want to destroy the church." Thirteen years later he described the origin of "atheistic communism" as "that criminal mafia that calls itself Freemasonry, and the hand that is guiding all that toward a clear goal is international Zionism." In 1934, as boycotts of Jewish businesses spread, Kolbe advised, "It would be better not to speak so much about the necessity of a systematic removal of Jews, but rather to contribute to the multiplication of Polish businesses, which would lead more speedily to the goal."[21] In 1936, he declared, "We have said many a time that the struggle against the influence of world Jewry and the Jews' economic supremacy must be waged in Poland for the good of all—in the name of the interests of the Polish nation and of Western, Christian civilization." That same year he wrote that "pornography, divorce, fraud and corruption are, for the most part, Jewish specialties. The poisoning of young souls is the work of Jewish agents." Occasionally, Kolbe also cautioned Catholic editors "not to accidentally arouse or deepen hatred in readers who are already hostile" to Jews.[22] There is little reason to regard Kolbe's views as at all exceptional among Catholic churchmen of his time.

Antisemitism among east European peasantries is usually taken for granted, especially when one also considers the traditional church influence in rural areas. This did not hold true in Poland, for the most part. Antisemitism was strongest in the cities and towns of Poland, particularly in middle-class circles. In the countryside, the Catholic church constituted one of the largest landowners, reluctant to effect land reforms that might reduce its holdings. Peasants knew this and had fewer illusions about the possible validity of church antisemitism. Heller writes unreservedly: "Since the Church was a huge landowner in a country of impoverished and landless peasants, the use of the Jews as an economic scapegoat served its interests well."[23] Lestschinsky characterizes the peasants as "not actively antisemitic" and holds that "the peasants realized that the landowners were utilizing the anti-Jewish campaigns for the purpose of drowning out the clamor for agrarian reforms."[24]

Fewer than four months before the Nazi attack on Poland, a Polish government spokesman, General Skwarczynski, declared: "We aspire to diminish the number of Jews in Poland." From 1939 to 1945, the number of Jews in Poland fell from 3,460,000 to 250,000. During that same time, however, a like number of non-Jewish Poles also met their deaths at the hands of Nazis and puppet forces.

During the Soviet-Nazi friendship period (August 1939–June 1941), Soviet troops occupied half of Poland and annexed all of Estonia, Latvia, and Lithuania. Many Jews, seeking to avoid Nazi occupation forces in western Poland, fled to the Soviet Union, as did even more non-Jewish Poles. At the time of the Nazi attack on the Soviet Union, some 2 million Polish refugees were on Soviet territory, 400,000 of them Jews. Many of the latter were barred from joining the Polish army in exile led by Polish General Anders. After Soviet-Jewish writer Ilya Ehrenburg informed Stalin that high Polish army officers were deeply anti-Soviet, Anders' forces were moved to Iran. Before that two all-Jewish companies, called the "Koltubianka," were organized with Anders' army. Somewhat later Stalin formed a second Polish force known as the Kosciuszko Legion in which Polish Jews played a very prominent role.[25]

In Poland, at the moment of German attack in 1939, Jewish participation in civil defense measures was welcomed. At the German prisoner-of-war camps, however, Jews suffered from discrimination by Polish comrades. "In Doessel, on the initiative of the Polish prisoners of war, a ghetto was set up for the Jewish prisoners."[26] Emmanuel Ringelblum, a trained historian who kept a contemporary record of relations between Jews and non-Jews, reported: "It was a common occurrence for Jews not to be allowed into the air-raid shelters in purely Polish blocks of flats, even during bombing."[27] (Before the war, it had been only rarely that apartments owned by non-Jews would be rented to Jews and so there were many "purely Polish" blocks.)

"Poland," wrote Ringelblum in 1943, "has given asylum at the most to one percent of the Jewish victims of Hitler's persecutions."[28] He estimated about 15,000 Jews were hiding in Warsaw and another 15,000 elsewhere in the country. Hiding Jews was a capital offense under Nazi rule. A number of non-Jewish Poles accepted Jews for hiding only if money was paid. "A sum of several tens of thousands of zloty was required to fix up a child on the Aryan side and only very wealthy people could afford to do so."[29] Even then, very frequently Jews were denounced to police by the recipients of the money; continuing blackmail was not uncommon. Working-class Polish homes were the safest for Jews. Ringelblum stressed that "in general Jews dream of getting into the homes of workers, because this guarantees them against blackmail or exploitation by their hosts."[30] It must be presumed that many such samaritan workers were of a leftist political persuasion.

After the Warsaw ghetto was created in October 1940, an extensive network of smuggling was established between Jews inside the walls and non-Jews on the outside. Food and other necessities were brought to the walls under great danger. Ringelblum does not restrain his praise: "Many Polish common people displayed human magnanimity...and were ready to make sacrifices for the sake of the Jews.... Polish-Jewish cooperation in the field of smuggling has been one of the finest pages in the history of mutual relations between the two peoples during the present war."[31] Referring to Poles who consented to hide Jews, he pledged: "Their name[s] will remain precious to us forever."[32]

In general, however, Ringelblum was deeply disappointed at the passivity of Poles in the face of Nazi atrocities against Jews. He asked, "Why do the few idealists who defend the Jews and give them refuge so rarely meet with cooperation from the community or the great majority of the community?"[33] The Polish underground was similarly passive with respect to Jews. He reproached "the Polish community with not having tried to dissociate itself, either in words—sermons in the churches, etc.—or in writing, from the antisemitic beasts that cooperated with the Germans, and for not having done anything whatsoever to weaken the impressions that the whole Polish population of all classes approved of the performances of the Polish antisemites."[34] (Ringelblum's life ended in 1943 when Nazis hunted him down and killed him.)

In November 1940, the Warsaw ghetto was suddenly sealed by Nazi troops. Entry and exit were strictly controlled. Some 70,000 Jews worked inside the walls of the ghetto, producing household goods, clothing, and other items, many of which were exchanged for food by smugglers. The poorest Jews, unable to draw on any financial resources, simply died of starvation. An economic and social elite within the ghetto, made up of top smugglers, selected Germans, and Jewish policemen, all of whom were partners in the smuggling operations, reproduced under extreme conditions a bit of upper-class life.

The Nazis, as customary, appointed a Jewish Council (*Judenrat*) to administer their orders. This extended to selection of individual Jews to be sent to "labor camps," in reality death camps. As Yisrael Gutman writes, "The *Judenrat* and the Jewish Police avoided causing injury to men of means and influence, so that the *Judenrat* in essence filled the obligation imposed on the community as a whole at the expense of its weakest and poorest members."[35]

Between July 22 and September 12, 1942, the Nazis sent 265,000 Jews from the Warsaw ghetto to the Treblinka death camps, although they took elaborate steps to disguise that destination. About 73,000 Jews remained in the ghetto. During a four-day period in January 1943, the Germans requisitioned 8,000 more Jews; only 5,000 were actually transported. Notable about this incident were two aspects that were unprecedented: (1) a few ghetto residents had somehow obtained revolvers and shot at German soldiers, and (2) unbeknown to the Germans, residents had dug a system of underground bunkers and tunnels where they hid from Germans. The use of firearms to assert Jewish interests "forged a bond of courage between the fighters and the rest of the ghetto's population and a consciousness that rather than bring ruin down on the ghetto, resistance might be the only solution to the existing situation."[36]

Around 700 young men and women, most of them between twenty and twenty-five years old, formed two separate though cooperative fighting groups. ZOB, the larger of the two, raised funds for weapons by whatever means it could, including threatening a member of the *Judenrat* with the death of his son if payments were not made. (Its initials stood for Zydowska Organizacja Bojowa [Jewish Fighting Organization].) Preparations for a revolt to facilitate escape were impracticable. Rather, their goal was to demonstrate the resolve of the ghetto community to assert some degree of control over their life—and death. On the early morning of Passover, April 18, 1943, battle stations were taken and soon the revolt began. (Passover commemorates the liberation of Jews from slavery in Egypt.) For three weeks ghetto fighters held off several thousand trained Nazi soldiers. As Gutman writes, "it took the Germans longer to quell the Warsaw ghetto uprising than it had taken them to defeat entire countries."[37]

How did Warsaw, and Poland for that matter, relate to the events in Warsaw? In general, according to Gutman, "the Poles' apathy and long-standing sense of hostility [toward Jews] intensified during the course of the war."[38] While many ordinary Poles admired the ghetto revolt, this admiration did not pervade the Polish exile government in London which controlled funds and arms in the Polish underground. At no time did the latter call upon Poles to oppose Nazi measures against the Jews. Repeatedly they ignored ghetto fighters' requests for arms. When they responded it was on an inconsiderable scale; moreover, such help proved abortive. Polish underground forces failed even once to conduct any joint actions with the ghetto uprising. Nor were there any Polish fighters in the actual revolt. The Polish Communist party praised the uprising and counseled Poles to follow its example. Both Ringelblum and Gutman cite Polish individuals and a handful of groups that helped Jews. Foremost among the latter was Zegota which succeeded in obtaining financial aid from the Polish underground. According to Joseph Kermish, Zegota operated between December 1942 and January 1945; at its peak it helped 4,000 Jews.[39]

Jewish fugitives from the ghetto revolt and elsewhere in the country tried to join Polish partisan groups to fight Germans but they were turned away; sometimes they were shot and killed and at other times handed over to the Germans.

In 1944, with the Red Army on Polish soil, a Soviet-backed Polish Committee of National Liberation was founded. The committee declared in its July 1944 manifesto: "The Jews, brutally oppressed by the [Nazi] occupiers, will be assured of reconstruction of their means of existence, as well as of actual equality of rights."[40] Until 1948 government policies were favorable to Jewish rights. In some 235 cities and towns, committees of Jews were formed. They organized Jewish and Hebrew schools, co-operatives, radio stations, synagogues, theaters and published periodicals in Yiddish, Hebrew, and Polish.

During the years 1944 to 1947, according to Lucjan Dobroszycki, some 1,500 Jews also lost their lives in antisemitic attacks: "Jews were killed when they came to ask for the return of their houses, workshops, farms, and other property. They were assaulted when they tried to open stores or workshops. Bombs were placed in orphanages and other Jewish public buildings. Jews were shot by unknown snipers and in full view of witnesses. Jews were attacked in their homes and forcibly removed from buses and trains. Jews were terrorized and forced to leave when they began to settle again in a small town or village."[41] Anti-Communist underground formations conducted some of these attacks. Local authorities frequently stood aside and failed to intervene in such attacks. In 1947, national policy on Jews shifted away from dependence on autonomous local bodies and toward more centralized control by government bodies. Also, policy grew more restrictive.

On July 4, 1946, a full-scale pogrom erupted in Kielce, a town notorious for its earlier antisemitism. During the war, townspeople had turned in many Jews in hiding to German authorities. In the postwar pogrom, around forty Jews were killed and about seventy-five wounded. According to eyewitness accounts, two army officers began the attacks by killing the chairperson of the town's Jewish committee after which soldiers threw Jews out the windows.[42] Nine persons were tried, found guilty, and sentenced to death for their activities in the pogrom. After these events Soviet authorities advised Jews not to try to regain their former property nor attempt to reclaim their old place of residence. The Catholic church hierarchy advised Jews not to join the new government. (As recently as 1983, Auxiliary Bishop Bronislaw Dabrowski told some Jewish visitors: "One could understand the resentment of the Polish people toward the Jews, because at the end of 1945, they were the first to adopt Communism.")[43]

The Constitution of 1952 proclaimed equal civil rights for persons of all nationalities and religions. Banned were any actions of hatred or contempt on racial or religious grounds having the effect of creating strife among groups. The Polish penal code called for the punishment of "whoever defames, derides, or degrades a group of the population or individual people on account of their national, religious or race affiliation." During the 1960s, Poland's 30,000 Jews saw these formal guarantees crumble under government and Communist party attacks. One reason for these easy collapses was the failure of postwar governments to conduct any educational or political campaigns against antisemitism. Rights were proclaimed resoundingly but no measures were taken to prepare the ground for implementation.

The mid-1960s saw a crisis within the Polish state and the Communist party. Central to these events was popular discontent over failing economic policy which tended to be identified with Wadyslaw Gomulka, the prime minister and party head. His principal critic was the minister of internal affairs, Mieczyslaw Moczar, who controlled the security apparatus of the country. Moczar charged the government was top heavy with Jews and called for their replacement. He declared that Jews had been responsible for installing Stalinist repression after World War II. Beginning in 1966, a "Jewish Section" in Moczar's ministry compiled "racial" family histories of Jews; over 200 employees did this work.

Even before the 1960s, the government had begun to enforce an exclusion policy for Jews in official positions. "By 1961," writes Josef Banas, "virtually all Jews had already been dismissed from the security apparatus, the police . . . , and many branches of the armed forces. . . . At first, the police were content to ban Jewish officials from business trips abroad, particularly to the West."[44] During 1966–68, the pace of official antisemitism grew frenzied as one Communist party faction and then another indulged in it. Each hoped to link its competitors with an alleged Jewish label and simultaneously to distract popular discontent from economic problems of the society as a whole.

Trybuna Luda, the party newspaper published in Warsaw, formulated the principal content of antisemitic doctrine. Six themes predominated: an international Jewish plot aimed to dominate the world; Jews were traitors to Poland and were subservient to a foreign power; Jews were foreign to Polish history and culture; Jews sought only to advance themselves, subordinating ideology to this goal; they were ungrateful; and Jews were "torturers of the innocent."[45] With a party congress approaching in 1968, Moczar's forces cracked down on demonstrators at the University of Warsaw who called for democratic reforms; many leaders bore Jewish names which were emphasized in press reports. Gomulka had already warned in 1967: "We do not want a Fifth Column in our country."[46] Government offices, the staffs of publications, and theaters were swept clean of Jews. The political organization that had attacked antisemitism without reserve in the harrowing 1930s and which had supported wholeheartedly the desperate Warsaw ghetto revolt in 1943, now, twenty-five years later, split into factions each of which obscenely sought to "out-Jew" the other.

Many Jews at whom this counterfeit fury was aimed were tested and loyal Communists minimally self-conceived as Jews. Most left the country during 1968–69. Exit papers came more readily if the exiles asked to go to Israel as the regime wished to identify Polish Jews as Zionists and thus not wholly loyal to Poland. The few Jews who remained in the country were subjected to explicit legal discrimination. One such measure excluded Jews from jobs paying more than 3,000 zlotys a month.[47] Many non-Jewish Poles directly benefited from Jewish losses: houses and apartments vacated by Jews became generally available; jobs, especially those in professional-level employment, were hastily acquired by middle-class persons who otherwise could not expect such promotions.

A few veteran Communists criticized the campaign; usually they were punished for dissenting. When the Soviet government cast its lot with Gomulka, factional struggles within the Polish Communist party waned. For about a decade afterward, the tiny collection—rather than a community—of Polish Jews existed on the margin of society. About 20,000 of the country's 30,000 Jews left Poland. While open antisemitism disappeared from the press and from party declarations, during the 1970s no rectifications were made of the blatant injustices of 1966–68. Jews and non-Jewish dissenters were not reinstated in official positions; exclusions from various public functions or employment were not remedied.

Antisemitism still had roots in the country. In 1978, for example, a small group, Polish Self-Defense, was organized to write and distribute antisemitic publications. The rise of the Solidarity movement, however, rekindled some antisemitic embers in Communist party circles as the latter attacked Polish political reformers for their alleged Jewish connections. In 1980, a group of Communists who had cooperated with General Moczar in the 1960s formed the Grunwald Patriotic Association, a nationalistic organization that portrayed Solidarity as part of a Zionist conspiracy against Poland. The next year, the Katowice Forum, another group of Communist right-wingers, proclaimed that "Trotskyist-Zionist" views were expanding in Poland.[48] The Communist party and other groups denounced the forum's statement. At the same time, a top leader of the party, Stefan Olszowski, publicly defended the forum.

Solidarity itself did not always resist the easy temptation to indulge in antisemitism. In 1981, for example, the head of Solidarity in Szczecin complained of the presence of so many "kikes" *(Zydki)* in the national government. (Actually, by this time the government was almost completely devoid of Jews.) For the most part, Solidarity openly opposed antisemitism. When the Grunwald group scheduled a rally in Warsaw, a day earlier Solidarity held a meeting to oppose it and denounced Grunwald's antisemitism as reminiscent of Tsarist and Nazi efforts. Lech Walesa, the Solidarity head, criticized the 1968 anti-Jewish campaign as "a mistake and a tragedy."

In March 1981, a leadership meeting of the Cultural and Communal Association of the Jews in Poland, met, along with party and government representatives. Leaders of the association spoke out with unparalleled candor and directness against "the inspirers of this inflamed anti-Jewish incitement [who] seek to turn the dissatisfaction of the masses, which is due to the bad economic situation, in a false direction."[49] Further, "the party leadership denounces the manifestation of antisemitism and the nationalistic-chauvinistic incitements [such as Grunwald and Katowice] that occurred recently."[50] At the same time, however, the party remained reluctant to conduct an all-out campaign against antisemitism as had also been the case directly after World War II.

During 1981–83, the Polish government courted world Jewish opinion by financing the reconstruction of Jewish cemeteries, community, and religious structures as well as preparing for commemoration ceremonies marking the fortieth anniversary of the Warsaw ghetto uprising.

The most chilling feature of the years after 1945 was the employment of deliberate antisemitism against the tattered remnants of a proud people who had before numbered 3.5 million and now were reduced to less than half of 1 percent that number. Anti-semitism was revealed as a useful tool of both rightist and leftist policies, all in the service of allegedly higher goals.

NOTES

1. S. M. Dubnov, *History of the Jews in Russia and Poland from the Earliest Times until the Present Day*, trans. I. Friedlaender (Philadelphia: Jewish Publication Society of America, 1916), p. 44.

2. Adam Vetulani, "The Jews in Medieval Poland," *Jewish Journal of Sociology*, 4 (1962), p. 287.

3. Ibid., p. 290.

4. Dubnov, *History of the Jews*, 1, p. 95.

5. Bernard D. Weinryb, *The Jews of Poland; a Social and Economic History of the Jewish Community in Poland from 1100 to 1800* (Philadelphia: Jewish Publication Society of America, 1973), p. 187.

6. Dubnov, *History of the Jews*, 1, p. 146.

7. Ibid., p. 172.

8. Ibid., pp. 274–75.

9. Ezra Mendelsohn, *The Jews of East Central Europe between the World Wars* (Bloomington: Indiana Univ. Press, 1983), p. 40.

10. Joseph Marcus, *Social and Political History of the Jews in Poland, 1919–1939* (Berlin: Mouton, 1983), pp. 47–49.

11. Celia S. Heller, *On the Edge of Destruction. Jews of Poland between the Two World Wars* (New York: Columbia Univ. Press, 1977), p. 104.

12. Harry M. Rabinowicz, *The Legacy of Polish Jewry. A History of Polish Jews in the Inter-War Years 1919–1939* (New York: Thomas Yoseloff, 1965), p. 99.

13. Heller, *On the Edge*, pp. 121, 123.

14. Marcus, *Social and Political History*, p. 355.

15. Jacob Lestschinsky, "The Anti-Jewish Program [Pogrom]: Tsarist Russia, the Third Reich and Independent Poland," *Jewish Social Studies*, 3 (1941), p. 153.

16. Heller, *On the Edge*, p. 290.

17. Emmanuel Ringelblum, *Polish-Jewish Relations during the Second World War*, ed. Joseph Kermish and Shmuel Krakowski, trans. Dafna Allon, Danuta Dabrowska, and Dana Keren (New York: Howard Fertig, 1976), pp. 31–32 n. 11.

18. Roseanne Axelrod, "Memories of Tarnow, 1925," *Jewish Currents* (June 1980), p. 22.

19. Marcus, *Social and Political History*, p. 384.

20. Heller, *On the Edge*, p. 112.

21. *New York Times*, November 19, 1982.

22. *Los Angeles Times*, June 19, 1983.

23. Heller, *On the Edge*, p. 111.

24. Lestschinsky, "The Anti-Jewish Program," p. 155.

25. Alexander Zvielli, "Jews of the Koltubianka," *Jerusalem Post Magazine*, August 18, 1978, p. 18.

26. Ringelblum, *Polish-Jewish Relations*, p. xxxvii.

27. Ibid., p. 35.

28. Ibid., p. 248.

29. Ibid., p. 140.

30. Ibid., p. 203.

31. Ibid., pp. 80, 86.

32. Ibid., p. 235.

33. Ibid., p. 9.

34. Ibid., p. 53.

35. Yisrael Gutman, *The Jews of Warsaw, 1939–1943. Ghetto, Underground, Revolt*, trans. Ina Friedman (Bloomington: Indiana Univ Press, 1982), p. 83.

36. Ibid., p. 320.

37. Ibid., p. 390.

38. Ibid., p. 252.

39. Ringelblum, *Polish-Jewish Relations*, p. 297.

40. Quoted in Josef Banas, *The Scapegoats. The Exodus of the Remnants of Polish Jewry*, trans. Tadeusz Szafar, ed. Lionel Kohan (London: Weidenfeld and Nicolson, 1979), p. 28.

41. Lucjan Dobroszycki, "Restoring Jewish Life in Post-War Poland," *Soviet-Jewish Affairs*, 3 (1972), p. 66.

42. Michael Checinski, "The Kielce Pogrom: Some Unanswered Questions," *Soviet Jewish Affairs*, 5 (1972), p. 57.

43. Mark R. Day, "U.S. Jews, Polish Church at Odds," *National Catholic Reporter*, May 20, 1983.

44. Banas, *The Scapegoats*, p. 73.

45. Heller, *On the Edge*, pp. 143–45.

46. Banas, *The Scapegoats*, p. 87.

47. Ibid., p. 158.

48. Sid Resnick, "Polish Jewry and Socialist 'Renewal,'" *Jewish Currents*, December 1981, p. 5.

49. Ibid., p. 8.

50. Ibid.

10

THE STRUGGLE FOR CIVIC STATUS: RUMANIA

> [Before World War I] Rumania had a well-deserved reputation
> for being, along with Russia, the most antisemitic country in Europe.
> —Ezra Mendelsohn, 1983

Rumania excelled in single-minded anti-Jewish activity during the century and a half before World War II. Yet in its history as a whole no other country matched the breadth of amplitude as Rumania swung from the extremes of antisemitism to the occasional heights of equal treatment.

Jews lived in Rumania even before the Roman conquest, but settled communities existed only by the latter half of the seventeenth century. In Bucharest, the largest Rumanian city, during the seventeenth and eighteenth centuries Jews "were confined to a suburb of the city, paid special taxes, and were compelled to wear black raiment, which made them conspicious."[1] Rumanian nobles (boyars), interested in developing economic resources, began in the late eighteenth and early nineteenth centuries to invite Jews to immigrate. They received certain privileges, including "exemption from taxes for several years, and free land for their synagogues, schools, baths, and cemeteries."[2] These Jews founded a number of small towns in Moldavia.

Some Rumanians, Jews and non-Jews, who lived in the country were not citizens or even residents. They placed themselves under the protection of certain foreign countries, especially Russia or Austro-Hungary. Among the Jews it was mainly the wealthy who made such a choice. The 1831 census showed that in Moldavia only 9 percent of Jews were in this status; the rest regarded themselves as Rumanians. After mid-century, the number of protected Jews declined almost to zero.

Nevertheless, Jews were not more accepted; if anything, they were even less so. Early in the nineteenth century, Rumanian nationalism began to develop just as the middle class began to grow rapidly. Anti-semitism started to rise as well. It was furthered especially from 1828 to 1834 when the country came under Russian occupation. During those years, the so-called organic laws were written under Russian tutelage. These were extremely harsh on Jews. Paragraph 94 provided for the expulsion of Jews from the country if they were found to have no "useful trade" or were "vagabonds." It was applied repeatedly in later years and did not lapse until nearly a century later. (The Russian-inspired laws also aroused the peasantry of the country by formally enacting serfdom.)

Later laws added to the civic burdens of Jews. In 1855 the *Manuel Administratif* provided that "all Jews, foreign or native, may be expelled if they do not fulfill the stipulated requirements." Daniel Labin explains what was covered by this phrase: "The requirements, in addition to a useful trade, were possession of 5,000 lei [a considerable amount of money at that time] and the obtaining of a pass from the authorities. Jews could travel from one place to another only when provided with this pass. The *Manuel* . . . excluded Jews from living in certain streets in the villages; they were not to rent stores in the neighborhood of churches, or trade in vegetables or leeches."[3]

The legal inferiority of Jews was a cause of agitation among them. From time to time, depending on the leanings of a specific ruler, a law might be eased. In general, however, this did not happen. In 1858, at the Congress of Paris, a gathering of European great powers concerned in Balkan affairs, European recognition was extended to Rumania but technically the country was still ruled as part of the Ottoman Empire. At Paris, a quasi-constitution was drawn up for Rumania. Paragraph 46 read: "Moldavians and Wallachians of all Christian denominations will enjoy political rights. Political rights may be extended to other elements of the population by legislation." This provision extended political rights to members of all Christian churches rather than only to Orthodox Christians, as had been the case. "Other elements," especially Jews, however, failed to receive any such rights as the Rumanian government never chose to honor them. The European powers did nothing about it.

Things took a turn for the worse when in 1866 Ion Bratianu, chief of the Liberal party, became head of the government. He hated Jews and referred to them collectively as a "social wound" and "leprosy." Article 7 of the constitution was amended to restrict the right of natu-ralization: "Only foreigners of Christian rite may obtain the quality of Rumania." In 1867, a Bratianu decree forbade the settlement of Jews in rural areas or villages. Many Jews were expelled as "vagabonds." These measures led to mass arrests of Jews and violent attacks upon them. When European governments protested against such outrages, Ruma-nian authorities denied they had occurred. A law passed in 1869 referred to Jews as the "scourge of peasants." In 1869 and 1870, Jews were expelled from the city of Ploesti and the following districts: Bacau, Vaslui, Tacuciu, and Botoshani. In order to eject Jews from an urban area it was reclassified as a rural area and thus no longer open to Jewish settlement. In some genuinely rural areas, peasants protected Jews from expulsion.

Whenever possible, Rumanian Jews sought help from fellow Jews elsewhere. They, in return, urged their home governments to intervene in Rumania. In 1870, when attacks on Jews mounted, the United States appointed an unpaid consul, Benjamin F. Peixotto, to be stationed in Bucharest. Max Kohler and Simon Wolf write that Peixotto "did not hesitate...to advise the Jews of Rumania to defend themselves with firearms, when necessary...the right of self-defense being recognized even by Rumanian law."[4] When, in 1875, Peixotto left for home, the situation of Jews in Rumania remained critical.

In 1877–78, Russia, Rumania, and Turkey fought a war. The peace treaty, drawn up at the Congress of Berlin in 1878, contained a special provision, Article 44, which stipulated: "In Rumania, distinction of religious faith and confession shall not be a hindrance to anyone or be regarded as a reason for exclusion or inability to acquire civil and political rights, to hold public office or honorary functions or to engage in the various industries and professions, wherever they may be."[5] Seemingly, Jews thereby gained equal treatment. Since Rumania now sought international recognition of its newly won independence, it was assumed by many that Article 44 would be implemented. But it was not. Instead, the following year, Rumania simply amended Article 7 of its constitution to make naturalization available to individuals only by vote of both legislative houses, signature of the king, and official publication. In a note sent later that year, Rumania "promised not to regard Jews as aliens in all matters of civil government, to allow them 'freedom in adopting whatever profession or trade' they desired, and to speed their naturalization."[6]

Three great powers, Germany, France, and Great Britain, acknowledged that while "Article 7 does not quite conform to the views of the Berlin Congress" that they nevertheless were "confident that Rumania will get closer to the spirit of liberalism which was that of the powers." Germany had hastened to recognize the independence of Rumania because that country had agreed to a financial settlement which was very favorable to German creditors of a failed enterprise in Rumania. The other powers had even less reason to object. The result was minimal since the Rumanian government once more violated its pledge. From 1880 to 1919, Jews continued to be regarded as legal aliens even if they were born in Rumania.

The nineteenth century as a whole was a disastrous time for Jews. While increasing numbers of Jews lived in Rumania and settled com-

munities multiplied, counterforces also operated. Thus, a rising non-
Jewish middle-class was eager to eliminate Jewish competition in the
marketplace, the professions, and employment in general. Many legal
enactments aimed to accomplish this end. In addition, a deeply chauvinistic trend within Rumanian nationalism fed the movement to exclude
Jews from any common civic experience. The state saw to it that the
operation of legal structures had just this effect. Major political parties
were openly antisemitic. The churches were not less so.

A vast number of anti-Jewish laws were passed during the century.
Here is a summary of the main ones, dated from 1803 to 1902:[7]

1803   Jews cannot rent farms
1804   Jews cannot buy farm products
1817   Jews cannot buy real property
1818   Jews cannot testify against Christians
1819   Jews cannot own land
1831   All Jews must register themselves and their occupations; Jews ruled
        nonuseful will be expelled
1839   Jews must pay a special tax
1850   Jews cannot enter country unless they have some money and a known
        occupation
1851   Commission appointed to study vagabondage and determine the right
        of entry of foreign Jews
1861   Jews cannot be innkeepers in rural areas
1864   Jews can be naturalized if they (1) served as noncommissioned officers
        in the army, (2) were college graduates, (3) had a recognized degree
        from a foreign university, or (4) had founded a factory
1864   Jews cannot be lawyers
1866   Jews cannot renew farm leases
1868   Jews must serve in the army
1868   Jews cannot practice as physicians
1869   Jews cannot be tax farmers in rural communes
1869   Jews are not to be considered Rumanians
1869   An extra tax was levied on the sale of kosher meat in two towns
1869   Jews can be apothecaries only if Christian ones are unavailable
1870   Serbian Jews in Rumania must serve in the army
1872   Jews cannot sell tobacco
1878   Jews cannot sell liquor in rural areas
1882   Jews cannot be customhouse officials
1882   All "inhabitants" (principally Jews) are liable to military service
1884   Strangers (mostly Jews) cannot petition Parliament
1884   Hawkers (peddlers) cannot trade in rural districts
1885   A pharmacy can be closed down if it is not directed by a recognized
        (that is, a non-Jewish) person
1886   The chairman of community electors must have political rights (which
        nearly no Jews had)
1886   Druggists must be Rumanians or naturalized citizens

1886	Books of account must be kept in Rumanian or other modern language (but not Yiddish)
1887	Within five years of the beginning of a factory, two-thirds of the workmen must be Rumanians (and not Jews)
1887	Children of Rumanians have preferential rights of admission to public schools (over Jews)
1892	Retired Jewish soldiers cannot serve as rural gendarmes
1893	Aliens (that is, Jews) can occupy only up to 10 percent of beds in free hospitals but must pay fees (while others need not)
1893	A Jewish apothecary apprentice may be employed only if a Rumanian (that is, non-Jewish) one is also employed
1895	Jews cannot be students in military hospitals nor can they be army doctors
1896	Children of strangers (that is, Jews) must pay fees to take entrance examinations
1898	Some 11,200 Jewish children were denied admission to various public educational institutions
1899	Jews cannot work on state-owned railroads
1899	Private Jewish schools must be closed on Sundays
1900	Quota for Jewish students in elementary schools further reduced to 5.5 percent; in secondary schools, from 10.5 to 7.5 percent
1900	Students in private Jewish schools must leave their heads uncovered while receiving instruction
1900	On privately owned railroads, at least 60 percent of employees must be Rumanian (that is, non-Jews)
1900	Private Jewish schools must remain open on Saturdays
1902	Artisans who are "aliens" can have their licenses renewed in "their own" countries (Jews had no "own" country except Rumania in which they were not regarded as Rumanians).

The overwhelming majority of these measures dealt with economic matters or issues that had considerable economic consequences. In every case they restricted the rights of Jews. Jews were plainly a politically oppressed group which was also subject to extreme economic exploitation. Antisemitism by the early twentieth century had become a highly effective political and economic tool. The possession of wealth saved some Jews from the worst effects of antisemitism. The factories and other enterprises they owned were valuable to the state. Also, since corruption was widespread in government, money bribes were quite common; exemptions might not be listed in the law but they were for sale. Another way out was to emigrate; between 1900 and 1906 alone, over 70,000 Jews left Rumania.

As a result of World War I, Rumania doubled its land area and population. It retained Dobrudja, which had been taken from Bulgaria in a war in 1913. During World War I, Bessarabia and Bukovina were taken from Russia and Transylvania from Hungary. The Jewish population of Rumania thus rose from about 240,000 to nearly 800,000.

During 1919–20, several general peace treaties were negotiated of which some were separate treaties dealing with the rights of minorities. To stave off these instruments, which were opposed by the Rumanian government, efforts were made to enable 75 percent of the Jews to become citizens. Despite this, the Allies insisted on a minority treaty which was signed and came into effect in September 1920. Two articles referred to Jews. Article 7 read: "Rumania undertakes to recognize as fully privileged Rumanian subjects without any formality the Jews living in all the Rumanian territories and who have no other nationality." Article 8 declared: "All Rumanian subjects are equal before the law and are in possession of the same civil and political rights without any distinction in race, language or religion."[8] For the first time in Rumanian history, Jews were equal citizens of the country in which they were born. They promptly began to assert their new rights, entering employments and institutions from which they had been barred. A greater Jewish presence was felt in government, the professions, the university, and elsewhere.

Antisemites deeply resented this. The former "aliens" and "strangers" were now fellow citizens. Nowhere was the reaction as extreme as in the universities. In 1920, Professor Alexander Cuza of the University of Jassy formed the League of National Christian Defense (NCD). It called for a quota on enrollment of Jews in higher education and a rule forbidding Jewish medical students to dissect corpses of Gentiles. During the 1920s, writes Ezra Mendelsohn, "Romanian students were the main perpetrators of violent antisemitism."[9] In 1922, anti-Jewish riots were staged by student groups financed by the interior ministry.[10] In 1927, Cornelius Codreanu founded the League of Archangel Michael which, according to Labin, was dedicated "to the extermination of the Jews through terrorism."[11] In 1927, student members of the league began a pogrom in Transylvania (Oradea Mare) "where they were holding a congress, for which they received a subsidy from the ministry of the interior; they were conveyed there in special trains put at their disposal free of charge by the government."[12] Anti-Jewish riots spread to various places throughout the country.

Violence against Jews became, if not the norm, then far less unacceptable: "In 1922 and 1923 anti-Jewish agitation increased. Windows of Jewish-owned houses and shops were broken, performances of Jewish theatrical troupes were disturbed, synagogues profaned, and Jewish passengers, including women and young girls, were pushed from moving trains.... In October, 1925 Codreanu assassinated Manciu, police prefect of Jassy, who had attempted to curb rioting antisemitic students."[13] During the years from 1920 to 1933, national Jewish legislators "were not only interrupted during their speeches but were often physically attacked by the deputies of the antisemitic parties."[14] In 1930, Codreanu created the Iron Guard out of the League of Archangel Michael. So-called gangs of death were set on Jews; few were punished for these acts.

The emancipation of Jews that came, finally, in 1920, thus lacked its first precondition—physical safety. In other respects, too, the promise of emancipation faded. "There are no Jewish prosecuting attorneys, judges or officials in Rumania," wrote Jacob Lestchinsky, "Jewish engineers and technicians are not employed on either municipal or state undertakings, the latter forming about one-fourth of all such projects in the entire country."[15] During the 1920s, "in practice, the magistracy, university chairs, and officers' corps remained closed to Jews."[16] During the 1930s "the examinations for admission to universities discriminated against all national minorities, including Jews, in order to prevent them from entering in great numbers."[17] Discrimination in the political realm also returned, despite the solemn peace treaties. In February 1924, revision of the citizenship status of Jews living in Bessarabia, Bukovina, and Transylvania was undertaken. As a result, many lost their political rights.

The economic depression of the 1930s proved a fruitful period for the political strengthening of Rumanian antisemitism: "Early in 1932 the Iron Guard, with 34,000 'nests' (sections) throughout the country, had become a political power. Officers, justices, public officials, clergymen, teachers, industrialists and merchants joined its ranks in great numbers.... Codreanu, Goga and Cuza established close relations with the Nazi organization at Berlin. Antisemitic propaganda increased. Not a city in Rumania, not a town of any importance, was without an anti-Jewish publication, and the antisemitic organizations were well provided with funds."[18]

While in 1933 the Duca government dissolved the Iron Guard—Duca was later assassinated—in the 1937 national elections one-sixth of the voters backed the party. During the years 1937 to 1940 "the slogan of the day was elimination of Jews from economic and cultural spheres, and their replacement by 'ethnic' Romanians."[19] The Goga administration served only about six weeks during late 1937 and early 1938. It began a "review" of Jewish citizenship which concluded in 1939 with declaring 270,073 Jews as non-citizens; this amounted to 36 percent of all Jews. "These Jews, thus having become aliens, were subjected to special taxation and deprived of the right to work."[20] In February 1938, a new premier, Patriarch Miron Cristea, took office; Jews expected little of him since he had once said "the Jews are sucking the marrow from the bones of the nation."[21] A week later he closed down the Yiddish and Hebrew language press. This was followed by a measure requiring that 75 to 80 percent of jobs in various industries be filled by "Rumanians"; as a result, many Jews were discharged.

Late in 1938, King Carol abolished constitutional government and established a personal dictatorship under the name of the Front of the Renaissance, complete with a Fascist salute. Jews alone were excluded from membership. Under Carol, anti-Jewish law-making went on apace. Jews could no longer be engineers on the railroads. "Jews were dismissed from the army and from the civil service; they lost their jobs as editors and company board members; they were restricted in the right to practice law and other professions; they lost their liquor licenses; they were prohibited from acquiring real estate, industrial enterprises in the provinces and so on. . . . [There were also] the prohibition of intermarriage and the revocation of name changes."[22]

In June 1940, after France fell to the Nazis, Carol dropped his "Front" and organized a "Party of the Nation, Christian, National, and Racial." Again, Jews were barred from membership. The next month, Carol declared Rumania a "neutral ally" of Germany. Premier Ion Gigurti, newly appointed, enacted a long series of anti-Jewish measures. Jews were now forbidden to sell any of their property, including real estate and securities, without government permission. In August, Gigurti's "Statute of the Jews" had the effect of equalizing government oppression against Jews: "During the two years following the publication of this statute, the entire Jewish population, irrespective of class difference, was subjected to the same procedure of expropriation and persecution."[23]

A coalition of Marshal Ion Antonescu and the Iron Guard overthrew King Carol in September 1940 and ruled together in an uneasy partnership. Prince Michael succeeded Carol and all political parties but the Iron Guard were dissolved. One hundred twenty thousand Nazi troops entered the country, presumably to protect the Ploesti oil fields, a vital source of German supplies. In November, Rumania became a full-fledged member of the Axis. That same year, the Soviet Union occupied Bessarabia and Bukovina and annexed the territories, thereby absorbing some 300,000 Jews. At the same time, the country's organized Jewish community remained in direct contact with Marshal Antonescu.

In January 1941, the Iron Guard attempted to overthrow Antonescu but was stopped. At the same time, however, the guard conducted a vicious pogrom in Bucharest. Raul Hilberg reports: "Jewish sources report that the victims had not merely been killed; they had been butchered. In the morgue bodies were so cut up that they no longer resembled anything human, and in the municipal slaughterhouse bodies were observed like carcasses of cattle."[24] Some remains bore signs identifying them as "kosher meat."[25] Thereafter, Antonescu ruled through the army.

Meanwhile, the Antonescu administration did not neglect its anti-Jewish program. The same month Antonescu took office, in September 1940, a number of measures were initiated. Jews were expelled from all schools and universities. The work permits of Jewish artisans—carpenters, shoemakers, tailors, and the like—were not renewed. Contracts between non-Jewish apprentices and Jewish employers were canceled. All Jewish-owned shipping was transferred to the state. Jewish physicians were no longer permitted to treat non-Jewish patients. Professional organizations, such as those for journalists, expelled Jewish members. Jewish-owned farm property was expropriated and in November 1940 Jews still employed in private industry were discharged. The following March, all Jewish-owned real estate was also expropriated.

The Union of Jewish Communities (UJC), led by the energetic Wilhelm Filderman, continued to protest and meet with Antonescu and lower officials. When Jews were forbidden to continue living in villages, UJC succeeded in arranging to send them to large cities where organized Jewish communities could help them. Jews also convinced the government that wearing a yellow star was not a necessity for Jews. UJC convinced the Romanian Orthodox Patriarch Nicodem to intervene with Marshal Antonescu on Jews' behalf. Toward the end of 1941 UJC was dissolved by the government and a puppet organization formed. While Jews cooperated, they also secretly reconstituted a coalition very much like UJC which continued until the end of the war. In July 1942, at the request of Chief Rabbi Alexander Safran, the Orthodox archbishop of Transylvania went to Bucharest and convinced the queen mother to intercede with Antonescu in the interest of the Jews.

These events, however, were still a sideshow for grave events which were developing in the military arena. In June 1941, Rumania joined the Nazi attack on the Soviet Union and soon recovered Bessarabia and Bukovina, as well as a strip in the southern Ukraine called Transnistria. There the Rumanian army built death camps, even before the Nazi death camps were constructed, and conducted large-scale murders of Jews from the recovered provinces. Rumanian troops cooperated with a Nazi unit whose special assignment was the destruction of Jews. So ghastly were the methods used by some Rumanians that Nazi officers sometimes stopped them. About 250,000 Jews were killed in Transnistria.

By late 1942, it had become clear that ultimate German success in the war was problematic. In the Battle of Stalingrad, which ended in February 1943, Rumania lost eighteen divisions. Reaction on the home front was unsettling to the regime. This affected Antonescu's Jewish policy. "During the second part of the war," writes Theodore Lavi, "there was a perceptible opposition to violence and murder [of Jews] even among the Rumanian population."[26] At the end of 1943, the Rumanians closed down the Transnistria camp and returned the remaining 50,000 Jews still there to Rumania proper. Lavi calls this action "one of the most extraordinary episodes in the history of the Holocaust."[27] Hilberg, on the other hand, supplies a rather straightforward reason for it: "The immediate cause of that total reversal was the Red Army's massive cross-

ing of the Dnieper River, the Soviet recapture of Kiev and Dneprope-
trovsk, and the sweeping Russian advance toward the Bug [River]."[28]
The nearer the Red Army, the more considerate of Jews the marshal
became. Early in 1944, Antonescu was meeting with an underground
Zionist executive group to discuss Jewish emigration, presumably to Palestine.[29] During the same period, 1943–44, Rumanians sought out Allied
representatives to explore possible peace terms. In April 1944, the Red
Army retook Bessarabia and Bukovina and in August was poised to enter
Rumania. Thereupon, King Michael arrested Antonescu and surrendered to the Russians. Rumania then declared war against Germany.

As of 1945, 430,000 Jews lived in Rumania. From 1944 to 1947, a
large number emigrated freely to Palestine. By 1970, only about 100,000
remained while some 200,000 had gone to Israel. During the immediate
postwar years, the new Communist government proclaimed and practiced equal rights for all religions. In 1946, 41,000 students attended
190 Jewish schools. Two years later there were fifty religious schools
(talmud torah schools) and five yeshivot. The war for Israeli independence ended the freedom of Zionists and other Jews to organize in Rumania. Almost all Jewish schools were closed, but Jewish-language
schools operated in Bucharest and Jassy until 1960–61. Synagogues remained open; in 1960, 153 communities had 841 of them. In that same
year, there were fifty-four talmud torah schools and a four-year-old
yeshivah. In 1967, when virtually the entire Soviet bloc of nations broke
diplomatic relations with Israel, Rumania refused to follow suit. It became the Soviet bloc country with the freest conditions for Jewish life.[30]

The remaining Jewish community, half or more of which was made
up of elderly persons, felt stigmatized when applying for visas to Israel.
In 1976, when some 50,000 or so Jews still lived in Rumania, Chief Rabbi
Moses Rosen said, "If I tell you that everyone who wants to go, goes, it
would be a lie. Those who seek exit visas . . . no longer have career possibilities. There are those who lose their jobs."[31] Visas were generally
forthcoming after a one-year wait. During the late 1970s, the American
Joint Distribution Committee was permitted to contribute some $3 mil-
lion a year for social services to Jews. In 1982, Rabbi Rosen wrote: "More
than 93 percent of the Jewish population has quietly and peacefully been
given the opportunity concretely to express their love of Zion and to go
to the Jewish state."[32]

Only rarely were specifically antisemitic incidents reported. On September 5, 1980, for example, *Septamana,* weekly publication of a Communist party committee, printed an antisemitic article. The next month,
after pressure by Rabbi Rosen, the publication issued an apology. Reportedly, Rabbi Rosen also objected to antisemitic material in the newly
published volume of the works of a nineteenth-century poet.[33] The first
eight volumes of this work of Michael Eminescu had contained none of

his antisemitic writings. In February 1981, Rabbi Rosen described as "the most disgraceful antisemitic pamphlet I have seen for 30 years" a publication distributed in Bucharest. Government spokespersons said it had been printed in Majorca by Rumanian Fascists and condemned it. Rabbi Rosen also said one of the pamphlet's distributors was in part responsible for publication of the *Septamana* article the year before.

Addressing the Rumanian Workers Conference on April 6, 1981, Rumanian President Nicolae Ceausescu declared:

We must combat decisively retrograde conceptions, mysticism and superstition as well as any nationalist, chauvinist, racist or antisemitic manifestations which were and are foreign to the revolutionary workers' ideals.... In conditions of a worsening international situation, of an economic crisis... we are now observing the intensification of creating animosity and disunity of the masses; the intensification of fascist organizations to end democratic liberty, acts of terrorism, international enmity and recrudescence of racism and antisemitism.[34]

These comments were reportedly widely disseminated in Rumania.

In May 1984, President Ceausescu personally apologized to Rabbi Rosen for publication of a book of poems by Corneliu Vadim Tudor which, among other things, attacked the rabbi. The book was withdrawn from sale in less than forty-eight hours of publication. Some poems in it attacked Jews who had gone to Israel in phrases such as "traitor... without a homeland" and "you'd better sell buttons and cheap brandy." The country's Jewish bimonthly published a criticism of the book but authorities refused to allow circulation of the issue, permitting only a single copy to be placed in the Jewish community hall in Bucharest.[35]

Rumania's postwar policy on Jews reflected in part its relatively independent foreign policy with regard to the USSR. No other member of the Soviet bloc rejected so decisively the general prohibition on friendly relations with Israel; nor did Rumania choose to practice either state antisemitism or permit an extralegal anti-Jewish group to gain permanence.

NOTES

1. Simon Mowshowitz, "Bucharest," *Universal Jewish Encyclopedia,* 2 (1940), p. 571.

2. Daniel Labin, "Roumania," *Universal Jewish Encyclopedia,* 9 (1943), p. 250.

3. Ibid., p. 252.

4. Max J. Kohler and Simon Wolf, "Jewish Disabilities in the Balkan States. American Contributions toward Their Removal, with Particular Reference to the Congress of Berlin," *Publications of the American Jewish Historical Society,* 24 (1916), p. 23.

5. Labin, "Roumania," p. 257.

6. Ibid.

7. Labin, "Roumania," p. 258. Almost all enactments were listed in a speech on the floor of the U.S. House of Representatives by Congressman Walter M. Chandler, on October 10, 1912; see Kohler and Wolf, "Jewish Disabilities in the Balkan States," pp. 116–17, 129–31.

8. Ibid., p. 259.

9. Ezra Mendelsohn, *The Jews of East Central Europe between the World Wars* (Bloomington: Indiana Univ. Press, 1983), p. 186.

10. *Encyclopedia Judaica,* 14, col. 394.

11. Labin, "Roumania," p. 260.

12. *Encyclopedia Judaica,* 14, col. 394.

13. Labin, "Roumania," pp. 259–60.

14. *Encyclopedia Judaica,* 14, col. 396.

15. Jacob Lestschinsky, "Bessarabia," *Universal Jewish Encyclopedia,* 2 (1940), pp. 247–48.

16. *Encyclopedia Judaica,* 14, col. 394.

17. Labin, "Roumania," p. 260.

18. Ibid.

19. Ibid.

20. Ibid.

21. Ibid.

22. Raul Hilberg, *The Destruction of the European Jews* (Chicago: Quadrangle, 1961), p. 488.

23. Labin, "Roumania," p. 261.

24. Hilberg, *The Destruction of the European Jews,* p. 489.

25. *Encyclopedia Judaica,* 14, col. 400. In 1982, Archbishop Valerian Trifa of the Rumanian Orthodox church was ordered deported from the United States. One of the charges was that he had made a speech on January 20, 1941, in Bucharest which had set off the three-day pogrom. See *New York Times,* October 8, 1982. Archbishop Trifa was finally deported to Portugal in August 1984. See Thomas O'Toole, "U.S. Deports Romanian as War Criminal," *Washington Post,* August 15, 1984.

26. Theodore Lavi, "The Background to the Rescue of Romanian Jewry during the Period of the Holocaust," in Bela Vago and George L. Mosse, eds., *Jews and Non-Jews in Eastern Europe 1918–1945* (New York: Wiley, 1974), p. 184.

27. Ibid., p. 178.

28. Hilberg, *The Destruction of the European Jews,* p. 505.

29. *Encyclopedia Judaica,* 14, col. 408.

30. Ibid., 14, col. 408. See also Mendelsohn, *The Jews of East Central Europe,* p. 211.

31. "Subtle Anti-Semitism Pervades Romania," *Los Angeles Times,* November 11, 1976 (UPI story).

32. Moses Rosen, "Using Rumanian Jews," *New York Times,* August 9, 1982.

33. "Romania," *Jewish Currents,* December 1980.

34. "Romania," *Jewish Currents,* June 1981.

35. Liora Moriel, "Ceausescu Calms Chief Rabbi over Anti-Semitic Poetry Book," *Jerusalem Post,* May 14, 1984.

11

LONG WINTERS OF DARK NIGHTS: RUSSIA/USSR

It was in the Russia of 1881 that, for the first time in nineteenth-century Europe, the Jews had to face antisemitism not simply as a permanent inconvenience but as an immediate threat to their established way of life, as an explosive force, as a dynamic rather than static phenomenon.

—Jonathan Frankel, 1981

Russian antisemitism came overwhelmingly from the top down. The throne and the pulpit cooperated. Jews were excluded altogether, proscribed from numerous employments and parts of the country, or subjected to official violence. Deep currents of popular antisemitism were encouraged. Social revolution promised an end to this oppression but turned out only to moderate it.

In eleventh-century Kievan Russia, anchored on the historically anti-Jewish Orthodox church, tension already existed between the state and the Jews. While a few Jewish merchants were permitted in Kiev, authorities worked actively to limit their numbers and settlements. Near the end of the fifteenth century, the Orthodox church was disrupted by the so-called Judaizing heresy, a movement largely from within the church, aimed, among other things, at denying the divinity of Jesus and rejecting belief in the Trinity. "Judaizers" translated works from the Hebrew. In time, their doctrines were rejected. The episode furthered the isolation of Jews and encouraged opposition to increased settlement by Jews.

The religious motive behind official exclusory policies was predominant. In state and church circles, deep fear was expressed at the possible influence of the Jewish anti-Christ; unceasing hatred of Jews was preached by the Orthodox clergy. Ivan the Terrible (1533–44) openly declared his hope of totally excluding Jews. A century later, under Peter the Great (1682–1725), Jews were all but barred from the empire. His successor, Catherine I (1725–27), banished Jews from all cities. Complete exclusion was achieved only under the religious zealot Elizabeth I (1741–62) when Jewish merchants and others were expelled from the country. "I do not want to have any income from the enemies of Christ," she declared.

Between 1772 and 1795, the Polish state was totally dismembered by Russia, Prussia, and Austria-Hungary. Nearly half the world's 2.5 million Jews residing in Poland suddenly came under Russian rule. They were greeted by a series of legal enactments that restricted their movement and severely diminished their ability to make a living. Russian merchants living in cities hastened to rid themselves of new competitors. Jews in cities were required to pay double the tax paid by non-Jews. More serious, however, was a merchant-initiated move to exclude Jews altogether from certain areas of the country. This eventuated in orders during 1790, 1791, 1794, and 1795 that created a Pale of Settlement for Jews. Essentially, the pale included formerly Polish territory in addition to a few other areas. Jews were to be concentrated in towns and cities even if this required them to be ordered out of the villages. The system of the pale lasted until 1915.

In 1804, under Alexander I (1801–25), the "Statute About Establishing Jews" was enacted. It was the first comprehensive legislation of its kind in Russia. The statute formalized the pale and prohibited Jews from leaseholding or distilling, two of the very few occupations then open to Jews living in villages and practiced by nearly one-half the Jewish population. Some Jews were allowed to enter agriculture at government expense and the rest were directed toward factory work and handicrafts. Jewish representative community bodies (the *kahal*) were recognized. All public schools and universities were declared open to Jews. Yiddish, however, was outlawed in public and in school. In Jewish schools, either Russian, Polish, or German was required as the language of instruction. Exceedingly few Jewish families accepted the invitation to send their children to such secular schools, preferring instead to continue using the religious schools.

"In Russian folklore and literature of the eighteenth and nineteenth centuries," writes Shmuel Ettinger, "everything connected with Jews... is associated with something negative."[1] During the first half of the nineteenth century, he continues, "the Russian intelligentsia entertained a negative attitude toward Jews."[2] In the mid-nineteenth century and later, Jews were regarded by the traditionalist Slavophiles as the enemies of Old Russia and as bearers of a capitalist order. This latter role was especially contradicted by widespread poverty among Jews and by their near exclusion from many branches of large-scale industry.

It was in such a hostile climate that the government continued its program of regulating Jews. When a legislative measure happened to work out well for Jews, it was discontinued. This occurred with government-financed agricultural settlements for Jews. After 10,000 Jewish colonists took up farming, and thousands more prepared to do so, the project was ended by the government.[3] In 1820, Jews were forbidden to employ non-Jewish domestics. Expulsion of Jews from villages continued. Most Jewish print shops were closed down. In 1835, Jewish males were forbidden to marry before age eighteen; for females the minimum age was set at sixteen. This was an effort to limit the population growth of the Jewish community. In 1843, in an action affecting hundreds of thousands, Jews were expelled from an area extending for thirty miles along the western border of Russia.

Under Nicholas I (1825–55) in 1827 Jews were made eligible for the standard twenty-five-year term of military service. The minimum age of recruits was twelve; it was all but certain that such young soldiers, placed under unremitting pressure to become Christians, would by term's end have converted. Jewish parents were terrified at the prospect of their sons being drafted. As Simon Dubnov points out, "the entire burden of recruitment duty devolved upon the poorest classes of Jews.... The more well-to-do were exempted from military service" either by law or by personal influence with the kahal, the Jewish self-ruling body (which was abolished in 1844).[4]

Indeed, a growing part of Russian state policy on Jews consisted of drawing distinctions between different groups of Jews. Bernard Weinryb points out that this approach was common to Prussia and Austria as well: "[They] had developed the policy of dividing the Jews into the rich and useful and the poor and useless or harmful. The first group was accorded privileges and given 'protection' of varying degrees in accordance with their usefulness and ability to pay; and eforts were made to get rid of the second group, or to limit their numbers and occupational opportunities."[5]

Such a class approach worked, in part, because it was consistent with the social structure of typical Jewish communities in eastern Europe. Dubnov explains: "Wealthy Jews exploited the poor Jewish working masses, just as the Polish gentry exploited the peasants. Rabbis were drawn to the rich, as the Polish clergy was drawn to the gentry. The secular and spiritual oligarchy that held sway in the [Jewish] communities ...oppressed the people with the tax instrument at its command. It imposed the heaviest burden of government and communal taxes upon the indigent strata of the people, and ruined them completely."[6]

The advent of Alexander II (1855–81) brought a change in emphasis of state policy on Jews. The conferring of privileges upon certain Jews was stepped up. A stress was to be placed on rewarding usefulness rather than penalizing uselessness. Certain classes of large-scale businessmen, such as guild merchants, and university graduates were permitted to live outside the pale, as were some artisans who produced services in short supply. Under certain conditions, some Jews could even become lawyers. This paper-thin privileged layer coexisted alongside a mountain of poverty and oppression.

In 1871, the first modern pogrom occurred in Odessa. It remained an isolated event for the next decade and was thus not thought to cast an ominous shadow. Ten years later, however, Alexander II was assassinated by revolutionists and soon thereafter a plague of pogroms erupted in about 200 different localities. The next year, an especially vicious one occurred in Balta; others were recorded in 1883, 1884, 1891, 1897, 1899, and afterward. While some suspected the silent hand of the central government lay behind the early attacks, little evidence of this appeared.[7]

But if the government had done little to ignite the fire, it did not hesitate to stoke it. In August 1881 a government memorandum blamed the pogroms not on their instigators but on their victims. It referred to "the detriment caused to the Christian population of the Empire by the activity of the Jews, their tribal exclusiveness and religious fanaticism." Further, it complained about an "exploitation [by Jews] of the indigenous population and mostly of the poorer classes."[8] Apparently, the tsarist state had lately experienced a conversion to the cause of poor workers and peasants. Its secret agents sped up their work. Another theme they spread was a supposed conspiracy of Jews to rule the world. In 1869, an apostate Jew and police spy, Jacob A. Branfman, had written a book setting forward such a thesis; the volume was unsullied by facts.

Tsarist officials used the pogrom crisis to install new legislation for Jews. In 1882 the so-called temporary laws were passed. (They lasted, in fact, until 1917.) Jews were forbidden to settle anew in villages. Outside towns and cities Jews could not own real estate. Work was not to be permitted on Sundays or certain holidays. Villages were granted authority to expel Jews. In 1884, a ministerial committee reported to the tsar "that the growing influx of the non-Christian element in the schools was exerting a deleterious influence in the ethico-religious phase, upon the Christian children." Three years later these sentiments were incorporated within a law that regulated the attendance of Jews in schools. Inside the pale, Jews could make up no more than 10 percent of total secondary school enrollment; outside the pale, only 5 percent; and in Moscow and St. Petersburg, only 3 percent. Quotas were later applied to higher education.

The new restrictive measures worked. Jewish enrollment in universities fell between 1887 and 1899 from 14.8 to 10.9 percent in Russia as a whole and from 12.7 to 4.4 percent in Moscow and St. Petersburg.[9] Quotas were lowered in 1901–2. In 1891, half the Jews in Moscow were expelled from the city. Two years earlier Jews were temporarily excluded from bar examinations. The next year they were no longer permitted to participate in local government. The pace of civic retrogression for Jews did not slacken. Indeed, with the reign of Nicholas II (1894–1917), the movement sped up.

Attacks on the Jews as an alien element grew just at the time they were becoming a more integral part of Russian society. The growth of industry and the abolition of serfdom in 1862 changed the role of Jews in many rural communities where they were replaced by Russians. Petty trade, small-scale industry, and artisan trades such as shoemaking, tailoring, and carpentry absorbed the energies of working Jews. As restrictions governing their movement and employment multiplied, their economic status fell. An official memorandum in 1883 said nine out of ten Jews "lived in poverty, in unhygienic conditions and poor housing."[10] Hundreds of thousands of Jews were dependent on communal Jewish charity.

Early in the nineteenth century, Jews had rejected tsarist invitations to send their children to secular public schools. Near century's end, however, Jews were protesting at the near-exclusion of their children from secular educational institutions. What happened inbetween was a series of changes that increased the integration of Jews into the national economy, loosened the hold of religious orthodoxy on them, and pushed them into radical opposition to an increasingly oppressive political system. All these changes occurred in a context of nationalist feeling among Jews, not as Russians but as Jews. Locked out of all formal institutions of governance, many Jews sought strength in national self-identity; others tried to combine such identity with a goal of revolutionizing Russian society.

Emigration was another Jewish response chosen by many. Between 1880 and 1914, nearly 2 million Jews left Russia, most of them for the United States. Hans Rogger notes that "more than half of Jewish immigrants arrived without any means."[11] The flow responded directly to the occurrence of pogroms and poverty.

The bedrock of the antisemitic movement continued to be the doctrines and teachings of the Orthodox church. In 1890, Alexander III wrote in the margin of a report on Jews: "But we must never forget that the Jews have crucified our Master, and have shed His precious blood."[12] The Russian press, some of it in the pay of the government, could be depended upon to attack Jews on whatever ground. On the eve of the 1881 pogroms, the press helped heat up the atmosphere of hatred. In 1890, Lev Tolstoy and other prominent writers signed a declaration

against antisemitism in the press. Many years earlier, in 1857, Ivan Turgenev was one of 140 eminent authors who protested the publication of
an antisemitic article in a St. Petersburg magazine.[13]

During the 1881 pogroms, Jewish victims felt abandoned and isolated.
Wherever possible, as in Kiev, Jews mounted self-defense measures—
but virtually no help was given by non-Jews. In fact, as Jonathan Frankel
points out, "two major revolutionary parties in Russia showed clear signs
of sympathy with the pogroms."[14] They viewed the admittedly destructive actions as a necessary first step toward the creation of a mass revolutionary movement to overthrow the tsarist system. Supporters of the
system, and these included the antisemites, rejoiced at the direction of
events.

Fewer than twenty years after the 1881 events, the situation had under-
gone a fundamental change. In 1897, Jewish socialists organized the
Bund, an organization uniting members in Russia, Poland, and Lithuania. The following year, Lenin and his supporters formed the Russian
Social Democratic Labor party (RSDLP). Both groups, who cooperated
from time to time, were resolutely opposed to pogroms. Lenin, who
regarded the Jews as the most oppressed people in Russia, attacked
pogroms as attempts to divert revolutionary energies from the over-
turning of the autocracy and capitalist rule. (See the appendix to this
chapter.) The Bund led Jews in self-defense measures. At times, RSDLP
members joined such efforts.

In the first decade of the twentieth century, the tsarist government
adopted the pogrom as a major instrument of its Jewish policy. Rallying
police, soldiers, editors, spies, hired thugs, and others, ministerial offices
became the headquarters of a national movement. While the auspices
of the pogroms to follow were never in doubt, elaborate efforts were
made to disguise them as indigenous and local in inspiration. The 1903
Kishinev pogrom, a particularly savage one, was followed by others even
more so. Official sponsorship encouraged the worst elements. By 1911,
Lenin was denouncing the government for letting "loose gangs of men
who seize hold of Jewish children by their legs and smash their heads
against stones, who rape Jewish and Georgian women and rip open the
bellies of old men."[15]

In October 1905, pogroms were occurring at the rate of about fifty
in a week. They failed, however, to distract popular attention from the
general failings of the regime. Jews could take little comfort from the
fact since they continued to suffer from the attacks. The Revolution of
1905 had involved numerous Jews in a common movement with many
more non-Jews. It was the single greatest integrative act of Jewish history
in Russia. As Frankel explains: "Whatever the social roots of antisemitism, its adoption as an instrument of concerted governmental policy
left the Jews no choice but to hope and work for the victory of the

opposition, and in 1905 that meant the victory, at least partial, of the revolution."[16]

Russia had absorbed a major part of Polish territory in 1772, 1793, and 1795. Let us review the course of antisemitism in Polish Russia in the years until 1918, when Poland once more became independent.

Poland itself did not have a "pale" but Jews were restricted to certain streets in cities like Warsaw. The principal part of the country, called Congress Poland, prospered from its access to the large Russian market. Industrialization attracted a growing Jewish community as well as a large Polish middle class. The two conflicted sharply over economic and other opportunities. Congress Poland became the gathering point of Polish antisemitism. In the borderlands, including the Lithuanian lands, and in Galicia, the underdeveloped agrarian region bordering on Austria-Hungary, antisemitism made less headway. Apparently, this was because in both places competition with the Jews was moderated by "the retarded nature of the local nationalities and their failure to develop an important commercial and professional class."[17]

In 1807, Napoleon's military victory was followed by creation of the Duchy of Warsaw. Jews gained little from this. In the Kingdom of Poland, which existed as an autonomous part of Russia from 1815 to 1830, laws were passed that closed more streets in Warsaw to Jewish residence. Jews were exempted from military service at a time when in Russia proper their fellow Jews were serving twenty-five-year terms. There was, however, no talk of equal rights for Jews in Congress Poland. Warsaw Jews, braving blatant antisemitism, volunteered in large numbers to fight Russia in the Polish Revolt of 1831. Jews sat out a similar insurrection in 1863 when they seemed to hope for concessions on their status from the tsar. None came. In 1881, when pogroms rent Russia, one broke out in Warsaw as well.

In 1897, the National Democratic party (NDP), founded by Roman Dmowski, was deeply antisemitic. Hoping to "free Poland from Jewish influence," it never ceased to advocate the expulsion of Jews from Poland. In the Duma, the Russian parliament, NDP deputies cooperated closely with right-wing Russian antisemites. Right after the 1905 revolution, Polish antisemites developed a movement whose first campaign was a national boycott of Jewish businesses. By 1911, according to Dubnov, "the boycott became a fierce economic pogrom."[18] By the outbreak of World War I in 1914, there was little to distinguish Polish from Russian antisemitism.

"When the war came in 1914," writes Rogger, "a spy scare led to indiscriminate mass expulsions of Jews from the Western territories of the Empire on the grounds that they were all traitors or potential traitors."[19] Picked up and immediately deported elsewhere in the country were up to half a million Jews living on the western frontier of Russia.

They had no chance to secure their belongings or their property. In 1915, the Russian censorship office banned all publications in Yiddish or Hebrew on the ground that these were especially difficult to review. The chief of staff of the supreme commander was the moving spirit behind these actions. In part, Russian military authorities feared a positive Jewish response to invitations by invading Germans for Russian Jews to set up Yiddish schools and other community institutions, all of which were illegal under the tsar. In some areas of German occupation, this was done. There was, however, no substance to the spy mania.[20] (The parallel between these events and those involving Japanese-Americans in World War II is striking.)

One unanticipated positive consequence of the spy mania was that Jews, when moved to the inner provinces, automatically left the pale. Similarly, wounded Jewish soldiers who were demobilized because of injuries could attend educational institutions regardless of quotas.

In February 1917 the provisional government headed by Kerensky took office. Within two weeks or so, a decree was published abolishing all anti-Jewish legislation. When the Bolshevik revolution triumphed in October, under the leadership of Lenin, the same action was taken. The most urgent matter confronting Jews was not, however, the issue of legal rights. Instead, it was the appearance of deadly pogroms in the Ukraine, where over 1 million of the country's 2.5 million Jews lived. Temporary independence enabled the creation of a Ukrainian army which in 1917 was massacring one Jewish community after another. After German troops retreated, late in 1918, an even worse wave of pogroms, led by Ukrainian leader Simon Petlura, a hater of Jews and of the new Communist government, occurred. The Red Army came to the rescue of many besieged Jews. As Dubnov wrote: "In many cities, Jews welcomed the Bolsheviks as saviors.... The Jewish self-defense was issued arms and fought heroically."[21] Between December 1918 and April 1921, according to Dubnov, 887 large-scale pogroms occurred in 530 Jewish communities. About 60,000 Jews perished in these years.

Special sections of government and Communist party bureaus were designated to deal with minority affairs, including Jews. While intense campaigns were waged by Communists against religious and nationalist chauvinism, the struggle was, as Isaac Deutscher notes, "conducted ... with complete impartiality."[22] Churches and synagogues were closed without distinction. The teaching of Hebrew, because of its special religious significance for Judaism, was all but illegalized. Religious schools and seminaries were closed down.

Yiddish-language culture experienced a great expansion with government encouragement. Yiddish schools, which had been illegal under tsarist rule, were now opened over the entire country. A shortage continued until the late 1920s. Between 1924 and 1928 the number of

Yiddish cultural and educational institutions doubled. Yiddish-language technical and professional schools were opened. Two Jewish state museums were in operation. At White Russia State University in Minsk, there was a Jewish section in the pedagogical faculty. Four divisions of the section prepared teachers for Jewish secondary schools. Jewish divisions were organized in the academies of science of the Ukraine and White Russia. In the former was a Jewish graduate school that was "the highest level institution in the Soviet Union conducting its work in Yiddish which offered degrees."[23]

The revolution opened the universities to new social circles. In 1927–28, for example, children of peasants made up one-fourth of all university students. Women, who had been excluded from universities in tsarist times, constituted 27 percent of all students in 1925.[24] Under prewar quotas, Jews had made up 10.7 percent of all university students in the Ukraine; in 1923, the figure rose to 47.4 percent; and by 1929 it had fallen to 23.3 percent.[25] The drop still left Jewish representation at over twice the prewar level. The main reason for the reduction was not a quota but the result of an affirmative-action policy that had been established in 1918. This policy admitted children of peasants and workers at or above the age of sixteen, whether or not they had graduated from secondary schools. In addition, more children of other national minorities began to attend universities; special measures were taken to encourage them.

Antisemitism did not disappear among all these developments. There is reason to believe, for example, that Stalin used antisemitism in his struggles during the 1920s against party leaders who differed with him. Lenin's spirited opposition to antisemitism remained a vital heritage after his death in 1924. Nevertheless, around the time of his death, antisemitism seemed on an upswing. In the late 1920s even some members of the Young Communist League were found indulging in the practice. In factories, which began employing Jews for the first time in the country's history, some workers were displeased and expressed their antisemitic sentiments. In 1929 an inquiry into antisemitism by the Moscow City Trade Union Council found further evidences. According to Solomon M. Schwarz, "antisemitism in the late 1920s had spread among groups dispossessed by the revolution, who incited the new industrial proletariat against the 'Jewish intruder'. . . . When the Five-Year Plan policy [in 1929] created millions of new jobs, recriminations against Jewish 'usurpers' became less frequent and lost their emotional meaning."[26]

Especially during the late 1920s, writes William Korey, "the regime continued to make strong efforts to contain the virus of anti-Jewish bigotry."[27] Books on antisemitism were issued by government presses. Non-Jewish industrial workers joined organized excursions to visit Jewish farm colonies. The project was "astonishingly popular."[28] Yet, there was less than complete mobilization of legal and political resources in the struggle against antisemitism. While Lenin had labeled antisemites "outlaws" in 1918, judges in the 1920s were reluctant to jail antisemites, even though specific statutes required it. Little was done in the schools or by the mass media to examine their own antisemitism. Schwarz writes that "the party was often irresolute and lethargic and fought antisemitism only when flagrant instances came to light; its activities seldom arose above the local level."[29]

During the first half of the 1930s, antisemitism seemed on the decline and at its lowest point since the revolution. Jewish cultural activities were near their peak. As Gerald Stillman reports: "In 1931, about half the Jewish children of school age in the Ukraine and Byelorussia [the areas of highest Jewish residence] attended Yiddish elementary schools.... In 1933, the State Yiddish Publishing House in Moscow printed 108 books in a total of 925,000 copies.... The Ukrainian Yiddish Publishing House that year printed 189 books in a total of 1¼ million copies.... In 1932, there were 40 Yiddish periodicals."[30] Continuing industrialization was helping break up many traditionally Jewish areas and Jews were dispersed ever more widely in the country. The Jewish petty trader class simply evaporated.

The Great Purges of the mid- and late 1930s changed all this. One old Bolshevik after another was charged with counterrevolutionary activities, found guilty, and executed. A disproportionately large part of them were Jewish. Entire staffs of Jewish institutions were arrested and executed. The Stalin regime then virtually destroyed the extensive cultural structure of Soviet Jewry. Jewish schooling was cut sharply. "By the end of 1940," Korey records, "there were some eighty-five thousand to ninety thousand Jewish children—about 20 percent of the Jewish student population—studying in schools where Yiddish was the language of instruction."[31] Yiddish theaters were closed down. All Yiddish publications were banned. The publishing of Yiddish books was reduced almost to nothing. Fatefully, as Korey observes, "from the late thirties and early forties on, if slowly and unevenly, anti-Jewish discrimination became an integral part of official state policy."[32] Schwarz stresses a different aspect: "The Great Purge virtually terminated the organized life of the Jewish group as a recognized cultural and ethnic minority."[33]

In August 1939, the Soviets and Nazis signed a nonaggression pact. A week later, Germany attacked Poland and World War II began. Within a few months, Soviet armed forces occupied the three Baltic republics (Estonia, Latvia, and Lithuania) and eastern Poland. In Lithuania, Jewish schools conducted in Hebrew were changed over to Yiddish or closed. The curriculum dropped all subjects related to religion, including Jewish history. Two leaders of the Polish Bund, Henryk Erlich and Wiktor Alter, were arrested by the Soviets in September 1939 and executed during December 1941–January 1942.

All this was evidence of an inexplicable change of Soviet state policy on Jewish affairs. While during the course of the war—the USSR was attacked by Nazi Germany in June 1941—the government did not relent, it nevertheless adopted a number of measures that were vital to the further existence of a Jewish community in the USSR. Soviet policy on Jews was, to say the least, ambiguous.

While 1.5 million Soviet Jews perished before the Nazi onslaught, at least a similar number were saved. Some, industrial workers, were evacuated eastward. Others were evacuated as civilians. A large number simply fled out of the Nazi path as news of the slaughter spread among Soviet citizens. Nazi commanders complained that they were occupying empty villages. Survivors of the invasion frequently referred to having participated in or witnessed evacuation. In Berdichev only one-third left. Jews in Taganrog were offered a chance to evacuate but refused. While Raul Hilberg writes that over 1.5 million Soviet Jews escaped death at the hands of the Nazis, Isaac Deutscher places the figure between 2.5 and 3 million.[34]

When Nazi armies entered the Ukraine and Byelorussia in mid-1941, they mounted an enormous campaign of antisemitism. Reports are conflicting as to how these efforts were received in the Ukraine, the site of the most extensive pogroms in Soviet history. Schwarz writes that "a passive attitude seems to have been the rule."[35] Hilberg agrees. Deutscher paints a very different picture: "In the Ukraine the population at first received Hitler and his occupation armies with relief and even joy. And this lasted up to the moment when the Nazis showed the Ukrainians what they were really capable of."[36] Ilya Ehrenburg, a Soviet writer of Jewish origin and a trusted associate of Stalin, reported that antisemitism among Russians was on the rise in territories occupied by the Nazis.[37] Stalin refused to mount a countercampaign because he did not want the war effort to appear to be a war on behalf of Jews. In fact, throughout the war the Soviet press deliberately censored any mention of Jews as special victims.

Soviet military victories saved large numbers of Jews in the USSR although 1.5 million Soviet Jews were killed. They also buoyed the spirits of Jews and others in the occupied countries of Europe. The great victory at Stalingrad was a pivotal event of continentwide proportions. Occurring in February 1943, it was the first demonstration that Nazi armed might was not invincible and that a complete Nazi defeat was possible. It moved some allies of the Nazis—Italy, Bulgaria, and Hungary—to heighten their resistance to Nazi pressure for a Final Solution in their countries.

In the first months of the war, when Nazi troops flooded the western part of the country, the Stalin regime sought aid overseas. Because Soviet Jews had family and communal ties with persons in allied countries, especially the United States, they were singled out for a special task. In the late 1930s, such ties had been regarded with suspicion by Soviet authorities and had helped undo numerous Jewish political and cultural functionaries. In August 1941, however, there was created, under supervision of the ministry of foreign affairs, the Jewish Antifascist Committee (JAC). Its work was carried on through a full-time staff, occasional plenary meetings, and numerous delegations to other countries. Beginning in the summer of 1942, a journal *Eynikayt* (unity) was published, at first every ten days and later three times a week. According to Shimon Redlich, "the tone of the journal was Jewish nationalism."[38] No other Soviet nationality organized its own committee.

In early JAC meetings, there was extensive discussion of reports on sufferings of Jews in the path of Nazi advance and of spreading antisemitism. Yet some principal leaders of the group opposed JAC dealing head-on with the issue of antisemitism in the USSR. In the second plenary session, however, held during February 1943—the month of the Stalingrad victory—"a number of participants hinted at the ominous anti-Jewish attitudes and accusations prevailing among the Soviet population and sought ways to reverse this trend."[39] At a JAC meeting in Moscow, held in 1944 and attended by 3,000 persons, some speakers "pointed to the dangers of antisemitic attitudes within the Soviet population, especially when held by those who had been exposed to Nazi rule and propaganda."[40]

JAC tended to become more of a communal voice as time wore on. It published Yiddish books. Yiddish literary events were held in its offices. It maintained an archive of Nazi offenses against Jews. Jewish soldiers and partisans were attracted to it. Complaints of discrimination against Jews were brought to JAC. In many ways, JAC was becoming an organization resembling the kinds of Jewish groups that had been abolished late in the previous decade.

Mid-1944 saw the clearing of all Nazis from Soviet soil. JAC tried to help Jews who were former residents of western Russia to return to their homes where they often met a hostile reception. Redlich charges that "outright and crude antisemitism prevailed in the highest Party circles in Belorussia after its liberation" and that "the Party leadership [in Minsk] was outspokenly antisemitic."[41] After the war the emergency that had given birth to JAC disappeared and the group's future became problematic. A damper was placed by the regime upon JAC activities that smacked of Jewish nationalism. Selected officials of the group attacked such activities and criticized an alleged preoccupation with the Holocaust.

Early in 1948, an outstanding leader of JAC, the actor Solomon Mikhoels, was killed in an accident in Minsk. The weight of evidence suggested the accident was ordered by the regime. Later that year, Ehrenburg published in *Pravda* an article that criticized those Jewish leaders who, according to him, tended to place Jewish nationalism above patriotic Russian concerns. In November, both JAC and *Eynikayt* were shut down. The group had emerged from a collapse of Jewish communal life; its demise threatened a new stage in the same direction.

In 1947–48, the issue of Jews in Russia became entwined with the birth of Israel. In 1947, the Soviets cooperated with the United States to pass a United Nations resolution calling for Arab and Jewish states to be created out of Palestine. The Soviets were the first to recognize the State of Israel in 1948. When, in 1948, war broke out between Arab and Israeli forces, writes John A. Armstrong, "Soviet agents dispatched a very substantial quantity of arms to Israel by air, in addition to recruiting and training Eastern European Jews for fighting in the Israeli forces."[42] (In 1948 and 1949 alone, fully two-thirds of Bulgaria's Jews were permitted to emigrate to Israel.) Whether Soviet Jews wanted to depart is not clear. Redlich reports that many Jews were eager to volunteer to fight for Israel.[43] On the other hand, Umberto Terracini contends that very few Soviet Jews moved to Israel when that state was created.[44] Perhaps many wished to go but were not permitted to do so.

Soviet support for Israel extended into 1949, as Korey notes: "In the Arab-Israeli War that . . . lasted until early 1949, the Soviet state was both a harsh critic of the Arab side and a vigorous supporter of Israel, enabling the latter to obtain great quantities of military supplies from Communist-dominated Czechoslovakia. Not until 1950 did the Soviet Government switch to a policy of overt antagonism toward Israel."[45] The USSR broke diplomatic relations with Israel only in 1953. The break, argues Korey, "was due far less to foreign policy considerations than to the need to justify an internal policy which required Israel, in the guise of Zionism, to be portrayed as an enemy. . . . The beginning of a pro-Arab policy on the part of the USSR did not emerge until 1954."[46]

The "internal policy" referred to a sweeping series of measures and actions of government origin against Jews that occupied the years from 1949 to 1953. In 1949, suppression of Jewish community cadre was completed. Even the most prominent of them was arrested and executed. Jews were criticized in the press as "cosmopolitans" and "antipatriots." When a Jew with a Russian-sounding name was discussed in a story, his Jewish name was placed in parentheses. During the early 1950s, rumors circulated that Stalin was planning to move European Jews to the Far East.

In January 1953, *Pravda* made a sensational announcement—nine physicians were arrested on charges that they had conspired to kill prominent politicians and military leaders under their care. *Pravda* stated that the physicians had "administered deleterious treatment to the patients and undermined their health." The story continued: "It has been established that all these doctor-murderers, who had become monsters of mankind, trampled the sacred banner of science, and defiled the honor of scientific workers, were hired agents of foreign intelligence services." Most doctors in the alleged conspiracy, charged *Pravda*, were connected with "the international Jewish bourgeois-nationalist organization, the Joint." (The Joint Distribution Committee is a worldwide organization that specializes in aiding needy Jews anywhere with relief funds for food, clothing, and shelter.) The same day, *Izvestia* referred to "this sordid Zionist espionage organization" and "corrupt Jewish bourgeois-nationalists." The next weeks were marked by a high-pitched campaign that terrified numerous Jews.

Amidst the campaign, Stalin died. The "Doctors' Plot" expired with him. His successor, Georgi Malenkov, called off the entire campaign and released everyone who had been arrested in connection with it. While the government thus acknowledged the entire affair rested on fake charges, no official comment was made on the antisemitic aspects of the affair. Little else changed. As Korey writes: "For the next fourteen years the ideology was absent but antisemitism remained as state policy in the form of discrimination against Jewish communal-cultural life, civil discrimination in the political-security area, and discrimination in administrative and cadre appointments and in quota systems in universities."[47]

Under the Khrushchev regime, an anti-Stalinist "thaw" set in. There was a sharp drop in police terror and arbitrary arrests. Many political prisoners were released from forced labor camps. In 1956, Khrushchev told the Twentieth Congress of the Communist party some of the details of Stalin's tyranny. He failed, however, to mention a single antisemitic action by Stalin; there was no reference to the recent doctors' plot.

In the country as a whole, the "thaw" had ambiguous effects on antisemitism. Ettinger holds that "the relative liberalization in Khrushchev's time, albeit weak, brought out strong public antisemitic feelings."[48] L. Dimerski-Tsigelman, however, points to another side of the matter: "The relaxation of censorship which took place during the period of liberalization created wider possibilities for having things published officially in the mid-1950s. It also led to the publication of a number of exposes which revealed, among other things, occasional truthful information about Jews' participation in World War II and about antisemitism. As the pressure of censorship increased, such works were gradually relegated to the pages of peripheral publications, finally to end up completely in the Samizdat, then the emigre press."[49]

The early 1960s saw a flurry of voiced concern about antisemitism. In a speech of March 1963, Khrushchev gave a Leninist interpretation of pogroms before the revolution: "The pogroms were instigated by the autocratic government, by capitalists, landlords, and by the bourgeoisie. They needed the pogroms as a means of diverting the working class from the revolutionary struggle."[50] (On the same occasion Khrushchev also told an anecdote that was arguably antisemitic.) Two years later Premier A. N. Kosygin stated in Riga: "The manifestation of nationalism, great-power chauvinism, racism, antisemitism is absolutely alien to us and in contradiction to our world view."[51] Less than two months later, a *Pravda* editorial referred positively to Lenin's call to "struggle against antisemitism, that malicious exaggeration of racial separateness and national enmity."[52] No such struggle is known to have ensued.

After the late 1940s, textbooks used by schoolchildren began to reflect the suppression of Jewish communal life. A standard reference work, the *Great Soviet Encyclopedia,* had devoted 117 pages to the Jews in its 1932 edition. Twenty years later, it was cut to *two* pages. Ruth Okuneva, a trained historian and curriculum specialist, reported on her study of the subject of Jewish history in Soviet textbooks. She found that during the years 1940–56 secondary-school history texts all but eliminated references to the subject. The same was done during 1954–56 in tenth-grade texts in ancient, medieval, modern, and Soviet history. Starting in the 1960s, she contends, texts were less likely to be written by academic experts. Perhaps not coincidentally, that was the same decade, according to Okuneva, when negatives about Jews began to appear and positives to disappear. It was her opinion that the texts and related popular literature were leading to "formation in the minds of schoolchildren of a stereotyped antisemitic view of Jewry."[53] In texts dealing with Germany during World War II, Jews are not mentioned; thus, the Holocaust is entirely passed over.[54]

To propagandize against religion is a constitutional imperative in the Soviet Union. Whether a specific attack upon Judaism is antisemitic depends on whether Jews are being singled out with special vehemence or frequency. Sources are at odds on this issue. In 1969, for instance, Alex Inkeles wrote: "The reviling of Jews in terms of their religion is . . . not greater than that of other religious groups, as far as basic practices go. The Jews are either incorporated in blanket attacks or particular aspects of Jewish ceremony and belief are picked out in a way that does not exceed . . . the lack of humaneness or consideration for human feelings involved in attacks on specific religious practices of other groups."[55] On the other hand, a study of a bibliographic compilation by B. Pinkus and A. A. Greenbaum leads William Korey to observe that between 1958 and 1967 "the number of copies of books attacking Judaism was seven times as great as the number of copies attacking Islam and twice as great as the number of copies attacking Christianity."[56]

In the 1960s, but especially during and after 1967, the year of Israel's Six-Day War, a new stage was reached in the official popularization of antisemitism in the Soviet Union. The new wave endured throughout the following decade as well. Seven or so authors, publicists for the most part, wrote a series of works that preached hatred of Judaism under the guise of Zionism, although oftentimes the attack was undisguised.[57] The spirit of the attacks followed the outlines of the tsarist police fabrication of 1903–5, *The Protocols of the Elders of Zion*. Jews were charged with conspiring to control the world. Their religion was denigrated. Zionism was said to be the true nationalism of Jews who were otherwise unpatriotic. Israel was declared to be the fountainhead of this world conspiracy.

Much of this new material directly contradicted writings by Lenin on Jews, but this fact was never stated by the writers. Lev Korneev, for example, wrote that "by the middle of the nineteenth century the bourgeoisie of Jewish origin in many countries—the Russian empire, Germany, France, Britain, the United States, Italy, Austria-Hungary, virtually controlled the policies of a number of states." Lenin, who regarded the Jews as the most oppressed national minority in tsarist Russia, would have rejected Korneev's characterization on this ground alone. In Italy Jews constituted a tiny minority and at mid-century had not even been emancipated. Full emancipation was yet to come in England and Germany. Korneev simply invented the influence of Jews in the mid-century United States.

V. Begun, another of the prominent antisemitic publicists, rejected—without noting so—the Leninist analysis of pogroms in tsarist Russia. Begun painted them as just retribution by workers and peasants against exploitation by Jews. He ignored Lenin's view that pogroms were aimed at Jews in order to use them as a scapegoat with which to distract worker and peasant dissatisfaction with the tsarist regime. As recently as 1979, Lydia Modzhorian wrote in *Zionism as a Form of Racism and Racist Discrimination* that "there were no anti-Jewish pogroms, but Jews continually interfered in the affairs of Tsars Nicholas I, Alexander II and Nicholas II."

Ye. Yevseev declared: "The peculiarities of the Jewish religion are hatred of mankind, preaching genocide, cultivating a love of power, and glorifying criminal means of achieving power." Begun assured his readers that "the Torah . . . proves to be an unsurpassed textbook of blood-thirstiness and hypocrisy, treachery, perfidy, and licentiousness—of every vile human quality."

Whereas Lenin stressed the true-blue revolutionary spirit among Jews during the early part of the century, the new writers simply declared the opposite and spoke of the very small Jewish capitalist class as though it were the whole of Jewry. Lenin had also viewed the Dreyfus affair in late nineteenth-century France as an attack on republicanism and the Jewish people. The new writers rejected this analysis—again, without saying so—and argued that the attack on Jews reflected worker-peasant anger at Jewish exploitation. (Actually, workers and peasants did not form the heart of French antisemitism.)

So blatantly at odds were these writings with classical Communist policies that objections to their antisemitism were voiced during 1964–78 by the Communist parties of Italy, Britain, Australia, and France. A former American Communist leader, Peggy Dennis, wrote after numerous visits to the USSR that "a government *glavlit* (censor) at each institution initials the contents of every publication. It is impossible for recurring antisemitic writings to appear accidentally, at the whim of some individual racist."[58] While in Moscow in 1972, she related, "the personal conversations of these bright, young party activists were punctuated with casual antisemitic remarks and jokes. The very casualness with which they were told indicated these comments had become ordinary."[59] She explained further: "The antisemitic expressions I personally heard came from Soviet-educated party ideologists and political cadres. The antisemitic incidents related to me were told by lifetime Comintern Communists."[60]

Partly in response to worldwide criticism, an antisemitic work published in 1963 was withdrawn the next year. (This was Trofim Kichko's *Judaism without Embellishment.*) Four years later, however, the Ukrainian Supreme Soviet awarded him a Diploma of Honor for "dissemination of atheist propaganda."

English historian Martin Gilbert visited the USSR in March 1983. He wrote:

My arrival in the Soviet Union . . . coincided with an article in the popular Leningrad history magazine *Neva* which made the astonishing claim that stories of the persecution of the Jews under the Tsars were nothing but "Zionist propaganda." According to the article, the much publicized pogroms of the Tsarist era arose, not from any irrational Jew hatred, but because the Jews themselves had provoked local and peasant anger by their economic dominance. No mention was made of the fact that much of Jewish life in the Pale of Settlement was marked by extreme poverty.[61]

Tsarist Russia, observed the article, "was always good for Jews."

It can be seen very readily that this distortion of Russian history went hand-in-hand with the policy over the past thirty years or so to omit Jews from the history curriculum. In this way, the silent repudiation of Lenin's authority on Jewish matters would meet with only the slightest objection. It is quite reminiscent of the stereotyped treatment until recently of the "happy slave" in U.S. history.

Sometime after World War II, Soviet authorities established unpublished quotas governing the number of Jews to be permitted in universities and certain employments. Armstrong, in fact, holds that secret quotas were begun as early as 1942, during the war.[62] In 1956, according to Korey, "the central government had consciously established quota systems to restrict Jewish employment, and even more rigid quotas were installed in the governments of the various union republics."[63] During the war, there were hundreds of Jewish generals. Since the war, apparently, no new ones have been appointed. Nor are there Jews in the Politburo or other key offices in national, provincial, or district party organizations. In the diplomatic service, or in the defense and foreign trade ministries, virtually no Jews serve at any level. Certain highly secret defense-related jobs are difficult for Jews to get.

Since the 1920s, Jews have attended universities far beyond their number in the population. In 1972, Joseph Braginsky wrote that "14 percent of the Jewish population ... has received a higher education, a percentage nine times higher than among the Russians and 12 times higher than among the Ukrainians."[64] Three factors have worked to reduce this historical advantage: (1) the opening of new universities in the eastern part of the country which enroll few Jews since not many live there; (2) the number of Jews is falling; between 1970 and 1979, the decline was 15.8 percent; and (3) there is evidence of increasing discrimination against Jewish students.

The number of all students in higher education grew between 1970 and 1976 by 8 percent while that of Jewish students fell by 36.8 percent.[65] The Jewish percentage of total enrollment thus declined from 2.3 percent in 1970 to 1.4 percent in 1976. In postgraduate studies, the picture was even worse. Between 1970 and 1975, while the number of all postgraduate students dropped by 3.8 percent, that of Jewish students fell by 42.5 percent.[66] The number of Jews among all postgraduates from 1970 to 1975 fell from 5 to 3 percent.

Jewish representation in university departments of science and mathematics, traditionally high, sank rapidly, especially during the 1970s. In 1970, Jewish authors of articles in the prime mathematical journal of the USSR numbered forty-three, nearly 40 percent of the total of 108. In 1977, the total had fallen to ninety-five but the number by Jews was only five, or 5.3 percent.[67] Anti-Jewish quotas were more moderate or even absent altogether in Siberian universities. The number of Jews employed as scientific workers continued to rise between 1970 and 1975 but the rate of growth lagged behind that for all scientific workers (7.7 percent and 21.1 percent). It is not clear how much of the lag reflected discrimination and how much was a ceiling effect.

Discrimination against Judaism continued into the 1980s. Unlike adherents of other religions in the USSR, Jews were forbidden to organize national or regional associations. Nor could they, as others, join world federations representing their faith. Similarly, alone of the major religions, Jews were forbidden to issue publications. Virtually no facilities existed for rabbinical training.[68]

An accumulation of antisemitism occurred in 1967 and thereafter, the time of the Six-Day War, won overwhelmingly by Israel. The Soviet press, followed by books, brochures, and broadcasts, portrayed Israel as the successor power to Nazi Germany. Zionism was said to be the equivalent of Nazism. Stereotypes of Jews, quite consonant with those generated by the Nazi press under Hitler, were outfitted in Israeli garb.[69] Arab forces, whom Soviets had criticized severely in 1948–49 when they fought Israel, were now hailed for their struggle. By the mid-1980s, the Soviet campaign against Zionism had not eased up.

Emigration from the USSR appeared to some Jews as the most effective means of escaping antisemitism. Between 1968 and 1981, 641,336 Soviet Jews received invitations to go to Israel. A total of 259,635, or 40.5 percent, permissions were granted by Soviet authorities.[70] Thus, about one out of ten Soviet Jews emigrated, a far lower percentage than under tsarist rule but itself a record outflow during the Soviet period.

By far most Jews in the Soviet Union chose to remain. One lesser reason was the immense difficulty placed by the government in the way of potential emigrants. Another was the high degree of assimilation among Jews. As Inkeles pointed out in 1969, "over the past twenty or thirty years, the Soviet Union has had one of the highest rates of social mobility in the world."[71] Four years later, Korey observed that "the continuing absolute increase in the numbers of Jews employed as specialists ... suggests that opportunities for Jews in the USSR are still great."[72] But Jews who wished to live a rich communal life as Jews faced difficult decisions. Although a law stipulated that any ten parents could request that their children be taught in a specific language of instruction, this was not enforced for Jews. To challenge the illegal practice was more than many Jews cared to undertake. (Lenin, by the way, had stressed the right of minorities to receive instruction in their language of choice and had mentioned Yiddish as a specific example.)

The effects of antisemitism on Jews are difficult but crucial to ascertain. In March 1983, a leading antisemitic writer, Lev Korneyev, wrote in a publication of the Young Communist League that the meaning of Zionism was "to turn every Jew, no matter where he lives, into an agent of the Jewish oligarchy, into a traitor to the country where he was born."[73] Two months later he wrote that "in the nineteenth century, Jews 'brought pogroms upon themselves' in order to stimulate emigration."[74] Those who remained were potential traitors while the ones who left were fleeing imaginary dangers, he declared.

An informed Jew, Grigory Vasserman, in an interview by Martin Gilbert, told him that "most of the Jews are willing to assimilate and are doing all they can to achieve that goal." Gilbert also related that "in ...

Odessa . . . [Vasserman] found that most Jews are not only indifferent to everything Jewish but hostile."[75] Little independent evidence is available to test Vasserman's statement. Dimerski-Tsigelman, an émigré, referred to "the growth of the shameless national apostasy characteristic of the anti-Zionist and anti-Semitic public utterances of the Jews themselves, in scientific treatises on the reactionary nature of Judaism and Zionism . . . in the newspapers . . . and in countless instances of personal testimony (press conferences, open letters, articles in periodicals). One sometimes gets the impression that this apostasy is assuming mass proportions."[76] The intimidating effect of mass media attacks on Jews, buttressed by an incessant stream of antisemitic and anti-Zionist books, can be seen at work here. In 1983 the regime organized an "Anti-Zionist Committee of the Soviet Public" on which a number of Jewish luminaries from various public spheres sat. It seemed to avoid any suggestion of antisemitism.

The most startling aspect of the situation in the Soviet Union was the sharp disjunction between open, unofficial Jew-baiting, on the one hand, and invisible, official antisemitism as well as occasional vacuous declarations against antisemitism by party and government, on the other. Both varieties, of course, were truly official since public authority is indispensable for mass communications to be employed.

APPENDIX

Vladimir Ilyich Lenin (1870–1924) was the organizer and leader of the Russian Social Democratic Labor party, later renamed the Russian Communist party, and the first premier of the Soviet Union. "Lenin never differentiated between people on the basis of their national or ethnic origins," according to the *Encyclopedia Judaica*. He wrote frequently on the subject of Jews and antisemitism.

In 1913 he described the Jews in tsarist Russia as "the most oppressed and persecuted nation."[77] The same year he declared that they were "condemned . . . to a condition worse than that of the Negroes."[78] In 1914 he returned to the matter: "No nationality is so oppressed and persecuted as the Jewish. . . . The Jewish workers are suffering under a double yoke, both as workers and Jews."[79] Lenin had struck this theme earlier, in 1905, when he wrote: "The Jewish workers, as a disfranchised nationality, not only suffer general economic and political oppression, but they also suffer under the yoke which deprives them of elementary civic rights."[80]

Government-inspired violence and private physical attacks upon Jews were condemned by Lenin without reserve. In 1911, he referred to the tsarist government as letting "loose gangs of men who seize hold of Jewish children by their legs and smash their heads against stones, who rape Jewish and Georgian women and rip open the bellies of old men."[81] Three months later, he recorded that "never before has there been such avid, ferocious, reckless persecution of the Jews, and after them of other peoples, not belonging to the dominant [Russian] nation."[82]

Lenin tended to explain the existence of such virulent antisemitism by dwelling on contemporary features of Russian society. The tsarist government, for example, was under a broadening attack from many sectors of the population and needed a scapegoat: "Governments that maintain themselves in power only by means of the bayonet, that have constantly to restrain or suppress the indignation of the people, have long realized the truism that popular discontent can never be removed and that it is necessary to divert the discontent from the government to some other object.... Hostility is being stirred up against the Jews; the gutter press carries on Jew-baiting campaigns, as if the Jewish workers do not suffer in exactly the same way as the Russian workers from the oppression of capital and the police government."[83] In addition, he charged the government tried to substitute ethnic hostility for class struggle and thus disrupt the revolutionary movement. Capitalist and other privileged classes, according to Lenin, similarly profited from ethnic hostility.

Lenin called upon workers without regard to ethnicity or religion to rally behind Jews under attack in pogroms. Referring to "legalized terrorism," he praised such an agreement in Ekaterinoslav which had been made in anticipation of a pogrom. Similarly, the Social Democrats in Borisoglebsk, during the revolutionary year of 1905, issued a leaflet calling for "a subscription for the organization of armed self-defense...to help in the organization of self-defense groups with money and arms."[84]

The Jews' lack of civil rights was an important issue to Lenin. When, in 1901, the government announced sale of some state lands, Jews and others were forbidden to buy any. Lenin commented acerbically: "The noble aristocrats, in alliance with the government, have prohibited Jews and other non-Russians (whom they try to present to the ignorant people as particularly outrageous exploiters) from acquiring state lands in Siberia, in order that they may *themselves* engage in the worst type of exploitation without hindrance."[85]

In 1914, a much broader approach to the issue of civil rights was outlined in a bill to be introduced into the Duma by the Bolsheviks. The measure was entitled "Bill for the Abolition of All Disabilities of the Jews and of All Restrictions on the Grounds of Origin or Nationality." In endorsing it, Lenin said the working class had "no more bitter enemy than the savage prejudices and superstitions which its enemies sow among the ignorant masses."[86] The hate campaign, Lenin added, was conducted not only by organized thugs but "this dirty and despicable work" was also carried on "by reactionary professors, scholars, journalists and members of the Duma. Millions and thousands of millions of rubles are spent on poisoning the minds of the people."[87]

The bill proclaimed legal equality for all nationalities. It forbade any discrimination: "No citizen of Russia, regardless of sex and religion, may be restricted in political or in any other rights on the grounds of origin or nationality." All laws restricting the rights of Jews were to be abolished; a list of these was appended.[88]

A major concern of Lenin's dealt with the nature of the Jewish people. Were Jews a nation, a nationality, or a national minority? Or a national caste? Centrally involved in such matters was the issue of assimilation which Lenin advocated. He opposed, however, any compulsory assimilation.

To Lenin, the "great world-progressive features of Jewish culture" consisted of "its internationalism, its identification with the advanced movements of the epoch (the percentage of Jews in the democratic and proletarian movements is everywhere higher than the percentage of Jews among the population)."[89] The best Jews, "those who are most celebrated in world history, and have given the world foremost leaders of democracy and socialism," he continued, "have never clamored against assimilation."[90] Lenin denied that the Jews were a nation. (Although from time to time he used the term "Jewish nation" he never presented an argument defending such usage.)

He took issue with Zionism on several occasions. In 1903 he spoke of "the Zionist fable about antisemitism being eternal."[91] He contended, instead, that a class-conscious alliance of Socialist workers could eliminate antisemitism. The Zionist conception of a Jewish nation he rejected since he believed that a national Jewish culture was incompatible with an international working-class culture. At no time, however, did Lenin deal with the specific Zionist idea of *a* national home for all the world's Jews.

On the other hand, an enigmatic statement of his, written in 1913, remains to be probed. "It is beyond doubt," he asserted, "that in order to eliminate all national oppression it is very important to create autonomous areas, however small, with entirely homogeneous populations, towards which members of the respective nationalities scattered all over the country, *or even all over the world,* could gravitate, and with which they could enter into relations and free associations of every kind."[92] Was this an indirect concession to a Zionist-like solution to Jewish oppression?

Much of Lenin's writing and speaking on Jewish matters involved the relation of his party to the General Jewish Workers Union or the "Bund" as it was popularly known. This Socialist group was organized in 1897 and affiliated, on and off, with the Russian Social Democratic Labor party, which was begun a year after the Bund. The Bund spoke of the Jews as a nation with its own language (Yiddish) and advocated the primacy of Jewish culture in a Socialist order. It fought Zionist doctrines and called upon Jewish workers to join the general movement for a Russian revolution. Bund leadership, as one historian put it, "could never finally decide whether its first duty lay with the international proletariat or with national liberation [of Jews]."[93]

Lenin took great issue with the Bund on whether it was to be autonomous within the Social Democratic party. He stressed that Jews within the party already had the right to publish materials in Yiddish, hold their own congresses, and adopt positions supplementary to the general party program. Under these conditions the certain consequence of autonomy would be a split between Jewish and non-Jewish Socialists. Lenin warned, for example, that Bundists were "stirring up distrust among Jewish towards non-Jewish proletarians, [and] fostering suspicion of the latter."[94] Governmental efforts to separate the nationalities and set them against one another underscored the need for unity among the Social Democrats; the Bund, he charged, was separatist. It favored the mandatory segregation of schools by national group, according to Lenin.

Outright advocacy of cultural assimilation by Lenin expressed the heart of his conflict with the Bund. Reviewing the history of legal emancipation of west European Jewry, he argued that this movement was accompanied by "the decline of medievalism [that is, of narrow religious influences] and the development of political liberty."[95] The abandonment of Yiddish and adoption of the national language followed emancipation. "Can we possibly attribute to chance," he asked, "the fact that it is the reactionary forces all over Europe, and especially in Russia, who *oppose* the assimilation of the Jews and try to perpetuate their isolation?"[96] Whoever raises an outmoded call for Jewish national culture is, Lenin declared, "an accomplice of the rabbis and the bourgeoisie."[97]

After the Russian Revolution of October 1917 and during the Civil War in 1919, a series of pogroms occurred in the Soviet Union. Lenin spoke on the subject and a phonograph record was made of his speech. He recalled the tsarist role in fomenting antisemitism before the revolution. "Presently," noted Lenin, "hatred toward Jews persists only in those countries where slavery to the landowners and capitalists has created abysmal ignorance among the workers and peasants. Only the most ignorant and downtrodden people can believe the lies and slander that are spread about the Jews."[98] Working people and Jews are not enemies; he stated: "Among the Jews there are working people, and they form the majority. They are our brothers, who, like us, are oppressed by capital; they are our comrades in the struggle for socialism."[99]

NOTES

1. Shmuel Ettinger, "The Historical Roots of Anti-Semitism in the USSR," in Theodore Freedman, ed., *Anti-Semitism in the Soviet Union: Its Roots and Consequences* (New York: Freedom Library Press of the Anti-Defamation League of B'nai B'rith, 1984), p. 9.

2. Ibid.

3. Simon Dubnov, *History of the Jews*, 4, trans. Moshe Spiegel (South Brunswick, N.J.: Thomas Yoseloff, 1967), p. 739.

4. Ibid., p. 161.

5. Bernard Weinryb, "East European Jewry (Since the Partitions of Poland, 1772–1795)," in Louis Finkelstein, ed., *The Jews. Their History, Culture, and Religion*, 1, 3d ed. (Philadelphia: Jewish Publication Society of America, 1960), p. 325.

6. Dubnov, *History of the Jews*, 4, p. 471.

7. See Jonathan Frankel, *Prophecy and Politics. Socialism, Nationalism, and the Russian Jews, 1862–1917* (New York: Cambridge Univ. Press, 1981), p. 53.

8. Ibid., p. 64.

9. Ilya Trotsky, "Jews in Russian Schools," in Jacob Frumkin et al., eds., *Russian Jewry (1860–1917)*, trans. Mirra Ginsburg, (New York: Thomas Yoseloff, 1966), p. 412.

10. Gregor Aronson, "Idelogical Trends among Russian Jews," in Frumkin et al., eds., *Russian Jewry*, p. 149.

11. Hans Rogger, "Tsarist Policy on Jewish Emigration," *Soviet Jewish Affairs*, 3 (1973), p. 32.

12. Dubnov, *History of the Jews*, 5, p. 559.

13. Ibid., pp. 341, 561 n. 51.

14. Frankel, *Prophecy and Politics*, p. 98.

15. V. I. Lenin, *Collected Works*, 17 (London: Lawrence and Wishart, 1960–70), p. 337.

16. Frankel, *Prophecy and Politics*, p. 139.

17. Ezra Mendelsohn, *The Jews of East Central Europe between the World Wars* (Bloomington: Indiana Univ. Press, 1983), p. 22.

18. S. M. Dubnov, *History of the Jews in Russia and Poland from the Earliest Times until the Present Day*, 3, trans. I. Friedlaender (Philadelphia: Jewish Publication Society of America, 1916), p. 167.

19. Hans Rogger, "The Beilis Case: Antisemitism and Politics in Reign of Nicholas II," *Slavic Review*, 25 (December 1966), p. 629.

20. Alexis Goldenweiser, "Legal Status of Jews in Russia," in Frumkin et al., eds., *Russian Jewry*, p. 113.

21. Dubnov, *History of the Jews*, 5, p. 844.

22. Isaac Deutscher, *The Non-Jewish Jew and Other Essays* (London: Oxford Univ. Press, 1968), p. 71.

23. Zvi Halevy, *Jewish Schools under Czarism and Communism. A Struggle for Cultural Identity* (New York: Springer, 1976), p. 174.

24. David Lane, "The Impact of Revolution: The Case of Selection of Students for Higher Education in Soviet Russia, 1917–1928," *Sociology*, 7 (May 1973), p. 248.

25. Zvi Halevy, "Jewish Students in Soviet Universities in the 1920s," *Soviet Jewish Affairs*, 6 (1976), pp. 58, 63.

26. Solomon M. Schwarz, *The Jews in the Soviet Union* (Syracuse, N.Y.: Syracuse Univ. Press, 1951), p. 293.

27. William Korey, "The Origins and Development of Soviet Anti-Semitism: An Analysis," *Slavic Review*, March 1972, p. 115.

28. Schwarz, *The Jews in the Soviet Union*, p. 289.

29. Ibid., p. 282.

30. Gerald Stillman, "The Yiddish Culture That Was Destroyed," *Jewish Currents*, 35 (June 1981), p. 6.

31. William Korey, *The Soviet Cage. Anti-Semitism in Russia* (New York: Viking, 1973), p. 30.

32. Ibid., p. 67.

33. Schwarz, *The Jews in the Soviet Union*, p. 298.

34. See Raul Hilberg, *The Destruction of the European Jews*, rev. and def. ed., 1 (New York: Holmes and Meier, 1985), p. 291; Ilya Ehrenburg and Vassily Grossman, eds., *The Black Book*, trans. John Glad and James S. Levine (New York: Holocaust Library, 1981) pp. 366, 368, 369, 549; Isaac Deutscher, *The Non-Jewish Jew and Other Essays*, ed. Tamara Deutscher (London: Oxford Univ. Press, 1968), pp. 78–79.

35. Schwarz, *The Jews in the Soviet Union*, p. 314.

36. Deutscher, *The Non-Jewish Jew*, pp. 76–77.

37. Shimon Redlich, *Propaganda and Nationalism in Wartime Russia. The Jewish Antifascist Committee in the USSR, 1941–1948* (Boulder, Colo.: East European Quarterly, 1982), p. 91.

38. Ibid., p. 47.

39. Ibid., p. 46.

40. Ibid., p. 51.

41. Ibid., pp. 163–64.

42. John A. Armstrong, "Soviet Foreign Policy and Anti-Semitism," in Nathan

Glazer et al., *Soviet Jewry: 1969* (New York: Academic Committee on Soviet Jewry, n.d.), p. 70.

43. Redlich, *Propaganda and Nationalism,* p. 166.

44. Umberto Terracini, "Israel as a Factor in Soviet Anti-Semitism," in Freedman, ed., *Anti-Semitism in the Soviet Union,* p. 169.

45. Korey, *The Soviet Cage,* p. 74.

46. Ibid., p. 76.

47. Ibid., p. 127.

48. Ettinger, "The Historical Roots of Anti-Semitism in the USSR," p. 15.

49. L. Dimerski-Tsigelman, "The Attitude toward Jews in the USSR," in Freedman, ed., *Anti-Semitism in the Soviet Union,* p. 82.

50. *Pravda,* March 10, 1963, quoted in Freedman, ed., *Anti-Semitism in the Soviet Union,* p. 551.

51. *Pravda,* July 19, 1965, quoted in Progressive Jewish Editors, "Memorandum to Soviet Officials on the Soviet Jewish Situation," *Jewish Currents,* 30 (December 1976), p. 10.

52. Ibid.

53. Ruth Okuneva, "Jews in the Soviet School Syllabus (What Soviet Schoolchildren Read about the History of the Jewish People)," in Freedman, ed., *Anti-Semitism in the Soviet Union,* pp. 422–48. See also Daniel Fish, "The Jews in Syllabuses of World and Russian History: What Soviet Schoolchildren Read about Jewish History," *Soviet Jewish Affairs,* 8 (Spring 1978), pp. 3–25. "Daniel Fish" is a pseudonym Ruth Okuneva used while still resident in the U.S.S.R. She now lives in Israel.

54. See Korey, *The Soviet Cage,* pp. 90–97.

55. Alex Inkeles, "Anti-Semitism as an Instrument of Soviet Policy," in Glazer et al., *Soviet Jewry: 1969,* p. 81.

56. Korey, *The Soviet Cage,* p. 45.

57. For numerous quotations from this literature, see Freedman, ed., *Anti-Semitism in the Soviet Union,* pp. 543–628. Some of the following quotations come from this source.

58. Peggy Dennis, "Anti-Semitism, Still Strong and Officially Sanctioned, Blights Soviet Society," *In These Times,* December 20, 1978.

59. Peggy Dennis, "Am I a Jew? Radical's Search for an Answer," *Nation,* July 12, 1980.

60. Peggy Dennis, reply to Lester Cole, "Russian Anti-Semitism," *Nation,* November 29, 1980, letter.

61. Martin Gilbert, *The Jews of Hope* (London: Macmillan, 1984), p. 111.

62. John Armstrong, "Soviet Foreign Policy and Anti-Semitism," p. 66.

63. Korey, *The Soviet Cage,* p. 52.

64. Joseph Braginsky, "Talking with Americans about Soviet Jews," *New World Review,* 40 (Fall 1972), p. 90.

65. World Conference on Soviet Jewry, *The Position of Soviet Jewry. 1977–1980.* Report on the Implementation of the Helsinki Final Act since the Belgrade Follow-up Conference (London: World Conference on Soviet Jewry), p. 47.

66. Ibid., p. 46.

67. Laurent Schwartz, "Soviet Anti-Semitism and Jewish Scientists," in Freed-

man, ed., *Anti-Semitism in the Soviet Union,* p. 180. See also G. A. Freiman, "I Am a Jew, It Turns Out," in ibid., pp. 200–65.

68. See World Conference on Soviet Jewry, *The Position of Soviet Jewry. 1977–1980,* pp. 17–21.

69. See Judith Vogt, "When Nazism Became Zionism. An Analysis of Political Cartoons," in Freedman, ed., *Anti-Semitism in the Soviet Union,* pp. 486–514.

70. Gilbert, *The Jews of Hope,* p. 76.

71. Alex Inkeles, "Anti-Semitism as an Instrument of Soviet Policy," p. 77.

72. Korey, *The Soviet Cage,* p. 60.

73. Quoted from *Komsomolskaya Pravda,* March 1, 1983, in Gilbert, *The Jews of Hope,* p. 117.

74. Ibid., p. 118.

75. Ibid., p. 167.

76. L. Dimerski-Tsigelman, "The Attitude toward Jews in the USSR," p. 97.

77. Lenin, *Collected Works,* 20, p. 26.

78. Ibid., p. 37.

79. Ibid., p. 172.

80. Ibid., 8, p. 349.

81. Ibid., 17, p. 337.

82. Ibid., p. 507.

83. Ibid., 4, p. 376.

84. Ibid., 9, p. 201.

85. Ibid., 5, pp. 98–99.

86. Ibid., 20, p. 237.

87. Ibid., p. 238.

88. Ibid., 20, p. 173.

89. Ibid., p. 26.

90. Ibid., p. 29.

91. Ibid., 6, p. 334.

92. Ibid., 20, p. 50, emphasis added.

93. Jonathan Frankel, *Prophecy and Politics. Socialism, Nationalism, and the Russian Jews, 1862–1917* (New York: Cambridge Univ. Press, 1981), p. 185.

94. Lenin, *Collected Works,* 7, p. 101.

95. Ibid.

96. Ibid., p. 101.

97. Ibid., 20, p. 26.

98. Ibid., 29, p. 252.

99. Ibid.

12

THE TOLERATION OF TOLERANCE: UNITED STATES

[American antisemitism differs from the European varieties in that in the United States] the main limitations imposed on Jews have been imposed by our "private governments"—industry and trade, banks and insurance companies, real estate boards and neighborhood associations, clubs and societies, colleges and universities.

—Carey McWilliams, 1948

In U.S. history, writes Michael Dobkowski, "no political or social movement, no religious development, no deep social crisis, has been associated with, or is significant because of antisemitism."[1] While evidences of antisemitism are plentiful, it has never occupied center stage in any sustained political movement. It is not, however, the relative quiescence of antisemitism that is unique to America. A number of countries have had the same experience, at least occasionally.

Most significant is the total absence of what was called elsewhere the Jewish question. This phrase signified doubt that Jews should be treated as equal and contributing members of the nation as a whole. The existence of the Jewish question made illegitimate any effort by Jews to participate in a common polity and economy. Instead, they were regarded as alien elements and deservedly subjects of discrimination.

Antisemitism in the United States was comparatively mild because it was not further poisoned by a Jewish question. In Germany, on the other hand, where antisemitism fed upon the Jewish question, interaction of the two was incessant.

Jews in colonial America were second-class citizens but for most of them this was an improvement. Granted the right to settle and to pursue a livelihood, Jews turned their attention to political and religious rights. As Richard Morris writes: "In colonial times naturalization was deemed to confer civil rights, but not political rights. Jews . . . were generally disqualified to vote in colony-wide elections for representatives to the legislature."[2] In the courts, Jews met with prejudice and were not treated as equal citizens, even after passage of the Naturalization Act of 1740. (In England itself, Jews remained ineligible for citizenship.) In colonial Pennsylvania, Jews and Christian believers were allowed to reside but not vote or hold office. Religious rights were protected by national legislation. In 1787, the Northwest Ordinance proclaimed: "No person . . . shall ever be molested on account of his mode of worship, or religious sentiments, in the said territory." The following year the newly ratified federal Constitution provided that "no religious test shall ever be required as a qualification to any office or public trust under the United States."

Yet, because of the distinctive federal nature of the government under the Constitution, rights granted to citizens of the United States might be—and were—withheld from the same persons within the confines of single states.

Among the original thirteen states, practices varied widely. Stanley Chyet notes: "New York was . . . the first state whose constitution imposed on the Jews no disabilities at all. . . . For the first time, Jews were full citizens in a North American polity."[3] Virginia accorded Jews all religious rights but withheld the right to vote. A number of states imposed a religious test for holding office. Most specified a belief in Christianity while others required affiliation with a Protestant church. In state after state, Jews and their allies pressed for changes. As a result, provisions for a religious test were dropped and bars on Jews' serving in public office were lifted. Newer states tended not to have any disabilities on Jews and generally omitted any religious test. Chyet sums up the resulting situation: "By the year 1840, only in five states—New Jersey, North Carolina, New Hampshire, Connecticut, and Rhode Island—did Jews continue subject to disabilities. While in twenty-one of the twenty-six states of the Union they generally enjoyed full religious and political equality."[4]

During roughly the same period, 1789–1840, Joseph Blau and Salo Baron report there was no quota for Jews in any occupation—except for lawyers in Maryland—and that no occupation was overcrowded, thus creating no basis for invidious competition between Jews and non-Jews.[5] Religious freedom came to mean the right to worship as one chose but also to have one's religion treated equally with all others. Given the European practice of official preferment of a church, American Jews welcomed the Jeffersonian conception of equality. In 1802, President Thomas Jefferson wrote of "building a wall of separation between church and state."[6] This conception also went far beyond the ancient practice of religious toleration. As an author wrote in 1820: "If any man tells me that he will *tolerate* my opinions, this implies that he claims the power of *restraining* them."[7] Early in the nineteenth century, New York State funds were paid Protestant schools but not those of Jews' and Catholics'. After a decade of lobbying, in 1811 payment to the Jewish school was approved.[8] Nobody seemed to protest at this scaling of Jefferson's wall.

Publicly expressed antisemitism was by no means rare. Antisemitic doggerel appeared in newspapers and antisemitic plays were presented. Antisemitism was injected into the political struggles of the 1790s with Federalists taking the offensive. In 1823, when a Jewish candidate ran for sheriff in New York City, the editor of the *New York American* opposed him, arguing that Jews lacked "that single national attachment, which binds a man to the soil of his nativity, and makes him the exclusive patriot of his own country."[9]

Around the mid-nineteenth century, a great many German-Jewish immigrants had become peddlers, a pursuit well fitted to the small capital they commanded. "Most of the bastions of economic privilege, the old established banks and business, were almost completely closed to Jews."[10] In line with the historical Jewish practice of searching out independent pursuits, few Jews entered the ranks of factory workers that were beginning to expand greatly around the 1860s.

The Civil War (1861–65) provided the first large-scale, if fleeting, instance of official antisemitism in American history. During the first year of the war, the Union government permitted a limited trade in southern cotton for which a large demand existed. In September 1862, for example, 14,000 bales were shipped up the Mississippi River. Among the speculators could be found many Gentiles and Jews. As Stephen Ash notes, however, "virtually every diatribe delivered against the speculators by army officers or others in the Mississippi Valley in 1862 betrayed a core of antisemitism."[11] General U. S. Grant, commander of Union forces in the District of West Tennessee, grew convinced that the Jewish traders were somehow more corrupt and greedy. This view was accentuated by the creation of a trading partnership between Grant's father and several Jews. On December 17, 1862, General Grant issued General Order No. 11 which expelled all Jews "as a class" from the military department; Jews were given twenty-four hours to clear out or face arrest and none was to be given a pass to apply for permits. Non-Jewish speculators were not affected by the order.

Not only was the order implemented but Provost Marshal L. J. Wardell plunged far beyond its literal terms and ordered all the Jews in Paducah, Kentucky, to leave the city. (None of those residents dealt in cotton.) Twelve days after issuance of General Order No. 11, all Jews had left Paducah. Almost immediately Jews complained to congressmen and to President Abraham Lincoln who promptly countermanded the order and directed General Henry W. Halleck to revoke it. President Lincoln told a complainant: "I do not like to hear a class or nationality condemned on account of a few sinners."[12] On January 6, twenty days after its issuance, Grant withdrew the measure.

Of some 7,800 Jews who fought in the Civil War, only about one-sixth joined the Confederate side. "Although antisemitism was widely felt in both camps," writes Morris Schappes, "it was more extensive in the South, especially as the Confederacy began to realize the inevitability of its defeat."[13] Antisemitic attacks were voiced on the floor of the Confederate Congress.

Jews also had to struggle for chaplains of their own faith in the Union armed forces. At first rejected, eventually the demand was granted. This episode, however, does not reflect any long-standing anti-Jewish tradition: A Jew, for example, was a member of the first graduating class at West Point. On the other hand, antisemitic attitudes pervaded the press. As Feldstein reports: "The *New York Herald* made it a point to identify Jews who were arrested as rebel spies but never mentioned religion when reporting casualty lists or acts of heroism by Jewish soldiers."[14]

Industrial capitalist America took shape during the half-century after the Civil War, a period that saw the Jewish population rise twentyfold from 150,000 to 3 million. Jews, however, failed to occupy the commanding heights of the American economy. Instead, they dwelled near the foothills and middle slopes. Neither as owners nor as chief executives could Jews be found in the steel, mining, and transportation industries. Mergers that created giant corporations were not managed by Jews. They were absent from new industries dependent upon advances in communication. Only the rarest commercial banker was Jewish, even in the largest cities. For a short time, a few Jews became investment bankers.

The Jewish absence from industry was especially striking but readily explained. For one thing, none stemmed from small manufacturing backgrounds that constituted the reservoir of growing industry in America. For another, their slender capital resources would not go far in heavy manufacturing. Further, Jews were simply not welcome in the industrial bastions of corporate America. Carey McWilliams correctly writes: "Generally speaking, the businesses in which Jews . . . concentrated are those in which a large risk-factor is involved; businesses peripheral to the economy; businesses originally regarded as unimportant; new industries and businesses; and businesses which have traditionally carried a certain element of social stigma, such, for example, as the amusement industry and the liquor industry."[15]

Clothing was the sole American industry in which Jewish ownership predominated. To flourish it required great quantities of low-paid, but skilled, labor, provided from the nearly 3 million Jews who entered the country before 1914. Since the shops were small, not much capital was needed. The industry made New York City the national center of American Jewry.

During the years of economic change, antisemitism also grew. The rise of new industries was inevitably accompanied by the decline of old employments and forms of wealth. Such movements endangered ancient supremacies and encouraged the emergence of new ones. As John Higham notes, in such a context "antisemitic discriminations offer another means of stabilizing the social ladder."[16] Well-to-do Jews were excluded from resort hotels, exclusive preparatory and finishing schools, and social circles that might suggest acceptance into intimate precincts of the powerful. In 1867, agents of some large insurance companies were directed secretly not to insure property owned by Jews. A series of protests by Jews reversed this antisemitic sally.[17] Thirteen years later, "America's first 'profesional' antisemite"—T. T. Timayenis—became the country's first publisher of antisemitic literature.[18] Translations of leading European antisemitic tracts were published by other firms.

On many fronts, Jews organized to oppose specific antisemitic acts and programs. Laws requiring the closing of businesses on Sunday affected religious Jews adversely. After a generation of objections, writes Allan Tarshish, by the 1880s "some 21 states had liberal Sunday laws, and in some others the Sunday closing laws were not enforced."[19] In 1874, the Merriam Company finally agreed to amend its standard Webster dictionary to omit "to Jew"; it had been defined as "to bargain."

Such viligance availed little, however, when it came to basic anti-Jewish stereotypes. Many of these were renewed weekly in "religious books [which]...often accepted the basic view of the Jew as despised Christ killer." In nineteenth-century novels, Jews were often portrayed as especially attracted to crime; sometimes this "tendency" was attributed to a peculiar shortcoming of Judaism. During the late nineteenth and early twentieth centuries so-called humor magazines "delighted in presenting full-page color cartoons and sketches of men, women, and children with huge hooked noses, gross lips, and crude ostentatious manners." In the dime novels, "Jews invariably appear...as secondhand clothing dealers and pawnbrokers, and their money-centered personalities complement their dialectal speech and grotesque physiognomies. They are *never* described as producers, contributors to the economy, or even as workers." It was not the popular character of these works that accounted for the antisemitism since the same sorely distorted images could be found in contemporaneous high-cultural works by Henry Adams, Henry James, Edith Wharton, Frederick Jackson Turner, and others.[20]

Attitudes like these were readily draped onto growing structures of antisemitism in the larger society. Education is one such example. In the years 1900–1914, most preparatory schools "established very small Jewish quotas." Higham adds: "After 1900 few Jews were elected to the Princeton clubs or to the fraternities at Yale and elsewhere. The literary and gymnastic societies at Columbia kept Jews out entirely." (In 1898, the first Jewish fraternity was organized at Columbia; eight years later black students at Cornell organized the first black fraternity.) Higham observes that "by 1910, there were complaints that few Jews could gain entry or advancement in academic circles. In the years before . . . [1914], a few colleges began to limit Jewish enrollment."[21] Thus, by 1917, antisemitic practice was embedded in a number of institutional structures. Similarly, antisemitic ideology fed on many literary sources and was widely accepted. What had not been provided yet was a social-political crisis that would mobilize the theory and practice of antisemitic exclusion.

Sociologist E. A. Ross wrote in 1914: "If the Czar . . . should succeed in driving out the bulk of his six million Jews to the United States, we shall see the rise of a Jewish question here, perhaps riots and anti-Jewish legislation. . . . The lump outgrows the leaven, and there will be trouble."[22] Nearly 3 million Jews did reach American shores, but three years after Ross wrote the only riots were those in St. Petersburg as the selfsame czar was overthrown by revolutionaries. Jews in the United States, regardless of their political orientation, celebrated the end of the world's most sweeping system of antisemitism. While the Bolsheviks were praised for this accomplishment, relatively few American Jews of Russian origin sympathized with the new Communist government. A new antisemitic line, however, gave an opposite impression: opponents of the Bolsheviks spread a false report that most Russian Communist leaders were Jews. Indeed, President Woodrow Wilson, while in Paris in 1919, stated that "the Bolshevist movement had been led by Jews."[23] Based on an examination of manuscript material, Zosa Szajkowski discovered that "as a rule, State Department lists of high Soviet officials noted which of them were Jews."[24] During the Red Scare of 1919–20, Jews were not singled out as dangerous. Reiteration of the alleged Jewish-Bolshevik identity, however, placed many Jews on the defensive. Some responded with energetic attacks on communism. This seemed to be the case with the rabbinate in general.[25] In attacking antisemitic writings in 1920, the American Jewish Committee also criticized communism.

In 1920, the officially sponsored Red Scare was joined by a privately sponsored "Jew Scare." That year, the automobile manufacturer Henry Ford began publishing the *Dearborn Independent*. In ninety-one consecutive weekly issues the paper "exposed" one after another supposed Jewish evil. Its circulation exceeded 250,000. The most fanciful of the pieces were then separately reprinted by Ford in a four-volume pamphlet edition entitled *The International Jew;* it was translated into sixteen languages including Arabic.

Article 10 of the series of ninety-one contained the first mention of

The Protocols of the Elders of Zion, a document that had been fabricated by tsarist agents in 1903 to smear Jews in the antitsarist movement. As Albert Lee, the principal historian of the Ford antisemitic venture, writes, according to the *Protocols* the "Jews had started the [first] world war in order to profit by it. Bolshevism was a Jewish invention, as were liberalism and unionism.... Negro jazz somehow became 'Yiddish moron music' in the [Ford] publication's vernacular."[26] Jews were portrayed as a universally corrupting influence. As Lee explained, *The International Jew* asserted that "the Jews seemed guilty because they refused to give up their Jewishness and become complete Americans.... The underlying message was clear: Beware of progress; it's a Jewish scheme."[27]

A key figure in Ford's antisemitic campaign was Boris Brasol, a Russian émigré who had served the tsar's government as a lawyer and a soldier during World War I. In 1919, he became a confidential advisor to the chief of military intelligence in the United States. In a book published the next year he declared that Jews formed a large part of the Soviet Communist government's leadership and portrayed the revolution as an outcome of a Jewish conspiracy. He did not find this difficult to square with a further argument that the Jews were also part of a worldwide conspiracy of bankers.[28] Ford's *Dearborn Independent* employed Brasol for two years and he remained in close touch with Ford personnel until 1939. It was Brasol who facilitated use of the *Protocols* by Ford.

Ford and *The International Jew* were highly praised by Adolf Hitler in 1923 and 1931. The latter year he told an American reporter: "I regard Heinrich Ford as my inspiration."[29] In the earlier year, some months before Hitler's ill-fated *Putsch,* a *Chicago Tribune* reporter wrote that the Nazi party organization in Munich was "sending out Mr. Ford's book [*The International Jew,* retitled in a German translation]... by the carload.[30] (In July 1933, Hitler sent Ford birthday congratulations and awarded him the Grand Cross of the German Eagle, reportedly the country's highest decoration.)

For whatever reason, antisemitic articles suddenly stopped appearing in 1922 but were resumed in 1924. An early article declared: "A band of Jews ... is on the back of the American farmer."[31] The article alleged that agricultural cooperatives were a Jewish plot. A Jew who had been maligned in the piece sued and in 1927 won a settlement. Ford retracted all the anti-Jewish articles that had appeared in the *Dearborn Independent,* and acknowledged that *The Protocols of the Elders of Zion* was "gross forgeries." Ford was helped to reach this point by a nationwide boycott of Ford products by Jews. The year 1927 was crucial to Ford, for that year his new Model A car was introduced. Over the years, however, American Jews simply patronized Ford's competitors.

The Ku Klux Klan, once praised by Ford, helped make the Jews a national issue in the 1920s. More a nuisance than a physical menace to

Jews, the Klan was found in high and low places alike. Chapters were
located at Harvard, Yale, and Syracuse universities as well as in many
small midwestern towns. In Denver, reports Kenneth Jackson, "the Klan
. . . frequently routed Friday evening automobile caravans past synagogues. Shouting insults from behind their white hoods."[32]

Imperial Wizard Hiram Wesley Evans asserted the group's goal as
"native, white, Protestant supremacy." He distinguished between Jews
from western Europe and those from eastern Europe, the far more
numerous and recent in arrival: "When freed from persecution these
Jews have shown a tendency to disintegrate and amalgamate. We may
hope that shortly, in the free atmosphere of America, Jews of this class
will cease to be a problem. Quite different are the Eastern Jews. . . . These,
unlike the true Hebrew, show a divergence from the American-type so
great that there seems little hope of their assimilation."[33] Referring to
Jews especially, Evans complained: "We found our great cities and the
control of much of our industry and commerce taken over by strangers,
who stacked the cards of success and prosperity against us."[34] In response
to the Klan's criticism of Jewish thought, the great black leader, W.E.B.
Du Bois, thundered: "For the alleged followers of Jesus Christ and wor-
shipers of the Old Testament to revile Hebrew culture is too impudent
for words."[35] He told of having visited Akron, Ohio, in 1925: "I found
the Klan calmly and openly in the saddle. The leader of the local Klan
was president of the Board of Education and had just been tremendously
busied in driving a Jew out of the public schools."[36]

The 1920s were the occasion for the national institutionalization of
antisemitism. As Feldstein puts it: "During this decade, employment
agencies openly advertised that 'No Jews need apply; quota systems were
adopted by universities, membership in social and professional organizations was limited to 'Christians only', and 'gentlemen's agreements'
were reached to keep the 'sheenies' out of the 'better' residential neighborhoods."[37] A New York City court ruled in 1927 Jews could be denied
a rental apartment "irrespective of their character and ability to pay the
rent."[38] During the decade, residential segregation of Jews in New York
City increased, in part because of their wishes. Handlin observes that in
the 1920s "whole areas of many cities, through voluntary covenants of
real-estate owners, were abruptly closed to 'Hebrew descent'."[39]

Higher education in the 1920s was still largely closed to Jewish faculty.
Lewis Feuer notes that "by the mid-twenties there were still probably
less than one hundred Jews among the college and university professors
in the liberal arts and sciences faculties in the United States."[40] He calls
sociology "a closed field to Jews during the first two decades of the
twentieth century."[41] In 1930, the Washington Square College of New
York University, enrolling "the largest Jewish student body in the world,"
did not employ any Jewish professors.

Jewish candidates for such positions were not lacking. Indeed, American universities at the outset of the 1920s took steps to reduce the supply of those candidates. Especially in elite universities, but among the lesser ranks as well, quotas were imposed to limit and then reduce the enrollment of Jews. Psychological tests and geographic representativeness were manipulated so as to result in maximum adverse impact upon Jewish students. In many institutions Jews tended to be placed on waiting lists—where they waited endlessly. The *Nation* magazine protested—as few American educators did—by charging in 1922: "Only the Russia of the Czars did what our universities are beginning to do; only Poland, Rumania, and Hungary do so today."[42]

Personal indignity was added to communal insult by imposing housing segregation upon the Jews who were admitted. At Syracuse University, for example, blacks were excluded altogether from living on campus. In 1926–27, the Dean of Women's Office called for the creation of a separate dormitory for Jewish women students. This was done. Four years later, it was closed and Jewish women students were redistributed among general dormitories for women, but only in proportion to their number in total enrollment. No dormitory was to hold more than 10 percent. This system or variants thereof persisted in the face of continued protests until 1935 when housing segregation of Jewish women ended at Syracuse.[43]

Despite quotas and other indignities, however, Jews succeeded in gaining a higher education. During 1916–17, for example, Jews made up 3 percent of all college students. (This was roughly in accord with their percentage of total population.) By 1937, the proportion had more than tripled, to 9.13 percent.[44] While Jews sorely resented quotas, quotas were usually set above the level of the average percentage of Jews in the country. Almost never were Jews excluded altogether, as was the case frequently for blacks. Jewish students also evaded the worst effects of quotas by attending colleges in other than traditional locations.

Jewish admission to professional schools was weakened severely during the 1920s and 1930s. New York City, in which more than half of the country's Jews lived, showed this most clearly. Alfred Shapiro writes: "At Columbia and Cornell Universities the approximate percentage of Jewish students dropped from 14 . . . in 1920 to less than 5 . . . by 1940. At New York University, the New York and Long Island Colleges of Medicine, always somewhat more liberal in this respect, percentages dropped from approximately 30 to 40 . . . to less than 20 . . . in the same period."[45] When Jewish medical graduates sought appropriate internships and residencies they were restricted to municipal institutions or hospitals operated by a Jewish community: "Almost a negligible fraction receive appointment in non-Jewish hospitals maintained by private philanthropy."[46]

German Nazism deeply disturbed American Jews and they sought an appropriate means of opposition. Jews throughout the world began in early 1933 a spontaneous boycott of German products and held mass rallies and protest marches. A prominent American Jewish lawyer, Samuel Untermyer, warned: "The Hitler party is bent upon the extermination of the Jews in Germany, or upon driving them out of the country."[47] A virtually unknown American Jew, Abraham Coralnik, shared the outlook: "This is no ordinary antisemitism, but an inexorable war against the Jewish race, unparalleled in the history of modern times."[48] Rabbi Stephen Wise of the American Jewish Congress declared, "It is not the German Jews who are being attacked. It is the Jews. We must speak out."[49] The three—Untermyer, Coralnik, and Wise—expressed a desperate urgency and soon succeeded in bringing about militant mass protests around the issue of a boycott of German goods and other measures.

The two oldest national organizations, the American Jewish Committee (AJC) and B'nai B'rith, rejected this path. An AJC official cautioned: "We ... believe that quieter and more realistic methods of dealing with the situation than mass agitation can be found and we are working on this principle."[50] Even at the outbreak of World War II in September 1939, however, AJC still failed to endorse the boycott; B'nai B'rith relented in 1937. The search for "more realistic methods" was fruitless and it denied the Jews a unity that might have lent crucial support to a concrete anti-Nazi step during a period of greatest Nazi vulnerability. Efforts to convince the Roosevelt administration to adopt an openly critical stance toward Hitler's Germany also failed.

Over only four years (1921–25), Jewish immigration to the United States fell from 119,036 to 10,292.[51] This was due primarily to passage of a new, highly restrictive law in 1924 the aim of which was to cut sharply the influx of people from southern and eastern Europe. Antisemitism was not a principal force behind the measure. Nevertheless, American immigration authorities reduced the inflow even more by adopting extremely stringent regulations.[52] This was especially the case when Jewish refugees from Hitler Germany pressed against the gates. Hitler taunted the United States for its obvious reluctance to admit the refugees. In April 1933 he declared, "Through its immigration law, America has inhibited the unwelcome influence of such races as it has been unable to tolerate within its midst. Nor is America ready now to open its doors to Jews fleeing from Germany."[53]

Non-Jewish opinion in the United States was strongly against any accommodation on quotas. David Wyman summarizes this evidence: "In 1938 ... four separate polls indicated that from 71 to 85 percent of the American public opposed increasing the quotas to help refugees.... In ... early 1939, 66 percent even objected to a one-time exception to allow

10,000 refugee children to enter outside the quota limits."[54] The Roosevelt administration chose to align its policy with these sentiments and made extremely few adjustments in favor of the refugees. Indeed, over the years from 1933 to 1939, federal authorities admitted a lesser number of German nationals than were eligible under the American quota system.

Nevertheless, American Jewish organizations were intimidated into near-silence by extreme nationalist and antisemitic agitation against easing immigration bars and by the obvious decision of government authorities to hold fast. Before the 1930s, Jewish publications regularly called for easing of the immigration laws. David Brody reports, however, that "almost nothing is to be found in the Jewish literature between 1938 and 1942 expressing significant dissatisfaction with the immigration laws."[55] Except for the Jewish Labor Committee, virtually every other major national Jewish group remained silent on the issue. (Jews were permitted to leave Germany and occupied Europe until late fall 1941.)

Undoubtedly, Jewish organizations had to take into account the practical politics of trying to pressure an administration which itself felt pressed by antisemitic and racist forces within the Democratic party. The depressed national economy proved unresponsive to New Deal recovery measures and mass unemployment persisted, thus perpetuating a political context in which antisemitism could thrive. Fascist groups were not slow to take advantage of the fact. As economic conditions worsened, anti-Jewish practices spread. Oscar Handlin writes: "By 1940 representative groups in the field of dentistry and psychiatry were going so far as to propose openly a quota system in those fields."[56] The Jewish-owned *New York Times,* Higham reminds us, "accepted help-wanted advertisements specifying 'Christians only.' "[57]

Father Charles E. Coughlin exemplified the political potential that lay within the accumulated tensions of the 1930s. After four years of preaching sermons over a Detroit radio station, in 1930 he began attacking socialism and communism, and even capitalists who, he said, "were providing fertile soil for the spread of leftist ideology because of their greed."[58] Later that year he switched to the CBS radio network and his audience expanded greatly. Within five years, he employed 100 clerks to handle his mail. Meanwhile, he began to attack "international bankers" for aiding communism. "Some weeks," Sheldon Marcus notes, "he received over 400,000 letters, most of which supported his attacks against the bankers."[59]

A year earlier, in 1934, Coughlin formed the National Union for Social Justice among whose principles were "a just, living, annual wage," "the chief concern of government shall be for the poor," and the right to form unions. He also favored limits on profits in every industry. In March 1936 he published the first issue of a press organ, *Social Justice.* Three months later, the Union party was organized to run Coughlin's candidate, Congressman William Lemke, for president. He attracted fewer than 900,000 votes out of nearly 46 million that were cast. In accordance with a preelection pledge, Coughlin thereupon withdrew from his broadcasting role and did not resume it until 1938.

During the 1936 election campaign Coughlin had begun to attack Jews openly. While he denied being antisemitic, *Social Justice* announced that "there was a 'Jewish Question' in the United States."[60] After a time, Coughlin became bolder and declared that the word "antisemitic" was "only another phase of castigation in communism's glossary of attack."

The year 1938 marked also the creation in Brooklyn and elsewhere of the Christian Front, a Coughlin group that excluded Jews from membership and was devoted to combatting communism. Most of its actions, however, seemed directed against Jews. Historians and observers have characterized the front accurately:

They organized "buy Christians only" movements and in 1938, 1939, and 1940 made the streets, subways and movie theaters of many cities . . . unsafe for Jews. . . . In many of America's large cities Christian Fronters were being arrested for attacking Jews who were frequently old men, children and women. . . . Street brawls involving Christian Fronters and Jews became frequent in New York City, and there were numerous complaints that the predominantly Irish Catholic police force was showing partiality to the Coughlinates. . . . On the streets of the nation's largest cities, it was not uncommon for Coughlin's storm troopers to assault Jews. . . . Each week the Christian Front . . . holds close to thirty open-air meetings in outlying districts and in the heart of Manhattan, attracting crowds as large as 2,000. . . . "Incidents"—brawls, beatings, brief but savage fist-fights—have inevitably multiplied. They have been almost uniformly ignored by the press, partly because it fears to tread on Catholic toes and partly because it still believes in the silent treatment for antisemitism.[61]

As Coughlin's antisemitism became more public, he began to soften reports of German Nazi outrages against Jews and then became an open apologist for the Nazis. Less than two weeks after *Kristallnacht* in late 1938, he stated: "German citizen Jews were not molested officially in the conduct of their business. . . . A few synagogues and stores were destroyed by mob violence. The children of German citizen Jews were permitted to attend public schools with other children."[62] Each sentence was false. At the end of 1938, the *New York Post* ran a story showing how Coughlin had copied, word-for-word, from a speech by the Nazi propaganda minister Joseph Goebbels. Even after the United States entered the war, Coughlin did not let up on his pro-Nazi writings. On March 16, 1942, *Social Justice* stated "that because one goal of the Jews was to involve the United States in a war against Germany, Hitler's persecution of the Jews in Europe was justified."[63] Some six weeks later, the Catholic church finally silenced Coughlin, after a private warning that otherwise the federal government would do so.

Marcus, the author of the ranking biography of Coughlin, concluded about his subject: "In a time of great frustration, he spawned discord, hate and violence.... He ... disseminate[d] his credo to millions and de-stroye[d] the confidence of men in their country and arouse[d] them against one another. He was a propagandist on behalf of fascism.... He stands as an illustration of how bigotry can emanate from religion."[64] One might also observe Coughlin's movement, from 1930 to 1936–38 away from a prolabor, equalitarian viewpoint to an outright antisemitic and extremely conservative stance.

From among ultraconservative, supernationalist sources during the 1930s sprang three separate leaders: William Dudley Pelley, Gerald B. Winrod, and Gerald L. K. Smith. Each organized a group based centrally on antisemitism some time during or after the decade. Pelley's Silver Shirts originated in 1933 with an antisemitic program that praised Hit-ler's policies toward the Jews. In its first year it grew from hundreds to 15,000; by 1938, however, it had declined to 5,000. Winrod organized the Defenders of the Christian Faith. In 1938, there were 110,000 sub-scribers to his publication, *Defender*. That same year he ran for the Re-publican nomination for senator in Kansas. He came in third with over 55,000 votes. During the campaign he soft-pedaled his antisemitism. Smith began his political career as an aide to Senator Huey Long of Louisiana whose "Share the Wealth" plan for a universal guaranteed annual income had made him a national figure. During World War II, Smith began to attack "organized Jewry." He began a magazine *Cross and the Flag* to publicize his views. That same year, he lost his race for the Republican senatorial nomination in Michigan; he attracted 120,000 votes. In the general election, running as an independent, over 32,000 voted for him.

Leo Ribuffo reports that Smith received "notable support from big businessmen" during the late 1930s.[65] This aid was highly consequential for Smith's program. According to Ribuffo, "Smith's alliance with big business ... helped to erode the anti-capitalist features of his program. ... Instead of a passionate advocate of redistributed income, by 1940 he was primarily a foe of subversion."[66] Soon, he added antisemitism, thus to be transformed into a certified member of the far Right. (In a memoir written late in his life, Smith boasted about the number of wealthy in-dustrialists who had admired and helped him.)[67]

All three antisemitic rightists reached many thousands of Americans. Ultimately, however, they were unable to translate their message into everyday political reality. Each effort to establish politically based anti-semitism failed.

The German American Bund was still another antisemitic group that flitted briefly through the 1930s. During 1933–35, it probably enrolled between 5,000 and 6,000 members. Its peak of influence was reached in 1937–38. In the Bund's 1938 program, the following goals, among others, were established:

1. A socially just, white, Gentile-ruled United States
4. Severance of diplomatic relations with Soviet Russia, outlawing of the Communist Party in the United States, prosecution of all known Communists for high treason[68]

Through its contacts in Nazi Germany, the Bund became a large-scale distributor of antisemitic literature in the United States. Perhaps at its peak it enrolled some 25,000 members. In February 1939 it sponsored a rally at Madison Square Garden attended by 22,000 persons. That same year, however, Fritz Kuhn, the group's *Fuehrer*, was arrested, tried, and convicted on charges of larceny and forgery. Under his successor, the Bund, now tied to the cause of Nazi arms in World War II, declined until by 1941 no public meetings were held.

Jews could take small comfort from the failure of organized antisemitism to make any significant political conquests. Instead, many were moved to wonder how secure their place was in the United States. Most troubling was repeated evidence of a silent, brooding antisemitism that could be moved but not mobilized. In the 1920s, when Ford was publishing antisemitic material, thousands of persons, including ministers, wrote for additional copies. Many thousands more voted for antisemitic candidacies during the 1930s. Millions heard the preachments of hate by Father Coughlin and hundreds of thousands responded with financial contributions. The growing system of discrimination and segregation against Jews was staffed by many.

It is no wonder, then, when the novel technique of public opinion polling was applied to the issue of antisemitism during the late 1930s, evidences of antipathy surfaced. Twice in 1938 national samples of Americans were asked: "Do you think the persecution of the Jews in Europe has been their own fault?" Responses were as follows, by percentage:[69]

	March 1938	May 1938
Entirely	12	10
Partly	49	48
Not at all	23	31
No opinion	16	11

Thus, a sizable majority of Americans believed, in a sense, that the Jews of Europe had it coming to them. This squares with the prevailing opinion, even more widespread among Americans, that no effort should be made to ease the entry of foreign Jews to the United States.

In March 1938, pollsters asked; "Do you think Jews have too much power in the United States?" Forty-one percent of respondents answered yes. During the next seven years the figure rose until it hit 58 percent in 1945. Similarly high percentages thought Jews were greedy, dishonest, and overly aggressive. About a seventh of respondents acknowledged they would have supported a campaign against Jews.

During the period of American participation in the war, 1941–45, anti-Jewish sentiment grew. The polls record as much. More important, established social patterns were unresistant. An unsigned article directed against Jews appeared in the first issue (January 1945) of the *Journal of Clinical Psychology:* "It . . . seems unwise to allow one group to dominate or take over any clinical specialty as has occurred in several instances."[70] The secretary of the Council on Dental Education of the American Dental Society, studying schools of dentistry at Columbia and New York University, observed too many students from "one racial strain." (He meant Jews.) Efforts to stimulate public awareness of antisemitism foundered. When, for example, Hollywood proposed a film, *Mrs. Skeffington,* to deal with American antisemitism, the Overseas Branch of the U.S. Office of War Information (OWI) rejected the script, writing, "This script . . . is gravely detrimental to the War Information Program. The most acute problem is the introduction of the anti-Semitic problem."[71] As a result of this objection, a scene was dropped in which a gentile woman married to a Jew is made unwelcome for that reason in a number of hotels. At the same time, OWI officials were well aware of the problem of antisemitism. In a report on a broad public opinion survey, dated July 27, 1942, OWI "found widespread antisemitic sentiment in half of the 42-states."[72] During 1938–42, for example, "the patriotism of Jews was consistently doubted by at least a quarter of the population."[73]

During the nearly four years of war between the United States and Germany, only 21,000 refugees were admitted, 10 percent of the number permitted by quota. Fundamentally, this poor record was the direct intended result of U.S. government policy. As Wyman relates: "Authenticated information that the Nazis were systematically exterminating European Jewry was made public in the United States in November 1942. President Roosevelt did nothing about the mass murder for fourteen months."[74] The State Department actually feared large numbers of Jews would be rescued and find their way into the United States. U.S. consular officials overseas were predominantly antisemitic and screened out thousands of Jewish refugees.

There was reason to believe that even President Roosevelt did not remain untouched by antisemitism. For instance, during January 1943, he and Winston Churchill were in Casablanca, Morocco. While there he met with two Vichy-appointed French colonial officials, Generals A. P. Nogues and H. Giraud. With Nogues, Roosevelt conducted an extended discussion of future French policy on Jews in North Africa (Algeria, Morocco, and Tunisia). In the words of the official account of the conversation, which was conducted mostly in French:

The President stated that he felt the whole Jewish problem should be studied very carefully and that progress should be definitely planned. In other words, the number of Jews engaged in the practice of the professions (law, medicine, etc.) should be definitely limited to the percentage that the Jewish population in North Africa bears to the whole of the North African population. Such a plan would therefore permit the Jews to engage in the professions, at the same time would not permit them to overcrowd the professions, and would present an unanswerable argument that they were being given their full rights.[75]

The discussion turned even uglier at this point, according to the transcript:

To the foregoing, General Nogues agreed generally, stating at the same time that it would be a sad thing for the French to win the war merely to open the way for the Jews to control the professions and the business world of North Africa. The President stated that his plan would further eliminate the specific and understandable complaints which the Germans bore toward the Jews in Germany, namely, that while they represented a small part of the population, over fifty percent of the lawyers, doctors, school teachers, college professors, etc. in Germany, were Jews.[76]

Several hours later, the president spoke along the same lines with General Giraud, although a detailed account is not available.

At Casablanca, Americans hoped for a pledge to revoke all French racist and antisemitic legislation. Also, presidential aide Harry Hopkins conveyed to a high Moroccan official Roosevelt's praise for the sultan's having refused a German demand that Morocco's Jews "be treated as they are in Germany."[77] At the same time, however, the President put forward the quota system, then under attack by the American Jewish community. These contradictions within American policy reappeared repeatedly.

Roosevelt's effort to placate French and German antisemites was based on misinformation. In 1933, Jews had made up about 1 percent of Germany's population and constituted 16.3 percent of its lawyers and 10.9 percent of its physicians. In 1925, Jews made up only 4 percent of the country's university teachers and 1.4 percent of Germany's teachers in elementary and secondary schools.[78] At the time Roosevelt grossly distorted these figures in Casablanca most of the German Jews had either fled the country or been killed in a death camp.

The gentile community in the United States was distinctly uninterested in rescuing Jews from the Holocaust, even when the basic facts were known. Thus, after conducting a study of fifty-two Protestant publications in the United States during the Nazi period, Robert Ross concluded: "I can say conclusively that American Protestant Christians did know what was happening to the Jews in Germany and later in occupied Europe under the Nazis."[79] Neither Protestant nor Catholic dignitaries made efforts to rescue Jews or to protest at the failure to rescue them.

Jews were themselves split on the issue between those most concerned with rescue and those more involved in creating a Jewish homeland after the war. Often the same person was involved in both. Zionists, who represented a growing element in American Jewry, did not accord rescue a high priority.

In January 1944, faced by internal administrative conflict that might soon expose the "do-nothing policy" of the federal government, President Roosevelt created by executive order the War Refugee Board. It was the first official American action of the war that established rescue as a principal aim. Curiously, however, nowhere near enough budgetary appropriations were made to finance the new body. In fact, Jewish organizations rescued the rescuers by supplying 90 percent of the WRB's funds. Rescue of Jewish and other victims of Nazism was thus almost an extralegal endeavor of the American government. Wyman estimates that the agency succeeded in rescuing some 200,000 Jews and about 20,000 non-Jewish refugees.[80] This was achieved despite refusal by many other government agencies to cooperate with the WRB. Included among these recalcitrants were the War Department, the Office of Strategic Services, the Office of War Information, and others.[81]

At war's end, American Jewry appeared to face a somber future. More than one out of every three Jews in the world had been exterminated as the American and other governments refused to save many Jews from a similar fate. At home, open antisemitic advocacy was growing common, structural discrimination had spread, government concern was minimal, and extreme right-wing groups operated freely. Yet the following forty years saw no repetition of the disastrous decade of 1935–45. In part, this beneficent outcome resulted from new tactics adopted in the service of a new broad social strategy adopted by Jewish organizations. For the most part, however, it was the consequence of extremely favorable economic and political circumstances that characterized the postwar years.

After World War II, the Jewish working class tended to evaporate as the older generation of immigrants died off. Their children and grandchildren came to inhabit the great American white middle class as never before. By 1970 educationally and occupationally, Jews had become one of the country's success stories. Jews aged twenty-five or over—that is, those who had been born in 1945 or earlier—had completed years of schooling as follows:

	Jewish	Total White
Less than 12 years	15.6	45.5
Twelve years	29.2	32.1
College		
1–3 years	19.2	11.1
4 years	14.2	6.4
5 or more years	18.2	4.9
Unknown	3.5	—

Occupationally, Jews were concentrated in the upper ranks. In 1970, they were distributed as follows by percentage:[82]

	Jewish	Total White
Professional and technical	27.4	15.5
Managers and administrators	32.2	9.0
Clerical	16.2	18.4
Sales	12.2	7.7
Crafts	4.2	14.4
Operatives	3.4	17.0
Service	2.0	11.0
Laborers	0.3	3.9
Agricultural	—	3.1
Unknown	2.2	—

By 1981, eleven years later, the same feature still held for Jews in the matter of family income, by percentage:[83]

	Jews	Non-Jews
Under $15,000	25	38
$15,000–$24,999	15	30
$25,000–$34,999	30	19
$35,000 and over	30	13

During the first postwar years, Jews attempted to counter discrimination by publicizing instances of it. Especially difficult to combat was systematic discrimination employed so as to appear neutral and nondiscriminatory. For example, Ruth Weintraub writes: "A report from Arizona indicates that the State Dental Board has discriminated against certain applicants. In June 1947 . . . 40 applicants took the examination for admission to the practice of dentistry, 26 were non-Jews and 14 Jews.

Of the 26 non-Jews, 22 were granted licenses. None of the 14 Jews was granted a license. In Arizona this did not represent an isolated instance, but instead was typical of a local pattern which has existed for a period of years."[84]

The first three postwar decades were a time of barely interrupted economic expansion in the United States. One of its effects was an unparalleled growth of higher education which led, in turn, to heightened demand for new faculty and administrators. For Jewish job applicants "the doors of universities did not really open until the 1950s."[85] Many other doors in the economy remained closed, however. Thus, the historical pattern of Jewish exclusion from high corporate office and major ownership in the biggest firms remained undisturbed.[86] On the other hand, all but eliminated were public specifications of religious preference for jobs.

Jews were on the defensive during the 1930s and the war years. Protest actions tended to emanate exclusively from Jewish sources and concerned Jews most directly. This stance of comparative narrowness was thrust upon organized Jewry by the lack of interest of non-Jewish groups. By the end of the 1930s, in Handlin's words, "the Jews no longer imagined their interests to lie in appeals to the powerful but in solidarity with the underprivileged."[87] The labor movement, which grew mightily during this period, became a close ally of Jewish demands for equality, as did national black groups. In return, Jewish groups were prominent in supporting basic demands of other groups—searching for economic and political equality. Legislation, both national and state, became a reality only when this strategy of coalition was underway. "The new approach of today," stated historian Jacob Rader Marcus, "is really the old Jewish socialistic approach of half a century ago: protect all groups, and the American people as a whole, through effective social action procedures."[88]

When, in the mid-1950s, the civil rights revolution erupted, advocates of the movement were found among Jews in greater numbers than among any other predominantly white group. This was most evident in large northern and western cities. In the South, many Jews and Jewish organizations first adopted a "strategy of silence."[89] In 1958, for example, Virginia editor James J. Kilpatrick attacked the Anti-Defamation League (ADL) with a vehemence that led many Jews to fear a resurgence of antisemitism should they openly oppose segregation. Statewide affiliates of ADL urged the national organization to mute its principled advocacy of desegregation. This was, in fact, done. The next year, a court struck down the Virginia laws that had led to closing of those schools under court order to desegregate. The schools reopened and ADL felt encouraged to resume public advocacy of desegregation.[90] Public opinion polls reflected these and related developments, as Charles Stember reports: "In 1959, almost as many persons had believed Jews to oppose school integration as believed them to favor it; in 1963, there were five respondents who thought Jews were helping Negro rights for every one who thought they were hindering them."[91] Jews, along with many other Americans, had been encouraged by the spirit of the times to declare their sympathies for civil rights.

Civil rights legislation by states and the federal government benefited Jews as well as other minorities. Quota restrictions in higher education disappeared; many middle-ranking executive positions in large industry opened; professions previously skittish about Jews began to admit them; residential exclusion ebbed. "Since the Second World War," writes Dennis Wrong, "Jews actually have been, as it were, institutionalized as part of American society."[92]

No black person has ever been a leader of a national antisemitic movement in the United States; nor have blacks belonged to such groups in any number. Antisemitic themes have not played a dominant role in the black churches as they have in the white ones. Because many antisemitic organizations are also racist—the Ku Klux Klan is a preeminent example—many more times than not blacks and Jews have cooperated against common enemies. Yet, antisemitism is a feature if also a minor note in American black life.

During World War II, L. D. Reddick, a black historian, noted that "antisemitism among Negroes in the United States is, in large measure, urban, Northern, and historically recent." He added, "There are no organized movements." In the South the color line acknowledged only blacks and whites; Jews were seen as whites. (Indeed, the one case of lynching violence in which a Jew was victimized occurred in Atlanta, Georgia, in 1916. Leo Frank, accused wrongfully of killing a gentile girl, was hanged by a mob of whites.) Reddick held that black-white relations in the North clustered around areas of competition and conflict: "These arise, in the main, from the face to face contacts with the landlord, the merchants, the employer of domestic labor and to a lesser degree, the professional man." While a number of blacks believe many "of the exploiting landlords are Jewish," Reddick wrote, "they also expect more from the Jewish landlord than from landlords in general, for the Jewish people, like the Negro people, have suffered." He added that black-Jewish relations should always be discussed in a context of both Jewish racism and black antisemitism. To encourage this process he made an unusual proposal: "All organizations for Jewish rights ought to incorporate the valid objectives of the Negro people in their programs. Likewise, all equivalent Negro organizations should incorporate all valid objectives of the Jewish people in their programs."[93]

Unfortunately, there are many fewer—perhaps no—public opinion studies of Jewish racism than of black antisemitism. Thus, it is difficult to apply Reddick's dictum about dealing with both together. Within that limitation, however, some relevant data are of value.

Harold Quinley and Charles Glock reviewed the findings of a mid-1960s national study of antisemitism which defined this concept as consisting of negative emphases on the Jews' wealth, dishonesty, clannishness, pridefulness, power-hunger, and pushiness. "Blacks," they found, "are distinguished from whites only by their more widespread feelings of economic hostility toward Jews." (This accords with Reddick's interpretation of thirty-seven years earlier.) Quinley and Glock continued: "They show no significantly greater tendency than whites to perceive Jews as aggressive, clannish, prideful, and conceited; they are somewhat less fearful than whites of Jewish power." Despite the salience of economic factors in black antisemitic attitudes, however, the researchers report that "urban blacks—whatever their other feelings toward Jews— would rather carry out their economic transactions with Jews than with other whites." This drawing toward Jews also emerged in the area of civil rights. Quinley and Glock found, for example, that "many blacks see Jews as especially supportive of civil rights, and those who do are consistently more disposed than those who do not to reject negative stereotypes of Jews and to condemn discriminatory behavior against them."[94]

Curiously, then, economic antisemitism seems detached from blacks' personal attitudes toward Jews. Many resent the Jewish merchant's practices without confusing those practices with Jewishness. In more recent years, when Korean-Americans and Arab-Americans bought and operated some of these same stores, black resentment at the formerly "Jewish" but now "Korean" and "Arab" practices remained. Now, however, the resentment was even more bitter because the practices were not moderated by civil rights attitudes as they had been between blacks and Jews.[95]

In 1981 a national survey on antisemitism was conducted for the American Jewish Committee by Yankelovich, Skelly, and White, Inc. Only a small part of it dealt with black-Jewish relations. Grouping the principal responses of both black and white non-Jews, the survey analysts found both groups related to antisemitism as follows, by percentage:[96]

	Prejudiced	Neutral	Unprejudiced
White non-Jews	21	30	49
Black non-Jews	37	41	22

Comparing attitudes during 1964 and 1981, whites had become somewhat less antisemitic (40.4 versus 32.7 percent) and blacks slightly more antisemitic (48.5 versus 57.6 percent).

Both whites and blacks strengthened their beliefs that Jews had too much power in the United States and were more loyal to Israel than to the United States. Both groups also had become less certain that Jews cared only about their own kind, controlled international banking, were shrewd and tricky in business, had a lot of irritating faults, used shady practices to get ahead, and always liked to head things. In two cases, blacks and Jews disagreed on the direction of change during 1964–81.

A third study was conducted by the Harris Survey from December 1984 to January 1985. It included several questions of special interest. One item asked for responses to the statement that "the same people who would like to keep the Jews down would also like to keep other minorities down." Blacks agreed by a percentage margin of 76 to 18; in 1978, the margin had been 67 to 10. To the same question, Jews responded affirmatively by a margin of 85 to 9. With respect to the statement "Jews are irritating because they are too aggressive," blacks and whites responded very closely together: about two-thirds negative and one quarter affirmative. In comparison with responses during 1976 and 1978, both blacks and whites had grown more accepting of Jews.[97]

Two themes pervade the polls: (1) black attitudes on Jews are especially harsh in the economic arena, yet this does not seem to eliminate the possibility of constructive black-Jewish relations; and (2) Jews and blacks are, in a real sense, in a similar political or civic boat, thus sharing a common destiny to a significant degree. Despite the distortion that frequently attends discussions of Jewish-black relations,[98] these themes have held up over the last forty years and constitute a solid foundation for future building. This is not to deny, however, that individual antisemitism can still be found in the black community and that it extends beyond economic issues.[99]

Historically, Jews and blacks have not competed for the same economic opportunities. During the past generation, however, this has ceased to be the case in public employment and in many levels of formal education. In these areas blacks attempted to enter while some Jews, enjoying the privilege of prior entry, adopted a defensive stance. This was a "white" view rather than a distinctively "Jewish" response. The consequence was a deepening of existing black sensitivity to economic factors in relations with Jews. Yet, when votes were counted in the 1984 elections, Jews and blacks emerged as the two largest groups of voters still loyal to traditional liberal programs including affirmative action.

During the early 1980s, violence against Jews became a more common topic in some far-right movements. Armed groups planned and carried out at least one execution of a Jew. A proliferation of such groups came into view by the mid-1980s. They were outnumbered by ideological antisemites who denied the historical reality of the Holocaust and/or gave new currency to the preachment of *The Protocols of the Elders of Zion*.

A much-delayed movement by federal authorities to deport war criminals who had helped the Nazis destroy Jews during World War II was
attacked by many small groups consisting of persons of Baltic origin.[100]
Some of these critics resorted to outright antisemitism in their
arguments.

National public opinion poll data gathered from 1981 to 1985 permit
both light and shadows to be remarked. In 1981 "a significant proportion
of Jews say that they have had recent experience (in the last year or two)
with such serious antisemitic incidents as the desecration of a temple (26
percent), a worker being passed over for a promotion because he or she
is Jewish (10 percent), or a club that excludes Jews from membership
(14 percent)."[101] While nearly eight out of ten Jews reported exposure
to an antisemitic incident, only half that proportion of non-Jews so
responded.

Of the entire non-Jewish sample, nearly one out of four were classified
as prejudiced against Jews while nearly one out of two were unprejud-
iced. Among the prejudiced, highly untrue stereotypes were believed by
sizable numbers. Thus, Jewish control of international banking was asserted by more than two out of five non-Jews who had opinions on the
matter. Certain unfavorable political attitudes toward Jews were widely
expressed. Fully 40 percent of non-Jews agreed that "Jews should stop
complaining about what happened to them in Nazi Germany." (Seventeen years earlier, 51 percent of non-Jewish respondents had felt this
way.) Nearly half (48 percent) believed "Jews were more loyal to Israel
than to America." (This represented an increase of 9 percent since 1964.)
In European history, antisemites had repeatedly tried to represent Jewry
as a "nation with a nation" and thus as somehow disloyal. This theme
has never gained many adherents in the United States. Nevertheless, its
impact is underscored by the parallel finding that non-Jews believing
that "Jews have too much power in the United States" rose from 13 to
23 percent between 1964 and 1981."[102]

While many individual Jews have been part of the civil rights movement in the United States, that movement has rarely included a struggle
against antisemitism in its program. In part, this is because these Jews
have not regarded antisemitism to be a critical threat. In larger part,
however, it has proved difficult for the movement to square the material
prosperity of American Jewry with the existence of discrimination
against Jews. There is a tendency to minimize the latter in the name of
the former. Since the major forms of racism most heavily impact on
poor blacks, Hispanics, and Indians, the civil rights movement tends to
identify discrimination with poverty. This mode of thought, however,
tends to ignore the reality of antisemitism in America. It also completely
sweeps away the centuries of suffering and struggle that are sketched

in this book. Ignorance of that history underlies a considerable part of the civil rights movement's present stance on antisemitism. Even among some Jews in the movement historical memories are dim.

Some twenty years ago, historian Ben Halpern wrote: "The situation of the Jews in America, however special its character, is not fundamentally different from what it has been elsewhere; and the configuration of Americans' attitudes toward them, however unique it may be, remains confined within the traditional framework of ambivalency between antisemitism and toleration."[103] Thus, while America's progress has been substantial it has not moved beyond toleration. During the 1930s, federal policy hardly reached even this limited goal. A half-century later, amid rising calls for a Christian America, more and more Jews began glancing over their historical shoulders. Toleration appeared increasingly attractive.

NOTES

1. Michael N. Dobkowski, "American Antisemitism and American Historians: A Critique," *Patterns of Prejudice*, 14 (April 1980), p. 34.

2. Richard B. Morris, "Civil Liberties and the Jewish Tradition in Early America," in Abraham J. Karp, ed., *The Jewish Experience in America*, 1 (New York: Ktav, 1969), p. 416.

3. Stanley F. Chyet, "The Political Rights of the Jews in the United States: 1776–1840," in *Critical Studies in American Jewish History*, 2 (New York: Ktav, 1971), pp. 44–45.

4. Ibid., p. 80.

5. Joseph L. Blau and Salo W. Baron, eds., *The Jews of the United States 1790–1840. A Documentary History*, 1 (New York: Columbia Univ. Press, 1963), pp. 3–4.

6. Ibid., p. 12.

7. Ibid., 3, p. 763.

8. Ibid., 2, pp. 445–46.

9. Morris U. Schappes, *A Pictorial History of the Jews in the United States*, rev. ed. (New York: Marzani and Munsell, 1965), p. 63; Morris V. Schappes, "Antisemitism and Reaction, 1795–1800," Karp, ed., *The Jewish Experience in America*, 1, pp. 362–90.

10. Allan Tarshish, "Jew and Christian in a New Society: Some Aspects of Jewish-Christian Relationships in the United States, 1848–1881," in Bertram W. Korn, ed., *A Bicentennial Festschrift for Jacob Rader Marcus* (New York: Ktav, 1976), p. 570.

11. Stephen V. Ash, "Civil War Exodus: The Jews and Grant's General Orders No. 11," *Historian*, 44 (August 1981), p. 508.

12. Ibid., p. 519.

13. Schappes, *A Pictorial History of the Jews*, p. 94.

14. Stanley Feldstein, *The Land That I Show You. Three Centuries of Jewish Life in America* (Garden City, N.Y.: Anchor Books, 1978), p. 108.

15. Carey McWilliams, *A Mask for Privilege. Anti-Semitism in America* (Boston: Little, Brown, 1948), pp. 147–48.

16. John Higham, *Send These to Me. Jews and Other Immigrants in Urban America* (New York: Atheneum, 1975), p. 148.

17. Tarshish, "Jew and Christian in a New Society," pp. 571–72.

18. Michael N. Dobkowski, *The Tarnished Dream. The Basis of American Anti-Semitism* (Westport, Conn.: Greenwood Press, 1979), p. 57.

19. Tarshish, "Jew and Christian in a New Society," p. 577.

20. Dobkowski, *The Tarnished Dream*, pp. 14, 69, 59, 84, 85–87. Compare, however, John J. Appel, "Jews in American Caricature: 1820–1914," *American Jewish History*, (September 1981), pp. 103–33. See also Naomi W. Cohen, "Anti-Semitism in the Gilded Age: The Jewish View," *Jewish Social Studies*, 41 (1979), pp. 187–210.

21. Higham, *Send These to Me*, pp. 152, 154, 155.

22. Quoted in Michael Selzer, ed., *"Kike!" A Documentary History of Anti-Semitism in America* (New York: World, 1972), p. 75.

23. Zosa Szajkowski, *Jews, Wars, and Communism*, 2, *The Impact of the 1919–20 Red Scare on American Jewish Life* (New York: Ktav, 1974), p. 153.

24. Ibid., p. 154.

25. Ibid., p. 192; a different impression can be gained from Leonard J. Mervis, "The Social Justice Movement and the American Reform Rabbi," in *Critical Studies in American Jewish History*, 3 (New York: Ktav, 1971), p. 128.

26. Albert Lee, *Henry Ford and the Jews* (New York: Stein and Day, 1980), p. 29.

27. Ibid., p. 31.

28. See Robert Singerman, "The American Career of the *Protocols of the Elders of Zion*," *American Jewish History* (September 1981), pp. 48–78.

29. Lee, *Henry Ford and the Jews*, p. 46.

30. Ibid., p. 51.

31. Ibid., p. 69.

32. Kenneth T. Jackson, *The Ku Klux Klan in the City 1915–1930* (New York: Oxford Univ. Press, 1967), p. 218.

33. Hiram Wesley Evans, "The Klan's Fight for Americanism," *North American Review*, 223 (1926), p. 60.

34. Ibid., p. 39.

35. W E. B. Du Bois, "The Shape of Fear," *North American Review*, 223 (1926), p. 301.

36. Ibid., p. 292.

37. Feldstein, *The Land That I Show You*, p. 283.

38. Deborah D. Moore, *At Home in America. Second Generation New York Jews* (New York: Columbia Univ. Press, 1981), p. 38. This is a quote from Moore's book, not from the court's opinion.

39. Oscar Handlin, *Adventure in Freedom. Three Hundred Years of Jewish Life in America* (New York: McGraw-Hill, 1954), p. 205.

40. Lewis S. Feuer, "The Stages in the Social History of Jewish Professors in American Colleges and Universities," *American Jewish History*, 71 (June 1982), p. 455.

41. Ibid., p. 461.

42. "May Jews Go to College?" *Nation,* 114 (June 14, 1922), p. 708. See also letters to the editor in *Nation,* July 12, 1922, pp. 45–46.

43. See Harvey Strum, "Louis Marshall and Anti-Semitism at Syracuse University," *American Jewish Archives,* 35 (April 1983), pp. 1–12. On the treatment of black students in American higher education, see Meyer Weinberg, *A Chance to Learn* (New York: Cambridge Univ. Press, 1977), ch. 7.

44. Feuer, "Stages," p. 456.

45. Alfred L. Shapiro, "Racial Discrimination in Medicine (With Special Reference to Medical and Specialty Education and Practice)," *Jewish Social Studies,* 10 (April 1948), p. 103.

46. Ibid., p. 109.

47. Moshe R. Gottlieb, *American Anti-Nazi Resistance, 1933–1941* (New York: Ktav, 1982), p. 61.

48. Ibid., p. 48.

49. Ibid., p. 31.

50. Ibid., p. 60.

51. Schappes, *A Pictorial History of the Jews,* p. 186.

52. See Alan M. Kraut et al., "The State Department, the Labor Department, and German Jewish Immigration, 1930–1940," *Journal of American Ethnic History,* 3 (1984), p. 24. "Of the approximately 300,000 persons who applied for visas under the German quota between 30 June 1933 and 30 June 1939, 74,858 received visas, although 158,000 were allowed under the quota law."

53. *New York Times,* April 7, 1933, quoted in Gottlieb, *American Anti-Nazi Resistance,* p. 24.

54. David S. Wyman, *The Abandonment of the Jews. America and Holocaust, 1941–1945* (New York: Pantheon, 1984), p. 8.

55. David Brody, "American Jewry, the Refugees and Immigration Restriction (1932–1942)," in Abraham J. Karp, ed., *The Jewish Experience in America,* 5 (New York: Ktav, 1969), p. 332.

56. Handlin, *Adventure in Freedom,* p. 205.

57. Higham, *Send These to Me,* p. 190.

58. Sheldon Marcus, *Father Coughlin. The Tumultuous Life of the Priest of the Little Flower* (Boston: Little, Brown, 1973), p. 32.

59. Ibid., p. 57.

60. Ibid., p. 126.

61. Ibid., p. 156; Charles J. Tull, *Father Coughlin and the New Deal* (Syracuse, N.Y.: Syracuse University Press, 1965), pp. 207–8; Feldstein, *The Land That I Show You,* p. 407; James Wechsler, "The Coughlin Terror," *Nation,* July 22, 1939.

62. Marcus, *Father Coughlin,* p. 160.

63. Ibid., p. 205.

64. Ibid., p. 230.

65. Leo P. Ribuffo, *The Old Christian Right. The Protestant Far Right from the Great Depression to the Cold War* (Philadelphia: Temple Univ. Press, 1983), p. 147.

66. Ibid., pp. 153–54.

67. Gerald L. K. Smith, *Besieged Patriot* (Eureka Springs, Ark.: Elna M. Smith Foundation, 1978), passim.

68. Leland V. Bell, *In Hitler's Shadow. The Anatomy of American Nazism* (Port Washington, N.Y.: Kennikat Press, 1973), p. 77. See also Sander A. Diamond,

The Nazi Movement in the United States, 1924–1941 (Ithaca, N.Y.: Cornell Univ. Press, 1974).

69. Charles H. Stember et al., *Jews in the Mind of America* (New York: Basic Books, 1966), p. 138.

70. Leonard Dinnerstein, "Anti-Semitism Exposed and Attacked, 1945–1950," *American Jewish History*, September 1981, p. 135.

71. K.R.M. Short, "Hollywood Fights Anti-Semitism, 1940–1945," in K.R.M. Short, ed., *Film and Radio Propaganda in World War II* (London: Croom Helm, 1983), p. 162.

72. Ibid., p. 164.

73. Stember et al., *Jews in the Mind of America*, p. 116.

74. Wyman, *The Abandonment of the Jews,* p. x.

75. U.S. State Department, *Foreign Relations of the United States. The Conferences at Washington, 1941–42, and Casablanca, 1943* (Washington, D.C.: Government Printing Office, 1968), p. 608.

76. Ibid.

77. Ibid., p. 702.

78. See Esra Bennathan, "Die Demographische und Wirtschaftliche Struktur der Juden," in Werner E. Mosse, ed., *Entscheidungsjahr 1932,* 2d rev. and enlarged ed. (Tübingen: J. C. B. Mohr [Paul Siebeck], 1966), pp. 11–12; American Jewish Committee, *The Jews in Nazi Germany. A Handbook Regarding Their Present Situation* (New York: Howard Fertig, 1982 [orig. 1933]), p. 10; Jacob R. Marcus, *The Rise and Destiny of the German Jew* (New York: Ktav, 1973 [orig. 1934]), p. 325.

79. Robert W. Ross, *So It Was True. The American Protestant* (Minneapolis: Univ. of Minnesota Press, 1980), p. 267.

80. Wyman, *The Abandonment of the Jews,* p. x.

81. See ibid., pp. 210, 294, 314–15.

82. Sidney Goldstein, "Jews in the United States: Perspectives from Demography," in Joseph B. Gittler, ed., *Jewish Life in the United States* (New York: New York Univ. Press, 1981), pp. 82, 89.

83. Gregory Martire and Ruth Clark, *Anti-Semitism in the United States. A Study of Prejudice in the 1980s* (New York: Praeger, 1982), p. 97.

84. Ruth G. Weintraub, *How Secure These Rights? Anti-Semitism in the United States in 1948. An Anti-Defamation League Survey* (Garden City, N.Y.: Doubleday, 1949), p. 64.

85. Lloyd P. Gartner, "Assimilation and American Jews," in Bela Vago, ed., *Jewish Assimilation in Modern Times* (Boulder, Colo.: Westview Press, 1981), p. 179. See also Feuer, "Stages," pp. 464–65; Stephen Steinberg, *The Academic Melting Pot. Catholics and Jews in American Higher Education* (New York: McGraw-Hill, 1974), p. 106.

86. See Stephen L. Slavin and Mary A. Pratt, *The Einstein Syndrome: Corporate Anti-Semitism in America Today* (Washington, D.C.: University Press of America, 1982); R. L. Zweigenhaft, "Recent Patterns of Jewish Representation in the Corporate and Social Elites," *Contemporary Jewry* (Spring–Summer 1982), pp. 36–46.

87. Handlin, *Adventure in Freedom,* p. 214.

88. Jacob Rader Marcus, "Background for the History of American Jewry," in Oscar I. Janowsky, ed., *The American Jew. A Reappraisal* (Philadelphia: Jewish Publication Society of America, 1964), p. 11.

89. Stember et al., *Jews in the Mind of America,* p. 202.

90. See Murray Friedman, "One Episode in Southern Jewry's Response to Desegregation: An Historical Memoir," *American Jewish Archives,* 33 (November 1981), pp. 170–83.

91. Stember et al., *Jews in the Mind of America,* p. 205.

92. Dennis H. Wrong, "The Psychology of Prejudice and the Future of Anti-Semitism in American," in Stember et al., *Jews in the Mind of America,* p. 331.

93. L. D. Reddick, "Anti-Semitism among Negroes," *Negro Quarterly* (Summer 1982), pp. 114, 115, 116, 121.

94. Harold E. Quinley and Charles Y. Glock, *Anti-Semitism in America* (New York: Free Press, 1979), pp. 57, 63, 68.

95. See La Barbara Bowman, "The Koreans: Corner Store Revolution," *Washington Post,* May 28, 1979; Peter Eng and Edward D. Sargent, "A Troubled American Dream," *Washington Post,* September 17, 1981; Carlyle C. Douglas, "Korean Merchants Are Target of Black Anger," *New York Times,* January 19, 1985; Salim Muwakkil, "Arab-Black Tensions Heat up over Urban Business Interests," *In These Times,* September 4, 1985.

96. See Gregory Martire and Ruth Clark, *Anti-Semitism in the United States. A Study of Prejudice in the 1980s* (New York: Praeger, 1982), pp. 36, 42. See also Martire and Clark, "Anti-Semitism in America," *Public Opinion,* 5 (April–May 1982), pp. 56–59.

97. Harris Survey, "Poll Results Contradict Claims That Prejudice Is Increasing," February 18, 1985 (mimeographed).

98. Three examples follow: (1) Halpern describes the Harlem riots of the 1930s, 1940s, and 1960s as equivalent to "pogroms" even though he goes on to describe the movements as "anti-white" rather than solely anti-Jewish (see Ben Halpern, "Self-Denial and Self-Preservation: Responses to Anti-Semitism among American Jews," in Salo W. Baron and George S. Wise, eds., *Violence and Defense in the Jewish Experience* [Philadelphia: Jewish Publication Society of America, 1977], pp. 280–81); (2) Dinnerstein writes that "by the early 1970s antisemitism in the United States seemed almost a thing of the past—except among blacks" (Leonard Dinnerstein, "Anti-Semitism Exposed and Attacked," *American Jewish History* September 1981, p. 148). Both historical reality and public opinion data contradict such a statement; (3) Avineri holds that "Jewish participation in ... the Civil Rights movement in the United States did not endear the Jews as a group to the ghetto Black" (Shlomo Avineri, "Aspects of Post-Holocaust Anti-Jewish Attitudes", in *World Jewry and the State of Israel* [New York: Arno Press, 1977], p. 5). Poll data contradict this assertion. The writer has an absurdly exaggerated view of the importance of Jews in the American civil rights movement.

99. See, for example, three antisemitic articles by LaVerne K. Mitchell in a black weekly published in Jackson, Mississippi, *The Jackson Advocate:* "The Zionist Conspiracy. The Black Connection," October 7, 1982; "The Fourth Reich," February 3, 1983; and "Blue Thunder," July 21, 1983. In addition, see her letter to the editor, December 9, 1982. See also the antisemitic article by Rev. F. D. Kirkpatrick, "Zionists and 'Honorary White' Negros Lead Protests to Re-enslave Africa," June 20, 1985, and reply by Meyer Weinberg, July 25, 1985. A better-known example is reported in "Louis Farrakhan. An Update," *ADL Facts* 30 (Spring 1985), pp. 1–14.

100. See Jerome Babst, *The Campaign against the U.S. Justice Department's Prosecution of Suspected Nazi War Criminals* (New York: Anti-Defamation League, June 1985).

101. Martire and Clark, *Anti-Semitism in the United States*, p. 105.

102. Ibid., p. 19.

103. Ben Halpern, "Anti-Semitism in the Perspective of Jewish History," in Stember et al., *Jews in the Mind of America*, p. 283.

13

SIMILARITIES AND DIFFERENCES

Do you need an opera glass to see antisemitism?
—Jacobo Timerman, 1981

What, besides the presence of antisemitism, binds the twelve countries together or sets them apart into groups? Let us summarize some of the highlights of each country and then see how distinctions can be drawn among the countries.

Argentinian antisemitism, indebted fundamentally to a close-minded medieval Spanish heritage, has neither forgiven nor accepted Jews for what they are. Fueled by a socially reactionary Catholic church, anti-Jewish measures and attitudes have been presented in a context of right-eousness that rejects moral protests by Satanic Jews. The church, the landowning aristocracy, and the military hierarchy, joined lately by large-scale industry, have led the country from one antisemitic excess to another. If the lower orders have not joined in exhuberantly, neither have they objected strenuously. Nazi doctrines of nation, blood, and force have dulled the keenness of public awareness. By the early 1980s, antisemitism was not resolved; rather, it simply ceased taking violent form.

Jews in Bulgaria, predating Slavic peoples in that country, were accepted as a native element. There was thus never a Jewish question in Bulgaria, rather an oddity in eastern Europe. Jews also benefited from a fairly evenhanded national policy to all minorities. Official antisemitism began to emerge as incidental to Bulgaria's allying with Nazi Germany in World War II. Anti-Jewish legislation was greeted by widespread opposition of non-Jewish Bulgarians. Christian church officials openly defended Jews as did a number of legislators. A nationwide protest succeeded in reducing sharply the number of Jews sent to death camps. After World War II, most Bulgarian Jews were allowed to move to Israel.

Alexandria, in Egypt, cradled antisemitism in the ancient world less because it was a highly Egyptian city and more so because of its character as a city of foreigners. Under Muslim rule after A.D. 640, Jews along with Christians were permitted to worship as they wished and suffered no discrimination in economic affairs. Antisemitic doctrines were imported from Europe by Christian Arabs near the end of the nineteenth century while Muslim Arabs largely resisted this trend. Zionism was received rather sympathetically in the 1920s but more circumspectly a decade later. An out-and-out antisemitic movement arose during the late 1930s, financed in part by the royal house and, perhaps, German funds. Little of a mass base, however, was created. After World War II, and especially the creation of Israel in 1948, Egyptian government authorities, prodded by hypernationalists and Muslim groups, promoted anti-Jewish measures both publicly and under cover. Anti-Zionism tended to merge with antisemitism. During the quarter-century after the late 1950s, a far-reaching program of antisemitic propaganda was undertaken by the Egyptian government. By the 1980s, the organized Jewish community had virtually disappeared through emigration.

Ethiopian Jews lived as an independent tribe for 2,000 years but were the object of unceasing attempts to defeat them, in wars by other Ethiopians, and to convert them to Christianity. In the seventeenth century, they suffered a final defeat and were deprived of the right to own farmland. Henceforward they became skilled artisans, attached to many villages of Christians. During the 1920s, appeals to worldwide Jewry were made for financial aid. Some slight progress ended abruptly with the Italian occupation from 1936 to 1941. During the 1950s and 1960s, appeals to the emperor were in vain as the Jews suffered persecution by Christians and heavy rental charges by landlords. Israel, out of diplomatic motives, refused to facilitate the emigration of these Jews. The Revolution of 1974 forced Haile Selassie from the throne and a land reform followed the next year. Jews were entitled to benefit, but landlords and other political opponents of the reform prevented them from sharing in it. Many Jews were beaten, enslaved, or killed. Only after a secret arrangement was concluded between Israel, Ethiopia, and Sudan were almost half the Jews in Ethiopia transported to Israel in 1984–85.

Antisemitism in France arose in the eleventh century under church auspices. The French throne exploited Jewish wealth through periodic exactions and, late in the fourteenth century, by expulsion from the country. The French Revolution of 1789 transformed the Jews from a separate people into citizens, although second-class ones. Antisemitism in local schooling was widespread during the nineteenth century. During the last third or so of the century, anti-Jewish publications multiplied. The Catholic church and the military officer corps, deeply antisemitic, were joined by small merchants and minor bureaucrats as well as professionals and university students. These and other Frenchmen became involved in the Dreyfus affair at century's end. After the affair, Jews became even more integrated into French society. During the 1930s, however, numerous Fascist groups attacked especially the immigrant Jews from eastern and central Europe. Before and during World War II, French authorities put together anti-Jewish legislation and cooperated with the Nazi program of extermination of Jews. After the war, little was said about this record and expressed antisemitism was comparatively low and declining.

Germany, the home of modern antisemitism, was the scene of church and state measures against Jews as early as the thirteenth century. Expulsions from individual towns were frequent. By the early eighteenth century, numerous anti-Jewish tracts had been published, chief of which were those written by Martin Luther in the mid-sixteenth century. Jewish emancipation was completed by 1871. Within a decade antisemitism had become an organized ideological movement. Exclusion of Jews from preferred employment, public and private, was widespread between 1870 and 1918. During these years, anti-Jewish planks were adopted by major parties although antisemitism was nurtured explicitly by ultra-conservative parties, including the Nazis, the Christian churches, university students, and the common schools.

Under Nazi rule, Jews suffered from intermittent physical violence. Laws and regulations excluded them from public employments and benefits, deprived them of their citizenship, and by 1939 effectively relieved them of their businesses or professional practices. More than half the country's Jews emigrated. In the autumn of 1941, further emigration was banned; plans for death camps were drawn up, and during the winter of 1941–42 gassings began. During the years 1933 to 1945, German public opinion shifted from a slight inattention to Nazi imprecations to an impersonalization toward Jewish affairs that verged on dehumanizing Jews.

Prior to World War I, Hungarian Jews were agents of Magyarization in the eastern rural provinces, populated by ethnic groups that collectively outnumbered Magyars in the country as a whole. Jews were also encouraged by the central government to help develop the national economy and some prospered greatly as a result. After the war, however, Hungary lost its eastern provinces and thus Jewish Magyarizers were no longer needed. Jews were increasingly replaced by Magyar jobseekers in various economic installations. During the 1930s, native and German Nazi groups took increasingly prominent parts in political life. Outright anti-Jewish laws were passed. Hungary allied itself with Germany which occupied the former in 1944. Soon, almost 500,000 Jews were shipped to Auschwitz; some 225,000 others remained in the country. After the war, Hungary was the least antisemitic nation of the eastern bloc.

Until the fifteenth century, Italian Jews lived under unusually hospitable conditions. Within the next two centuries, some of the most barbaric massacres in Europe were in force. Church leaders initiated most of them. Jews were compulsorily segregated in ghettos, their trading opportunities were restricted, and manufacturing and certain trades were entirely closed to them. In 1775, these oppressive regulations were resurrected by a pope. Momentarily emancipated under Napoleonic rule, Jews were thrown back into civil servitude by the end of the first quarter of the nineteenth century. In 1870, when Italy was unified, all religions were given equal recognition. After World War I, Jews joined the Fascist party along with non-Jews. Anti-Jewish measures materialized under Mussolini only in 1938 and after. During World War II, however, few Jews were sent to their deaths and Italian authorities rescued a number from such a fate.

Anti-Jewish trends in Poland were set in motion during the thirteenth century by Catholic church circles. During the next six centuries, the church was at the forefront in such movements. Jews were invited to Poland upon being expelled from Spain in 1492 and filled many useful economic positions. Their civic status rose accordingly. In the mid-seventeenth century, many Jews were slaughtered as they fought alongside Poles in wars ignited by Cossacks, Ukrainians, and Tatars. Outright antisemitic political movements emerged at the close of the nineteenth century. In independent Poland (1918–39) the government took an active role in anti-Jewish affairs. It refused to enforce minority rights for Jews who were also excluded from government employment. (Private employers in industry also largely barred Jews.) Licenses for numerous small traders and peddlers were managed so as to disadvantage Jewish holders and applicants. Universities discriminated against Jewish students through quotas and other practices. Church preaching against Jews heightened during the 1930s.

The Nazi attack on Poland in September 1939 set off a vast process of destruction of Jews. In 1943, residents of the Warsaw Ghetto revolted. Few Poles helped Jews. Pogroms and isolated attacks on Jews reappeared at war's end. While new laws banned national and religious strife, Jews did not benefit since their rights remained purely formal. During the 1960s, various warring factions in the Communist party made political use of antisemitism. They "accused" liberal reformers, many of whom were Jews, of acting out a Zionist conspiracy of some sort. Remnants of the issue arose during the 1980s.

Rumanian antisemites were centrally concerned with maintaining the civic inferiority of Jews. At the same time, they wished to deprive Jews of any economic advantage they might have gained or to impose upon them restrictions that would preclude economic gain. Except for that of Russia, Rumania's statutory antisemitica was closely interlocked with the issue of Jewish rights because the great powers of Europe compelled Rumania to grant such rights as the price of recognition. This happened only in 1920, some seventy years after such pressures were first exerted. During the 1930s, many of these advances were retracted by the Rumanian government. Allied with Germany in World War II, Rumania administered the cruelest program of extermination of Jews. In 1944, it switched sides and reversed its anti-Jewish policy. After the war, Rumania adopted the most enlightened policy on Jews within the Soviet bloc.

Tsarist Russia dealt with the Jews first by restricting their numbers, then by expelling them altogether, and, finally, when they reentered the empire as an incident of war, by forcing them to live within a severely policed section of the country. Within the pale, as it was called, Jews had few rights. Favoring a tiny group of wealthy, educated Jews, the government bore down heavily on the rest. Access to secondary and higher education was limited by quotas. From 1881 to 1906, numerous pogroms, many secretly organized by the government, afflicted the Jews. The revolutions of 1917 abolished the entire body of tsarist restrictions on Jews. During the 1920s and early 1930s, antisemitism was opposed actively by the Soviet government but the Stalinist purges of the Communist party in the mid- and late 1930s expressed, in part, a new infusion of antisemitism. After World War II severely anti-Jewish measures were implemented; many of these disappeared with the death of Stalin. An official process of employment and university quotas, however, was strengthened into the present. Much of the history of Jews in Russia and the USSR was either suppressed or distorted. A new antisemitism appeared in which distaste for Jews and Judaism was disguised as a movement against Zionism. Much of Lenin's heritage of thought on Jews and antisemitism was ignored or distorted by the purveyors of the new hate.

Antisemitism appeared in the United States only fitfully before the Civil War. Unlike Europe, America offered few occasions for economic or religious conflict between Jews and Gentiles. Particularly significant was the absence of a Christian state church. While religion-engendered anti-Jewish stereotypes thrived, antisemitism never became a theological imperative. Between the Civil War and World War I (1865–1914) economic opportunities expanded as industrialism swept all before it. Children of the large Jewish immigrant working class entered the growing middle class after acquiring higher education rather readily. Outright anti-Jewish measures emerged under private auspices in employment, housing, education, and recreation. During the 1930s and early 1940s, political antisemitism entered the scene momentarily. Like other Western countries, the United States resisted rescuing refugee Jews and maintained rigid immigration barriers. Despite an economically expansive postwar period, and in the face of a stable social situation, a sizable undercurrent of antisemitism continued to flow. It was matched by the persistence of apprehension among Jews.

Does geography matter? Not much. Among the three western European countries can be found the country of the Final Solution, the country which hastened to install an antisemitic program before Germany ordered a repetition of its own, and a dictatorship that proved most protective of Jews during the Holocaust. In eastern Europe before World War II, there was little to choose from any single country except Bulgaria and, intermittently, the USSR. By the 1930s Poland, Rumania, and Hungary were uniformly anti-Jewish.

Was there a popular tradition of antisemitism in any of the countries? If we mean a grass-roots variety, the answer must be yes. In Germany, Poland, Russia/USSR, and, much less so, France, there was a traditional belief that Jews somehow did not measure up to the standard for full membership in the nation. In other words, a Jewish question existed. During the nineteenth century, antisemitic legislation descended from the top ranks of society and so we find little antisemitism among Rumanian peasants. After World War I, somewhat the same was true in Hungary. In Ethiopia, during the nineteenth and twentieth centuries, antisemitism became populist mainly under pressure of the Christian churches. Neither Egypt nor the United States has a significant history of popular antisemitism, undoubtedly for very different reasons.

Few of the twelve countries may be said to have had a uniform tendency toward antisemitism during the entire course of their histories. Much more often they shifted and turned, expanded and contracted. Germany during the 1920s was a favored refuge of Jewish university students who were not permitted to attend schools in Hungary, Poland, or Rumania. Soviet policy on Jews was dizzying from one decade to another. Rumania and Hungary, which had treated Jews brutally in World War II, suddenly became exemplars after the war, while their political masters in the Soviet Union turned in the other direction. Bulgaria departed for a few years during the late 1930s from its historical policy of friendship toward Jews, but it, too, returned shortly to its older stance.

How important for antisemitic policy was the presence of a state Christian church? Such churches were critically significant in Poland, Rumania, Argentina, and Ethiopia where in each case prominent church leaders were known antisemites. In Germany and France, the Catholic churches, though not state bodies, found little to object to in anti-Jewish measures or even the final solution. The Protestant churches of Germany followed the same path, but this was not the case in France where Protestant churchpersons drew on an old tradition of dissent. In Italy, the Catholic church adopted an ambiguous policy toward Jews. In Rumania and Hungary Christian church leaders occasionally lent a hand—or more likely, a private word—to Jews in need. Only in Bulgaria did the Orthodox church take a clear position against antisemitic policies. Elsewhere, they were silent (as in the United States during the Holocaust) or irrelevent (as in the USSR).

Gentile opposition to antisemitism was most persistent in Bulgaria and perhaps least so in Argentina. Judging from explicit findings by historians, one measures the number of gentiles who aided Jews during the Holocaust by fractions of fractions. Poland seems to excel in bad taste when it comes to making excessive claims of having helped Jews. On the other hand, historical evidence suggests strongly that Italy's positive record has been greatly underestimated. All too often we reserve the words "heroes" or "heroines" for such persons. Interestingly, however, many of these very people do not view themselves in this light. At Yad Vashem, the museum of the Holocaust located in Israel, non-Jews who risked their lives in helping save the lives of Jews during the Holocaust are honored as the "Righteous." According to the director of this work at the museum: "In half of the cases we investigate, we receive no reply or people say, 'I just did my duty as a good person; I don't need to be honored.'"[1] In any event, between 1962 and 1983 only some 5,000 persons received the honor.[2]

How did the effectiveness of Jewish community organization vary, crisis by crisis and country by country? While detailed studies are almost wholly lacking, impressionistic evidence permits some observations to be made. Sometimes, as in the case of wartime Rumania, a single leader—Wilhelm Filderman, head of the national Jewish organization—proved to be a powerhouse who alternatively coordinated, wheedled, begged, and demanded concessions from the government. His influence was indispensable. In other cases, concern for the sensibilities of Jews led leaders to withhold upsetting news from the rank and file, thus contributing to their lack of preparation for the worst that was to come. This, for example, was true of Rabbi Leo Baeck of Berlin as well as much of the Jewish leadership in Budapest. In both cases, news of the gassings in death camps was kept secret. The Bulgarian Jewish leadership had more elbow room in which to operate inasmuch as numerous gentile figures of influence cooperated. In Argentina, as we saw, the leadership was intimidated so severely that during the "disappearances" it was incapacitated, spending whatever energies it had in dissuading others from protesting too loudly. Jewish leaders in Ethiopia were as effective as a stringent situation permitted; they did not believe in silence. During the Holocaust years, American Jewish leaders failed to challenge the restrictive immigration laws nor did they, during the 1930s, agree on a boycott of German trade. The Jewish Anti-Fascist Committee, the nearest thing to a nationally representative body Soviet Jews ever had under Stalin's

rule, spoke in the name of Jewish communal interests but did not dare
to bargain with or make demands of the government.

All twelve countries were alike in one negative respect: outside of
Jewish circles, antisemitism was rarely regarded as a *national* problem.
Enlightened leaders might openly speak against national hatreds or racism, but parallel, explicit denunciations of antisemitism were—and are—
scarce. Ultranationalists on the far Right, however, did not hesitate to
label the Jews themselves as a national problem. Thus, in 1879 the German historian Heinrich von Treitschke declared: "The Jews are our
national misfortune." Similar sentiments were voiced by conservative
Russian nationalists in the USSR a century later. Examples in other
countries and times are numerous.

NOTES

1. Mordecai Paldiel, quoted in Joy Horowitz, "Legacies of Holocaust: Hope,
Heart," *Los Angeles Times*, March 9, 1983.
2. Ibid.

14

THE WORLD OF ANTISEMITISM

If you can assume that any particular minority, however defined, does not have a claim on the enjoyment of equal rights, you have already destroyed the very moral and philosophical basis upon which the rights of Jews depend as well.

—Hans J. Morgenthau, 1967

Judging by the twelve countries studied in this book, by far most antisemitism has been deliberately cultivated and planned by governments and dominant social groups for their political and other advantage. Very little of it arose from individual prejudice, although such sentiments do facilitate the application of deliberate antisemitism. In other words, antisemitism usually proceeds from the top down rather than from the grass roots up. As is clear from the chapter on Egypt, that country is only the most recent example of the deliberate manufacture of antisemitism by a government. Both church and state in Poland are more ancient practitioners of the art. In U.S. legal vocabulary, most antisemitism tends to be de jure (created by official action) rather than de facto (it just happens to happen as a result of individual decisions). The official action can originate wholly from government leaders or in cooperation with private groups. And it may combine affirmative acts and conscious failure to enforce existing protective legislation.

Political parties formed principally to advance antisemitism are rare. A few were first to be found in western Europe during the last quarter of the nineteenth century. These tended to be viewed as marginal extremist groups and attracted little support. More successful were efforts to convince standard conservative groups to adopt antisemitic planks in their platforms. These could be found in Germany, Egypt, Poland, and Hungary. With some degree of political influence or control, organized antisemitism was able to push for passage of restrictive legislation. Jewish defense organizations, quite aware of this, counteracted the tendency by forming Jewish parties or collaborating with parties consisting mainly of non-Jews, or contributing financially to parties that worked in practical ways against antisemitism. (It will be recalled that in Germany the Socialists were the beneficiaries of such aid.) In none of the twelve countries was organized Jewry any more than just another pressure group. Often, it was an ineffectual one when it came to critical issues of Jewish welfare.

Is antisemitism least likely to thrive under a democratic form of government? Our dozen cases suggest the answer is not altogether clear. It is supported in the case of the United States but not in Italy. Under the Fascist rule of Mussolini, from 1922 to 1938, antisemitism was hardly known in Italy. Even from 1938 on—when antisemitic decrees were issued—many Italians refused to honor such measures. As we saw above, this included high government and military officials. During World War II, the allies of Germany—Bulgaria, Hungary, and Rumania—collectively accounted for 1.25 million Jews in 1929 and 677,000 in 1945, a loss of 45.8 percent. Poland, ruled by a modified military dictatorship until 1939, lost 98.5 percent of its Jews during the same period. In the Soviet Union, about half were lost.

Revolutions have affected antisemitism in various ways. Both Russian revolutions of 1917 proclaimed the end of tsarist oppression of Jews and for nearly the next twenty years antisemitism was combated by the Soviet government. Policies were reversed abruptly during the mid-1930s, however. The American and French revolutions contributed to transforming Jews into equal citizens, as did the English Civil War of the seventeenth century in a much more gradual process. Twentieth-century revolutions that proved unsuccessful were suppressed with extraordinary violence by extreme right-wing forces that extended their attacks onto Jews as well. Such events transpired during 1918–19 in Germany (Berlin and Munich), Hungary (Budapest), and Argentina (Buenos Aires). During the next decades, conservatives nursed the legend that all Jews were wild revolutionaries. Undoubtedly, revolutions, even if they did not triumph, sometimes loosened certain restrictive practices if only momentarily. Thus, in the 1905 Russian Revolution, soviets (councils) of college professors began ignoring official attendance quotas for Jewish students. With defeat of the revolution, however, the quotas were reinstated.

Pogroms were another mark of political weakness on the part of Jews. The essence of a pogrom is not the scope of the violence but the official inattention accorded it. It is a deadly public disorder aimed directly at outnumbered and defenseless Jews. Government often chooses not to know of the action, or its representatives may actually participate in it. Pogroms were much more typical of antisemitism in Russia, Rumania, and Ethiopia than in Poland where group attacks were generally avoided, or Germany before the 1930s. They were almost unknown in the United States or in France. In Argentina, except during the frenzied Tragic Week, killings of individual Jews have prevailed over group murders.

In view of the physical victimization and political weakness of Jews, assertions about their reputed power are baseless. Every major antisemitic ideology of the past century posited the existence of a conspiracy of Jews aimed at controlling the world. *The Protocols of the Elders of Zion,* fabricated in order to "demonstrate" the truth of the charge, is a classic statement of the thesis. Yet, history has contradicted the charge at every turn. Between 1939 and 1945, the number of Jews in the world fell from approximately 16 million to 10 million. Even today, nearly fifty years later, the number has not returned to its 1939 level. The allegedly all-powerful Jews proved unable to stave off a demographic catastrophe.

Another area of factual powerlessness lay in the area of immigration during the 1930s. Both in the enlightened United States or the benighted Argentina loud charges of Jewish control were voiced at a time when the Jews were too intimidated even to attack publicly the refusal of governments to receive refugees from Nazi tyranny. There Jews were shunted from one port to another, even as their vessels broke apart and they themselves sank in the ocean waters. Doors remained locked.

Allegations of economic control were also directed at owners of mass communications media who happened to be Jewish. As Jews, however, such ownership was meaningless. For example, the *New York Times* was owned by a Jewish family but this did not prevent the newspaper's editorialists in 1933 from adopting a laid-back view of Hitler's chancellorship. Undoubtedly, Jewish ownership in the movie industry was widespread. But this, too, had no communal significance, since during World War II Hollywood filmmakers were afraid to mention the word "Jew" in films about the Nazis and did not insist upon restoring scenes about antisemitic behavior in censored scripts. When, occasionally, Jewish owners of mass media brought their newspapers to bear on problems of antisemitism—as Jacobo Timerman in Argentina did in the 1970s—their essential powerlessness was underscored by arrests and silencing in prison. In Egypt, during the 1930s, some Jewish publishers began magazines that printed spirited attacks on Nazi oppression of Jews as well as Nazis in Egypt. These publications, however, were not mass media and were read by a narrow circle of people. Jews were thus only powerful enough to speak with each other about antisemitism.

If antisemitism in modern times is largely a product of conscious government action, what role has government taken to eradicate it? Apparently, in only one of the twelve countries studied were there even short-term efforts by the government to attack antisemitism and advocate the right of Jews to live as Jews. This was the Soviet government during the decade from the early 1920s to the early 1930s. As pointed out, both government and party officials convened meetings and conferences on antisemitism. Many books and pamphlets against antisemitism were published under government auspices. While this activity is sometimes attributed to the influence of Lenin, it should be noted that he died in 1924 and was succeeded by Joseph Stalin. It was therefore under Stalin that much of this publishing and discussion occurred. Between the mid-1930s and the decade's end, however, the movement was stilled. Between 1949 and 1953, Stalin's last years, he reinstituted a viciously antisemitic campaign that culminated in the cooked-up "Doctor's Plot." After Stalin's death, his successors largely succeeded in ignoring the idea of antisemitism. Neither Stalin's one-time struggle against it nor his indulgence in it were mentioned, at least not publicly.

In the absence of detailed histories of antisemitism in the USSR and of public opinion polls in the USSR on the subject, one question at least is difficult to answer: What are the effects of shifting policies about antisemitism on ordinary people? Russian history is filled with official denunciations of Jews and legislation to limit their freedom. But the Soviet period has its ups and downs on the subject. How successfully was the older historical antisemitic attitude changed beginning in the 1920s? When, from 1939 to 1953, Jews were painted as dangers to the nation, did ordinary citizens resist the stereotype because a decade or so earlier a much more benevolent conception of Jews had been advanced by the government?

A related question arises with respect to the attempt of recent Egyptian governments to spread antisemitism among their people. Historically, as we have seen, antisemitism was not strongly rooted there. Only after the mid-1940s did governments try to change this. School textbooks in religious seminaries began to propagate the crudest kind of antisemitism, most of it imported directly from European models. Mass media including radio, television, and newspapers were mobilized for the same purpose. Government leaders spoke with the authority of their offices on behalf of anti-Jewish policies. Never before have such resources been concentrated in Egypt's history to achieve such a low objective. The effort might not only succeed in corrupting a basically wholesome interrelation of Jews and Arabs but also poison the atmosphere beyond repair.

Does, in fact, the general history of antisemitism suggest which policy—positive or negative—tends to last longer in popular thought? Some recent experiences suggest that portions of the militant Left in Italy and France employed anti-Jewish language and sentiments in mid-1982 when protesting against Israel's invasion of Lebanon. In both cases, however, when challenged, they seemed hurriedly to leave this rather new territory. In both countries, the historical position of leftist support for Jewish causes was resumed rather promptly. On the other hand, in Germany of the 1920s, the highest public offices were for the first time made available to Jews, who discharged these responsibilities not less well than others. Yet conservative Germans ignored this rather obvious fact and regarded the period of Weimar democracy as a national calamity. In Bulgaria, official antisemitic policies during the late 1930s and the early 1940s did not prevent, although they may have deterred, the spontaneous expression of opposition for measures to ship Jews to death camps.

In the chapter on Argentina we found that upper-class persons were preeminent in propagating antisemitism. Is this typical of the other eleven countries? Americans would reject such a finding since they tend to identify antisemitism (and racism) with little education and low income. Antisemitism, in other words, is regarded as an individual expression of rather backward, materially deprived persons. Well-to-do persons, on the other hand, having had the advantage of education and other benefits, are expected to be more personally enlightened. On public opinion polls, in fact, this is often, though not invariably, the pattern recorded. Yet severe doubts have been expressed about the presumed education-attitude relationship. David Thursz, a high official of the American B'nai B'rith, has written: "Our assumption is that education reduced antisemitism and we in B'nai B'rith spend millions of dollars on education as a result. There is no evidence of that; on the contrary, there seems to be a good deal of evidence that today's antisemitism comes from people who are extremely knowledgeable and well-educated, and I need not remind you of the part played by academics during Hitler's Holocaust."[1] Upper-class persons, being more aware of the social unacceptability of antisemitism, can easily mask their views.

We ought to distinguish between thinking antisemitically and organizing antisemitic actions. There may or may not be a congruence between the two. Barring of Jews from socially exclusive clubs is still widespread in the United States, for example. The excluders are upper-class, often business executives. Two objectives are served by the restrictive action: the Jewish persons involved learn that they are disvalued and that they cannot participate in various deals that customarily transpire in these settings. Frequently, the excluders are the same ones who manage to maintain residential areas as white or Christian and who enforce discriminatory employment in their own establishments. Upper-class antisemitism is the active kind, requiring close attention to the details of exclusion and the sifting of exceptions. It may be seen at work in most of the countries studied in this book.

Class solidarity among the well-to-do, both Jews and non-Jews, was promoted in a number of countries. In tsarist Russia, for example, wealthy, educated Jews were exempted from the restriction to the pale. In none of the dozen countries, however, were there efforts to foster class solidarity among the poor Jews and non-Jews. Both were true of pre−World War I Austria-Hungary as well as Russia. During the Holocaust years, except for the rarest instances, bribery and ransoming through high Nazi officials were the sole ways open to the purchase of privilege. In the end, nothing made any difference for most rich or poor Jews.

To escape from severe antisemitism one could emigrate, but it was a confession of defeat. During the nineteenth and early twentieth centuries, when Jews were emancipated from second-class citizenship, they celebrated their newly won equality. As has been written, however, for many emancipation meant the acquisition of a stepfatherland. The pogrom era in tsarist Russia saw the emigration of hundreds of thousands of unemancipated Jews. During the 1920s, emancipated Jews from Poland streamed to the United States, Palestine, and elsewhere. (Since the 1890s, the dominant Constitutional Democratic party had advocated clearing Jews out of Poland, so their departure was not lamented.)

The advent of Nazism ultimately changed the significance of emigration. As we have seen, from 1933 to 1938, Jews hastened to leave mainly in spurts. The enactment of the racist Nuremberg Laws in 1935 and the occurrence of the *Kristallnacht* three years later sent thousands overseas. An emergency program to spur Jewish emigration was mounted by the Gestapo and the SS in 1938–39. Not until October 1941 was emigration from the German war zone altogether stopped. Contrary to a widespread impression, over half of Germany's Jews left while they could. Many who moved to other European countries, especially France, were captured and executed when Nazi armies invaded, so that their escape had been made in vain.

Wherever German (and Austrian) refugees found themselves in Europe, they constituted an inferior rank of Jew. When the Nazis demanded these "foreign" Jews be shipped to Auschwitz, compliance followed in Hungary, France, Bulgaria, Italy, and Rumania. Even before the Holocaust years, Western countries turned the Jewish refugees away, admitting only those they could not manage to ignore. After the end of the war the immigration of "displaced persons" who were Jews was similarly hobbled in Western countries. The situation changed only slowly.

Somewhat related to immigration were efforts by Jews in various countries to gain the support of their governments to stop anti-Jewish actions in tsarist Russia and elsewhere. Since there was no Jewish government to call on, efforts were made to arouse public opinion among Jews and Christians in France, England, the United States, and whatever countries could be moved. What most frequently happened, however, was that foreign governments, solicitous of their own relations with the offending government, contented themselves with a formal note of remonstrance, if that. In 1882 and 1890, when pogroms in Russia were very numerous,

European powers simply banned anti-Russian demonstrations within their own borders. Only England allowed such mass protests, even though Anglo-Russian diplomatic relations suffered for it.[2] Jews in the United States tried to convince the American government not to renew a commercial treaty with Russia near the beginning of the twentieth century, but as the volume of Russo-American trade expanded, the humanitarian ardor of American authorities cooled.

At the close of World War I, in response to Jews and others, so-called minorities treaties were signed at the Versailles peace conference. These guaranteed that public facilities for minorities would be equally supported and provided for appeals to be made directly to the League of Nations. England and France, which dominated the League, paid little heed to the complaints that were made. Even when a government decided to cancel its minorities treaty, there was no collective response. During the 1930s the solemn documents were mocked by governments that discriminated against many minorities, including Jews.

Total exclusion from a trade or educational institution is a zero quota. Assigning a fraction of the available opportunities to a group establishes a maximum claim or quota that may be put forward by that group. Because Jews usually constitute a relatively small percentage of a country's population a quota based on that percentage would be disadvantageous. In the United States, which has the world's largest contingent of Jews, Jews make up around 3 percent of the population. Yet their representation in various professions and highly paid employments well exceeds that level. Thus, to be restricted to 3 percent admission to elite universities and medical and law schools would require a severe reduction in the number of Jews attending such institutions. (For blacks in the United States to be assured a 10 percent representation in these same institutions would, on the other hand, call for a considerable expansion over present levels.)

But the precise levels of quotas are not the whole story. Even more important is whether there are any alternatives available. In Europe most universities are public institutions managed by a central authority. A quota covers any and all public institutions in that authority's span. Under these conditions, there is no evading the restriction of the quota. This was the case, for the most part, in Germany, Poland, Russia, Rumania, and Hungary.

In the United States, however, where the tradition of higher education has a strong private component and public higher education is regulated in a highly decentralized fashion, Jewish students had many opportunities to escape the worst effects of quotas. If Institution A established a quota on Jews—as many did in the 1920s and 1930s—applicants could go instead to Institution B which had no quota. (Black students, con-

fronted often with zero quotas—that is exclusion—had many fewer alternatives; quotas for blacks were also very tiny, frequently admitting
only handfuls.)

During the late 1960s and after, when affirmative action programs
began in the United States, many Jews feared they would lose their
favorable position. In fact, however, this did not happen, for at least two
reasons: (1) half the Jews were women, who clearly benefited under
affirmative action, and (2) male Jews found many new fields in which
to be employed and thus were not as dependent on the kinds of careers
that blacks and other minorities were now entering.[3]

Common wisdom about antisemitism holds it rises during periods of
economic difficulties and falls during so-called good times. This relationship is treated as though it were inevitable and automatic. It is, in
fact, neither. Experience in our twelve countries suggests as much. Antisemitism rose during the 1920s in the United States, although this
period is commonly called a period of high prosperity. During the depressed 1930s, on the other hand, mass antisemitism in Egypt did not
grow significantly. At the same time, during the many periods of economic depression when antisemitism grew, this was not a mechanical
automatic response to the lack of jobs and falling living standards.
Rather, it involved a definite cognitive process: people had to learn how
to think and act antisemitically and someone had to point out how it was
to be done.

It must be recalled that the worldwide depression of the 1930s came
rather suddenly and unexpectedly, following a period when economists
and business and government leaders had predicted unending prosperity. In a number of countries unemployment spread and bankruptcies
mounted. Many of those affected were puzzled and sought explanations.
Establishment theories were viewed skeptically. In Germany, the United
States, Poland, France, and elsewhere, antisemites arose to point to the
Jews as the alleged causes of people's distress. Explanations like these
were couched in language sympathetic to destitute workers and dis-
traught small businessmen and clerks. Listeners might be swept off their
feet by an occasional extraordinary phrase but they also reflected on the
substance of their problems. One view promised an end to unemployment, a renewal of national spirit, and a supposed end to alleged Jewish
domination of the economy. Another might say more or less the same
without mention of Jews. In any event, the critical factor was the listener's
capacity for weighing arguments. Many of the unemployed and bank-
rupted were not swept away by demagogues. But of those who were,
undoubtedly economic circumstance was a powerful predisposing factor.
Clearly, however, so was the failure of the dominant society to supply
more satisfactory answers or reforms.

The search for correlations between specific social circumstances and

changes in the level of antisemitism has produced little other than hom-
ilies about antisemitism growing during periods of social conflict and
distress. One problem lies in definitions. What is distress and how difficult must a situation be before becoming conflictual? The reason historians date modern antisemitism from the last third or so of the
nineteenth century is not because social conditions worsened then.
Rather, it is because at that time antisemitism first became a mass movement, unified by a conscious ideology and propagated by formal organizations which sought out the arenas of public opinion and politics. In
other words, whatever social circumstances arose could now be glimpsed
through a consistent worldview.

One of the core ideas of modern antisemitism is the manufactured
conception of a Jewish conspiracy to rule the world. *The Protocols of the
Elders of Zion,* which centers on this theme, arose, it is true, during the
years preceding the outbreak of the Russian Revolution of 1905. These
were especially stressful times. But *Protocols* enjoyed its contemporary
high point during the 1960s and 1970s when Middle Eastern states such
as Saudi Arabia and Kuwait became the world's greatest purveyors of
anti-Jewish literature, including the *Protocols.* These same years, of
course, were the most prosperous those reigns had yet seen. Clearly,
ideology rather than distress is the more significant explanation of the
course of antisemitism in the Middle East. To be sure, various ideologies
serve different interests. Thus, an ideology may emerge to protect a
group which is under pressure. Upper-class groups have had a special
attraction for world-conspiracy theories if only because these (1) distract
attention from their own considerable—and undoubted—power, and (2)
because of their vagueness permit unlimited inferences to be drawn
about the power of Jews.

World-conspiracy theories present the Jews as a tiny group, scattered
over the world, occupying—until recently—no fixed location or territory,
regulated by no government of their own, with no special body of rights,
and having no armed forces. How, in a world of change, have the Jews
been able to endure? The theorists reply: by a conspiracy each of whose
terms is self-explanatory. It is alleged to be a combination of persons
who embody very different life-roles (bankers and Communists), who
are united by an evil purpose (to rule the world), who are planning
numerous hostile actions against the gentile world (wars, depressions,
revolutions), and who operate in secrecy. By repetition, the charges take
on the color of familiarity which is misconstrued as proof.

The creation of Israel has challenged the conspiracy-theorists who
have responded with a new myth in which the word "Zionist" has replaced the word "Jew." In the Soviet Union and Middle East, this became
the dominant image by the 1960s. Since Israel did not operate any more
secretly than other governments, the purely conspiratorial aspect has

retracted somewhat. World domination is still alleged as an evil purpose but now it is said by antisemitic theorists to proceed by military power. No longer is as much made of the supposed alliance of bankers and Communists, at least when Israel is discussed. As previously, allegations of world domination are propounded even when they fly in the face of the simple facts of Israel's size and lack of war potential on a world scale.

The creation of Israel in 1948 was a major landmark in Jewish history. How significant, however, has it been for the history of antisemitism?

Zionist theory predicted that a Jewish state would in time attract all but a few Jews from the Diaspora. Antisemitism would decline as the gentile world came to respect this new factor in international relations. Meanwhile, the state could serve as a refuge for oppressed Jews everywhere; in 1950, the Knesset enacted the Law of Return under which Jews anywhere had the right to live in Israel. Thirty-five years later about a quarter of the world's Jews lived in Israel with no further major immigrant movement underway. The Diaspora persisted.

Apparently, few persons reflected on the fact that with the presence of Israel there was now one country without antisemitism. (When a number of persons asked what countries the present author was covering and were told, many asked: "What about Israel?" Upon being informed that the country had no history of antisemitism, a rather sheepish grin of acknowledgment followed.)

The nature of Israel's state interests was also partly affected by communal concerns; in larger part, however, Israel's international behavior was indistinguishable from that of other states. It sought to enter into diplomatic and commercial relations with just about all countries, whatever their internal policies on Jews. In Argentina, Israeli diplomatic officers intervened on behalf of certain Jews who had been imprisoned or maltreated for their Jewishness while refusing to protest publicly against Argentina's general anti-Jewish policy, or even explicitly denying the existence of such a policy. In Ethiopia, Israeli representatives for years muted the deep-rooted desire of that country's indigenous Jews to emigrate to Israel. It was hoped thereby to serve other foreign-policy objectives which required the favor of Emperor Haile Selassie. In 1953, the Federal Republic of Germany and Israel signed an agreement that provided for German reparations payments to Israel in the form of vitally needed industrial goods. Two other treaties set into motion a process whereby the German government would compensate individual German Jews for their losses under the Nazi regime. Internal political conflicts over dealing with the former oppressor country split the Jews of Israel. In the event, however, the agreements were ratified and honored.

At other times, Israel claimed a communal purpose in a foreign-affairs episode when its state interest actually prevailed. In sending secret agents into Egypt to bomb foreign-owned installations, and then blaming the Egyptians for the deeds, the Israeli government hoped to convince Great Britain not to withdraw its troops from the Suez Canal area. Upon being informed of the arrests of the agents in 1954, however, Israeli Prime Minister Moshe Sharett publicly objected to the "despicable slanders designed to harass the Jews in Egypt."[4] Israel never acknowledged its actual goal in Egypt.

Israel has affected antisemitism only indirectly. It is, at most, a regional power, and even within its area cannot grapple with the specifics of Middle Eastern anti-Jewish policy. Only in Egypt since the peace treaty did the frequency and vehemence of official antisemitism slack off somewhat. Israel largely failed to moderate the profoundly anti-Jewish climate of Argentina. Lacking diplomatic relations with the USSR and most other east European powers, Israel could only consult privately from time to time.

Anti-Zionism is almost as old as Zionism but any connection between Zionism and antisemitism is much more recent. As we saw in the chapter on Egypt, Jewish celebrations of the Balfour Declaration of 1917 were joined in by Muslims. A decade later Palestine was not an important issue in Egyptian politics. During the 1930s the situation began to change but even at decade's end the Egyptian government saw itself merely as an impartial conciliator between Arabs and Jews in Palestine rather than as a partisan of the former. During the late 1930s, the most embittered anti-Zionists in Egypt—the Muslim Brotherhood and Young Egypt— had moved beyond that position to antisemitism. Jews in Egypt were penalized, as Jews, for their support of a Jewish national home in Palestine.

With the end of World War II in 1945 and the organizing of the Arab League that same year, anti-Zionist campaigns were increasingly tinged with anti-Jewish themes. During United Nations debates over partition of Palestine in 1947–48, broad hints by Arab spokesmen of anti-Jewish consequences that would flow from the creation of Israel were heard. Both the United States and the Soviet Union supported the partition proposal as well as the making of a Jewish state and defended these positions against Arab protests. Both Soviet and American representatives dwelt on the special sufferings experienced by the Jewish people during the Holocaust.

During the 1950s, verbal attacks on Israel were phrased as opposition to Zionism. In Egypt, at least early in the decade, government spokespersons took pains to avoid slipping over from anti-Zionism to antisemitism. This was far less the case in other Arabic countries. By the late 1950s, however, Egypt had also made the switch. When the 1967 war against Israel broke out, the USSR also began in earnest a practice of identifying Israel as a Zionist imperialist power and, through cartoons in publications, utilized blatantly anti-Jewish stereotypes linked with Israel. It was thus the Arab countries that led the Russians rather than the reverse in this matter. The Soviets, for example, never attacked Vatican II's 1965 declaration that Jews as a group were not responsible for the death of Jesus Christ. A number of Arab spokespersons, on the other hand, did attack it.

In 1975, the UN General Assembly declared Zionism to be a form of racism. During the following decade, numerous attacks were launched against Israel on this ground. Whether or not Israeli authorities committed specific acts of racist oppression against Palestinians did not seem to be paramount to the critics. Instead, they denied the very legitimacy of Israel itself. In this demonology, Jews became the only people in the world who were denied the right of national self-determination. In this sense, anti-Zionism is antisemitism. Why should Jews be denied an otherwise universal right simply because they are Jews? Is this not the essence of antisemitism?

At the same time, a national sample of Israeli Jews was split down the middle when asked in November 1982, five months after the invasion of Lebanon: "There are those who claim that Israel's policies of late have caused antisemitism to increase in the world. Do you agree or disagree?" Nearly a third of the pro-Likud respondents agreed, even though their party controlled the national government. Over three-fourths of pro-Labor respondents also agreed.[5] It would be preposterous to label these critics antisemitic or even anti-Zionist. They were questioning Israel's state actions, not the legitimacy of the state. What cannot be learned from the poll is whether the respondents thought the heightened antisemitism was justified. By context alone, however, this can be discounted. Non-Israeli critics of Israel's Lebanon war should be evaluated no differently. A positive opinion of Israel's actions says nothing of the respondent's possible antisemitism; nor do negative ones. As for exaggerations of Israeli's negative actions, there is nothing distinctively antisemitic about them. Virtues can also be exaggerated.

When anti-Zionism becomes antisemitism it is a form of bigotry, not any the less to be rejected than other forms of racism. When an anti-Zionist approves of all other nationalisms in principle but denies the same right only to Jews, this is antisemitic. And when an Israeli government oppresses its own Arab or other minorities it is neither anti-Zionist nor antisemitic to say so.

During the past century or so, it is almost axiomatic that antisemitism has been a product of the political Right. This descriptive term covers varying combinations of conservatism, vested rights attached to wealth, hypernationalism, religious orthodoxy, xenophobia, and mystical notions of historical origins. These elements were represented most amply in German antisemitism and least so in the Italian movement.[6]

The Left, on the other hand, could most frequently be found alongside the Jews. In part, this was because of situational factors; the class interests of industrial workers led them to oppose wealthy rightists who also happened to be antisemites, as in France. German workers, heavily Socialist, were not religious in any devotional sense and thus were estranged from church influences. In other words, sectors of the Left opposed the delirium of any of their enemies, including antisemitism. A desire to show up their political opposition as socially backward also led leftist elements to campaign against especially blatant examples of antisemitism. The Socialists in Argentina and in pre-Hitler Germany played such a role.

Left parties and groupings, though by no means all of them, were a consistent source of aid to Jews in resisting physical attacks in the twentieth century. During the tsarist-sponsored pogroms around 1903–5, Lenin successfully called upon his party for volunteers to join in the defense of Jews. In the early 1930s, the Reichsbanner, a political militia made up primarily of Socialists, cooperated with the Jewish war veterans organization. Polish Socialists performed a similar task during the 1930s. Emmanuel Ringelblum, the historian of the Jewish ghetto in Warsaw, stressed how relieved Jews were to find a hiding place in homes of Polish workers, presumably those on the left. During the Holocaust and earlier, Communists were among the few who conducted underground opposition to the Nazis, both in Germany and France, as well as in the Netherlands. It must be reported that no instance of organized assistance to Jews by organized forces of the Right is to be found in the principal literature of the subject. Undoubtedly, individual examples, even of rare Nazi soldiers, appears in isolated accounts.

One surprising exception to the rule was the case of Karl Marx whose father was a converted Jew. Marx, who lived between 1818 and 1883, favored the civic emancipation of Jews but regarded Judaism as a hopelessly reactionary worldview. His characterizations of individual Jewish persons were downright insulting whether they appeared in his essays on Jews or in general political and economic treatises. The fairest characterization is to say he was a personal antisemite. He never participated in an antisemitic movement. Most commentators on the matter explain it as an instance of self-hate, a characterization subject almost unavoidably to circular reasoning.

Perhaps a more "Marxist" explanation would dwell on the stage of German capitalism in the 1840s, when Marx wrote his best-known pieces on Jews. At this time, the German artisan class was being disrupted by the growth of machine industry and being displaced by less-skilled hands. These hard-pressed artisans were open to explanations of their plight that attributed the new economic system to Jewish designs. Indeed, in the 1860s, when the first Socialist party in Germany was formed, the presence of many distressed artisans among the members assured that antisemitism would express itself as it did. A split occurred within this party and its successor over the question. By the late 1880s, after Marx died, the antisemitic group, now far outnumbered by industrial workers lacking artisan origins, lost out. In 1889, socialist leader August Bebel dubbed antisemitism "the socialism of the fools," referring to a contention that opposing Jewish capitalists, rather than capitalists as a whole, would suffice to bring down the capitalist system. While the Socialists in Germany never reverted to this view, German Communists during the 1920s and early 1930s did. In the latter period they hoped to win away those radical followers of the Nazis who thought economic recovery would follow the elimination of Jewish capitalists but not any others.[7]

We could not truly honor the dead of the Holocaust if (1) we did not know how the Final Solution was related to the centuries of antisemitism that preceded it, (2) we could not say that those persons principally responsible for the catastrophe had been duly punished, and (3) we had not provided against a repetition of the slaughter. Has the world done any of these things?

The first task challenges our intellectual concern and imagination and charges us to go beyond the horror to search out cause and effects. For example, many writers have distinguished sharply between antisemitism and the Final Solution, arguing that the latter was in a special category of human behavior that altogether exceeded such matters as discrimination and racial stereotypes. This overlooks several important points. As Raul Hilberg writes, "The German Nazis . . . did not discard the past; they built upon it. They did not begin a development, they completed it."[8] Traditional antisemitic policies during the years from 1933 to 1939 helped dehumanize the German Jew in the eyes of Germans. By 1941, when mass extermination began, the process deepened and a merely uncomfortable silence descended on all.

Further, it is well-known that the Nazis lacked the labor resources to implement fully the Final Solution. Aid came from hundreds of thousands in occupied countries. In the death camps, guards were recruited from among Baltic and other east Europeans. In France the police force rounded up Jews and sent them off to Auschwitz. Many of these Nazi auxiliaries had been trained in Fascist and antisemitic movements in their native countries. Here, too, was another connection between traditional antisemitism and the Holocaust.

In occupied countries as well as in Germany itself, the Final Solution was organized bureaucratically. "No Jew," writes Hilberg, "was left alive for lack of transport to a killing center."[9] Hungary, which held out for some time against Nazi demands for shipment of Jews to death camps, finally capitulated when a pro-Nazi solution did not lag in Hungary— or elsewhere—for lack of bureaucratic cooperation of indigenous personnel. Pre-war antisemitism was the great training ground for the Holocaust. The Nazi murderers could depend until the end upon recruits from this source.

As we saw in the chapter on Germany, a clear progression is visible in Germans' ability to think less and less of Jews as fellow human beings. This was one of the greatest triumphs of Nazi policy. But there is still a large unexplained gap between losing one's sense of empathy, on the one hand, and acceding to or even participating in the mass killings of the Jews, on the other. Historians, seeking to understand the emergence of various kinds of movements and eras, often search for earlier developments that presage the later ones. Thus, in recent years many historians, hoping to explain the rise of the Industrial Revolution, have begun studying what they call Proto-Industrialization. This is less a dress rehearsal than a prelude to the later main drama. Some of what later became principal elements can be viewed in their rough outlines. Initial traces of new ways of thinking are discernible.

Was there in any meaningful sense a Proto-Holocaust in Germany during the years from 1933 to 1941? The answer appears to be yes. The first sizable group subjected to large-scale arrests and executions was the German Left, especially Communists and Socialists, with greater emphasis upon the former. The evil of communism was described as part of a demonic worldwide conspiracy. Communists were portrayed by the Nazis during the 1920s as the greatest danger confronting Germany. In every succeeding election campaign, Nazism was put forward as the most reliable barrier to Communist progress. Upon taking state power in 1933, Nazi hate for Communists led to indulgence in unrestrained terror, both official and unofficial. The first concentration camps, built soon after Hitler took office, were designated for political—that is, left-oriented—opponents of the regime. Both on the streets and in early concentration camps such as Dachau, murder of Communists was regarded as almost a national honor.

Even before 1933 ended, it is likely that Communists had already been dehumanized in German public opinion. When in 1941–42, the Final Solution began, both Jews and Communists became the favorite victims of the Nazis. Very few accounts of the Holocaust, however, deal with this aspect of the subject. Because of the continuing political viability of the contemporary Communist issue, commentators and politicians on both sides of the Atlantic have continued to ignore its role as a precursor of the Holocaust.

In 1985, Richard von Weizsäcker, president of the Federal Republic of Germany, addressed the federal parliament on the occasion of the fortieth anniversary of the end of World War II in Europe. After referring to that day in 1945 as "a day of liberation" of Germans, Weizsäcker declared: "In particular we commemorate the six million Jews who were murdered in German concentration camps.... As Germans, we pay homage to the victims in the German resistance, among the public, the military, the churches, the workers and trade unions *and the Communists.*"[10] This may have been the first mention by a West German official of Communists as a legitimate element in the German resistance to the Nazis. Apparently, the point was not commented on in the American press which largely ignored the speech. The *New York Times* in noting the speech did not refer to the mention of Communists.

The dehumanization and extermination of the Communists demonstrated the feasibility of similar outcomes with other groups, including the Jews. The history of the Holocaust should be broadened to include not only more ethnic groups than the Jews but also politically outcast groups such as the Communists.

In 1943, the American Jewish Conference resolved that "the non-punishment of the Germans for their crimes against an entire people would 'signify the acquiescence of the democratic nations in the act of Jewish extermination.' "[11] This is very nearly what did happen. While some of the highest-placed Nazi war criminals were put to death or were imprisoned, many more in the West escaped with nominal or no punishment. As part of the severe crackdown on the Jews of the USSR, beginning in 1949, prosecution of German war criminals was suspended in the Soviet Union. They were not resumed until more than a decade later.[12] Although the Nuremberg trials found the SS to have been a criminal organization, SS members did not find their past affiliation a handicap to their rehabilitation within Germany. (We saw how a number entered government service in Egypt and Argentina.) They were entitled to military pensions covering the period of SS service. After 1949, when the Federal Republic of Germany organized a defense force, former SS members joined up in droves. When veterans joined their special Waffen SS ex-servicemen's organization, the dues were tax-deductible. After they died many were buried in regular military cemeteries.

The general slackness pervading American and German efforts to arrest and try suspected war criminals arose from political judgments. Between 1945 and 1949, American policy on Germany developed rapidly. As Theo Sommer, editor of *Die Zeit,* later recalled: "All of a sudden West Germany was promoted to a kind of guest victor. Its support was sought, its youngsters were wanted as soldiers again, its industrial prowess was needed in the emerging struggle with the Soviet bloc. Necessity prompted indulgence, if not forgiveness."[13] Western allies forgave frantically as their political memories precluded forgetting.

This tendency was stretched to its utmost when, in May 1985, President Ronald Reagan visited a German military cemetery at Bitburg. Preceding the trip, Reagan equated the SS veterans buried there with Jews who perished in the Holocaust: "They were victims, just as surely as the victims in the concentration camps."[14] Immediately upon learning of this statement, the United States Holocaust Memorial Council wrote Reagan: "If no immediate correction is offered by you, it will mean you see no difference between war and genocide."[15] No correction ensued. A former Waffen SS officer, Major General Otto Ernest Remer, commented: "After all we are all sitting in one boat, in NATO."[16] Some commentators embroidered the historical record of postwar Germany as did McGeorge Bundy, former U.S. foreign policy official, when he wrote of the Germans' "unflinching recognition of the Holocaust as Hitler's most monstrous crime and of the guilt shared by all who had any part in it."[17]

Numerous representatives of Jewish groups attacked the president for his benign conception of Hitler's legions. An Israeli newspaper criticized the Bitburg visit as the "virtual legitimization of the SS."[18] Another writer, countering the idea of Germans coming to terms with their Nazi heritage, commented that "it was . . . not until the mid-1960s that the syllabus and history books were altered to give West German teenagers even a modicum of information about the Third Reich and the preceding Weimar Republic."[19]

In other editorial quarters, ideological confusion reigned. Thus, *Newsweek* wrote: "In truth, Reagan had stumbled headlong into one of the deepest moral quandaries of modern times—the tension between world Judaism's need to remember the crimes of the Holocaust and post-Nazi Germany's need to forget."[20] By treating both sides of the equation as "needs" in a moral quandary, it left the impression that both sides were equally moral. For a country to seek to forget its central role in the Holocaust is deeply immoral. Bitburg was another step in that direction. It also was an admission that while the Holocaust was not yet forgotten, its lessons sorely needed to be recalled.

Bitburg reawakened the ancient issue of collective guilt, that is, whether responsibility for the Holocaust could justly be laid atop the entire German nation. Advocates of such a view were seldom heard. On the other hand, a creative variant of it was voiced by Meir Merhav, an Israeli Jewish journalist: "If there is collective guilt and responsibility— and there is—it belongs to the omissions and commissions of the *present*, not the crimes of the *past*."[21] In other words, the entire German society needs to create the conditions that would preclude another Holocaust. This collective responsibility is owed to every victim of the Final Solution. An analogy is the issue of slavery in the United States. Whites who helped perpetuate the system of black slavery owed each slave a moral responsibility to end the system. Their responsibilities continued in the postemancipation period during which they must work to preclude the return of slavery or any of its semifree disguises. This is entirely aside from the question of whether they personally ever owned slaves.

The Holocaust is often treated by historians as inevitable. Each development is fitted into a pattern set by its predecessor and helps make the matrix of its successor. The train of events appears to chug on apart from any enveloping currents of political and economic struggle. Indeed, mention of such factors is regarded as an intrusion if not an obscenity. Thus, even Hitler's Final Solution is portrayed as a thing in itself, not subject to alternative paths of development or to the lurches of political policy. Our study of the twelve countries, however, does not support this view. Antisemitic policy arises from human conflict rather than from a cocoon. Clashing political and economic perspectives give shape to policy directions. There is no predetermined, preshaped combination of circumstances that automatically produces certain policies.

Consider, for example, the rise of Nazi rule in Germany. We have seen that the Jewish issue was secondary in Hitler's electiontime rallies during the late 1920s and early 1930s. Upon taking power, the Nazis initiated a sporadic rise in violence against Jews. This, in turn, brought retaliatory trade boycotts against Germany by Jews and others in various countries. During the years 1933 to 1936, especially, the weakened German economy was highly vulnerable to such pressures. Few if any governments, however, joined in the boycotts. A slight number of non-Jews participated. The Jews themselves were split, in France, England, and the United States. The major Western powers abstained from either military or economic sanctions against Hitler. Germany was tided over. A rag-tailed world boycott proved inadequate to compel policy changes. All this says nothing about inevitablity.

Another dimension of the question concerns the powerful tendency of Jewish leadership during the Holocaust to comply with Nazi orders. Hilberg writes: "On a Europeanwide scale the Jews had no resistance organization, no blue print for armed action, no plan even for psychological warfare. They were completely unprepared." The Nazi-created Jewish Councils became part of the process of destruction: "Day by day they were reliable agents in the eyes of the German perpetrators while still retaining the trust of Jews." As a historical minority, Jews had endured by compliance. Now, compliance meant the end of the Jews. To be sure, evidences of armed resistance by Jews can be found all over Europe, as well as in Argentina and Egypt. But this was not the general pattern. On the other hand, Jews were by no means pacifists. Where the opportunity arose, Jews resorted to armed resistance far beyond their numbers. In the immediate prewar days in France, we have seen how Jewish volunteers poured into the national army when ranks were opened momentarily to persons of foreign birth. During the war itself, Jews joined the French underground in highly disproportionate numbers, perhaps ten times their proportion in the population.

During the 1930s, Jewish community leaders looked upon the organization of militant and armed resistance to Nazism with disfavor. As a result, the pattern of nonresistance prevailed up to the eve of the Holocaust. The Jewish leadership, frequently conservative, tended not to challenge the reactionary political currents that increasingly gained power in the 1930s. An extreme example occurred in Salonika, Greece, "where the Jewish leadership cooperated with the German deportation agencies upon the assurance that only 'Communist' elements from the poor sections would be deported, while the 'middle-class' would be left alone.' "[22] Here, again, one is confronted by political conflict rather than inevitability.

Few historians have compared the course of antisemitism in more than one or two countries. As a result, this book has been more venturesome than most in trying to measure one country against others with respect to various problems in the history of antisemitism. Yet, this chapter and the preceding one are necessarily less complete and final than I—or the reader—might wish. A number of explanations and theories have been examined and the lack of historical support for them has been indicated. It is always important to speak plainly about mistaken views, no matter how hallowed they might be.

At the same time, however, we are not left completely adrift. Historical evidence is quite sufficient to support, if not definitively establish, the following generalizations:

1. Antisemitism is in no sense natural, spontaneous, and inevitable. Wherever it emerged as a social movement, it was preceded by prolonged, conscious, organized efforts.

2. Antisemitism as a social movement is not the product of personally cruel individuals; it is the product of actions by privileged sectors of a society attempting to preserve their prerogatives and to deny equality to others.

3. The weight of government power has never been fully mobilized against antisemitism in any country or for any long, sustained period of years. Therefore, we do not know how successful such campaigns might be.

4. Actually living, working, and being educated together under roughly equal conditions for all groups seems to be an effective way of promoting constructive social relations among Jews and non-Jews.

5. While many persons undoubtedly become antisemitic under pressure of unemployment, inflation, and other adverse conditions, quite possibly as many or more others similarly situated do not. Thus, one should be careful not to underestimate the potential of resistance to antisemitism.

6. The long-term position of minorities is more secure with cooperation among them all than by one seeking an alliance with government against the others. Fundamentally, this is because it is easier for equals to share a common interest than to bend and twist one's own to fit those of a much stronger party.

7. To those who employ antisemitism to advance their own interests it is a matter of indifference whether antisemitism or some other movement is utilized. Racism may do as well. Choice of a specific minority may be a matter of historical accident or infernal convenience. What Jews were spared in the

United States afflicted blacks and Indians, for example. In Europe, Jews caught the brunt of it.

NOTES

1. David Thursz, in Proceedings of International Conference on Anti-Semitism held at the Thirtieth Zionist Congress, Jerusalem, December 1982, *Forum on the Jewish People, Zionism and Israel,* 49 (Summer 1983), p. 44.

2. Simon Dubnov, *History of the Jews,* 5, trans. Moshe Spiegel (South Brunswick, N.J.: Thomas Yoseloff, 1973), p. 619.

3. Nathan Glazer, "On Jewish Forebodings," *Commentary,* 80 (August 1985), p. 34.

4. Howard M. Sachar, *A History of Israel from the Rise of Zionism to Our Time* (New York: Knopf, 1976), p. 480. At the time of this statement Sharett did not know of the plan to use secret agents. After his statement, he was so informed and no longer mentioned the matter publicly. He did not, however, retract his earlier statement.

5. Mark Segal, "One of Two Israelis Blames Gov't. for Anti-Semitism Rise," *Jerusalem Post,* December 8, 1982.

6. George Mosse, in discussing the development of antisemitism in Germany, writes of "the anti-Jewish orientation of the Right as a whole since 1918." See George L. Mosse, "Die Deutsche Rechte und Die Juden," in Werner E. Mosse, ed., *Entscheidungsjahr 1932,* 2d rev. and enlarged ed. (Tübingen: J.C.B. Mohr [Paul Siebeck], 1966), p. 244.

7. Referring to the Social Democrats and the Communists, Hans-Helmuth Knutter writes: "The socialist parties of Germany, who certainly underestimated the daemonic power of antisemitic slogans and their effect on the spirit of many workers, were free of antisemitism, as such." See Hans-Helmuth Knutter, "Die Linksparteien," in Mosse, ed., *Entscheidungsjahr 1932,* p. 345.

8. Raul Hilberg, *The Destruction of the European Jews,* 1, rev. and def. ed. (New York: Holmes and Meier, 1985), p. 9.

9. Ibid., 3, p. 1003.

10. *New York Times,* May 9, 1985 (emphasis added). See also Allan Merson, *Communist Reistance in Nazi Germany* (London: Lawrence and Wishart, 1985).

11. Hilberg, *The Destruction of the European Jews,* 3, p. 1062.

12. See Tom Bower, *The Pledge Betrayed* and Joseph Kermish, "The History of the Manuscript of the Black Book," in Ehrenburg and Grossman, eds., *The Black Book,* p. xxiii.

13. *Newsweek,* May 6, 1985.

14. *New York Times,* April 19, 1985.

15. *Boston Globe,* April 19, 1985.

16. *New York Times,* May 3, 1985.

17. Ibid., May 2, 1985.

18. *Jerusalem Post,* May 6, 1985 (editorial).

19. John Dornberg, "The Bitburg Bungle," *Jerusalem Post,* April 30, 1985.

20. *Newsweek,* April 29, 1985.

21. Meir Merhav, "Honoring Evil," *Jerusalem Post,* May 3, 1985.

22. Hilberg, *The Destruction of the European Jews,* 3, pp. 1030, 1038, 1042.

BIBLIOGRAPHIC ESSAY

The best starting place for study is Leon Poliakov's *The History of Anti-Semitism*, 4 vols. (New York: Vanguard Press, 1965–86). Almost entirely oriented to western Europe, it begins with ancient history and ends with the Nazi accession to power. Two general histories of the Jewish people are indispensable for reading and reference. Salo W. Baron's *A Social and Religious History of the Jews*, 19 vols. 2d ed. (New York: Columbia Univ. Press, 1952–83), reports straightforwardly on antisemitism, but this is not the central thread in his story. In general, Baron ends his analysis around 1750. Simon M. Dubnov's *History of the Jews*, 5 vols., trans. Moshe Spiegel (South Brunswick, N.J.: Thomas Yoseloff 1967–73), is a classic of European historiography. Its learning and passion are refreshing in these days of sciolism and coolness. This work ends with the 1920s, although revisions entered in 1938 presaged the author's murder by a Nazi officer who had once been Dubnov's student at Heidelberg. The main articles on antisemitism in three encyclopedias are worth reviewing: (1) *Encyclopedia Judaica*, vol. 3, cols. 87–160; (2) *Universal Jewish Encyclopedia*, vol. 1, pp. 341–409; and (3) *Jewish Encyclopedia*, pp. 641–49. In *From Prejudice to Destruction. Anti-Semitism, 1700–1933* by Jacob Katz (Cambridger, Mass.: Harvard Univ. Press, 1980), a distinctive analysis of the subject in Europe is presented.

The history of antisemitism in Argentina can be traced in detail in Robert Weisbrot, *The Jews of Argentina from the Inquisition to Peron* (Philadelphia: Jewish Publication Society of America, 1979), and in Eugene F. Sofer, *From Pale to Pampa. A Social History of the Jews of Buenos Aires* (New York: Holmes and Meier, 1982). Bulgarian antisemitism, such as it was, is analyzed in books by Frederic B. Chary, *The Bulgarian Jews and the Final Solution 1940–1944* (Pittsburgh, Pa.: Univ. of Pittsburgh Press, 1972), and Vicki Tamir, *Bulgaria and Her Jews. The History of a Dubious Symbiosis* (New York: Sepher-Hermon Press, 1979). Tamir rejects the image of an age-old Bulgarian friendship toward Jews.

The position of the Jews in ancient, medieval, and early modern Egypt has to be picked out from works on broader subjects. Two items by S. D. F. Goitein are basic: *A Mediterranean Society*, 4 vol. (Berkeley: Univ. of California Press, 1968–83), and *Jews and Arabs: Their Contacts through the Ages*, rev. ed. (New York:

Schocken, 1974). Another important work is Bernard Lewis, *The Jews of Islam* (Princeton, N.J.: Princeton Univ. Press, 1984). A book by the same author, *Semites and Anti-Semites: An Inquiry into Conflict and Prejudice* (New York: Norton, 1986), deals with The Middle East. In another, Benjamin Braude and Bernard Lewis, ed., *Christians and Jews in the Ottoman Empire. The Functioning of a Plural Society*, 2 vols. (New York: Holmes and Meier, 1982), can be found material on specific eras.

Antisemitism in Egypt is treated in two works by Jacob M. Landau: *Jews in Nineteenth-Century Egypt* (New York: New York Univ. Press, 1969), and "Ritual Murder Accusations in Nineteenth-Century Egypt," in his *Middle Eastern Themes. Papers in History and Politics* (London: Frank Cass, 1973). Lukasz Hirszowicz, *The Third Reich and the Arab East* (London: Routledge and Kegan Paul, 1966), touches on high Egyptian involvement with the Nazi movement. The history of two outright antisemitic organizations active in Egypt in the 1930s and 1940s is analyzed in James P. Jankowski, *Egypt's Young Rebels. Young Egypt: 1933–1952* (Stanford, Calif.: Hoover Institution Press, 1975), and Richard P. Mitchell, *The Society of the Muslim Brothers* (London: Oxford Univ. Press, 1969). A succinct account on Egypt may be found in Siegfried Landshut, *Jewish Communities in the Muslim Countries of the Middle East* (London: Jewish Chronicle, 1950). The single most detailed account is in Gudrun Krämer, *Minderheit, Millet, Nation? Die Juden in Ägypten 1914–1952* (Wiesbaden: Verlag Otto Harrassowitz, 1982).

In volume 22 of the *American Jewish Year Book* appears a short essay by Jacques Faitlovitch, "The Falashas," which is a summary statement by the most influential Western scholar of Ethiopian Jewry. Two works stressing the more recent years are Louis Rapoport, *The Last Jews. Last of the Ethiopian Falashas* (New York: Stein and Day, 1979), and David Kessler, *The Falashas. The Forgotten Jews of Ethiopia* (London: George Allen and Unwin, 1982). A recent work by Tudor Parfitt, *Operation Moses* (London: Weidenfeld and Nicolson, 1985), is valuable principally for its firsthand description of conditions in the refugee camps of Sudan, preceding the airlift of Ethiopian Jews. See also Louis Rapoport, *Redemption Song. The Story of Operation Moses* (New York: Harcourt Brace Jovanovich, 1986). James A. Quirin's "The Process of Caste Formation in Ethiopia: A Study of the Beta Israel (Falasha), 1270–1868," *International Journal of African Historical Studies*, 12 (1979), is a useful integration of historical materials.

Material on the precarious position of Jews in early France can be found in Robert Chazan, *Medieval Jewry in Northern France. A Political and Social History* (Baltimore, Md.: Johns Hopkins Univ. Press, 1973). Arthur Hertzberg's *The French Enlightenment and the Jews* (New York: Columbia Univ. Press, 1968) stresses the anti-Jewish element among eminent thinkers of that movement. The development of antisemitism in nineteenth-century France, before Dreyfus, is detailed in Robert F. Byrnes' *Antisemitism in Modern France* (New York: Howard Fertig, 1969). Two works on the Dreyfus affair are Stephen Wilson, *Ideology and Experience. Anti-Semitism in France at the Time of the Dreyfus Affair* (Rutherford, N.J.: Farleigh Dickinson Univ. Press, 1982), and Jean-Denis Bredin, *The Affair. The Case of Alfred Dreyfus*, trans. Jeffrey Mehlman (New York: George Braziller, 1986). Antisemitism in France of the 1930s is examined with great insight in David H. Weinberg's *A Community on Trial. The Jews of Paris in the 1930s* (Chicago: Univ. of Chicago Press, 1977). Michael R. Marrus and Robert O. Paxton, *Vichy*

France and the Jews (New York: Schocken, 1983), recreate comprehensively a largely shameful story.

The beginnings of German antisemitism are set out authoritatively in Guido Kisch, *The Jews in Medieval Germany. A Study of Their Legal and Social Status* (Chicago: Univ. of Chicago Press, 1949). Relevant sections of Dubnov's, Poliakov's, and Baron's works should be consulted. Jacob Katz's *From Prejudice to Destruction* is also highly relevant. A volume of essays of varying value is David Bronsen, ed., *Jews and Germans from 1860 to 1933: The Problematic Symbiosis* (Heidelberg: Carl Winter, 1979). Organized Jewish responses to antisemitism are examined in Ismar Schorsch, *Jewish Reactions to German Anti-Semitism, 1870–1914* (New York: Columbia Univ. Press, 1972). Donald L. Niewyk's *The Jews in Weimar Germany* (Baton Rouge: Louisiana State Univ. Press, 1980) is a standard authority. The Nazi period is covered by Karl A. Schleunes, *The Twisted Road to Auschwitz. Nazi Policy toward German Jews, 1933–1939* (Urbana: Univ. of Illinois Press, 1970), and Raul Hilberg, *The Destruction of the European Jews,* 3 vol., rev. and def. ed. (Holmes and Meier, 1985). The postwar failure to extirpate Nazi influences from German public life is viewed critically in Tom Bower, *The Pledge Betrayed. America and Britain and the Denazification of Postwar Germany* (Garden City, N.Y.: Doubleday, 1982).

Randolph L. Braham's towering work, *The Politics of Genocide. The Holocaust in Hungary,* 2 vols. (New York: Columbia Univ. Press, 1983), contains an excellent overview of the half-century before the Holocaust. The events in Hungary during 1919–39 are presented in a thoughtful context in Ezra Mendelsohn, *The Jews of East Central Europe between the World Wars* (Bloomington: Indiana Univ. Press, 1983). A short account of the near-disappearance of antisemitism in post–World War II Hungary is in Paul Lendvai, *Anti-Semitism without Jews. Communist Eastern Europe* (Garden City, N.Y.: Doubleday, 1971). With respect to Italy, two books are of prime value: Cecil Roth, *The History of Jews in Italy* (Philadelphia: Jewish Publication Society of America, 1946), and Meir Michaelis, *Mussolini and the Jews. German-Italian Relations and the Jewish Question in Italy, 1922–1945* (Oxford: Clarendon Press, 1978).

The earlier years of antisemitism in Poland are viewed critically in S. M. Dubnov, *History of the Jews in Russia and Poland from the Earliest Times until the Present Day,* 3 vols., trans. I. Friedlaender (Philadelphia: Jewish Publication Society of America, 1916), and relevant sections in Dubnov's *History of the Jews.* The very beginnings are examined in Adam Vetulani's article "The Jews in Medieval Poland," *Jewish Journal of Sociology,* 4 (1962). Historians have been attracted to interwar Poland (1919–39) in large numbers. A sketch of the principal events can be found in Mendelsohn's *The Jews of East Central Europe between the World Wars.* Full-length treatments are in Joseph Marcus, *Social and Political History of the Jews in Poland, 1919–1939* (Berlin: Mouton, 1983), and Harry M. Rabinowicz, *The Legacy of Polish Jewry. A History of Polish Jews in the Inter-War Years 1919–1939* (New York: Thomas Yoseloff, 1965). In Yisrael Gutman's profoundly moving *The Jews of Warsaw, 1939–1943. Ghetto, Underground, Revolt,* trans. Ina Friedman (Bloomington: Indiana Univ. Press, 1982), can be found a rare historical work that is fully respectful of the people whose history is narrated. The hounding of Jews out of Poland in the late 1960s is depicted in Josef Banas, *The Scapegoats. The Exodus of the Remnants of Polish Jewry,* trans. Tadeusz Szafar (London: Weidenfeld and Nicolson, 1979). (A recent work, received after completion of the present book, is Yisrael Gutman, *The Jews in Poland after World War II* (Jerusalem: Zalman Shazar Center for Jewish History, 1985).

Rumanian Jews are not well represented in English-language materials. A highly informative, long periodical account is Max J. Kohler and Simon Wolf, "Jewish Disabilities in the Balkan States. American Contributions toward Their Removal, with Particular Reference to the Congress of Berlin," *Publication of the American Jewish Historical Society*, 24 (1916). Relevant sections of two books should be consulted: Bela Vago and George L. Mosse, ed., *Jews and Non-Jews in Eastern Europe 1918–1945* (New York: Wiley, 1974), and Mendelsohn, *The Jews of East Central Europe between the World Wars*. For detailed accounts of the Rumanian government's actions during World War II, see Hilberg, *The Destruction of the European Jews*, vols. 1–3 (references in index).

Historical materials on Russian/Soviet antisemitism are plentiful. Dubnov's works are important: *History of the Jews in Russia and Poland from the Earliest Times until the Present Day* and *History of the Jews*. A number of excellent essays are located in Jacob Frumkin et al., eds., *Russian Jewry (1800–1917)*, trans. Mirra Ginsburg (New York: Thomas Yoseloff, 1966). Two outstanding works that stress the role of social factors are Ezra Mendelsohn, *Class Struggle in the Pale* (New York: Cambridge Univ. Press, 1970), and Jonathan Frankel, *Prophecy and Politics. Socialism, Nationalism, and the Russian Jews, 1862–1917* (New York: Cambridge Univ. Press, 1981). A full and fair-minded account is that of William Korey, *The Soviet Cage. Anti-Semitism in Russia* (New York: Viking, 1973). Theodore Freedman, ed., *Anti-Semitism in the Soviet Union: Its Roots and Consequences* (New York: Freedom Library Press of the Anti-Defamation League of B'nai B'rith, 1984), has edited a collection of materials touching on many aspects of the subject. Solomon M. Schwarz's *The Jews in the Soviet Union* (Syracuse, N.Y.: Syracuse Univ. Press, 1951) is a consistently harsh, informed treatment. The record of Jews in the Soviet Union during and immediately after World War II is set forth in Shimon Redlich, *Propaganda and Nationalism in Wartime Russia. The Jewish Antifascist Committee in the USSR, 1941–1948* (Boulder, Colo.: East European Quarterly, 1982). Isaac Deutscher, the critical biographer of Joseph Stalin, has written incisively about Jews and the Russian Revolution in *The Non-Jewish Jew and Other Essays* (London: Oxford Univ. Press, 1968).

General historical surveys of American antisemitism are few. One is Michael N. Dobkowski, *The Tarnished Dream. The Basis of American Anti-Semitism* (Westport, Conn.: Greenwood Press, 1979). Another is Michael Selzer, ed., *"Kike!" A Documentary History of Anti-Semitism in America* (New York: World, 1972). Carey McWilliams' *A Mask for Privilege. Anti-Semitism in America* (Boston: Little, Brown, 1948) is still relevant. (A work published after the present book was completed is David A. Gerber, ed., *Anti-Semitism in American History* [Urbana: Univ. of Illinois Press, 1986].) The rise of antisemitism in the 1930s has helped produce several useful works. Sheldon Marcus's *Father Coughlin. The Tumultuous Life of the Priest of the Little Flower* (Boston: Little, Brown, 1973) is the best of the biographies. Moshe R. Gottlieb's *American Anti-Nazi Resistance, 1933–1941* (New York Ktav, 1982) is a thoroughly documented analysis of conflicting currents within the Jewish community. Two books deal with the Nazis in the United States: Sander A. Diamond, *The Nazi Movement in the United States, 1924–1941* (Ithaca, N.Y.:

Cornell Univ. Press, 1974), and Leland V. Bell, *In Hitler's Shadow. The Anatomy of American Nazism* (Port Washington, N.Y.: Kennikat Press, 1973). Two studies of public opinion polls about Jews are Harold E. Quinley and Charles Y. Glock, *Anti-Semitism in America* (New York: Free Press, 1979), and Gregory Martire and Ruth Clark, *Anti-Semitism in the United States. A Study of Prejudice in the 1980s* (New York: Praeger, 1982).

The *American Jewish Year Book*, published annually since 1899, is a storehouse of information on antisemitism and other matters related to Jewish life in many countries. A basic bibliography is Robert Singerman, comp., *Antisemitic Propaganda* (New York: Garland, 1982). The English journal *Patterns of Prejudice* lists current research literature on antisemitism and allied topics at the end of each issue. The Bowker publication *Weekly Record* lists books in English published in the United States but is completely unindexed. *Dissertation Abstracts* is, on the other hand, well indexed and should be checked regularly.

The following are indexes to subjects bearing directly or indirectly on the history of antisemitism: *Index of Articles on Jewish Studies; Index to Jewish Periodicals; Kiryat Sefer; Contemporary Mideast Backgrounder.*

INDEX

A Cool Million, xvi
Action Française (France), 74
Adams, Henry, 211
Affirmative action, 189, 228, 252
Against the Jews and Their Lies, 86
Agrarian League (Germany), 98
Al-Azhar University, 41, 42
Albert, Phyllis Cohen, 69, 70
Alexander the Great, 33
Alexander I, 182
Alexander II, 183, 196
Alexander III, 185
Alfonsin, Raul, 22
Alianza Libertadora Nacionalista (Argentina), 12
Ali Bey, 35
al-Manar, 38
Alter, Wiktor, 190
American Dental Society (USA), 221
American Jewish Committee (USA), 212, 216, 227
American Jewish Conference (USA), 260
American Jewish Congress (USA), 216
American Jewish Joint Distribution Committee (USA), 59
Anar affair (Argentina), 18
Angress, Werner, 95, 100
Anschluss, 73, 74
Anti-Defamation League (USA), 225
Antisemitism: and antizionism, 238,

255–56; class base of, 71, 72, 249; definition of, xiv; as deliberate movement, 245; economic motivations of, 33, 38; as evasion of real social problems, xvii; not eternal, xv; pattern of, xiv; and revolutions, 246; as social movement, 93; and social stress, xvii, 252–53
"Anti-Zionist Committee of the Soviet Public" (Russia/USSR), 200
Antonescu, Ion, 176, 177, 178
Apion, 34
Arabic-Palestinian Information Bureau (Egypt), 40
Arab-Israeli War (1948–49), 44–45, 199
Arab League, 13, 43, 60, 255
Aramburu, Pedro, 13
Argentine Patriotic League, 5
Armstrong, John A., 193, 198
Arnold, Karl, 9
Aron, Raymond, 78
Aryanization Law, 75, 77, 108
Ash, Stephen, 209
Assimilation, 73, 91, 135, 199, 201, 202
Association for Work (Argentina), 6
Association of Ethiopian Jews in Israel, 58
Auschwitz, 74, 76, 77, 78, 137, 149, 239, 250, 258
Auschwitz Myth—Legend or Reality?, 123

Avineri, Shlomo, 234 n.98
Avni, Haim, 3, 7
Azariah, Asa, 57

Baeck, Leo, 243
Baer, Gabriel, 36
Balfour Declaration, 38, 42, 44, 255
Banas, Josef, 164
"Bar Kochba" (Germany), 104
Baron, Salo, xix, 208
Baron Jehovah, 70
Bartok, Bela, 136
Bartys, Julian, 90
Bauer, Yehuda, xiii
Baum Group (Germany), 111, 112
Bebel, August, 258
Begin, Menachim, 57
Begun, V., 196
Bell, H. I., 33, 34
Beta Israel (Ethiopia), 53
Bieber, Hans-Joachim, 83, 101, 105
Bill for the Abolition of All Disabili-
    ties of the Jews and of All Restric-
    tions on the Grounds of Origin or
    Nationality, 201
Bishop, Hugo, 102
Bismarck, Otto, 100
Black Death, xviii, 85
Blacks and Jews, 226–27, 228
Blacks as buffers, xix
Blau, Joseph, 208
Bloody Friday (Argentina), 5
B'nai B'rith (Egypt), 43
B'nai B'rith (USA), 216, 249
Bodin, Jean, 67
Bogale, Yona, 56
Boleslaw the Pious, 153–54
Bonaparte, Napoleon, 36, 68, 69, 90,
    145, 187
Bonner Scandal (Argentina), 18
Book-burning, 66
Boris III, 29
Bormann, Martin, 12
Bossman, Dieter, 120
Boston Globe, 59
Boussuet, Jacques, 67
Bower, Tom, 122
Boycott against Germany, 9, 216

Braginsky, Joseph, 198
Braham, Randolph L., 133, 136, 138
Branfman, Jacob A., 184
Brasol, Boris, 213
Bratianu, Ion, 170
Brody, David, 217
Brown Shirts (Germany), 105, 123
Buenos Aires Herald, 18
Bund, 186, 202
Bund (Polish), 158, 190
Bundy, McGeorge, 261
Byrnes, Robert, 70

Carol, King, 176
Carsten, F. L., 87
Catherine I, 182
Catholic Center party (Germany),
    104
Catholic Circles of Workers (Argen-
    tina), 4
Catholic People's party (Hungary),
    134
Caza de los Rusor (Argentina), 5
CBS, 217
Ceausescu, Nicolae, 179
Cecil, Lamar, 96, 100
Central Union of German Citizens of
    the Jewish Faith (Germany), 99,
    100, 104
Chary, Frederick, 28
Chazan, Robert, 66
Chicago Tribune, 213
Christian Front (USA), 218
Christian rule over Jews, xix, 34, 53,
    181, 185
Christian Socialist Workers' party
    (Germany), 93
Churches and antisemitism, 29, 94,
    102, 117, 121, 136, 138, 139, 242–
    43
Churchill, Winston, 221
Chyet, Stanley, 208
Citizenship rights of Jews, xvi, 6, 33,
    36, 37, 43, 65, 68, 69, 74, 75, 85,
    96, 100, 102, 106, 107, 145, 171,
    175, 201
Civic Guard (Argentina), 5
Civil rights movement, 225, 229, 230

Civil War (USA), 36, 209, 210
Civil War (Russia/USSR), 203
Clarinada, 10
Class structure of Jewish communities, 69, 72, 87, 88, 90, 156, 157, 162, 173, 183
Clermont-Tonnerre, 68
Codreanu, Cornelius, 174, 175
Cofindustria (Italy), 147
Collective crimes of omission, 261
Columbia University, 212, 215, 221
Commissariat for Jewish Questions (Bulgaria), 28, 29
Commissariat-General of Jewish Affairs (France), 75
Commission for Defense of Order (Argentina), 6
Committee Against Anti-Semitism and Racism (Argentina), 9
Committee for the Boycott of Jewish Commerce (Egypt), 41
Communism and Communists, 73, 75–76, 79, 104, 111–12, 115, 135, 139, 140, 150, 158, 159, 163, 164, 165, 166, 188, 194, 197, 200, 212, 213, 220, 259–60
"Company Law No. 138", 43
Concentration camps, 29, 74, 75, 76, 77, 109, 120, 259
Conservative party (Germany), 98
Constitutional Democratic party (Poland), 250
Coralnik, Abraham, 216
Cornell University, 212, 215
Cossacks, 155
Coughlin, Charles E., 217, 218, 219, 220
Council on Dental Education (USA), 221
Courts and the rights of Jews, 103, 121, 158, 190, 208, 214
Cox, Robert, 18
Cremieux Decree, 75
Cristea, Miron, 175
Croix de Feu (France), 73
Cross and the Flag, 219
Crusades, the, 66, 83–84

Cultural and Communal Association of the Jews in Poland, 166
Cuza, Alexander, 174, 175
Cyril, 34

Dabrowski, Bronislaw, 164
Dachau, 259
Dayan, Moshe, 57
Dearborn Independent, 212, 213
Deeb, Marius, 36
Defender, 219
Defenders of the Christian Faith (USA), 219
De Hirsch, Baron, 3
Deicide (killing of Christ), xvi, 47, 67, 86
Delegacion de Asociaciones Israelitas Argentinas, 9, 10, 13, 19, 20, 22
Democratic party (Germany), 104
Democratic party (USA), 217
Denazification, 118, 121, 122, 125
Dennis, Peggy, 197
Department of Jewish Affairs (Germany), 97
Department of Warfare Against Jewry (Germany), 116
Depersonalization, of Jews, 115, 117, 125, 259
Derian, Patricia, 21
Der Stürmer, 114
Der Weg, 12
Desegregation, 72, 225
Deutscher, Isaac, 188, 191
Deutscher Vortrupp (Germany), 107
Dhimmi status, 34, 35
Die Zeit, 260
Dimerski-Tsigelman, L., 194, 200
Dimitrov, Georgi, 30
Dinnerstein, Leonard, 234 n.98
Dirlewanger, Oskar, 46, 50 n.63
Discrimination, economic, 69, 74, 84, 87, 88, 106, 108, 136, 144, 148, 149, 156, 165, 172–73, 175, 176, 177, 182, 184, 185, 187, 198, 201, 209, 210, 211, 224–75, 229
Dmowski, Roman, 187
Dobkowski, Michael, 207
Dobroszycki, Lucan, 163

"Doctor's Plot" (Russia/USSR), 194,
   248
Drancy camp, 76, 77
Dreyfus, Alfred, 71
Dreyfus affair, 71–72, 196
Drumont, Edouard, 71
Dubnov, Simon, 66, 69, 83, 154, 155,
   156, 183, 187, 188
Du Bois, W. E. B., 214
Dulzin, Arye, 20

Ebert, Hans, 114
"Edict of Emancipation", 146
Ehrenburg, Ilya, 160, 191, 193
Eichberger, Eugen, 46
Eichmann, Adolf, 12, 13, 76, 110,
   137
Eicke, Theodore, 122
Eisenmenger, A. I, 88
Elizabeth I, 182
Elkin, Judith, 19
El Pampero, 9, 10
Emancipation of Jews, 68, 89–90, 91–
   92, 175, 202
Eminescu, Michael, 178
Encyclopedia Judaica, 78, 200
Erlich, Henryk, 190
Ethiopian Democratic Union, 57
Ethiopian Peoples Revolutionary
   party, 58
Ettinger, Shmuel, 182, 194
Evans, Hiram Wesley, 214
Evil eye (*buda*), 54
Evil Found in the Talmud, 48
Expulsion of Jews, 66–67, 86–87,
   170, 185, 187
Eynikayt, 192, 193

Fain, Bernardo, 20
Faitlovitch, Jacques, 53, 54, 55, 56
Falcoff, Mark, 12
Farouk, King, 41, 42, 45
Fascieux Nationalistes European
   (France), 78
Fascism, 146–47, 159, 176, 179, 217
Fascist party (Italy), 146, 147
Fatherland Front (Bulgaria), 29, 30
Fatherland party (Germany), 101

Federation of Commercial Employees
   (Argentina), 8
Federation of German Jews (Ger-
   many), 99
Federation of German Welfare and
   Cultural Clubs (Argentina), 10
Feldstein, Stanley, 210, 214
Feuer, Lewis, 214
Field, Geoffrey, 103
Filderman, Wilhelm, 177, 243
Filipo, Virgilio, 8
Final Solution, xv, 76, 78, 110, 111,
   115, 117, 125, 138, 139, 149, 191,
   242, 258, 259, 261, 262
Finzi, Aldo, 147
Fischerman, Joaquin, 15
Five-Year Plan policy (USSR 1929),
   189
Fleury, Abbe, 67
Ford, Henry, 10, 12, 212, 213, 220
Fourth Latern Council, 84
Frank, Leo, 226
Frankel, Jonathan, 181, 186
Freimark, Peter, 91
French Revolution of 1789, 67
Frondizi, Arturo, 13
Front of the Renaissance (Rumania),
   176
Fuhrmann, Arnulf, 10

Garcia, Domecg, 5
Gelbard scandal (Argentina), 18
General Confederation of Labor (Ar-
   gentina), 8
General Jewish Workers Union, 186,
   202
German American Bund (USA), 219,
   220
German Federation of Commercial
   Employees (Germany), 98
Germani, Gino, 14, 15
German-Israelite Community League
   (Germany), 97
German Nationalist People's Party
   (Germany), 102
German Social Democratic party
   (Germany), 95, 97, 104
Gestapo (Germany), 109, 111, 250

Ghetto benches (Poland), 158
Gigurti, Ion, 176
Gilbert, Martin, 197, 199
Gioldi, Americo, 9
Giraud, H., 222
Gleim, Leopold, 46
Glock, Charles, 227
Goebbels, Joseph, 109, 113, 115, 218
Goitein, S. D. F., 34, 35
Gömbös, Gyula, 136
Gomulka, Wadyslaw, 164, 165
Gordon, Sarah, 109, 112, 113, 114,
   115, 117, 119
Göring, Hermann, 106, 109
Graetz, Roberto, 19
Graiver, David, 24 n.79
Graiver scandal (Argentina), 18
Grand Cross of the German Eagle,
   213
Grant, U. S., 209, 210
Great Britain and Jews, 37
Great Power protection of Jews, 170,
   171, 250–51
Great Purges (Russia/USSR), 190
Great Sanhedrin (France), 69
Great Soviet Encyclopedia, 195
Greenbaum, A. A., 195
Green Shirts (Egypt), 40
Grunwald Patriotic Association, 166
Guardia Blanca (Argentina), 5
Guida, J. M., 13
Gutman, Yisrael, 163

Haim, Syulvia G., 38
Hakim, al, 35
Halleck, Henry W., 209
Halpern, Ben, 230, 234 n.98
Hamburger, Ernest, 95
Handlin, Oscar, 214, 217, 225
Harris Survey, 79, 228
Harvard University, 214
Haykal Pasha, 43
Hebert, John, 5, 6
Hebrew language, 97, 144, 163, 175,
   181, 188, 190
Hecker, Friedrich, 91
Heller, Celia, 158, 159, 160

Help received by Jews, 113, 119, 161,
   163, 243
"Hep, Hep" riots (Germany), 90
Hertzberg, Arthur, 67, 68
Herzl, Theodore, 38
Heydrich, Reinhardt, 109, 110
Higham, John, 211, 212, 217
Higher education, 10, 17, 102, 113–
   14, 121, 125, 174, 175, 182, 189,
   214, 251–52
Hilberg, Raul, 122, 176, 177–78, 191,
   258, 262
Himmler, Heinrich, 76, 111
Hindenburg, Paul von, 101
Hirszowicz, Lukasz, 42
Hitler, Adolf, 40, 102, 105, 106, 109,
   110, 118, 119, 120, 122, 125, 191,
   213, 216, 219
Hitler Youth (Germany), 107, 131
Hlond, Cardinal, 159
Holeczek, Heinz, 92
Hollywood, 221
Holocaust, xix, 20, 177, 195, 223,
   228, 242, 243, 250, 258, 260, 261,
   262
"Holocaust" (television series), 123–
   25
Hopkins, Harry, 222
Horthy, Admiral, 137, 138
Housing segregation of Jews, xvi, 54,
   88, 95–96, 144, 154, 169, 187, 214
Humboldt, Wilhelm von, 89
Husayn, Ahmad, 40
Hyman, Paula, 73

Ilman Lake Travel Club (Germany),
   122
Inkeles, Alex, 195, 199
Inquisition, 3
Institute for Public Opinion (Ger-
   many), 117
Institute Français de l'Opinion Pub-
   lique, 78
Intellectuals and antisemitism, 76
International Committee of Educa-
   tors to Combat Racism, Anti-Semi-
   tism and Apartheid, xix
International Jew, 10, 12, 212, 213

Irigoyen, Hipólito, 5, 6
Iron Guard (Rumania), 175, 176
Islam and antisemitism, xvi–xv, xix, 27, 34, 39, 41
Islamic Nationalist party (Egypt), 42
Islamic Youth Organization of Palestine (Palestine), 39
Israel, migration to, 30, 46, 56, 58, 59–61, 165, 178, 193
Israeli policy, 253–56; in Argentina, 20–21; in Egypt, 46; in Ethiopia, 56, 57, 58, 59–61
Ivan the Terrible, 181
Izvestia, 194

Jackson, Kenneth, 214
James, Henry, 211
Jankowski, James, 38
Jefferson, Thomas, 208
Jersch-Wenzel, Stefi, 88
Jesus Christ Was Born A Jew, 86
Jew, Don't Get Angry, 123
Jew in the Mysteries of History, 13
Jewish Agency (Israel), 20, 56
Jewish Antifascist Committee (Russia/USSR), 192, 193, 243
Jewish Boxing Club (Germany), 104
Jewish Colonization Association (Argentina), 10
Jewish conspiracy, charges of, xvi, 70, 94, 165, 184, 196, 253
Jewish council (*Judenrat*), 139, 162, 262
Jewish defense organizations, 97–98, 99–100, 104, 177, 246
Jewish Defense Service (Germany), 104
Jewish Labor Committee (USA), 217
Jewish question, 207, 218, 237, 242
Jewish Scientific Institute (Bulgaria), 30
Jewish self-defense actions, 6, 9, 11, 34, 73, 74, 104, 158, 159, 186, 188, 201
Jewish World, 59
Jews: and other minorities, xix, 28, 36, 37, 39, 134, 155, 175, 251; and radicalism, 4

"Jew Scare" (USA), 212
Joint Distribution Committee, 194
Joseph II, 145
Journal of Clinical Psychology, 221
Judaism Unmasked, a True and Accurate Report, 88
Judaism without Embellishment, 197
"Judaizers" (Russia/USSR), 181
Judenrat, 139, 162, 262

Katowice Forum, 166
Katz, Jacob, 93
Katzburg, Nathaniel, 134
Kennedy, John F., 47
Kerensky, Alexander, 188
Kermish, Joseph, 163
Kershaw, Jan, 112, 115, 116, 117, 119
Khrushchev, Nikita, 194
Kichko, Trofim, 197
Kilpatrick, James J., 225
Kisch, Guido, 84, 85
Kishinev pogrom (Russia/USSR), 186
Knutter, Hans-Helmuth, 264 n.7
Kohler, Max, 171
Kolbe, Maximilian Maria (St. Maximilian), 159–60
Koltubianka, 160
Korey, William, 189, 190, 193, 194, 195, 198, 199
Korneyev, Lev (*also* Korneev), 196, 199
Kosciuszko Legion, 160
Kosygin, A. N., 195
Kovacs, Andras, 140
Krämer, Gudrun, 43, 44
Kristallnacht (Germany), 9, 109, 111, 113, 115, 116, 123, 218, 250
Kuhn, Fritz, 220
Ku Klux Klan (USA), 213, 214, 226
Kulka, Otto Dov, 112, 115, 116, 117, 119
Kwiet, Konrad, 111, 112

Labin, Daniel, 170, 174
La France Juive, 71
La Libre Parole, 71
Landau, Jacob M., 37

Landshut, Siegfried, 44, 45, 47
La Opinion, 17
La Prensa, 10
La Protesta, 4
La Vanguardia, 4
Lavi, Theodore, 177
"Law for the Defense of the Nation", 28
Law of Return, 56, 57, 254
League Against German Antisemitism (Egypt), 40
League for Defense and Defiance (Germany), 101
League of Archangel Michael, 174, 175
League of National Christian Defense (Rumania), 174
League of Nations, 147, 251
Ledeen, Michael, 147
Lee, Albert, 213
Leers, Johann von, 46
Left, Jews and the, 74, 167, 257–58
Lemke, William, 218
Lendvai, Paul, 139, 140
Lenin, Vladimir Ilyich, 186, 189, 190, 195, 196, 197, 200–203, 241, 248, 257
Lernoux, Penny, 24, 25 n.97
Les Juives, nos maitres, 70
Lestchinsky, Jacob, 158, 160, 175
Lewis, Bernard, 33, 38
Liebman, Seymour B., 24 n.82
Ligue International contre l'Antisemitisme (France), 73
Lincoln, Abraham, 209
Literature, discrimination in, 70, 88, 209, 211
Loch, Theo Maria, 123
Loi Marchandeau, 74
Long, Huey, 219
Lopez Rega, Jose, 17
Los Angeles Examiner, xvi
Louis IV, 85
Louis IX, the Pious, 66
Louis XVI, 68
Lowenstein, Steven, 95
Ludendorff, Erich, 101, 102

Ludovic, 65
Luther, Martin, 86, 87, 239

"Maccabi" (Germany), 104
McWilliams, Carey, 207, 210
Malenkov, Georgi, 194
Malino, Frances, 68, 69
Man, Don't Get Angry, 123
Manetho, 33
"Manifesto of the Race", 148
Manuel Administratif (Rumania), 170
Marcus, Jacob Rader, 225
Marcus, Sheldon, 217, 219
Marr, Wilhelm, 93
Marrus, Michael R., 65, 75, 76, 77, 78
Marx, Karl, 257, 258
Mason, Carlos G. Suarez, 18
Mein Kampf, 40
Meinveille, Julio, 13
Mekonnen, Ras Tafari, 55
Mellibovsky, Santiago, 25 n.95
Mendelsohn, Ezra, 135, 156, 174
Menelik, 53
Mengele, Josef, 12
Merhav, Meir, 261
Merriam Company, 211
Meyer, Marshall T., 19, 20, 21
Michael, King (Rumania), 176, 178
Michaelis, Meir, 143, 147, 148, 149
Mikhoels, Solomon, 192
Minorities Treaty, 156, 159, 174, 251
Mirelman, Victor, 5, 6
Moczar, Mieczyslaw, 164, 165, 166
Modzhorian, Lydia, 196
Mohammad Ali, 36, 37
Money and Jewry, 85
Monteneros (Argentina), 24 n.79
Morgenthau, Hans J., 105, 245
Morris, Richard, 207
Mosaic persuasion, 68
Moscow City Trade Union Council (Russia/USSR), 189
Moser, Alois, 46
Mosse, George, 264 n.6
Mousseaux, Henri Gougenot des, 70
Mrs. Skeffington, 221

Muslim Brotherhood (Egypt), 39, 40, 41, 42, 43, 44, 45, 255
Muslim Congress (Egypt), 45
Mussolini, Benito, 55, 77, 146, 147, 148, 149, 240, 246

Naguib, Mohammed, 45
Napoleon, Bonaparte, 36, 68, 69, 90, 145, 187
Nasser, Abdel, 45, 46, 47
Nation, 215
National Association of Manufacturers (Argentina), 18
National Democratic party (Russia/USSR), 187
Nationalist Youth Alliance (Argentina), 8
Nationalization Act of 1740, 208
National League of Jewish Frontline Veterans (Germany), 103, 106
National rights of Jews, 68, 69, 185, 192, 202
National Socialist Workers party (Germany), 102, 107, 108, 112, 116, 121, 125
National Union for Social Justice (USA), 217
Nazi government, activities in: Argentina, 7, 8, 9, 10; Egypt, 40, 41–42; Hungary, 136; USSR, 191
Nazi party (Argentina), 7
Nazi party (Egypt), 40
Neva, 197
New Deal, 217
Newsweek, 261
New York American, 209
New York Herald, 210
New York Post, 218
New York Times, 59, 217, 247, 260
New York University, 214, 215, 221
Nicholas I, 183, 196
Nicholas II, 185, 196
Nielson, James, 18
Niemiery, Jaafar, 60
Niewyk, Donald, 102, 103, 104
Nirgad, Ram, 21, 25 n.100
Noah's Ark of bigotry (Argentina), 3
Nogues, A. P., 222

Northwest Ordinance, 208
Nuremberg Laws, 107, 111, 113, 115, 116, 148, 250
Nuremberg trials, 260

October, 47
Okuneva, Ruth (Daniel Fish), 195
Olivetti, Gino, 147
Olszowski, Stefan, 166
"Operation Moses", 59, 60, 61, 63
ORT, 58
Orthodox church (Russia), 181, 185
Oschlies, Wolf, 27, 30
Ottoman empire, 35, 36, 133

Pale of Settlement, xvi, 182, 197
Palestine, partition of, 43–44, 193
Panahi, Badi, 120
Pan German League (Germany), 99
Parliamentary World Congress for the Protection of Palestine, 40
Party of the Nation, Christian, National, and Racial (Rumania), 176
Patriarch Miodem, 177
Patriotic Front (Bulgaria), 30
Paxton, Robert O., 65, 75, 76, 77, 78
Peasants and antisemitism, 160, 171
Peixotto, Benjamin F., 171
Pelley, William Dudley, 219
People's Organization Against Anti-Semitism (Argentina), 9
People's party (Germany), 104
Peres, Shimon, 60
Perón, Isabel, 16, 17
Perón, Juan, 10, 11, 12, 13, 16
Peshev, V. P., 29
Petain, Henri-Philippe, 74, 76
Peter the Great, 182
Petlura, Simon, 188
Philip the Fair, 67
Pichon-Riviere, 14, 15
Pinkus, B., 195
Pioneering Youth, 158
Pogroms, 246–47; Argentina, 4, 5, 6, 11, 13; Bulgaria, 28; Egypt, 33, 43; Ethiopia, 57–58; France, 68, 71; Germany, 83, 90, 91, 109, 115; Hungary, 139; Poland, 156, 158,

164; Rumania, 174, 176; Russia/
USSR, 184, 186, 187, 188, 194–95,
196, 199, 201
Poliakov, Leon, 33, 65, 66, 85, 149
Polish Committee of National Libera-
tion, 163
Polish Self-Defense, 166
Political parties, antisemitic, 71, 98–
99, 101, 176, 207, 218, 219, 245–
46
Pope Benedict XIV, 145
Pope Gregory IX, 85
Pope Innocent III, 84
Pope John XXIII, 29
Pope Leo XII, 146
Pope Paul III, 144
Pope Paul IV, 144
Pope Pius IV, 144
Pope Pius V, 144
Pope Pius VI, 145
Pope Pius IX, 146
Pope Pius XI, 148
Pope Pius XII, 74, 137, 149
Pope Sixtus IV, 144
Pope Sixtus V, 144
Powerlessness of Jews, 247
Pravda, 193, 194, 195
Preziosi, Giovanni, 147
Princeton clubs, 212
*Prisoner without a Name, Cell without a
Number*, 20
Proclamation No. 2, 44
Protestantism and antisemitism, 86–
87, 242
Protestant Reformation, 86
Protocols of the Elders of Zion, 12, 40,
47, 196, 213, 228, 247, 253
Proto-Holocaust, 259
Prussian Reserve Corps, 94
Public office, religion and, 10, 18, 28,
94, 101, 156, 198, 208
Public opinion: in Argentina, 14–16;
in France, 76, 78, 79; in Germany,
107, 116, 117–21; in the United
States, 220–21, 226–28
Public schools, 11, 69–70, 72, 95,
103, 145, 184, 190, 202, 214
Pulzer, Peter, 94, 100

Quinley, Harold, 227
Quotas, 28, 75, 106, 136, 157, 174,
184, 189, 194, 197, 208, 212, 214,
215, 217, 222, 251–52

Racist doctrine, 55, 68, 136, 148, 229
Rapoport, Louis, 62 n.5
Reagan, Ronald, 260
Red Army (Russia/USSR), 29, 137,
138, 188
Reddick L. D., 226, 227
Redlich, Shimon, 192, 193
Red Scare of 1919–20 (USA), 212
Reichsbanner (Germany), 104, 257
Reichsvertretung der Juden in
Deutschland, 107
Reinefarth, Heinz, 121
Remer, Otto Ernest, 261
Rescue of Jews from Nazi Germany,
7, 9, 12, 216–17, 221
"Rescue" of Nazis from defeated
Germany, 12, 46, 63, 50
Residence Law of 1902, 4
Revised General Privilege, 88
Ribuffo, Leo, 219
Right, Jews and the, 256; Argentina,
6, 17, 20; Bulgaria, 28; France, 73,
74; Germany, 93–94, 101–2, 106–
7, 244; Poland, 167; United States,
219
Right to be Jews, xviii
Ringelblum, Emmanuel, 161, 162,
163, 257
Ringer, Fritz, 103
Ritual murder charges, 37, 55, 86,
154
Rogger, Hans, 185, 187
Roman Catholic church and antisem-
itism, 242; Argentina, 3–4, 7, 8, 11,
13, 19, 22, 38–39, 237; France, 65–
67, 70–71, 72, 76; Germany, 84–
85, 113, 115; Italy, 144, 145, 146;
Poland, 154, 159–60, 164; United
States, 217, 218–19
Rommel, Erwin, 42
Roncalli, Angelo, 29
Roosevelt, Franklin D., 10, 137, 221,
222, 223

Rosen, Moses, 178, 179
Rosenberg, Alfred, 47
Ross, E. A., 212
Ross, Robert, 223
Roth, Cecil, 145, 146, 147
Roth, Stephen J., 120
Royall, Kenneth, 122
Rudel, Hans Ulrich, 12
Rürup, Reinhard, 89, 91
Russian Communist party (Russia/
    USSR), 200
Russian Revolution: of 1905, 186; of
    1917, 188, 203
Russian Social Democratic Labor
    party (Russia/USSR), 186, 200, 202

Sachsenspiegel, 86
Sadat, Anwar, 45, 47, 48
Safran Alexander, 177
Salamah, Albert, 47
Salgo, Laszlo, 140
Samizdat, 194
Sapieha, Adam Cardinal, 159
Schappes, Morris, 210
Schleunes, Karl, 108
Schoeps, Hans Joachim, 106
Scholem, Gershom, 96
Schorsch, Ismar, 90, 91, 97, 98, 99
Schwarz, Solomon M., 189, 190, 191
Schwarze, Hans Werner, 125
Segregation, social, 69, 84, 96, 154
Selassie, Haile, 55, 56, 57, 61, 238,
    254
Septamana, 178, 179
Servitus Judeorum, 85
Shamir, Yitzhak, 21
Shapiro, Alfred, 215
Sharett, Moshe, 255
Silver Shirts (USA), 219
Sinus Institute (Germany), 120
Sirat, Rene Shmuel, 79
Sirota, Graciela, N., 13
Six-Day War, 195, 199
Slave labor, 114
Smith, Gerald L. K., 45, 219
Sochatzky, Klaus, 120
Socialism and Socialist: Argentina, 4,
    9; France, 70, 72; Germany, 93,

95, 97, 104, 246; Italy, 147; Po-
    land, 158, 159; Russia/USSR, 200,
    201
Socialist International Organization,
    70
Socialist party (Germany), 93
Social Justice, 217, 218
Social Party of Restoration (Argen-
    tina), 8
Soiza Reilly, Juan Jose de, 5
Solidarity (Poland), 166
Sommer, Theo, 260
*Special Information about the Incarcer-
    ated and the Disappeared Jews*, 19
SS (Germany), 113, 116, 121–23,
    149, 250, 260
Stakes, burning at the, 66, 154
Stalin, Joseph, 30, 189, 190, 191,
    192, 193, 194, 243, 248
Stalingrad, battle of, 42, 112, 137,
    177, 191, 192
State Yiddish Publishing House in
    Moscow (Russia/USSR), 190
Statut des juifs, 75, 76
"Statute About Establishing Jews",
    182
Statute of the Jews, 1940 (Rumania),
    176
Stefan, Metropolitan, 29
Stein, Gertrude, xiv
Stember, Charles, 225
Stern, Henry, 56
Stillman, Gerald, 190
Stöcker, Adolf, 93
Strauss, Herbert A., 108
Streicher, Julius, 114
Students, antisemitic, 102, 174
Sturm Abteilung (Germany), 105,
    106, 107, 109
Suchy, Barbara, 98
Sunday laws (USA), 211
Syracuse University, 214, 215
Szajkowski, Zosa, 72, 212
Szlachta, 155, 156

Tacuara (Argentina), 13, 15
Talmud, portrayed as source of evil,
    47, 48, 66

Talmudic Sacrifices, 47

Tamir, Vicki, 28

Tarshish, Allan, 211

Tatars, Crimean, 155

Teffera, Melaku, 58

Terracini, Umberto, 193

Thirty Years' War, 87

Thursz, David, 249

Tignor, Robert, 43

Timayenis, T. T., 211

Timerman, Jacobo, 17, 18, 19, 20, 21, 24 n.78, 237

Toaff, Elio, 150

Toleration, 208–9, 230

Tolstoy, Lev, 185

Tragic Week (Argentina), 4, 5, 6, 9, 247

Treitschke, Heinrich von, 93, 244

Trianon peace treaty of 1920, 135

Trifa, Valerian, 180 n.25

Trybuna Luda, 165

Tsur, Yascov, 63 n.36

Tudor, Corneliu Vadim, 179

Turgenev, Ivan, 186

Turner, Frederick Jackson, 211

Ukrainians, 155

Ukrainian Yiddish Publishing House (USSR), 190

Union for Defense Against Antisemitism (Germany), 98

Union Generale des Israelites de France, 75

Union of Clothing Cutters, Measurers, and Finishers (Argentina), 8

Union of Jewish Communities (Rumania), 177

Union of Jewish Communities of Italy (Italy), 55

Union of Jewish Students in Germany (Germany), 122

Union party (USA), 218

UN General Assembly, 44, 256

United Nations Mission for Egypt, 45

United States Holocaust Memorial Council (USA), 261

United States Office of War Information, 221, 223

Universities, Jewish attendance in, 5, 13, 96–97, 135, 146, 147, 148, 158, 176, 184–85, 188, 194, 197–98, 212, 214, 215, 251–52

Universities, Jewish employment in, 90–91, 94–95, 103, 146, 189, 214, 225

University of Berlin, 103

University of Budapest, 135

University of Buenos Aires, 5, 10

University of Jena, 102

University of Munich, 102

Untermyer, Samuel, 216

Variety, 124

Vasserman, Grigory, 199, 200

Vatican and Jews, 29, 76, 137, 138, 149

Versailles peace conference, 251

Vetulani, Adam, 154

Vigneaux, Simon, 70

"Viking Youth" (Germany), 123

Vogel, Werner, 123

Voltaire, xviii, 67, 68

Vorwärts, 97

Waffen SS, 260

Walesa, Lech, 166

Wallenberg, Raoul, 137

War crimes trials, 122, 229, 260–61

Wardell, Marshal L. J., 209

War Information Program, 221

War Refugee Board, 223

Warsaw ghetto revolt, 162–63

Washington Jewish Week, 59

Washington Square College, 214

Webster's dictionary, 211

Weinberg, David H., 73, 74

Weinryb, Bernard, 183

Weintraub, Ruth, 224

Weisbrot, Robert, 3, 5, 13, 17, 19

Weizsäcker, Richard von, 259

Weltsch, Robert, 106

Wertheimer, Jack, 96

West, Nathanael, xvi

West German Broadcasting Service, 123

Wharton, Edith, 211

White Russia State University in Minsk, 189

Wilson, Stephen, 71, 72

Wilson, Woodrow, 212

Winrod, Gerald B., 219

Wise, Stephen, 216

Wolf, Simon, 171

Wolff, Karl, 121

World Jewish Congress, 59

Wrong, Dennis, 226

Wyman, David, 216, 221, 223

Yad Vashem (Israel), 243

Yale University, 212, 214

Yankelovich, Skelly, and White, Inc., 227

Yardai, Avraham, 58

Yesayahu, Yisrael, 56

Yevssev, Ye, 196

Yiddish language, 8, 10, 72, 91, 97, 163, 173, 175, 188, 189, 190, 192, 199, 202, 203

Yom Kippur War, 57

Young Communist League (Russia/ USSR), 189, 199

Young Egypt (Egypt), 40, 41, 42, 255

Zegota (Poland), 163

Zionism and Zionists, 6, 20, 30, 38, 39, 41, 42, 43, 44, 47, 58, 110, 111, 112, 158, 159, 166, 178, 194, 196, 197, 199, 200, 202, 238, 254, 256

Zionism as a Form of Racism and Racist Discrimination, 196

Zionist-Socialists, 158

Zionist Sports Association (Germany), 104

Zydowska Organizacja Bojowa-Jewish Fighting Organization (ZOB), 162

About the Author

MEYER WEINBERG has had a distinguished career as a teacher, editor, and author. Currently he is both a professor at the University of Massachusetts, Amherst, and the director of the Horace Mann Bond Center for Equal Education. His writings include *Race and Place: A Legal History of the Neighborhood School*, *The Search for Quality Integrated Education*, *America's Economic Heritage: From a Colonial to a Capitalistic Economy, 1634–1900* (Vol. I) and *A Mature Economy, Post 1900* (Vol. II), and *The Education of Poor and Minority Children: A World Bibliography. Supplement, 1979–1985* (1986).